Sustainable Growth and Global Social Development in Competitive Economies

Andrei Jean Vasile
Petroleum-Gas University of Ploiesti, Romania & Romanian Academy, National Institute for Economic Research "Costin C. Kirițescu", Romania

Mile Vasić
European Marketing and Management Association, Banja Luka, Bosnia and Herzegovina

Predrag Vukovic
Institute of Agricultural Economics, Belgrade, Serbia

A volume in the Advances in Finance, Accounting, and Economics (AFAE) Book Series

Published in the United States of America by
IGI Global
Business Science Reference (an imprint of IGI Global)
701 E. Chocolate Avenue
Hershey PA, USA 17033
Tel: 717-533-8845
Fax: 717-533-8661
E-mail: cust@igi-global.com
Web site: http://www.igi-global.com

Copyright © 2023 by IGI Global. All rights reserved. No part of this publication may be reproduced, stored or distributed in any form or by any means, electronic or mechanical, including photocopying, without written permission from the publisher.
Product or company names used in this set are for identification purposes only. Inclusion of the names of the products or companies does not indicate a claim of ownership by IGI Global of the trademark or registered trademark.

Library of Congress Cataloging-in-Publication Data

Names: Jean-Vasile, Andrei, 1982- editor. | Vasic, Mile, 1972- editor. | Vukovic, Predrag Miroslav, 1971- editor.
Title: Sustainable growth and global social development in competitive economies / edited by Jean Vasile Andrei, Mile Vasic, Predrag Vukovic.
Description: Hershey, PA : Business Science Reference, [2023] | Includes bibliographical references and index. | Summary: "Despite this research topic is a very actual and some books are published including by IGI Global, some major aspects are neglected. This book proposal fulfills a gap between theory and practice in field of the resilient economies, sustainable growth and global social development in the New Normal. Usually, there are books treating economic crisis but less on transformative economic aspects. Implementing the outcomes and solutions designed in the book to various collaboration formats will let to increase the visibility of the publication and to elaborate new practices and solutions in the sphere of constraints and opportunities in shaping the future in terms of business models, development patterns and transformations in the New Normal paradigm. This current book project will try to provide some holistic approaches regarding the business models, development patterns and transformations in the New Normal paradigm. The research subject addresses to a very actual and debate full aspect as: business models and integration business process, modeling and development, consumption patterns and transformations, tourism, development patterns and transformations, digital transformation and education, e-business and e-governance in translational countries, economic diversity and resilience"-- Provided by publisher.
Identifiers: LCCN 2022062316 (print) | LCCN 2022062317 (ebook) | ISBN 9781668488102 (hardcover) | ISBN 9781668488119 (paperback) | ISBN 9781668488126 (ebook)
Subjects: LCSH: Sustainable development. | Organizational change.
Classification: LCC HC79.E5 S864934 2023 (print) | LCC HC79.E5 (ebook) | DDC 338.9/27--dc23/eng/20230105
LC record available at https://lccn.loc.gov/2022062316
LC ebook record available at https://lccn.loc.gov/2022062317

This book is published in the IGI Global book series Advances in Finance, Accounting, and Economics (AFAE) (ISSN: 2327-5677; eISSN: 2327-5685)

British Cataloguing in Publication Data
A Cataloguing in Publication record for this book is available from the British Library.

All work contributed to this book is new, previously-unpublished material.
The views expressed in this book are those of the authors, but not necessarily of the publisher.

For electronic access to this publication, please contact: eresources@igi-global.com.

Advances in Finance, Accounting, and Economics (AFAE) Book Series

ISSN:2327-5677
EISSN:2327-5685

Editor-in-Chief: Ahmed Driouchi, Al Akhawayn University, Morocco

MISSION

In our changing economic and business environment, it is important to consider the financial changes occurring internationally as well as within individual organizations and business environments. Understanding these changes as well as the factors that influence them is crucial in preparing for our financial future and ensuring economic sustainability and growth.

The **Advances in Finance, Accounting, and Economics (AFAE)** book series aims to publish comprehensive and informative titles in all areas of economics and economic theory, finance, and accounting to assist in advancing the available knowledge and providing for further research development in these dynamic fields.

COVERAGE

- Accounting information systems
- Finance and Accounting in SMEs
- Stock Market
- Economics of Risks, Uncertainty, Ambiguity, and Insurance
- Public Finance
- Risk Analysis and Management
- Macroeconomics
- Economic Theory
- Statistical Analysis
- Taxes

IGI Global is currently accepting manuscripts for publication within this series. To submit a proposal for a volume in this series, please contact our Acquisition Editors at Acquisitions@igi-global.com or visit: http://www.igi-global.com/publish/.

The Advances in Finance, Accounting, and Economics (AFAE) Book Series (ISSN 2327-5677) is published by IGI Global, 701 E. Chocolate Avenue, Hershey, PA 17033-1240, USA, www.igi-global.com. This series is composed of titles available for purchase individually; each title is edited to be contextually exclusive from any other title within the series. For pricing and ordering information please visit http://www.igi-global.com/book-series/advances-finance-accounting-economics/73685. Postmaster: Send all address changes to above address. Copyright © 2023 IGI Global. All rights, including translation in other languages reserved by the publisher. No part of this series may be reproduced or used in any form or by any means – graphics, electronic, or mechanical, including photocopying, recording, taping, or information and retrieval systems – without written permission from the publisher, except for non commercial, educational use, including classroom teaching purposes. The views expressed in this series are those of the authors, but not necessarily of IGI Global.

Titles in this Series

For a list of additional titles in this series, please visit:
http://www.igi-global.com/book-series/advances-finance-accounting-economics/73685

Concepts and Cases of Illicit Finance
Abdul Rafay (University of Management and Technology, Pakistan)
Business Science Reference • copyright 2023 • 273pp • H/C (ISBN: 9781668485873) • US $250.00 (our price)

The Importance of Entrepreneurship in Fostering Economic Progress
Mohammed El Amine Abdelli (University of Western Brittany, France) Naima Bentouir (Ain Temouchent University, Algeria) and Esra Sipahi Döngül (Aksaray University, Turkey)
Business Science Reference • copyright 2024 • 300pp • H/C (ISBN: 9781668471272) • US $240.00 (our price)

Perspectives on the Transition Toward Green and Climate Neutral Economies in Asia
Patricia Ordóñez de Pablos (The University of Oviedo, Spain) Mohammad Nabil Almunawar (Universiti Brunei Darussalam, Brunei) and Muhammad Anshari (Universiti Brunei Darussalam, Brunei)
Business Science Reference • copyright 2023 • 465pp • H/C (ISBN: 9781668486139) • US $325.00 (our price)

Revolutionizing Financial Services and Markets Through FinTech and Blockchain
Kiran Mehta (Chitkara Business School, Chitkara University, India) Renuka Sharma (Chitkara Business School, Chitkara University, India) and Poshan Yu (Soochow University, China & Australian Studies Centre, Shanghai University, China)
Business Science Reference • copyright 2023 • 340pp • H/C (ISBN: 9781668486245) • US $265.00 (our price)

The Past, Present, and Future of Accountancy Education and Professions
Nina T. Dorata (St. John's University, USA) Richard C. Jones (Hofstra University, USA) Jennifer Mensche (St. Joseph's University, USA) and Mark M. Ulrich (CUNY Queensborough Community College, USA)
Business Science Reference • copyright 2023 • 240pp • H/C (ISBN: 9781668454831) • US $215.00 (our price)

For an entire list of titles in this series, please visit:
http://www.igi-global.com/book-series/advances-finance-accounting-economics/73685

701 East Chocolate Avenue, Hershey, PA 17033, USA
Tel: 717-533-8845 x100 • Fax: 717-533-8661
E-Mail: cust@igi-global.com • www.igi-global.com

Editorial Advisory Board

Laurentiu Ciornei, *Center for Study and Research for AgroForestry Biodiversity "Acad. David Davidescu", Romanian Academy, Romania*
Drago Cvijanovic, *University of Kragujevac, Serbia*
Ignacio De Los Ríos Carmenado, *Universidad Politécnica de Madrid, Spain*
Mircea Duica, *Valahia University of Târgoviște, Romania*
Dorel Dusmanescu, *Petroleum-Gas University of Ploiești, Romania*
Vasilii Erokhin, *Harbin Engineering University, China*
Tianming Gao, *Harbin Engineering University, China*
Ileana Gheorghe, *Petroleum-Gas University of Ploiești, Romania*
Iza Gigauri, *St. Andrew the First-Called Georgian University, Georgia*
Félix Puime Guillén, *University of A Coruña, Spain*
Eglantina Hysa, *Epoka University, Albania*
Marko Jelocnik, *Institute of Agricultural Economics, Serbia*
Mehmet Kalgi, *Ardahan University, Turkey*
Syed Abdul Rehman Khan, *Xuzhou University of Technology, China*
Boris Kuzman, *Institute of Agricultural Economics, Serbia*
Chivu Luminita, *National Institute for Economic Research "Costin C. Kirițescu", Romanian Academy, Romania*
Vladescu Mihaela, *National Institute for Economic Research "Costin C. Kirițescu", Romanian Academy, Romania*
Panait Mirela, *Petrolum-Gas University of Ploiesti, Romania*
Mihaela Georgiana Oprea, *National Institute for Economic Research "Costin C. Kirițescu", Romanian Academy, Romania*
Catalin Popescu, *Petroleum-Gas University of Ploiești, Romania*
Donatella Privitera, *University of Catania, Italy*
Lazar Raković, *University of Novi Sad, Serbia*
Violeta Sima, *Petroleum-Gas University of Ploiești, Romania*

Alexandru Sin-Schneider, *National Institute for Economic Research "Costin C. Kirițescu", Romanian Academy, Romania*
Adrian Stancu, *Petroleum-Gas University of Ploiești, Romania*
Jonel Subić, *Institute of Economics Agriculture, Serbia*
Carmen Veronica Zefinescu, *Petroleum-Gas University of Ploiești, Romania*
Jovan Zubovic, *Institute of Economic Sciences, Serbia*

Table of Contents

Preface xvii

Acknowledgment xxiv

Chapter 1
The Concept of Global Growth and Development With the New Normal 1
    Vladimir M. Ristanović, Institute of European Studies, Belgrade, Serbia
    Berislav Andrlić, Faculty of Tourism and Rural Development Pozega, J.
        J. Strossmayer University of Osijek, Croatia

Chapter 2
Paradigm Shift in Corporate Responsibility to the New Era of ESG and
Social Entrepreneurship 22
    Iza Gigauri, St. Andrew the First-Called Georgian University, Georgia
    Valentin Penchev Vasilev, Higher School of Security and Economics,
        Bulgaria

Chapter 3
Toward Understanding the Underlying Causes of Scope Creep 42
    Simon Cleveland, Purdue University Global, USA
    Marisa Cleveland, Northeastern University, USA

Chapter 4
Does Financial Globalization Have a Benign or Malignant Effect on
Development and Growth? 51
    Fatma Taşdemir, Sinop University, Turkey

Chapter 5
Tourism Is an Essential Trade: VR and AR Technologies Make It Profitable 79
    C. V. Suresh Babu, Hindustan Institute of Technolgy and Science, India
    T. Jeyavasan, Hindustan Institute of Technology and Science, India

Chapter 6
Distribution of Mechanization by Regions and Areas in the Republic of Serbia 97
    Irina Marina, Institute of Agricultural Economics, Beilgrade, Serbia
    Biljana Grujić Vučkovski, Institute of Agricultural Economics, Belgrade, Serbia
    Marijana Jovanović Todorović, Institute of Agricultural Economics, Belgrade, Serbia

Chapter 7
Impact of Financial Literacy on the Risk Tolerance Behavior of Females Working in the Unorganized Sector 122
    Anushree Srivastava, Dr. A.P.J. Abdul Kalam Technical University, India
    Neha Yadav, Babu Banarasi Das University, India
    Anuradha Maurya, Babu Banarasi Das University, India

Chapter 8
Rural Tourism Destinations and the Sustainable Development of Tourism in the Republic of Serbia: Analysis of Variables Affecting the Competitiveness .. 136
    Predrag Miroslav Vuković, Institute of Agricultural Economics, Belgrade, Serbia
    Natatasa Kljajic, Institute of Agricultural Economics, Belgrade, Serbia

Chapter 9
Short Food Supply Chains for Achieving Sustainable Growth in Central and Eastern European Countries 157
    Vesna Paraušić, Institute of Agricultural Economics, Belgrade, Serbia
    Vlado Kovačević, Institute of Agricultural Economics, Belgrade, Serbia

Chapter 10
The Analysis of the Relationship Between Renewable Energy and Human Development 180
    Mustafa Batuhan Tufaner, Beykent University, Turkey

Chapter 11
The Complementary Effect of Network Capability and Learning Orientation on Firm Performance: Evidence From SMEs in Türkiye 193
    Pelin Karaca Kalkan, Ankara Science University, Turkey
    Nilay Aluftekin Sakarya, Genta Pty., Turkey

Chapter 12
Women Entrepreneurship in Multifunctional Agriculture for Rural Revival in Serbia 225
    Vesna Popović, Institute of Agricultural Economics, Belgrade, Serbia
    Branko Mihailović, Institute of Agricultural Economics, Belgrade, Serbia

Chapter 13
The Influence of Financial Incentives and Other Socio-Economic Factors on Two-Wheeler EV Adoption in the NCR Region..248
    Farah Siraj, Amity University, India
    Pooja Mehra, Amity School of Economics, Amity University, India

Compilation of References 280

About the Contributors 322

Index 328

Detailed Table of Contents

Preface xvii

Acknowledgment xxiv

Chapter 1
The Concept of Global Growth and Development With the New Normal 1
    Vladimir M. Ristanović, Institute of European Studies, Belgrade, Serbia
    Berislav Andrlić, Faculty of Tourism and Rural Development Pozega, J.
        J. Strossmayer University of Osijek, Croatia

The chapter presents a new view of global changes. The new normal paradigm is based on economic premises but, essentially, constitutes a new scheme. It is a concept that necessarily requires transformations within the entire society. The focus, however, is on a new life and work pattern. Adaptation to changes will be realized quicker than expected. Numerous processes have already been prepared and implemented, such as international standards implementation in social, political, and business spheres, which is sometimes ignored or forgotten. At the same time, this chapter will show the chronology of the events that preceded the new normal paradigm, and which went in the direction of its final manifestation. It will confirm that these efforts in the developed world have existed for decades.

Chapter 2
Paradigm Shift in Corporate Responsibility to the New Era of ESG and
Social Entrepreneurship 22
    Iza Gigauri, St. Andrew the First-Called Georgian University, Georgia
    Valentin Penchev Vasilev, Higher School of Security and Economics,
        Bulgaria

Since the business purpose to serve shareholders' interests changed to a more balanced view of serving all stakeholders, companies' focus shifted towards corporate social responsibility (CSR) to meet the expectations of society. Corporations recognize that a profit-driven mission is not making them the best companies as information about unethical behavior spreads rapidly. Digital resources can be used in corporate strategy to create value for consumers and shareholders. Digital transformation impacts CSR while paving the way for digital CSR. Increasingly, companies admit the need for sustainability and proactive steps to contribute to Sustainable Development Goals. In this regard, ESG—environmental, social, and governance—issues aim to connect financial value to social responsibility. Furthermore, social entrepreneurship has received special attention worldwide as pressing social and environmental problems requiring complex solutions. Therefore, the research trends regarding CSR, ESG, sustainability, social entrepreneurship, and digitalization have been growing.

Chapter 3
Toward Understanding the Underlying Causes of Scope Creep 42
Simon Cleveland, Purdue University Global, USA
Marisa Cleveland, Northeastern University, USA

Scope creep is an issue project managers must address across various industries. When scope creep is not addressed, the project becomes troubled or fails. Because scope creep appears to be a challenge for emerging and existing project managers, having an introductory understanding of the underlying causes of scope creep will add to the body of literature with particular focus on providing individuals new to projects a foundation to prevent being part of the problem. This includes new project managers, as well as new stakeholders and leaders who are unfamiliar with how projects operate and are best managed. This literature review provides a summation of an analysis of the underlying causes of scope creep and identifies a host of factors that contribute to it.

Chapter 4
Does Financial Globalization Have a Benign or Malignant Effect on
Development and Growth? 51
Fatma Taşdemir, Sinop University, Turkey

Globalization with trade and financial linkages is beneficial for countries, as indicated by theory. The literature often finds that these are less clear for financial globalization. This chapter examines the association amongst financial globalization, growth, sectoral value added, and employment in emerging market and developing economies. Accordingly, financial globalization tends to lower growth, based on the main descriptive analysis. Financial globalization encourages industrialization in Asian economies while it leads to de-industrialization in African and Latin American countries. The services sector is positively associated with financial globalization in all regional country groupings. The analysis in this chapter indicates that financial globalization directs the allocation of resources across and within sectors. A strategic and systematic industrial policy that channels selective foreign savings into the finance of critical industrial projects also contributes to Sustainable Development Goals by minimizing the side effects of financial globalization.

Chapter 5
Tourism Is an Essential Trade: VR and AR Technologies Make It Profitable 79
    C. V. Suresh Babu, Hindustan Institute of Technolgy and Science, India
    T. Jeyavasan, Hindustan Institute of Technology and Science, India

This chapter aims to present a sustainable growth solution for the tourism industry by utilizing virtual reality (VR) technology. The chapter focuses on creating a platform similar to a VR metaverse that offers users an immersive and compelling tourism experience of well-known tourist attractions worldwide. The platform aims to enable sustainable growth for the tourism industry while also promoting global social development. The chapter discusses the importance of such a platform, addressing key issues in VR tourism and providing recommendations for its effective implementation. The proposed solution offers a viable alternative to traditional tourism that has a significant environmental impact, such as carbon emissions and overcrowding. Through the VR-based platform, tourists can travel virtually, reducing the need for physical travel while still enjoying the beauty and culture of different locations worldwide. Overall, this chapter aims to present a solution that can promote sustainable tourism while simultaneously contributing to global social development.

Chapter 6
Distribution of Mechanization by Regions and Areas in the Republic of Serbia 97
    Irina Marina, Institute of Agricultural Economics, Beilgrade, Serbia
    Biljana Grujić Vučkovski, Institute of Agricultural Economics, Belgrade,
        Serbia
    Marijana Jovanović Todorović, Institute of Agricultural Economics,
        Belgrade, Serbia

The goal of writing the chapter is to analyze the distribution of agricultural mechanization, which is the most common in the Republic of Serbia (single-axle tractors, two-axle tractors, universal combine harvesters). The purpose of this chapter is to analyze the used mechanization by regions and areas in Serbia during 2012 and 2018, as well as by the number of holdings at its disposal. Principal component analysis (PCA) was used in the research, and the results were presented both tabularly and graphically (loading plot and biplot). The results of the PCA method showed that the situation has not changed in the observed years when it comes to the distribution of mechanization by regions. The PCA method was also applied to mechanization that were used at the level of 25 areas in Serbia only in 2012 because the Statistical Office of the Republic of Serbia (SORS) does not have data for 2018. Based on the biplot presentation, the authors concluded the dominant representation of certain types of mechanization in certain regions and areas of Serbia.

Chapter 7
Impact of Financial Literacy on the Risk Tolerance Behavior of Females
Working in the Unorganized Sector 122
    Anushree Srivastava, Dr. A.P.J. Abdul Kalam Technical University,
        India
    Neha Yadav, Babu Banarasi Das University, India
    Anuradha Maurya, Babu Banarasi Das University, India

Risk and return are the two terms which are used while making investments. Financial literacy is an important indicator of measuring risk tolerance level as it helps in making sound financial decisions and planned investment choices. Financial literacy not only broadens the scope of investment choices and financial planning but also helps in the process of rotating money and diversification of funds. This study helps to explore the impact of financial literacy on risk tolerance behavior of females. Risk tolerance is an important indicator which helps in looking at the amount of surplus funds with the people, the preferred tool of investment, and how well they are managing and diversifying funds. As per the authors, 200 females working in the unorganized sector were surveyed in Uttar Pradesh region. Data was collected through a questionnaire which was designed to test the financial literacy, financial prudence, and investment pattern of females and how the access to financial products, services, and wealth impacts the confidence and risk-taking aptitude of females.

Chapter 8
Rural Tourism Destinations and the Sustainable Development of Tourism in
the Republic of Serbia: Analysis of Variables Affecting the Competitiveness..136
    Predrag Miroslav Vuković, Institute of Agricultural Economics,
        Belgrade, Serbia
    Natatasa Kljajic, Institute of Agricultural Economics, Belgrade, Serbia

The problem of rural development is present in a large number of countries. Rural areas today are characterized by negative trends of population migration to urban centers, depopulation, aging of the rural population, reduction of macro-economic indicators, etc. The aim of the chapter is to identify the variables that influence the current situation in the sector of rural tourism based on the theoretical analysis of the management of rural tourist destinations and the conducted empirical research on the perceptions of tourists as consumers and domestic stakeholders on the quality of tourist offers in rural destinations in Serbia and the potential offer of rural tourist destinations in Serbia to propose strategic directions for the development of rural destinations and to present a sustainable management model for improving the competitiveness of the rural tourist destinations.

Chapter 9
Short Food Supply Chains for Achieving Sustainable Growth in Central and
Eastern European Countries..157
    Vesna Paraušić, Institute of Agricultural Economics, Belgrade, Serbia
    Vlado Kovačević, Institute of Agricultural Economics, Belgrade, Serbia

Traditional types of short food supply chains have represented a significant part of food systems in most Central and Eastern European countries for centuries. In these countries, direct sales are the result of the dominance of small-scale family farms with subsistence and semi-subsistence farming, and their insufficient market integration in global food supply chains. The literature highlights that "short supply circuits" have undeniably contributed to reaching the sustainable growth of local communities and securing sustainable income of farmers. However, the authors' clear and critical opinion is that the positive contribution of short food supply chains to sustainable growth should not be generalised or excessively glorified. This attitude relies on the fact that the contribution of short food supply chains to all sustainability dimensions is determined by numerous factors and assumptions, and that the combination of different marketing channels is frequently required to maximise their total contribution to sustainable growth.

Chapter 10
The Analysis of the Relationship Between Renewable Energy and Human
Development 180
    Mustafa Batuhan Tufaner, Beykent University, Turkey

As in all areas of human life, energy plays a vital role in these areas as well. However, reasons such as the risk of depletion of traditional energy sources, damage to the environment, and supply shocks have led to more discussion of renewable energy sources. The aim of the study is to analyze the relationship between renewable energy and human development for 37 OECD countries for the period 1990-2018. For this purpose, Gengenbach, Urbain, and Westerlund panel cointegration test and Dumitrescu-Hurlin panel causality tests were applied. Empirical results reveal that the increase in the rate of renewable energy consumption in total energy consumption positively affects human development. Also, the Dumitrescu-Hurlin panel causality test shows that there is no causality between human development and renewable energy consumption. These results will help policy makers and government officials in OECD countries better understand the role of renewable energy in the human development process.

Chapter 11

The Complementary Effect of Network Capability and Learning Orientation
on Firm Performance: Evidence From SMEs in Türkiye 193
    Pelin Karaca Kalkan, Ankara Science University, Turkey
    Nilay Aluftekin Sakarya, Genta Pty., Turkey

It is widely accepted that network capability (NC) and learning orientation (LO) directly enhance small and medium-sized enterprises' (SMEs) performance. Yet relatively little attention has been paid to the study of the complementary effects of internal and external capabilities on innovation and firm performance. Drawing on the dynamic capabilities theory, this study investigates the complementary effect of NC and LO on SME performance. Moreover, this research examines how product and process innovation capability mediates the complementary effect of NC and LO on SME performance. The hypotheses were tested on 309 high-technology manufacturing SMEs in Türkiye. Empirical results revealed that NC and LO jointly influence product innovation capability. The results also suggested that only process innovation capability performs a mediating role in the complementary effect of NC and LO on firm performance. This study contributes to the literature by providing a comprehensive analysis of the relationships between NC, LO, innovation capabilities, and SME performance.

Chapter 12

Women Entrepreneurship in Multifunctional Agriculture for Rural Revival in
Serbia 225
    Vesna Popović, Institute of Agricultural Economics, Belgrade, Serbia
    Branko Mihailović, Institute of Agricultural Economics, Belgrade,
       Serbia

The COVID-19 crisis has revealed the benefits of rural living and underlined the importance of strengthening local food systems and empowering family farming and women farmers given the crucial role they play in multifunctional agriculture, climate resilience, and recovery from the pandemic. Multifunctional agriculture is an effective framework for a set of business models that integrate economic, environmental, and socio-cultural impacts of agriculture and food production on sustainable rural development. Innovative business models in multifunctional agriculture give new opportunities for women farmers only if they enjoy gender equality and have access to work-life balance services. This chapter per the authors analyzes women entrepreneurship in Serbian agriculture using business model canvas analysis of a case study farm from the Homolje area (East Serbia). Research results, solutions, and recommendations aim to raise awareness of the role of women's multifunctional entrepreneurship and collaborative business strategies in rural revival within the new normal paradigm.

Chapter 13
The Influence of Financial Incentives and Other Socio-Economic Factors on
Two-Wheeler EV Adoption in the NCR Region 248
    Farah Siraj, Amity University, India
    Pooja Mehra, Amity School of Economics, Amity University, India

Electric vehicles are a technological advancement that has the potential to reduce greenhouse gas emissions and lessen the effects of climate change. However, externalities like knowledge appropriability and pollution reduction produce societal and economic benefits that are not reflected in the cost of electric vehicles. Governments have implemented a few strategies to solve the ensuing market failures. The authors identified a few additional socio-economic parameters based on the research that are anticipated to have an impact on the adoption rates of electric vehicles. They investigated the link between those variables and the effect of socio-economic factors on these variables using structural equation modelling. The model discovered that there is no correlation between financial incentives awareness and two-wheeler EV uptake. The findings indicate that among these socioeconomic characteristics, adoption of two-wheeled electric vehicles was most strongly correlated with age, gender, education, married status, and yearly family income.

Compilation of References 280

About the Contributors 322

Index 328

Preface

In an era of unprecedented global interconnectivity and the ever-present challenges that accompany it, the dynamics of business models, development patterns, and societal transformations have taken center stage in discussions surrounding the New Normal paradigm. The world is undergoing a profound shift, and as we navigate this transition, it is imperative to comprehensively comprehend the reshaping of economic landscapes and the emergence of new realities. It is within this context that we proudly present the edited reference volume: *Sustainable Growth and Global Social Development in Competitive Economies*.

This collaborative effort, authored by esteemed experts Andrei Jean Vasile, Mile Vasić, and Predrag Vukovic, delves into the intricate tapestry of sustainable economic development in the face of modern challenges. The authors bring to light the imperative of not only restructuring conventional frameworks but also recalibrating our understanding of economic paradigms and fostering sustainable entrepreneurship. While the research community has directed its focus toward business models, development patterns, and transformations within the New Normal paradigm, certain critical aspects have remained underexplored.

This book endeavors to bridge the gap between theoretical discourse and practical implementation in the realm of resilient economies, sustainable growth, and global social development within the New Normal. While numerous works address economic crises, few offer comprehensive insights into transformative economic dynamics. Our aim is to not only address this gap but to provide holistic approaches that shed light on the multifaceted dimensions of the New Normal paradigm.

The book's thematic landscape encompasses diverse subjects, including business models, integrated business processes, consumption patterns, digital transformation, education, economic diversity, and more. By examining these facets through the lens of real-world cases spanning various continents and economies, including Europe, North America, and Asia, this volume serves as a valuable resource for professionals, researchers, policymakers, business strategists, and investors alike.

In addition to its academic contributions, this book benefits from the support of influential partners, including RebResNet and EUMMAS, as well as collaborations with universities and research institutions. This collaborative ethos ensures that the book not only disseminates knowledge but also fosters a vibrant dialogue between stakeholders.

The chapters within this volume encapsulate a range of crucial themes, offering solutions and insights into resilient economies, sustainable growth, and global social development within the New Normal paradigm. From business process modeling to rural startups, from economic diversity to tourism and hospitality, the chapters coalesce to form a comprehensive tapestry that addresses the urgent questions of our times.

We extend our heartfelt gratitude to the authors, contributors, and partners who have collectively woven together this volume's rich and diverse tapestry of knowledge. As editors, we are honored to present this compendium to scholars, practitioners, and enthusiasts who are committed to deciphering the complexities of our rapidly evolving economic and social landscapes.

CHAPTER OVERVIEW

Chapter 1: The Concept of Global Growth and Development With the New Normal

Authored by Vladimir Ristanović and Berislav Andrlić, this chapter introduces readers to a fresh perspective on global shifts in the context of the New Normal paradigm. Emphasizing the societal transformations required by this paradigm, the authors delve into the novel life and work patterns it entails. The chapter chronicles the evolution leading to the New Normal and showcases existing initiatives in social, political, and business realms. By spotlighting these efforts, the authors establish the foundation for comprehending the decades-long endeavors driving the New Normal's emergence.

Chapter 2: Paradigm Shift in Corporate Responsibility to New Era of ESG and Social Entrepreneurship

Iza Gigauri and Valentin Vasilev contribute to the discourse on corporate social responsibility (CSR) in this chapter. They illuminate the transition from profit-centric business purposes to a stakeholder-centric approach, emphasizing ethical behavior and sustainable practices. The authors explore the interplay between digital transformation and CSR, highlighting the significance of ESG (environmental, social, and governance) considerations. The chapter also delves into the burgeoning concept of social entrepreneurship, underlining the increasing relevance of sustainability and societal impact in corporate strategies.

Chapter 3: Toward Understanding the Underlying Causes of Scope Creep

Simon Cleveland and Marisa Cleveland address the prevalent issue of scope creep in project management. This chapter provides an accessible analysis of the factors underlying this challenge, catering to both novice and experienced project managers. By identifying the root causes of scope creep, the authors equip readers with foundational insights to proactively manage projects and prevent its detrimental effects.

Chapter 4: Does Financial Globalization Have a Benign or Malignant Effect on Development and Growth?

Authored by Fatma Taşdemir, this chapter critically examines the complex relationship between financial globalization, growth, and sectoral dynamics in emerging market economies. Through comprehensive analysis, the chapter uncovers varying impacts across regions and sectors. The author delves into the nuanced effects of financial globalization on growth trajectories, industrialization, and economic diversity, offering valuable insights for policymakers and researchers alike.

Chapter 5: Tourism Is an Essential Trade – VR and AR Technologies Make It Profitable

C.V. Suresh Babu and Jeyavasan T present an innovative solution to sustainable tourism growth through the application of Virtual Reality (VR) technology. The authors propose a VR metaverse platform that offers immersive tourism experiences, minimizing the environmental impact associated with traditional travel. By exploring the intersection of technology and sustainable tourism, this chapter pioneers a novel approach to both economic growth and global social development.

Chapter 6: Distribution of Mechanization by Regions and Areas in the Republic of Serbia

In this chapter, Irina Marina, Biljana Grujić Vučkovski, and Marijana Jovanović Todorović offer an in-depth analysis of agricultural mechanization distribution in Serbia. Employing rigorous statistical methods, the authors uncover patterns in mechanization adoption across regions and over time. By presenting empirical data and visualizations, the chapter sheds light on the prevailing trends and highlights the factors contributing to the observed distribution patterns.

Chapter 7: Impact of Financial Literacy on Risk Tolerance Behavior of Females Working in the Unorganized Sector

Anushree Srivastava, Neha Yadav, and Anuradha Maurya delve into the relationship between financial literacy and risk tolerance among female workers in the unorganized sector. Examining the intricate interplay between financial literacy, investment behavior, and risk tolerance, the chapter contributes to our understanding of how financial knowledge influences decision-making and economic outcomes.

Chapter 8: Rural Tourist Destinations and Sustainable Development of Tourism in the Republic of Serbia – Analysis of Variables Affecting the Competitiveness

Predrag Vuković and Natatasa Kljajic focus on the rural tourism sector in Serbia, analyzing the variables influencing its competitiveness. Through empirical research and theoretical analysis, the authors identify key factors affecting the quality of tourist offerings in rural destinations. By proposing strategic directions for sustainable development, the chapter advocates for a holistic approach to enhancing the attractiveness and competitiveness of rural tourism.

Chapter 9: Short Food Supply Chains for Achieving Sustainable Growth in Central and Eastern European Countries

Vesna Paraušić and Vlado Kovačević navigate the realm of short food supply chains in Central and Eastern European countries. The chapter unpacks the multifaceted impacts of these chains on local communities and farmers, dissecting their contributions to sustainable growth. Through a balanced assessment, the authors underscore the nuanced relationship between short food supply chains and various dimensions of sustainability.

Chapter 10: The Analysis of the Relationship Between Renewable Energy and Human Development

Mustafa Batuhan Tufaner's chapter delves into the intricate interplay between renewable energy adoption and human development. Using empirical analysis, the author uncovers the associations between these factors in OECD countries. By shedding light on the impact of renewable energy on various dimensions of human development, the chapter enriches the discourse surrounding sustainable growth.

Preface

Chapter 11: The Complementary Effect of Network Capability and Learning Orientation on Firm Performance Evidence From SMEs in Türkiye

Authored by Pelin Karaca Kalkan and Nilay Aluftekin Sakarya, this chapter explores the interconnectedness of network capability and learning orientation in the context of SME performance. By employing the lens of dynamic capabilities theory, the authors investigate the mutual influence of these factors and their role in fostering innovation. The chapter underscores the significance of both internal and external capabilities in shaping SME success.

Chapter 12: Women Entrepreneurship in Multifunctional Agriculture for Rural Revival in Serbia

Vesna Popović and Branko Mihailović illuminate the pivotal role of women entrepreneurship in revitalizing rural areas through multifunctional agriculture. By analyzing a case study from Serbia, the authors demonstrate how collaborative business strategies and gender equality contribute to sustainable rural development. This chapter offers a pragmatic perspective on empowering women entrepreneurs to drive positive change within the New Normal paradigm.

Chapter 13: The Influence of Financial Incentives and Other Socio-Economic Factors on Two-Wheeler EV Adoption in NCR Region

Electric Vehicles are a technological advancement that has the potential to reduce greenhouse gas emissions and lessen the effects of climate change. However, externalities like knowledge appropriability and pollution reduction produce societal and economic benefits that are not reflected in the cost of electric vehicles. Governments have implemented a few strategies to solve the ensuing market failures. We identified a few additional socio-economic parameters based on the research that are anticipated to have an impact on the adoption rates of electric vehicles. We investigated the link between those variables and the effect of socio-economic factors on these variables using structural equation modelling. The model discovered that there is no correlation between financial incentives awareness and two-wheeler EV uptake. The findings indicate that among these socioeconomic characteristics, adoption of two-wheeled electric vehicles was most strongly correlated with age, gender, education, married status, and yearly family income.

IN SUMMARY

As editors of *Sustainable Growth and Global Social Development in Competitive Economies*, we stand at the intersection of knowledge and transformation. The journey through the chapters of this book has been a remarkable exploration of diverse dimensions that collectively shape our understanding of the New Normal paradigm. The contributors, each an expert in their field, have illuminated critical aspects that define the course of economies, societies, and human endeavors in this rapidly evolving era.

The chapters presented in this volume form a tapestry of insights that expand our comprehension of sustainable growth, entrepreneurship, innovation, and societal progress. From redefining corporate responsibility to harnessing technological advancements in tourism, from deciphering the nuances of financial globalization to unraveling the relationship between renewable energy and human development, these chapters offer profound perspectives that guide us towards a more resilient and inclusive future.

Through empirical analysis, theoretical frameworks, and case studies, the book's authors have collectively enriched our discourse on global challenges and opportunities. The exploration of business models, development patterns, and transformations within the New Normal paradigm has illuminated paths towards sustainable economic growth, social development, and environmental stewardship.

In a world marked by uncertainties and rapid changes, the collaborative nature of this book mirrors the collaborative spirit required to overcome challenges and seize opportunities. The insights presented here do not merely reside within these pages; they have the potential to catalyze discussions, influence policies, and drive innovations that shape the trajectories of businesses, economies, and societies.

Preface

As we conclude this journey through the chapters, we extend our deepest gratitude to the authors who have contributed their expertise and insights, and to the readers who engage with these pages. May the ideas within this book inspire ongoing dialogue, research, and action, ultimately guiding us towards a future where sustainable growth and global social development harmoniously coexist in the competitive economies of our New Normal.

Andrei Jean Vasile
Petroleum-Gas University of Ploiesti, Romania & Romanian Academy, National Institute for Economic Research "Costin C. Kirițescu", Romania

Mile Vasic
European Marketing and Management Association, Banja Luka, Bosnia and Herzegovina

Predrag Vukovic
Institute of Agricultural Economics, Belgrade, Serbia

Acknowledgment

The editors would like to express their special thanks and acknowledgements to all the contributors who make possible and gave the opportunity to develop this book project on sustainable growth and global social development in competitive economies.

We would also like to give special thanks to Prof. Luminita Chivu, General director of National Institute for Economic Research "Costin C. Kirițescu" within the Romanian Academy and Prof. Teodor Sedlarski, Academic Director of the Centre for Economic Strategies and Competitiveness at Sofia University, affiliated with the Institute for Strategy and Competitiveness at Harvard Business School (Bulgaria) for their continuous support when undertaking this publishing project and editing the book.

Finally, we are grateful to IGI Global for providing us with the opportunity to publish this edited and for all and support provided. We would like to extend a special thanks to Ms. Jocelynn Hessler for her direct implication in making possible this book.

The editors are grateful to everyone who has been involved directly in supporting this book among the entire process. Without their contribution, reviews, comments and dissemination, help and guidance, this book would not have been possible nowadays.

Chapter 1
The Concept of Global Growth and Development With the New Normal

Vladimir M. Ristanović
https://orcid.org/0000-0002-2957-3465
Institute of European Studies, Belgrade, Serbia

Berislav Andrlić
Faculty of Tourism and Rural Development Pozega, J. J. Strossmayer University of Osijek, Croatia

ABSTRACT

The chapter presents a new view of global changes. The new normal paradigm is based on economic premises but, essentially, constitutes a new scheme. It is a concept that necessarily requires transformations within the entire society. The focus, however, is on a new life and work pattern. Adaptation to changes will be realized quicker than expected. Numerous processes have already been prepared and implemented, such as international standards implementation in social, political, and business spheres, which is sometimes ignored or forgotten. At the same time, this chapter will show the chronology of the events that preceded the new normal paradigm, and which went in the direction of its final manifestation. It will confirm that these efforts in the developed world have existed for decades.

DOI: 10.4018/978-1-6684-8810-2.ch001

INTRODUCTION

The New Normal Paradigm implies a new approach, substantive transformation from old business models to new sustainable business ideas, new development patterns, and a new concept of entrepreneurship. It's a transition process towards a new model of society and economy, which will rearrange existing classic structures.

The essence is in a holistic approach. This approach implies the existence of a potentially large number of connections that exist between different social, economic, and environmental values. Today, a holistic approach to development is represented, according to which the formation of a coherent development policy is the priority. It has become part of international relations. Almost every international meeting begins and ends with conclusions on some of the sustainable development issues. Topics such as the environment, renewable energy sources, poverty reduction, equality, and sustainable development, are central issues of collective debate at the highest international level (Ristanović, 2022b). The negotiations are based on a common global development concept, with the preservation of the environment, technology, innovative industry, digital transformation of education, healthcare, and labor market, integration of business processes, and adequate regulation.

The mission of the New Normal Paradigm is to achieve a macroeconomic environment based on inclusive growth, without GDP, but with an ecological component, technological solutions, and new social norms, among which there should be a balance between the market, the state, and the community, and everything would be built on the expected global common concept of development. Paradigm's biggest flaw is also its mission. It is almost impossible to give a general social picture that is identical for everyone. So, it needs to be changed to manifest the value of well-being for all countries, including the most vulnerable. Thus, they would minimize the failed effects without any consequences. Technically, it could be achieved. Innovative solutions can provide development production processes almost everywhere, certainly where there are objective and time prerequisites for it. But the simple question arises, to whom will equality correspond?

New concepts should respond to the existence of a new environment in which the world is positioned, new approaches that correspond to the business moment, and a new regulatory framework that will respond to everyday needs. It is important to note that these changes have existed since before, far before the emergence of the paradigm. It could be said that the changes started with the entry into the new millennium. In the literature, new approaches and concepts are mostly related to the outbreak of the COVID-19 pandemic and the period of restricted movement and business during the lockdown. However, this attitude is wrong. Why? For the reason that the social phenomena during the pandemic are actually just a manifestation of the changes that were announced earlier and which the developed world hinted at. For example, digitalization was announced much earlier as the basis of the transformation of society, and today it is a concept that will be incorporated into the new "operating system" of every country (WTO, 2020). The education system with digitization will receive a new format that must be more efficient, flexible, and socially useful. It is similar to healthcare. These are two parts of the public sector that were, until recently, the exclusive expense of the state budget. In the new concept, this will no longer be the case. Both sectors will contribute to economic growth and give a new framework to the social system.

The chapter will present a new business concept based on outcomes and impact on the social community rather than the business cycle results. Several decades ago, economic theory has been analyzing the business process through three key elements. The first is input, as an incoming element of the production process. The second one represents the activities carried out by the company. The last, third element represents the final or finished product due to the production process. In recent times, this concept would have been incomplete. Unfinished! The process itself is much more complex and should include, in addition to the economic, the context of the company's impact on society and the environment. Specifically, two more elements should be added to the previous concept. These are outcomes and impacts. With outcomes, it is important to emphasize that outcomes can have beneficial as well as unwanted effects. The former must dominate over the latter. As a result of outcomes, impacts can cause structural and long-term social changes. Therefore, it is up to the policymakers to use economic policy measures and instruments to make these outcomes and impacts more beneficial to society at a minimal cost. Electricity production in Serbia will illustrate an example of a new business concept.

ANNOUNCEMENT OF THE NEW NORMAL PARADIGM

The entry into the new millennium was presented dramatically in the years leading up to it. Announcements that problems in the information telecommunication sector would paralyze the entire world were placed everywhere. In fact, from this distance, the millennium bug was only a threat to the future state of the global economy. The mix we live in today, twenty years later. And that is a world in the uncertainty of work, knowledge, innovation, artificial intelligence, capital, investments, exchange rates, interest rates, stock markets, regulation, etc. Uncertainty exists due to ambivalent solutions, frequent crises, problems in all spheres of life (energy, water, food, weapons, currencies, viruses, pandemics, etc.), economic imbalances, turbulent periods, political turmoils, etc.

Frequent changes to the game rules at the global level have become a daily occurrence. New regulation at the national level and competition at the supranational level deepens the uncertainty. The world is increasingly burdened by growing protectionism. The new order was not created. We are still in the old global order, growing in deep inequality. Growing debts. Only some parts of the existing order were changed. They only changed the roles and participation of certain actors in the global cake. Only cosmetic changes were made, which led the rich to even more wealth and the poor to greater poverty.

The announcement of future system changes already exists in the public domain. For the past two or three decades, radical changes in societies have been underway in the direction of a new assessment of sustainable development and less and less application of conventional theories of economic growth and development. Economics has been taught in schools for over a century, regardless of ecology, sustainable energy, and the environment. Circumstances impose new directions, and expectations accelerate the pace to start with more concrete actions in the new millennium (Table 1). The first initiatives were launched by relevant international institutions such as the United Nations and the World Bank. That was to be expected! The first step forward came with the Millennium Goals, at that time, a new approach to the growth and development of the economies of poor and underdeveloped countries on the African continent. Available data up to the world financial crisis in 2008 show that the global economy was growing. However, even in that period, numerous problems existed, which indicated that a crisis was coming. The energy crisis of 2003-2008 had a significant impact on the auto industry. The period of rapid technological advancement coincided with the age of vehicle mega-platforms. The growing supply of cars was accompanied by an increasing number of loans, which were not so cheap. It was similar to the real estate market, where the bubble that caused the global crisis in 2008 was created. The outlines of that crisis are still visible today.

In the years of the financial crisis, the initiative for implementing these goals was additionally strengthened, with pressure for stronger financing of sustainable development. A turnaround in terms of new and broader goals followed, and in 2012 the implementation of the concept of sustainable development goals began, which was valid for all countries of the world, regardless of their level of development. The fight against poverty, equality, social justice, and environmental protection. A new approach was adopted in measuring the quality of economies. Thus, GNP, GDP, GDP per capita, and GDP purchasing power parity go down in history, and new measures of country development dominate, such as inclusive development, green economy, circular economy, renewable energy, technology in production, and innovation, which is followed by the new regulatory framework. The latter was incorporated in the Stockholm Declaration in 2014, which definitively ended the Washington Consensus. Next, in 2016, Agenda 2030 defined complex scopes

Table 1. Evolution of the new normal

Year	Description
2000.	Criticism of the Washington Consensus (Stigliz, World Bank)
	Millennium Goals - MDGs (created only for the African continent)
2007.	The financial crisis (appeared on the demand side - solved by wrongly chosen measures on the supply side)
2014.	The era of sustainable development begins (green economy, circular economy, instead of GDP, GDP, GDP pc, GDP PPP)
	The Stockholm Declaration (definitive collapse of the Washington Consensus)
2016.	Impelmentation of the sustainable development goals and Agenda 2030
2019.	COVID-19 virus
2020.	Schwab's Big Reset
	The defeat of the free market and the creation of a new operating system for every country – WTO
2021.	„New Normal" paradigm
2022.	Ukrainian and energy crisis (appeared on the suply side - solved by wrongly chosen measures on the demand side)

Source: Own contribution

for sustainable development, an energy-neutral and healthy green planet. New confirmation that the invisible hand of the market is not producing the results that were expected decades ago, guided by neoliberal policies, came with the annual report of the World Trade Organization in 2020. The conclusion is that the state is the key to economic development in a triangle with the market and the community. The state's new operating system would consist of three units: financial system, legal structure, and regulatory framework. In which an industry based on ideas and competition will be clearly defined, and where finally, the public sector (education, health, employment), with the help of digitalization, will be a positive component of the country's development. The benefits of digital education have already been explored and recognized around the world (Andrlić et al., 2023).

The business changes went in the direction of changing the management concept instead of establishing a market balance. A focus on market actors rather than market support has led to the spread of protectionist measures by many. Increasing protectionism has threatened business in markets, especially in fast-growing economies. The creation of various trade agreements raised the question of the sustainability of globalization. The protection of certain financial giants, support for powerful corporations, and insufficiently strict regulation has influenced weakened market tools. Measures and instruments of economic policies have become insufficiently powerful to respond to uncertainty, risk, and crisis. Selective measures, which have been applied in several countries, have only benefited certain players rather than targeting market performance. That forced business actors to modify their business processes. Changing economic conditions, changing consumer behavior and the development of new technologies will cause the emergence of new or growth of existing markets (Andrlić et al., 2022a).

A good example is the transition to the long-tail economy. It's a new business concept that first undermined supply chains and came to the fore with the pandemic in the following years. The concept is designed to sell less current and expensive products to the detriment of classic production and sales. Avoiding inventory, late delivery, third-party financing, limited assortment, and forced demand has become a new business model. The best example of this concept is car sales. Today, there is almost no example of a customer being able to walk into a car dealership with cash, pay the car bill and drive home. There are no cars in the showroom, but only in the online car catalog. There are no finished cars in the warehouse either. Only pre-ordered cars can be found on the factory lines. So, this is not about breaking the supply chain or stopping production (due to the delay of spare parts). The choice of equipment in the car is almost pre-defined, and the buyer can choose only what is in the narrow assortment. Similar to the menu in restaurants! Brands have lost their dominance. Sellers are less and less able to influence traffic. Today, customers dominate the market - where and which products to buy.

In recent years, the redistribution of globalization is also becoming a considerable aspect of global changes to the existing order. Global changes recognize new business models, such as nearshoring or friend-shoring models. Protectionist measures are again in force. Selective state policy dominates and goes to the detriment of the market balance. Wrong activities in banks and financial institutions are bailed out with taxpayer money, while regulations and business practices are ignored. That contributes to the collapse of the business environment. A parallel cryptocurrency market also functions. Largely unregulated, this market is becoming global with high daily turnover. We are facing a new face of globalization: friendly partners are sought, and decisions are made with a common interest. In other words, there is a noticeable trend to move from nearshoring to friend-shoring of the business model (collective sanctions against Russia, joint pressure on China).

The banking sector is always attractive. Throughout history, it has been slow to accept changes but successfully adapted. For example, the banking sector has responded adequately to digitization and new strategies. The introduction of the Fintech industry into the banking sector has significantly increased the role of innovation (Basole & Patel, 2018). They contributed to the emergence of new business models, namely peer-to-peer lending, digital wallets, and crowdfunding (Leong et al., 2017). Today, the dominant risk in the banking business has become an operational risk, ahead of market and interest rate risks (Ristanović & Knežević, 2023; Cristea, 2021; Vasiliev et al., 2018). Uncertainty from the market was transferred to banking management structures. Management, labor, and the principal-agent problem create more risk than the market. Only major business mistakes can lead banks to bankruptcy. At the beginning of the financial crisis in 2008, the interest rate and exchange rate, as economic variables, began to distort the results of econometric models. Unscrupulously conducted monetary policy at the global level has influenced expectations, investments, and planning to be determined by short-term stock market movements. Daily fluctuations of the exchange rate and interest rates on the financial market distort the real picture. Big financial players are given special treatment by national and supranational institutions. Banks develop their new products over time and offer them to clients long before these products are recognized in regulations. The Basel standards are being accepted and implemented satisfactorily (BIS, 2021; BIS, 2020; Ferreira et al., 2019). However, their application is not by the regulations. Insufficiently fast adjustments threaten the stability of the banking sector. Also, the new regulation must accompany the new banking business related to the new approach to sustainable development. For example, delay or slow inclusion of ESG activities in banking strategies will negatively affect the profitability of banks and the banking sector (Menicucci & Paolucci, 2023; Dragomir et al., 2022).

Trade flows are taking on new dimensions. Trade in goods is increasingly determined by trends in daily business rather than global trade flows. Trade flows are increasingly linked to political rather than trade partners (Ristanović, 2022a). Reaching for protectionist measures increased dramatically (Pelevic & Ristanovic, 2011), even more so in the second decade of the new millennium during the pandemic and energy crisis periods. Hence, there is a continuous disequilibrium in the commodity market (Ricci, 2016). For years, this imbalance spilled over into the market of production factors. The labor market suffered the most, and its lack of flexibility only fueled the global market imbalance. Several times during the first two decades of the new millennium, international trade recorded a significantly greater decline than the global gross domestic product (ECB, 2016). In the first decade, services were affordable and accessible for the majority, while they became unavailable and expensive in the next decade. In the pandemic years, they were limited. That hurt global economic growth (UNCTAD, 2021). By reducing disposable income, due to the pandemic, energy crisis, and inflation in recent years, there has been a drop in international trade. Big businesses remained in the hands of wealthy actors, and the secondary market trade was increasingly intense (for example, public debt purchase). The prices of foreign currencies have become so volatile that even currency wars have become meaningless (dollar-yuan, dollar-ruble).

Leadership takes on a new dimension with the New Normal paradigm. Namely, new leaders must change their approach in the business world. The elite's power has been overcome because the supremacy of individuals will be overcome by social power. Achieving the set goals will not be the only task of the new leaders. The key will be how well the objectives reach the end users. Therefore, profit will not be the only goal in the new normal, but an added value that will benefit the social community. Doherty et al. (2020) state that new business models will primarily focus on the individual, the environment, and the social community. Bhattacharya et al. (2017) have already defined new business models in commercial circles: "These models rely less on the physical movement of goods and fixed investments in markets and more on using digital connectivity and ecosystems to expand across borders." Even earlier, Rickart (2015) pointed out that assessing how innovations will contribute to future business models is difficult. He classified them into three groups. The first group of models that do not create value for the consumer and that such models should be removed immediately. The second group is platform models that simultaneously serve two or more markets. The third group represents a global business that opens on the international market.

Trade in today's global world will be based on completely different assumptions. The backbone of trade will be marketing. And marketing will be carried out through numerous niches and not aggressively on the mass market. Access to consumers will have a completely different format than before. Thus, trade flows and directions will also change. However, in numerous less-developed economies, trade directions will remain determined by the old practice of trading only with countries that are major foreign trade or political partners (Ristanović, 2022a). So, the idea is to form a trade in the future so that the mass sale of each developed product is realized through marketing niches. The goal will not be to enter the market with one product and create a hit. Internet provides the opportunity to promote a number of post-purchase services and the opportunity to spread propaganda with the aim of creating loyalty and eventual repeat purchases (Andrlić et al., 2022b)

Creating new business models will put the customer in a dominant position. The numerous options available to the consumer leave room for choice. This will lead to new alternatives. Shopping in small shops will be a disincentive, especially after the possibility of online shopping. It's the same with entertainment, as there are numerous ways to consume entertainment content. Even their availability may lead consumers to prefer a home theater over a movie theater. That will affect the change in the business policy of film distribution. Schwab (2020) announced during the COVID-19 pandemic that incarceration will selectively affect behavioral changes. Individuals will even be forced to continue working for themselves (do it yourself - DIY), as was the case during the lockdown (baking bread, cooking, cutting hair, etc.). And students will question the high price of education they pay in some countries. What is the importance of the previous way of acquiring knowledge, its later use, the profitability of studying, the types of learning, and the role of the teacher/professor?

According to McKinsey (2017), digital customer expectations are growing in every industry, both directly for digital products and services and indirectly for the speed, accuracy, productivity, and convenience that digital technology enables. This means it's necessary to transform management into operational management adapted to the digital world.

Sustainable development takes over the role of a measure of economic growth from GDP. Since 2014, a new concept has been launched based on a holistic approach considering numerous social, economic, and environmental categories. A concept that transcends national borders and becomes a global topic. The procedures for achieving the UN sustainable development goals (SDGs) are defined by simple procedures and specific economic and political processes (Ristanović, 2023). Achieving the SDGs includes social, environmental, and economic issues. Conservative quantitative measures of the economy remain benchmarks for comparison and analysis. The new criteria are based on more inclusive criteria, summarizing numerous indicators apart from economic ones. Criteria such as sustainable development and inclusive development are taking over. People from public life, especially politicians, have neglected conventional economic theories in previous years, apostrophizing that they fail to explain new economic flows. It makes sense if you look at the role of business in environmental issues, education, water protection, etc. However, these topics, such as the circular or green economy, have only recently been opened up. In such circumstances, a new approach is needed, new theoretical concepts that are not based on doctrines.

DIGITALIZATION HELPS THE NEW NORMAL

The introduction of digitization aimed to improve business, speed up some processes, facilitate administration, reduce costs, etc. Digitization did contribute to global progress, bringing global benefits for the growth of economies and their development. It also led to individuals not using technology but managing it. Problems arise when individuals or groups misuse digitization and technology. At the global level, the abuse of technology or digitization necessarily imposes the need to create a unique global strategy for growth, development, and world order from one center. In other words, they impose a centralized approach that would prevent the misuse of technology and digitization in society. However, centralization can limit individual freedoms and represent a slippery slope. It is, therefore, necessary to create a new approach that includes innovations in management, control, regulations, business, and market. That is why the legislation will be complicated, as well as complex. Let's try to make it purposeful!

The creation of new types of learning began much earlier, before the COVID-19 pandemic, especially in the developed countries of the Western Hemisphere. Research on new learning tools has been developing for almost two decades. Their application intensified after the 2010s. The largest universities in the world developed their learning software. So, they smoothly responded to the crisis years and the years during and immediately after the pandemic. Creating virtual networks where participants socialize, play, and learn is widespread. Several networks are publicly available. When Mr. Zuckerman talked about the future of Facebook, he meant a parallel virtual environment where it would be possible to jump in and take advantage of such networking. Long before him, the digital oasis was mentioned in Ernest Klein's novel. Even further in the past, Neal Stevenson, in his 1992 novel "Snowfall" described the Metaverse as a virtual world composed of unique environments which have a specific purpose: entertainment, socializing, education, etc. We are all part of virtual reality. We live it! We are unconsciously drawn into it. And access is about more than simple – You have a smartphone, don't you? The individual user falls along a continuum within the spectrum of virtuality (on a scale from low to high, there is augmented reality, mixed reality, and virtual reality) (Pimentel et al., 2022).

Digitization has long since entered the educational system of developed countries. The application of online learning has been developing for more than ten years. Distance learning systems and adequate software have been developed, enabling a new approach to education. Education is an investment that is becoming unsustainable. Why? Because it is an investment of 3, 5, or 6 years, and it is uncertain. Several key questions arise. What after that period? Will the acquired knowledge be in demand after that period? What about the expected application of knowledge? Will the skills match the needs of the market? What is the expected return on investment? Here the situation is specific - the service is paid immediately (annually), and the outcome comes only after the end of the study cycle (3 or 5, or 6 years). New forms of education must focus on the students as an individual, innovations in science, technology advance, application of knowledge, good practice for acquiring skills, and numerous paid courses. Worldwide, the trend is for the cost of education to fall entirely on the individual. The tendency is to reduce government expenditures and provide programs someone is willing to pay for. Experience has shown a low rate of finishing free courses, even if the topics are current and attractive.

Digitization raises the question of including gender equality in the gender and social context. Women's participation in the digital economy has been increasing in recent years, and this trend has been particularly pronounced in the last two decades. Women are also gaining greater participation in the labor force and are becoming a higher part of the active population.

Advances in digitization have undoubtedly changed people's lives and work. Sousa et al. (2020) show that digital technologies are relevant in various areas: management, science, education, etc. In a business sense, digitization has helped improve business processes, increase labor productivity, and reduce labor costs. The advancement of artificial intelligence (AI) is a leap into the future of business and social life. AI develops numerous positive effects. Expectations show they would contribute to GDP growth of 7% and labor productivity growth of 1.5% in the next ten years. The other side of the coin is the hidden costs of artificial intelligence. These are the consumption of energy and materials (Nordgren, 2023; van Winsberghe, 2022; Coeckelbergh, 2021) but also the costs of regulation (Barczentevicz & Mueller, 2021). At the same time, the question of the impact of AI on the labor market is becoming increasingly prominent in the public eye.

Why is it important? Several jobs are under pressure to shift due to the introduction of artificial intelligence into business processes. There is a fear that the world will face the abolition of certain jobs in specific professions. Another problem facing the world is that the global demographic picture is unfavorable. According to data from the World Bank (WB, 2016), the world is facing a decline in the working population and an aging population. The correlation between AI and the labor market can be estimated. In other words, will the application of AI succeed in replacing the shortage of the working population in the labor market? If this possibility exists, why is the further progress of AI controversial? Goldman Sachs (2023) predicts that about 25% of jobs in the US and Europe could be covered by AI, equivalent to approximately 300 million full-time workers. That's a huge number! If the world faced such a dramatic scenario, it would have a doubly negative effect on the labor market. On the one hand, the number of workers would be reduced, and on the other, the salaries of the remaining employees would be reduced. A few occupations susceptible to rapid replacement by artificial intelligence are lawyers, translators, accountants, data entry clerks, financial analysts, administrative staff, software developers, and customer service representatives.

The process of business standardization began to be applied in the 1980s, and a series of global changes transformed employment and work (ILO, 2019). They were introduced with a clear emphasis on the advantages of standardized business - greater efficiency, security, better communication, and better finances. Employed workers were less prone to mistakes and were more satisfied. Managers found their way around more easily, communicated better with workers, and increased work productivity thanks to established procedures. Control was simpler. End users knew what quality of product or service they expected, with shorter waiting times. However, when these processes are analyzed in more detail today, they were only an introduction to today's artificial intelligence application. International standards are needed to make AI work as well as possible and help solve problems. The standards were refined over decades, and when they reached a suitable form, they became part of the AI algorithm. The vast majority of the world's population has not seen far enough. Everyday topics occupied people - politics, crises, wars, diseases, sports, forums, Miss World, Eurovision songs, prices, stocks, etc.

Today, the global public insists on slowing down the development and application of AI for six months out of fear for the labor market and the social community. The Institute for the Future of Life (2023) launched an initiative in professional circles through an open letter expressing disagreement with the further development of AI. Threatening jobs is a serious social and business problem. It can also be a macroeconomic problem. Why? For example, one of the benchmarks for conducting economic policy in the US is the creation of new monthly jobs. The development and application of AI during the last decade exceed the current capacities of states and societies. In conditions of depopulation, rigorous migration measures, protectionism, etc., the problem of artificial intelligence becomes even more complicated. The degree of commercial competition is estimated to have increased manifold in the last few years [with the development of generative pre-trained transformers (GPT) from the family of large language models (LLM) introduced in 2018]. Proponents of slowing down the progress of AI argue that it violates prudential and ethical principles, creating national and supranational frameworks to increase public protection. Among this group of experts, there is a growing fear that artificial intelligence can be misused. Artificial intelligence systems can deviate from human goals and values by spreading misinformation and manipulating public opinion. Their key point is that societies need time to adapt to new changes and regulations to be established. The initial idea of creating artificial intelligence was to work for the benefit of humanity. Is today's application of generative artificial intelligence, which solves complex problems, art, and assists in scientific research, also aimed at the benefit of humanity? These are issues that will require a specific holistic approach, ethical application of AI, and adequate regulation in the future. However, like every revolutionary change so far, this one will create new jobs, and the development of AI will enable new concepts that will keep pace with global business flows, science, and research, with a greater degree of transparency and oversight of AI systems (see also van Wynsberghe et al., 2022). The short-term limitations that AI can cause will, already in the medium term, be adapted to everyday activities. It takes time to adjust to the new trends the world is exposed to today. When the circle is turned and the time savings thanks to the application of AI are creatively used, a sustainable global picture will emerge.

AN ANALOGY WITH THE LUDDITE MOVEMENT

There have always been individuals or groups opposed to the coming changes, innovations, and technical solutions, which were fueled by technological progress. Such resistance in people manifests a more psychological than economic dimension. Recently, during the financial crisis and the COVID-19 pandemic, some research has shown that job loss harms mental and physical health without financial strain

(Blustein & Guarino, 2020; Breslau et al., 2020; Coile et al., 2014; Blustein, 2013; Libby, 2010). From that point of view, there is justification for individual resistance to change. However, this point of view has another side. On that side, the question arises, how much will the extension of resistance slow down concrete progress? What is the lesser evil for the community? Where are the minor consequences? The answer is very complex. A similar problem exists in France today. Protests against structural changes can be justified when it comes to the motive of workers to keep the length of their working life unchanged. However, they can hardly be justified if some other issues are taken into account, such as the economic system (budget), the health system (healthier population), or demography (longer life expectancy).

At the beginning of the 19th century, the greatest workers' resistance was in England. Textile workers, fearing job losses, protested against the introduction of mechanical looms and weaving machines. It was a significant technological advance in the textile industry. The movement was named after Ned Ludd, who began breaking machines with a large hammer. There was a fear among artisans that unskilled machine operators would take away their jobs and livelihoods.

The outcome of the protest was inevitable. Collapse! Artisans could either stay in manual work with lower productivity or use new machines and increase productivity. How ready were the artisans for change? Was there much interest in them embracing technological advances and working on weaving machines? Obviously, not enough. Much time was spent in vain, although the outcome was not uncertain. The creators of the new technological advancement should have been patient enough to allow time for workers to accept the foundations of the new solution. The system was established a few years later the machines were no longer the enemy of the artisans. They increased their productivity, and there was no more fear for their work and earnings. The outcome of these protests brought trade unions to the fore (Matias, 1969), whose organization was already tolerated (Morton & Tate, 1956). The strengthening of trade unions helped make the foundations of the new order easier to accept. Unions had a dual role - they protected capital and pacified workers. All this shows that the Luddite movement should be seen in a deeper context - as a step towards the development of modern society, not only as a revolt of artisans.

Is it acceptable to make an analogy between the Luddist movement and today's trends? Are today's changes with "the new normal" a real threat that numerous people will lose their jobs? Yes. Indeed, it will! In various professions, many jobs will be lost. Someone will say that it is all because of modern technologies. However, a counterargument is always missing - new technology will inevitably create new jobs in these and other professions. It will be like that in the future. Sooner or later, there will be further progress in society, with less or more resistance to change. Namely, it is human nature not to accept changes to what is already established and functioning well. Experimentation in conditions of stable earnings is not acceptable to anyone, even if there is a justification and social benefit. Social progress must have both losers and winners. The best scenario would be to have less of the former and more of the latter. New changes within the existing global order should be given time and space to establish themselves and contribute to the well-being of humanity.

CLASSIC PRODUCTION PROCESS VERSUS THE "NEW NORMAL" SUSTAINABLE PRODUCTION PROCESS

The classic production process is a multi-phase process. In the first phase, companies acquire resources as inputs into the production process. They then undertake various production activities to transform resources into products. The final product is quantitatively and qualitatively measurable and represents the result of the production process. Future production processes will be based on the concept of sustainable development. It means, in the future, they have to respond to greater demands from those end users. In addition to the three stages of the mentioned production process, sustainable production processes will contain two more key ones. The finished product is an output for the end user but, at the same time, an outcome for the social community. Therefore, the company must have some outcome type throughout the production process. It is how it communicates with the community in which it operates. At the same time, that outcome can be positive or negative. These outcomes can be generated at multiple levels – corporate social responsibility, philanthropic activities, local growth, entrepreneurship, etc. Today, numerous tools for measuring outcomes have been developed. Measurement is realized in several ways. For example, it is related to a specific UN Sustainable Development Goal (gender equality, planet, poverty...), stakeholder mapping, inclusion in "ESG" (environmental, social or governance) categories, etc., in another key phase, these outcomes can lead to structural impacts and long-term social change.

Hereafter, the transition from classical to sustainable production will be presented. It's a global trend! Global changes require this adaptation of the production process because producing a finished product for the end user is becoming a thing of the past. In the future, production processes will include two more dimensions, the impact on the community and the environment. Here we will present both production processes, classic and sustainable, using a concrete example of electricity production in Serbia. In the best form, their differences and specificities will be highlighted. Why was the electricity system chosen in Serbia? For the reason that the largest share of electricity production is still based on non-renewable forms of energy and that the commitment to green energy is being introduced at a slow pace. According to official data from the Energy Agency of Serbia (2021), as much as 60.4% of production in 2021 came from thermal power plants (down from 68.6% in 2020). It is important to note that

Figure 1. The business framework through which companies create impact
Source: Own contribution

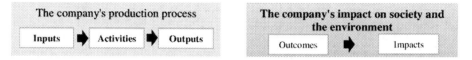

the goal of this analysis is not the analysis of EPS's operations or the current energy development strategy. The goal is to analyze the premises of the existing classic production process and the future expected sustainable electricity production. This concept is presented in Figure 1.

As previously emphasized, thermal power plants are the main actors in electricity production in Serbia. They use coal as an input. Coal is a non-renewable resource, and its exploitation threatens the environment. From the production process, electricity is created as a final product. End users are companies, households, and individuals. According to the classical production process, the story ends here - EPS produces, delivers, and bills the electricity. Therefore, the production process is completed with the delivery of the final product. However, the process does not end here. It continues with the "New Normal" paradigm. The outcome and impact of the final product on the social community and the environment are evaluated. This is where a problem for sustainable development arises. Electricity is produced from non-renewable sources by mining coal. This implies damage to the environment. First, at the level of the mine or the pit itself, it becomes devastated. Then, during the production process, air pollution occurs. This means that every kilowatt of electricity produced satisfies end-users with a service (electricity) but harms society (environmental and air pollution) and hurts the economy in the long term (wasting non-renewable resources).

From the end user's point of view, the situation is also dramatic. The user pays the electricity bill. He gets adequate service, i.e. electricity. He directly pays for electricity as a final product. But indirectly, he pays for air pollution in the amount of the cost of kilowatts of electricity consumed from the bill. In other words, when the viewing angle changes, which comes with the new normal, the end user gets electricity and pays for air pollution.

Positive long-term effects (outcomes and impacts) on the economy, society, and ecology can only be expected if a part of the price of electricity from the bill is directed to the installation of adequate and modern filters, to modernize the production process, encourage and develop green energy, increase the share of electricity production from renewable sources, i.e. reduction of production from non-renewable sources, and adjustment of regulations.

Relying on classic electricity production, if an increase in labor productivity does not accompany an increase in the price of energy, the effect on the total income of the company will be low. From the perspective of sustainable production, any increase in energy prices should be converted into investment in adequate environmental protection systems or reinvestment through renewable energy sources. Only then will sustainable development not be absent. Therefore, the future business focus must be determined for the outcomes and impacts of the final product, which is the result of the production process.

CONCLUSION

In times of global geostrategic changes, corporate strategies, and changing societal values, governments will be forced to offer individuals and households more alternatives. Rapid and frequent changes will require stronger cooperation of corporate sectors with governments in the country and abroad in the future. Market uncertainty and geopolitical shocks are forcing economic policymakers to revise their approaches, create advanced analyzes and offer sophisticated strategies. The emphasis must be on effective demand rather than imagined demand. In this regard, it is necessary to accelerate investments, focus on clean energy, sustainable development, accelerate deregulation, etc. It is an adaptation to the new business model of the global economy. McKinsey (2017) highlights the importance of introducing a next-generation operating model in the world of digital services, which is completely customer-oriented. All new business models will be focused on the individual, as the end user, and the protection of the planet. From the social side, perhaps all this is justified. Finally, the individual will perform everyday tasks more successfully, stimulate creativity even more and improve their competencies, living on a preserved planet in healthy conditions.

Global changes in the future mean applying each country, company, and individual to global trends established through all activities and processes so far. The adjustment result will be better only with maximum use of the national potential for sustainable development, adequate business models, a transparent control system, and adequate regulation. Everything mentioned in this article is intended to look at trends that have been partially neglected, to cover a wide range of things that will necessarily change in the future, and to present changes that are inevitable and that have already been prepared. The point is to adapt to the wheel that has begun to turn and which needs to be arranged from an ethical, social, economic, and ecological point of view for the benefit of all humanity.

The changes that are expected in the future would be easier to accept, i.e. they would be easier to adapt if the lens through which it is observed were changed. Advocates of paradigm could emphasize that! Therein lies the puzzle to be solved. It is how to change the approach that will strengthen the impact and contribution to the community instead of focusing on making a profit. Does such a leap indicate an intergenerational problem? New generations accept the transition easier and faster than the old ones. Obviously, the former will implement the process, and the latter will provide the experience. It could even be said that the total costs will remain the same. How is it possible? Through the process of adaptation, everything that at first glance seems complicated, expensive, and even unfathomable will only be a common feature of future models of behavior or business. Opponents will oppose even the slightest change, declaratively refusing to implement it. Often only until the moment when they are forced to adhere to the adopted solution without alternatives (chips, codes, e-applications, e-purchases, e-payments, etc.). Patience takes time! But we should not forget that a missed moment can create a negative outcome and impact.

Conceptually, the "New Normal" covers the gap between already established standardized processes and their application in a new format. The observations presented in the text suggest the existence of different forms that will allow greater visibility of different approaches, hint at potential problems or provide new solutions, develop new practices, etc. At the same time, it will enable a look into the future of shaping new business models, behavioral patterns, social norms, and sustainable processes through adaptation to the New Normal paradigm. Moreover, the observations from the article can be conducive to policy-makers, decision-makers, companies, citizens, and investors.

REFERENCES

Andrlić, B., Ariwa, E., & Gonçalves Rodrigo Franco. (2022a) Corporate Promotion in the Digital Era: A Conceptual Framework of Tourism Sector. In *Proceedings of IX International Scientific Conference of students and young scholars "Actual problems of Management in Marketing- Current Challenges"*. Lutsk National Technical University. https://doi.org/658.8:338(066)

Andrlić, B., Pandas, A., & Hak, M. (2022b). Market Valuation Models in the Function of Sustainable Rural Tourism. *5th International Rural Tourism Congress*, 772-782.

Andrlić, B., Priyashantha, K., & De Alwis Adambarage, C. (2023). Employee Engagement Management in the COVID-19 Pandemic: A Systematic Literature Review. *Sustainability (Basel), 15*(2), 1–22. doi:10.3390u15020987

Barczentewicz, M. & Mueller, B. (2021). *More Than Meets The AI: The Hidden Costs of a European Software Law*. Center for Data Innovation. Information Technology and Innovation Foundation (ITIF).

Basole, R. C., & Patel, S. S. (2018). Transformation through unbundling: Visualizing the global FinTech ecosystem. *Service Science*, *10*(4), 379–396. doi:10.1287erv.2018.0210

Bhattacharya, A., Reeves, M., Lang, N., & Augustinraj, R. (2017). *New Business Models for a New Global Landscape*. Boston Consulting Group.

BIS. (2020). *Implementation of Basel standards A report to G20 Leaders on implementation of the Basel III regulatory reforms*. Basel Committee on Banking Supervision.

BIS (2021). *Progress report on adoption of the Basel regulatory framework*. Basel Committee on Banking Supervision.

Blustein, D. L., & Guarino, P. A. (2020). Work and Unemployment in the Time of COVID-19: The Existential Experience of Loss and Fear. *Journal of Humanistic Psychology*, *60*(5), 702–709. doi:10.1177/0022167820934229

Blustein, D. L., Kozan, S., & Connors-Kellgren, A. (2013). Unemployment and underemployment: A narrative analysis about loss. *Journal of Vocational Behavior*, *82*(3), 256-265. doi:10.1016/j.jvb.2013.02.005

Breslau, J., Finucane, M. L., Locker, A. R., Baird, M. D., Roth, E. A., & Collins, R. L. (2021). A longitudinal study of psychological distress in the United States before and during the COVID-19 pandemic. *Preventive Medicine*, *143*. doi:10.1016/j.ypmed.2020.106362

Coeckelbergh, M. (2021). AI for climate: Freedom, justice, and other ethical and political challenges. *AI and Ethics*, *1*(1), 67–72. doi:10.100743681-020-00007-2

Coile, C. C., Levine, P. B., & McKnight, R. (2014). Recessions, Older Workers, and Longevity: How Long Are Recessions Good for Your Health? *American Economic Journal. Economic Policy*, *6*(3), 92–119. doi:10.1257/pol.6.3.92

Cristea, M.-A. (2021). Operational Risk Management in Banking Activity. *Journal of Eastern Europe Research in Business and Economics*, 1–16. Advance online publication. doi:10.5171/2021.969612

Doherty, R., Haugh, H., Sahan, E., Wills, T., & Croft, S. (2020). *Creating the new economy: business models that put people and planet first*. WFTO and Traidcraft.

Dragomir, V. D., Bătae, O. M., Ionescu, B. S., & Ionescu-Feleagă, L. (2022). The Influence of ESG Factors on Financial Performance in the Banking Sector during the Covid-19 Pandemic. *Economic Computation and Economic Cybernetics Studies and Research*, *56*(4), 71–88. doi:10.24818/18423264/56.4.22.05

EARS. (2021). *2021 Energy Agency Annual Report*. Energy Agency of the Republic of Serbia.

Ferreira, Jenkinson, & Wilson. (2019). *From Basel I to Basel III: Sequencing Implementation in Developing Economies*. IMF WP/19/127

Future of Life Institute. (2023). Pause Giant AI Experiments: An Open Letter, ECB. (2016). Understanding the weakness in global trade. What is the new normal? *Occasional Paper Series*, 178. European Central Bank.

ILO. (2019). *Rules of the game: An introduction to the standards-related work of the International Labour Organization. International Labour Office*.

Kindylidi, I., & Cabral, T. S. (2021). Sustainability of AI: The Case of Provision of Information to Consumers. *Sustainability (Basel)*, *13*(21), 12064. doi:10.3390u132112064

Leong, C., Tan, B., Xiao, X., Ter Chian Tan, F., & Sun, Y. (2017). Nurturing a FinTech ecosystem: The case of a youth microloan startup in China. *International Journal of Information Management*, *37*(2), 92–97. doi:10.1016/j.ijinfomgt.2016.11.006

Libby, A. M., Ghushchyan, V., McQueen, R. B., & Campbell, J. D. (2010). Economic grand rounds: Psychological distress and depression associated with job loss and gain: The social costs of job instability. *Psychiatric Services (Washington, D.C.)*, *61*(12), 1178–1180. doi:10.1176/ps.2010.61.12.1178 PMID:21123399

Mathias, P. (1969). *The First Industrial Nation: The Economic History of Britain 1700–1914*. Methuen & Co. Ltd.

McKinsey. (2017). *Introducing the next-generation operating model*. McKinsey & Company. www.mckinsey.com

Menicucci, E., & Paolucci, G. (2023). ESG dimensions and bank performance: An empirical investigation in Italy. *Corporate Governance (Bradford)*, *23*(3), 563–586. doi:10.1108/CG-03-2022-0094

Morton, A. L., & Tate, G. (1956). *The British Labour Movement 1770–1920*. Lawrence and Wishart.

Nordgren, A. (2023). Artificial intelligence and climate change: Ethical issues. *Journal of Information. Communication and Ethics in Society, 21*(1), 1–15. doi:10.1108/JICES-11-2021-0106

Pelević, B. & Ristanović, V. (2011). (Neo)protekcionizam i svetska ekonomska kriza, *Srpska politička misao, 4*, 237-255. doi:10.22182/spm.3442011.12

Pimentel, D., Fauville, G., Frazier, K., McGivney, E., Rosas, S., & Woolsey, E. (2022). *An Introduction to Learning in the Metaverse*. Meridian Treehouse.

Ricart, J.E. (2015). *Business Models for the Companies of the Future, Reinventing the Company in the Digital Age*. Academic Press.

Ricci, A. (2016). *Unequal Exchange in International Trade: A General Model*. WP-EMS no 2016/05, University of Urbino.

Ristanović, V. (2022a, January–April). International Trade Flows of the Balkan States. *The Review of International Affairs, 73*(1184), 1184. doi:10.18485/iipe_ria.2022.73.1184.1

Ristanović, V. (2022b). Sustainable Development – Where is Serbia in Fulfilling Agenda 2030 Goals? *Serbian Review of European Studies, I*(1), 119–152.

Ristanović, V. (2023). Sustainable development in the new methodology of Serbia's accession to the EU. *International Problems, 75*(1), 7–37. doi:10.2298/MEDJP2301007R

Ristanović, V., & Knežević, G. (2023). Multi-criteria Decision-Making on Operational Risk in Banks. *Proceedings of the 1st International Conference on Innovation in Information Technology and Business (ICIITB 2022)*, 5–21. doi:10.2991/978-94-6463-110-4_2

Sachs, G. (2023). *Generative AI could raise global GDP by 7%*. Author.

Schwab, K., & Malleret, T. (2020). *COVID-19: The Great Reset*. World Economic Forum.

Sousa, R. D., Karimova, B. & Gorlov, S. (2020). Digitalization as a New Direction in Education Sphere. *E3S Web of Conferences, 159*. doi:10.1051/e3sconf/202015909014

UNCTAD. (2021). Handbook of Statistics 2021. doi:10.18356/9789210010610

van Wynsberghe, A., Vandemeulebroucke, T., Bolte, L., & Nachid, J. (2022). Towards the Sustainability of AI; Multi-Disciplinary Approaches to Investigate the Hidden Costs of AI. *Sustainability (Basel), 14*(24), 16352. doi:10.3390u142416352

Vasiliev, I. I., Smelov, P. A., Klimovskih, N. V., Shevashkevich, M. G., & Donskaya, E. N. (2018). Operational Risk Management in A Commercial Bank. *International Journal of Engineering and Technology (UAE), 7*, 524–529. doi:10.14419/ijet.v7i4.36.24130

WB. (2016). *Development Goals in an Era of Demographic Change*. Global Monitoring Report 2015/2016, The World Bank. doi:10.1596/978-1-4648-0669-8

WTO. (2020). World Trade Report 2020. World Trade Organisation.

KEY TERMS AND DEFINITIONS

Friend-Shoring Business Model: Trade with countries that share the same common values. Friendship gives them access to global markets with less business risk.

Immersive Learning: Learning based on practice, in which the environment is improvised for the student through real-life scenarios, where he receives and processes information based on individual characteristics.

Long-Tail Economy: Is a business strategy where manufacturers sell small quantities of hard-to-find products to many customers, instead of selling only large quantities of a reduced number of popular products, through a developed distribution chain (online sales, distributor network).

Megaplatforms: Automated assembly lines that produce different models and classes of cars from the same family, networked with locally produced parts.

Metaverse: An advanced generation of the Internet with a hard-to-see difference between offline and online, and the space allows users to socialize, learn and play.

Nearshoring Business Model: Represents a part of the business process that is transferred to a neighboring country or region, in the same or similar time zone, due to greater business efficiency and better communication (from Germany to Slovakia).

New Normal Paradigm: It basically implies business changes that simultaneously identify key changes in the wider socio-political environment.

Operational Risks: Today, the dominant risk in the bank's operations arises as a result of increasingly ineffective internal processes, above all people, but also systems or external events.

Chapter 2
Paradigm Shift in Corporate Responsibility to the New Era of ESG and Social Entrepreneurship

Iza Gigauri
https://orcid.org/0000-0001-6394-6416
St. Andrew the First-Called Georgian University, Georgia

Valentin Penchev Vasilev
Higher School of Security and Economics, Bulgaria

ABSTRACT

Since the business purpose to serve shareholders' interests changed to a more balanced view of serving all stakeholders, companies' focus shifted towards corporate social responsibility (CSR) to meet the expectations of society. Corporations recognize that a profit-driven mission is not making them the best companies as information about unethical behavior spreads rapidly. Digital resources can be used in corporate strategy to create value for consumers and shareholders. Digital transformation impacts CSR while paving the way for digital CSR. Increasingly, companies admit the need for sustainability and proactive steps to contribute to Sustainable Development Goals. In this regard, ESG—environmental, social, and governance—issues aim to connect financial value to social responsibility. Furthermore, social entrepreneurship has received special attention worldwide as pressing social and environmental problems requiring complex solutions. Therefore, the research trends regarding CSR, ESG, sustainability, social entrepreneurship, and digitalization have been growing.

DOI: 10.4018/978-1-6684-8810-2.ch002

1. INTRODUCTION

The business purpose to serve shareholders' interests changed to a more balanced view of serving all stakeholders. Accordingly, companies' focus shifted towards corporate social responsibility to meet the expectations of society. Corporations recognize that reputation can be an important risk factor. Moreover, digital transformation impacts CSR while paving the way for digital CSR. Digitalization affects the organizational approach toward CSR disclosure and communication (Esposito & Ricci, 2020). Digital transformation is conceptually defined as "a process that aims to improve an entity by triggering significant changes to its properties through combinations of information, computing, communication, and connectivity technologies" (Vial, 2019). It should increase organizational performance and potential for innovation. Through digitalization, companies can influence society. Digital resources can be used in corporate strategy to create value for consumers and shareholders. Companies need to consider the possible impacts of digital technologies on CSR to implement responsible digitalization goals. Responsible digitalization takes into account digital systems and technologies to be in compliance with CSR goals (Cardinali & De Giovanni, 2022), especially when energy consumption, emissions, or privacy, are the focus of sustainability.

The field of corporate social responsibility has evolved based on the research contributing to various models and theories from voluntary social initiatives to CSR incorporated into business strategies and is relevant to the Sustainable Development Goals (Rodriguez-Gomez et al., 2020). Increasingly, companies admit the need for sustainability and proactive steps to contribute to Sustainable Development Goals (SDGs). For this reason, policies and strategies are required to be integrated into the objective of sustainability while taking into consideration the complexity of business decisions and the interdependence of various business strategies.

Recently, CSR has been transforming into ESG - environmental, social, and governance issues, which are interconnected and aim at linking financial value to social responsibility. The analysis of 120 reports illustrated that companies use CSR to decrease their ESG and reputational risk factors (Karwowski & Raulinajtys-Grzybek, 2021). The concept strives to balance resources, human capital, financial resources, and sustainable business decisions. Thus, sustainability measures play a significant role. KPIs and targets should be created in order to measure progress, mitigate risks, and improve performance. Appropriate metrics for the holistic performance of a company are paramount for ESG. Companies implement CSR programs to avoid ESG - Environment, Social, corporate governance and reputational risks (Karwowski & Raulinajtys-Grzybek, 2021).

Furthermore, social entrepreneurship along with sustainable entrepreneurship has received special attention worldwide as pressing social and environmental problems requiring complex solutions. The phenomenon of Social Entrepreneurship centers on people and the planet rather than profit. The various definitions of the concept highlight innovative solutions to social problems while satisfying the needs of disadvantaged groups of society by providing them with goods and services. Social enterprises use business activities to generate profit that is used for achieving the social mission. Some scholars regard social entrepreneurship as a development of CSR (Buendía-Martínez & Carrasco Monteagudo, 2020). In spite of differences, particularly in terms of profit orientation, the concepts share notable similarities. Social entrepreneurship like CSR promotes SDGs and facilitates tackling grand challenges.

Moreover, the COVID-19 pandemic as a Black Swan event has shaken the economy and society on a global scale. Values have been reevaluated and businesses reassessed their missions and purpose in this light. Therefore, the research trends regarding CSR, ESG, sustainability, social entrepreneurship, and digitalization have been growing. Digital transformation in conjunction with sustainable development goals, emerging changes in consumption patterns, and consumer behavior in the New Normal is reflected in the direction of CSR. In this respect, studying the evolution of CSR and existing management tools can enable the business sector to apply the concepts in practice.

This chapter deals with the CSR concept in the digital era and its relationship with sustainability through ESG. It also discusses social entrepreneurship through the lens of corporate responsibility and sustainable development in the New Normal. In addition, the chapter provides practical examples from various countries and companies.

2. CSR, ESG, AND DIGITALIZATION

2.1. Corporate Social Responsibility in Light of Sustainability and ESG

Apart from corporate citizenship reflecting a responsible behavior of a company towards all stakeholders, CSR comprises sustainability indicating simultaneous achievement of economic growth and environmental protections (Ramos-González et al., 2017). In addition, the Brundtland report emphasizes that sustainable development should take into account the needs of the next generations and their ability to satisfy them while meeting the needs of the current generation (WCED, 1987). Elkington (1994) initiated the concept of the Triple Bottom Line (TBL) - people, planet, and profit (Elkington, 1994), followed by the idea of ESG - Environment, Social, and Governance, to measure a company's non-financial performance (Elkington, 2020).

Figure 1. CSR domains
Source: Authors' elaboration based on Baskentli et al. (2019)

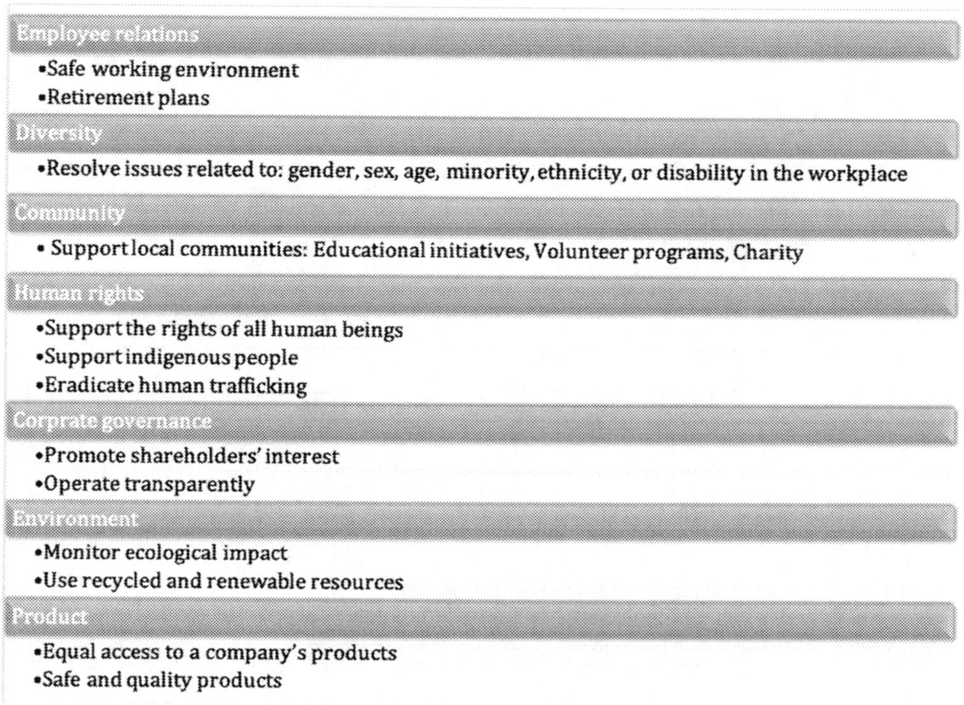

Employee relations
- Safe working environment
- Retirement plans

Diversity
- Resolve issues related to: gender, sex, age, minority, ethnicity, or disability in the workplace

Community
- Support local communities: Educational initiatives, Volunteer programs, Charity

Human rights
- Support the rights of all human beings
- Support indigenous people
- Eradicate human trafficking

Corprate governance
- Promote shareholders' interest
- Operate transparently

Environment
- Monitor ecological impact
- Use recycled and renewable resources

Product
- Equal access to a company's products
- Safe and quality products

CSR reporting has become obligatory and investors consider ESG scores along with other CSR-related criteria to make investment decisions (Valls Martínez et al., 2022). However, it still requires studies to confirm the real impact of those conceptions on evaluating the sustainability of businesses (Elkington, 2018).

The widely used classification of CSR domains is MSCIKLD (Du et al., 2017), which is used to measure ESG risks and opportunities (MSCI, n.d.). Companies can focus on one to several of all seven areas CSR is encompassing: Relations with employees, Corporate governance, Human rights, Diversity, Community relations, Environment protection, and Product issues (Figure 1) (Baskentli et al., 2019). These areas are included in a company's CSR programs and policies (Wood, 1991) and aim to contribute to economic, environmental, and social welfare (Sen & Bhattacharya, 2001).

2.2. Digital Transformation and Corporate Digital Responsibility

Digitalization is seen as an enabler of sustainable development. In the era of digital transformation, researchers emphasize the need for a special focus on ethics. Vial

(2019) points to using digital technologies for innovations and value propositions, which must be based on moral views even if they may seem contradictory to short-term financial goals. Accordingly, ethical considerations should be included at the strategic level within CSR to guide the adoption of digital technologies or design products and services using digital technologies (Vial, 2019).

The Covid-19 pandemic speed up the digitalization of business as companies had to move online to sell goods and services, communicate with customers, build relationships with stakeholders, and work remotely. Thus, they have increasingly used digital tools and technologies, which, on the other hand, creates issues related to the privacy and security of online presence. Companies need to decide how to implement responsibility in the digital economy (Grigore et al., 2017).

Worldwide, digital transformation has brought changes in the economy and society while offering new opportunities for business. Digitalization gave rise to the discussion about the responsibility in using digital technologies, disclosure practices of a firm as well as online communication of CSR issues (Grigore et al., 2017). In a similar vein, CSR needs to follow this trend and therefore the concept of Corporate Digital Responsibility (CDR) emerged to define responsibilities regarding business digital impact (Herden et al., 2021; Bednarova & Serpeninova, 2023). Corporate responsibility includes ethical behavior in terms of using customer data, monitoring digital products, using artificial intelligence, and digitally surveilling employees (Grigore et al., 2017). When codes and algorithms control and manage processes, ethics, and responsibility can be avoided since they are not human (Grigore et al., 2017).

CDR is defined as "voluntary entrepreneurial activities that go beyond what is legally required, particularly in the interests of consumers, and actively help to shape the digital world for the benefit of society. CDR can make a significant contribution to making digital transformation fair and to the benefit of all. It thus promotes sustainable development" (BMVJ, 2018).

Some authors emphasize digital sustainability as well as social, economic, and environmental aspects when describing CDR as "a voluntary commitment by organizations fulfilling the corporate rationalizers' role in representing community interests to inform "good" digital corporate actions and digital sustainability (i.e. data and algorithms) via collaborative guidance and addressing social, economic, and ecological impacts on digital society" (Elliott et al., 2021).

According to Wade (2020), CDR is "a set of practices and behaviors that help an organization use data and digital technologies in a way that is socially, economically, technologically, and environmentally responsible".

However, scholars argue that instead of "digital CSR" or "Online CSR", there are only new responsibilities linked to corporate responsibility of using digital technologies (Grigore et al., 2017).

From 2017 to 2022, research on CDR has dramatically increased in the literature (Bednarova & Serpeninova, 2023) confirming the ongoing discussion and the growing importance of the field. Herden and colleagues (2021) surveyed 509 respondents in the USA and displayed that digitalization requires a strategic attitude to CDR which can be defined in the ESG framework. The study illustrated that CDR strategy can facilitate a company's goals and use opportunities while dealing with threats in the digitalized world (Herden et al., 2021).

Overall, CSR should include emerging domains of responsibility that have originated as a result of digitalization (Grigore et al., 2017). Thanks to digital transformation trends, CSR shifting towards ESG includes digital factors leading to the concept of CDR (Bednarova & Serpeninova, 2023). In addition, CDR influences ESG dimensions and hence, plays a significant role in sustainable development goals, as bibliometric analysis has demonstrated the relationship between CSR and CDR (Bednarova & Serpeninova, 2023).

3. FROM CSR TO SUSTAINABLE AND SOCIAL ENTREPRENEURSHIP

3.1. Corporate Social Responsibility for Sustainable Business

In 2015, the United Nations announced the 17 Sustainable Development Goals aiming at eliminating poverty, protecting the Earth, and ensuring peace and prosperity, implementing of which all member states agreed (UN, 2020). Accordingly, companies are increasingly using SDGs to modify their strategies and policies to contribute to sustainable development (Peterson et al., 2021; Andrei et al., 2021; Akkaya et al., 2022). In 2019, the Business Roundtable changed its principles primarily focused on shareholders towards corporate responsibility emphasizing stakeholders - consumers, employees, contractors, communities, owners, and shareholders (Business Roundtable, 2019). This statement demands companies shift their efforts toward society and not serve solely their stakeholder interests (Peterson et al., 2021).

Corporate social responsibility highlights a company's responsibility towards society (Smith, 2003). In addition, businesses can be conducted successfully only in a flourishing society as the social environment is essential for competitiveness (Porter & Kramer, 2006; Peterson et al., 2021). Researchers link strategic CSR to innovation as the latter stimulates sustainability and facilitates addressing global challenges of urbanization, poverty, environmental degradation, and other crises (Hlioui & Yousfi, 2022). Empirical research of companies in France between 2010-2016 shows that innovation has an impact on CSR (Hlioui & Yousfi, 2022).

Scholars connect sustainability with CSR and link it to the strategic performance and competitiveness of a firm (Feng & Ngai, 2020; Wei et al., 2020; Panait et al., 2022; Weber, 2008). In this respect CSR is defined as "'doing good' (the normative case) or 'doing well' (in terms of firm performance) by 'doing good' (the business case)" (Peterson et al., 2021). Furthermore, Carroll (1991) explains CSR through a pyramid that includes economic, legal, ethical, and philanthropic responsibilities. The economic category is the basis of a company as it involves profitability, while legal responsibility covers business actions within the legal system; ethical responsibility follows fair and just activities, and philanthropic responsibility of a company encompasses charity programs (Peterson et al., 2021). Although socially responsible companies must be economically profitable, greed or excessive financial gain is discouraged in order for CSR to enhance reputation, and promote sustainability and innovation while recognizing the diverse needs of stakeholder groups (Hlioui & Yousfi, 2022).

Philanthropy is seen as a contribution of business to society and a marketing tool for companies (Bishop & Green, 2010; Bloom et al., 2006). Examples of corporate philanthropy include matching gifts when donating money to not-for-profit organizations, and volunteer grants when employees of a firm donate their time and perform work for nonprofit organizations (Double the Donation, n.d). Google, Microsoft, Dell, Apple, Walmart, General Electric, Verizon, Expedia, and other corporations are engaging in philanthropic programs to support communities and make (Double the Donation, n.d).

Furthermore, consumers determine companies' CSR as their loyalty is growing regarding purchasing from companies with ethical and sustainable behavior (Baskentli et al., 2019). Consequently, business strategies, production, purchasing, and consumption behaviors as well as demand have been altered in line with SDGs (Andrei et al., 2021; Andrei & Drăgoi, 2021). Studies revealed that when consumers' morality corresponds to a company's CSR, consumers' positive attitude towards a company increases (Baskentli et al., 2019). However, consumers' reactions to a firm's CSR failures can differ according to their political views as left-wing consumers can have more negative reactions to avoiding taxes by a company than right-wing consumers (Antonetti & Anesa, 2017).

The research results uncovered that CSR improves corporate strategic performance in four aspects: stakeholder relationships, business opportunities, brand capital, media, and communication strategies (Mochales & Blanch, 2022). Companies began implementing CSR programs with the purpose to improve reputation and reduce risks (Hlioui & Yousfi, 2022). However, Enron is an example of a company with CSR practices that eventually failed due to greed, as well as other well-known brands - such as Volkswagen, Mitsubishi, General Motors, and Siemens were involved in moral scandals (Hlioui & Yousfi, 2022). Therefore, CSR should be integrated into a firm's strategy and guide the managerial mindset to create shared value. CSR efforts must help companies avoid unethical behavior.

Corporate reputation can be improved by positive media reports. In this sense, CSR helps companies to maintain a positive image, which is especially important during a crisis. Previous studies uncovered that crisis communication strategies affect media reports and corporate image, while media coverages influence corporate reputation (Gunawan et al., 2015). Especially, social media is embraced to communicate CSR-related issues, for example, to educate consumers about sustainable development or engage in dialogue with stakeholders (Grigore et al., 2017)

3.2. Corporate Social Responsibility in Connection With Social Entrepreneurship

The current shift of the paradigm towards sustainable business is focusing on addressing global issues and supporting sustainable development (Ramos-González et al., 2017). Companies have to create long-term value and contribute to just, equal, and prosperous development (Ramos-González et al., 2017).

The empirical research of 104 sustainable companies according to MERCO ranking in Spain demonstrated that sustainable entrepreneurship as well as good governance and ethical conduct have a positive impact on corporate reputation (Ramos-González et al., 2017). Sustainable entrepreneurship highlights long-term values and solving social and ecological issues through clean technologies, offering jobs, creating prosperity, considering the environment, and obeying the law and fiscal obligations (Ramos-González et al., 2017). Scholars indicate that companies with a strategic CSR can be seen as social enterprises as they strive to achieve financial and societal sustainability while adopting innovative solutions (Szeged et al., 2016).

Unlike a traditional business concentrating solely on financial gain, sustainable entrepreneurship involves social entrepreneurship and eco- or environmental entrepreneurship (Ramos-González et al., 2017). The main goal of social entrepreneurship like CSR is the development of society and the contribution of a country's economy. Both concepts are united by social innovation. Such new business models suggest that not only economic goals can be implemented but also positive social impacts can be created (Szeged et al., 2016). Although both visions aim to solve social problems, the expansion of CSR can hinder market opportunities for social enterprises (Buendía-Martínez & Carrasco Monteagudo, 2020).

Social enterprise can use a business model to achieve social and financial goals simultaneously, while social entrepreneur refers to a person with innovative skills who tries to fulfill a social mission (Szeged et al., 2016). Social entrepreneurship differs from commercial entrepreneurship in the view towards profit: commercial enterprise is profit-oriented whereas social enterprise is mission-oriented. For social entrepreneurship, profit is an instrument to fulfill social objectives; contrariwise companies adopt CSR strategy to ultimately increase profit (Buendía-Martínez & Carrasco Monteagudo, 2020). Yet the two notions are interconnected and scholars indicate that CSR can be developed into social entrepreneurship (Buendía-Martínez & Carrasco Monteagudo, 2020). Research results conducted by Buendía-Martínez and Carrasco Monteagudo (2020) confirm that CSR directly influences social entrepreneurship in terms of social and economic standpoints, as well as CSR can have a social impact on communities and stakeholder relationships through social entrepreneurship.

Obviously, the role of management is crucial to achieving responsible, sustainable, and ethical behavior to generate not only profit but also reputation and increase consumer reliability and employee retention (Ramos-González et al., 2017).

4. EXAMPLES OF CSR INITIATIVES AND SOCIAL ENTREPRENEURSHIP IN DIFFERENT COUNTRIES

4.1. Practices From Hungary, Georgia, and Poland

In Hungary, the implemented CSR projects aim at regional development, charity, contribution to education, collaboration with civil organizations, and providing support to social enterprises in terms of business education and financial aid (Szeged et al., 2016). Social enterprises in the country mainly help disadvantaged groups of people to get involved in the labor market (Szeged et al., 2016).

In Georgia, CSR programs helped companies to mitigate social, health, and economic challenges that emerged after the pandemic outbreak (Gigauri, 2021). The empirical research emphasized the importance of CSR practice and confirmed that CSR improves the communication, brand equity, and crisis management ability of companies (Gigauri, 2021). In general, CSR has been increasingly adopted by Georgian companies last few years since the concept and practice have gained the attention of nonprofit organizations and media.

According to the Associate Agreement between the European Union and Georgia, CSR should be promoted and contributed to economic, social, and environmental dimensions of sustainable development goals. It is noteworthy that education has a crucial role to play in sustainable development (Gigauri et al., 2022; Coşkun et al., 2022). However, Georgian higher education institutions are not offering courses in sustainability nor are SDGs integrated into the curriculum, and even CSR courses are not delivered in all universities or educational programs (Gigauri et al., 2021).

In Poland, social enterprises are more oriented on the social dimension, which enforce them to depend on public funds, grants, and the support of local governments

(Ciepielewska-Kowalik et al., 2015). They differ in their objectives and can be Work Integration social enterprises aiming to provide jobs for vulnerable people; Social enterprises that aim at local development to improve the quality of life; and Enterprises that provide health care or cultural services to residents (Bogacz-Wojtanowska et al., 2014).

According to recent research, the goals of Georgian social enterprises are similar to Polish counterparts (Gigauri & Bogacz-Wojtanowska, 2022). In particular, in both countries, social entrepreneurs try to hinder the outflow of inhabitants, especially young people from rural areas and villages. Besides, they strive to create jobs for disadvantaged groups and facilitate their economic and social integration and inclusion. In Georgia, social enterprises have not achieved economic independence and often rely on grants and support from local and international governmental and donor organizations. They help disadvantaged groups of people to integrate into social and economic life by producing various goods and services (Gigauri et al., 2021; Gigauri, 2021).

4.2. Social Enterprises in Bulgaria

There are several models of social enterprises in Bulgaria, for instance, which are described in the framework of the presentation of practices of individual countries:

1. The model for employment creation and workforce development is founded on the prospect of providing jobs for people with limited opportunities. The concept is tied to what is known as "protected employment," in which a nonprofit organization hires disabled people.
2. An approach to entrepreneurship in which the social enterprise serves as an intermediary between the market and those in need. In this occupational therapy approach, people with disabilities take part in the creation of goods that the social enterprise then markets and distributes.
3. The direct service model, which has the closest ties to social care providers. It allows the social enterprise to offer social services to outside clients in exchange for money while also offering social services to its own members, with payment coming from a contract with the municipality or the state.

The social enterprise in this model develops the same services, but they are aimed at separate users and customers, which is an essential point to make.

The multidisciplinary and global trust study and analysis performed by Edelman Data & Intelligence, the Edelman Trust Barometer, and the 2021 Edelman Trust Barometer Special Report: The Covid-19 pandemic changed values for workers, according to a study called Belief-Driven Employe that was performed in early

August 2021 in seven countries. As a result, higher salaries are no longer a sufficient motivation to work longer and harder. The employee now chooses and stays with the business based on his values, just as the consumer chooses and sticks with the employer brand. The modern era is characterized by social care, flexible work schedules and remote work, increased power delegation, and company commitment to acting in the best interests of both employees and society. A new agreement between employee and employer requires business to adopt a more ambitious social role while essentially reviewing employee motivations. a contract that calls for more frequent, two-way contact in order to advance both parties' interests. 'Social contract' in a time of chaos. We should consider the term "social contract" to refer to an agreement that management and employees voluntarily enter into after determining that they share a shared objective and are subject to its direction and control. At the core are social interest and common happiness. The perspectives established in this manner can serve as a foundation for the creation of concepts and initiatives relating to organizational changes that improve people's active, dialogical, motivated, and constructive participation in the life of organizations in conflict with the move of time. They can also outline new paradigms in the effectiveness of organizational changes.

On the other hand, it can be claimed based on analyses and empirical research in recent years that all the contributing factors that led to the crises suggest new difficulties in the efficient management of human resources that must be resolved through new methods. In order to improve outcomes for both the company and the workforce, it is crucial to understand the connection between social responsibility and employee engagement and how it relates to motivation levels.

Social businesses in Bulgaria exist as for-profit corporations, cooperatives, and non-profit legal organizations in such management dynamics. For vulnerable groups, they have all experienced socially important results. Legal organizations that are nonprofits are the most common type. Through priority line 5 of the European Union's Operational Program for Human Resources Development, social entrepreneurship in Bulgaria has recently received support. Due to administrative challenges and worries about the long-term sustainability of the measures taken, many municipalities choose not to adopt similar projects during the program periods. Leading experts agree that social businesses face competition when they first join a market because, for example, their social purpose is not what makes them tolerated but rather becomes a burden. The statistics demonstrate that initiatives like "Friends in Silence," a social business for unique hand knits in Stara Zagora, the "Transitional Jobs" program, and others have been carried out through similar financing in recent years.

These efforts share a social purpose, as well as the people who they aim to serve, which are individuals with disabilities.

The "Counterpart International" Program additionally supports the growth of social business in Bulgaria. More than 30 social enterprises have opened since 2002, focusing their operations on a variety of areas including manufacturing and trade, training and consulting, social and health services, child care, children's services, and more.

An "Institute of Social Entrepreneurship" was established with the goal of advancing good practices and concepts in the area of this relationship in order to support the notion of developing the "social responsibility-social entrepreneurship" relationship (Bulgarian Institute of Social Entrepreneurship, n.d.).

For instance, in Varna, the first "Social Store" opened in 2019. The shop sells goods created by people with disabilities, including handcrafted trinkets created by blind people. The "Catalog of typical Varna souvenirs" also advertises the goods that are sold in the social store and produced by socially vulnerable groups (VarnaUtre, 2013). The program is a component of the "Social Shop - Living Heritage" project, which the "My City" Association is putting into action with the help of funding from the Municipality of Varna.

"Pass on" is a brand-new type of social business that seeks to assist vulnerable groups by organizing various events and making sales of the products created by the participants (BegoodToday, n.d.).

The Public Laundry "Zelena" at the Complex for Mental Health Services in the Community, Sofia, Slatina district is another social activity that is especially common in Bulgaria. It hires individuals who are housed there and make use of the facilities.

The concept of occupational therapy for drug addicts using the creation and restoration of antique furniture, which has a positive impact on drug addicts and revitalizes out-of-date furniture in the context of a sustainable circular economy, is unquestionably novel (BetelBulgaria, n.d.).

It is evident that social business has grown in Bulgaria in recent years. Entrepreneurship activities typically rely on the experience of developed nations but are filtered through the prism of the Bulgarian setting. Theoretically, there is still a lack of study on the topic of social entrepreneurship, making it difficult to identify specific trends or predict potential outcomes. The absence of highly qualified entrepreneurs who have the desire to create such projects is a major issue in Bulgarian practice.

Another factor preventing the spread of entrepreneurial practices is a lack of commitment on the part of municipal and state governments. As has already been mentioned, educational institutions fall short in this respect when it comes to finding and providing relevant educational services and materials to support the growth of knowledge and abilities in the areas of social entrepreneurship and social responsibility.

4.3. CSR in Bulgaria

In Bulgaria, the number of academic studies in the area of corporate social responsibility has greatly increased in recent years, and a new CSR strategy was implemented in 2019 (Ministry of Labor and Social Policy of Bulgaria, 2019). This document of a strategic nature also set out important management principles. For instance, business management, the management divisions of public institutions, employees, and employees are the main beneficiaries in the implementation of the Strategy. In a broader context, we can include those who directly benefit from the public administration's provision of goods, services, and administrative services, as well as corporate clients and subcontractors along the supply chain and every aspect of their system, social partners, civil society organizations, academic institutions, and, last but not least, the environment and its surrounding ecosystems. In a complex world, ethical judgment and speedy decision-making are increasingly needed across the full spectrum of stakeholders. By transforming this privilege into individual responsibility for choices made, business organizations and public structures enable the informed option of the individual. A culture of socially responsible supply, consumption, and attitude is formed as a result of the creation of reciprocal relationships between socially responsible behavior. Despite significant changes and developments, particularly in the field of human resource management, "the challenges of motivation, dedication, and the use of technology to deliver effective public services continue to confront the public sphere (Icheva & Vasilev, 2021).

It should be noted that competitions in different areas of social entrepreneurship and corporate social responsibility are organized to further the interest in these topics. For instance, the Annual Awards for Responsible Business are presented by the Bulgarian Forum of Business Leaders (BFBL, 2022). The 19th annual Corporate Social Responsibility and Sustainable Development Awards, with the theme "Set a Good Example," featured more than 100 cause-related projects competing in seven categories in 2022.

The Institute of Public Administration in Bulgaria hosts a yearly competition for best practices in state administration, which is another reputable competition. More than 30 institutions participated in the competition for 2022 in one of the three categories connected to socially responsible practices. To increase their visibility and chances that they will be used in other organizations, all nominated and winning practices are published in specialized collections (Institute of Public Administration, 2021).

Leadership behavior develops leadership style and skills. Skills, by themselves, do not make a leader - manner and action do. If you have an interest in learning and developing as a leader - look at leadership behavior (Chankova & Vasilev, 2021).

Next, leaders will be required to send very "powerful" messages to employees, given that one of the most difficult tasks of human resource management is to retain employees in the age of globalization. Last but not least, human resource management will have more and more direct access to the most valuable capital of the organization - human. And for this reason, the most effective ways to increase this value of capital will be sought (Stoykov & Vasilev, 2021).

All the above-mentioned examples are identification for one thing – leadership in the search for innovative solutions.

Moreover, employees encourage employers who are committed to sustainable development, which is another trend that needs to be highlighted in the present research. Long-term employee loyalty is a major driver for employers to engage in greater sustainability, and for increasing numbers of employees, sustainability is a crucial factor when selecting an employer. This has been demonstrated in a number of recent scientific papers, as the strategic approach in communication processes is a particularly delicate component. (Vasilev & Stefanova, 2021).

In conclusion, the greater attention paid to sustainability in recent years has changed the corporate cultures of many organizations, especially those that are going through transformation.

5. CONCLUSION

The chapter offered an overview of CSR in relation to ESG, Sustainability, and Social Entrepreneurship. For sustainable growth and social development, CSR presents an essential tool for the business to integrate environmental, social, and governance factors into core strategies. CSR initiatives enhance brand equity leading to improved performance of a company (Mochales & Blanch, 2022).

In the same vein, digital transformation is regarded as a contributor to sustainable development through innovation and disruptive technologies.

Companies undertaking socially responsible activities measuring and reporting their progress using ESG that improves their reputation and attractiveness. Non-financial aspects have become an integral part of investment analysis relating to risks and opportunities. Furthermore, ESG criteria contribute to sustainable development.

Social enterprises go beyond CSR to solve social problems. The main difference between the two is their preference for social or financial achievements. However, every business in the future ought to be a social enterprise in terms of balancing economic, social, and ecological goals (Szeged et al., 2016). Social entrepreneurship that prefers achieving social goals over financial profit offers a sustainable business model for a sustainable future.

REFERENCES

Akkaya, B., Guah, M. W., Jermsittiparsert, K., Bulinska-Stangrecka, H., & Koçyiğit, Y. K. (2022). *Agile Management and VUCA-RR*. Emerald Group Publishing. doi:10.1108/9781802623253

Andrei, J., & Drăgoi, M. (2020). A brief analysis of tourism economics in the EU – is there a massive economic potential change? *Tourism International Scientific Conference Vrnjačka Banja - TISC*, *5*(1), 59-76. Retrieved February 3, 2023 from http://www.tisc.rs/proceedings/index.php/hitmc/article/view/329

Andrei, J. V., Constantin, M., & de los Ríos Carmenado, I. (2021). Assessing EU's Progress and Performance with Regard to SDG-12 Targets and Indicators. In C. J. Chiappetta Jabbour & S. A. R. Khan (Eds.), *Sustainable Production and Consumption Systems. Industrial Ecology*. Springer. doi:10.1007/978-981-16-4760-4_1

Antonetti, P., & Anesa, M. (2017). Consumer reactions to corporate tax strategies: The role of political ideology. *Journal of Business Research*, *74*, 1–10. doi:10.1016/j.jbusres.2016.12.011

Baskentli, S., Sen, S., Du, S., & Bhattacharya, C. (2019). Consumer reactions to corporate social responsibility: The role of CSR domains. *Journal of Business Research*, *95*, 502–513. doi:10.1016/j.jbusres.2018.07.046

Bednarova, M., & Serpeninova, Y. (2023). Corporate digital responsibility: Bibliometric landscape – chronological literature review. *The International Journal of Digital Accounting Research*, Michaela, Bednarova. Advance online publication. doi:10.4192/1577-8517-v23_1

BegoodToday. (n.d.). https://www.begood.today/cvete-s-kauza/?fbclid=IwAR0U_jCxAqtctK3lNYGGad6y6IoUymyV_K011YjISkTkMcLlaYi-TDY-M0g

BetelBulgaria. (n.d.). https://betelbulgaria.org/bg/

BFBL. (2022). *Bulgarian Business Leader Forum*. Retrieved March 21, 2023 from https://bblf.bg/bg/sabitiya/1637/obyavihme-kso-shampionite-za-2021-a

Bishop, M., & Green, M. (2010). *Philanthrocapitalism: How giving can save the world*. Bloomsbury Publishing USA.

Bloom, P. N., Hoeffler, S., Keller, K. L., & Meza, C. E. B. (2006). How socialcause marketing affects consumer perceptions. *MIT Sloan Management Review*, *47*(2), 49. Retrieved February 2, 2023, from https://sloanreview.mit.edu/article/how-socialcause-marketing-affects-consumer-perceptions

BMVJ. (2018). Corporate Digital Responsibility Initiative. *Federal Ministry of Justice and Consumer Protection*. Retrieved February 2, 2023 from https://cdr-initiative.de/en/initiative

Bogacz-Wojtanowska, E., Przybysz, I., & Lendzion, M. (2014). Sukces i trwałość ekonomii społecznej w warunkach polskich [Success and sustainability of the social economy in Polish conditions]. Fundacja Instytut Spraw Publicznych.

Buendía-Martínez, I., & Carrasco Monteagudo, I. (2020). The Role of CSR on Social Entrepreneurship: An International Analysis. *Sustainability (Basel)*, *12*(17), 6976. doi:10.3390u12176976

Bulgarian Institute of Social Entrepreneurship. (n.d.). https://sites.google.com/a/piamater.org/theinstistute/examples

Business Roundtable. (2019). *Business roundtable redefines the purpose of a corporation to promote 'an economy that serves all Americans'*. Retrieved February 3, 2023 from https://www.businessroundtable.org/business-roundtable-redefines-the-purpose-of-a-corporation-to-promote-an-economy-that-serves-all-americans

Cardinali, P. G., & De Giovanni, P. (2022). Responsible digitalization through digital technologies and green practices. *Corporate Social Responsibility and Environmental Management*, *29*(4), 984–995. doi:10.1002/csr.2249

Carroll, A. B. (1991). The pyramid of corporate social responsibility: Toward the moral management of organizational stakeholders. *Business Horizons*, *34*(4), 39–48. doi:10.1016/0007-6813(91)90005-G

Chankova, D., & Vasilev, V. (2020). Leadership and deliberative democracy in the changing world: compatible or reconcilable paradigms. *Perspectives of Law and Public Administration*, *9*(2), 209-218. Retrieved March 20, 2023 from http://www.adjuris.ro/revista/an9nr2.html

Ciepielewska-Kowalik, A., Pieliński, B., Starnawska, M., & Szymańska, A. (2015). *Social Enterprise in Poland: Institutional and Historical Context*. ICSEM Working Papers, No. 11, Liege: The International Comparative Social Enterprise Models (ICSEM) Project.

Coşkun, H. E., Popescu, C., Şahin Samaraz, D., Tabak, A., & Akkaya, B. (2022). Entrepreneurial University Concept Review from the Perspective of Academicians: A Mixed Method Research Analysis. *Sustainability (Basel)*, *14*(16), 10110. doi:10.3390u141610110

Double the Donation. (n.d.). *Corporate Philanthropy examples: 15 companies doing it right*. https://doublethedonation.com/corporate-philanthropy-examples/

Du, S., Yu, K., Bhattacharya, C. B., & Sen, S. (2017). The business case for sustainability reporting: Evidence from stock market reactions. *Journal of Public Policy & Marketing*, *36*(2), 313–330. doi:10.1509/jppm.16.112

Elkington, J. (1994). Towards the sustainable corporation: Win-win-win business strategies for sustainable development. *California Management Review*, *36*(2), 90–100. doi:10.2307/41165746

Elkington, J. (2018). 25 years ago I coined the phrase "triple bottom line." Here's why it's time to rethink it. *Harvard Business Review*, *25*, 2–5. Retrieved February 3, 2023, from https://hbr.org/2018/06/25-years-ago-i-coined-the-phrase-triple-bottom-line-heres-why-im-giving-up-on-it

Elkington, J. (2020). *Green Swans: The coming boom in regenerative capitalism*. Fast Company Press.

Elliott, K., Price, R., Shaw, P., Spiliotopoulos, T., Ng, M., Coopamootoo, K., & Van Moorsel, A. (2021). Towards an Equitable Digital Society: Artificial Intelligence (AI) and Corporate Digital Responsibility (CDR). *Society*, *58*(3), 179–188. doi:10.100712115-021-00594-8 PMID:34149122

Esposito, P., & Ricci, P. (2020). Cultural organizations, digital Corporate Social Responsibility and stakeholder engagement in virtual museums: A multiple case study. How digitization is influencing the attitude toward CSR. *Corporate Social Responsibility and Environmental Management*, *28*(2), 953–964. doi:10.1002/csr.2074

Feng, P., & Ngai, C. (2020). Doing more on the corporate sustainability front: A longitudinal analysis of CSR reporting of global fashion companies. *Sustainability (Basel)*, *12*(6), 2477. doi:10.3390u12062477

Gigauri, I. (2021). Corporate Social Responsibility and COVID-19 Pandemic Crisis: Evidence from Georgia. *International Journal of Sustainable Entrepreneurship and Corporate Social Responsibility*, *6*(1), 30–47. doi:10.4018/IJSECSR.2021010103

Gigauri, I., & Bogacz-Wojtanowska, E. (2022). Effects of the Pandemic Crisis on Social Enterprise: A Case Study from Georgia. *Economics & Sociology (Ternopil)*, *15*(2), 312–334. doi:10.14254/2071-789X.2022/15-2/19

Gigauri, I., Panait, M., & Palazzo, M. (2021). Teaching Corporate Social Responsibility and Business Ethics at Economic Programs. *LUMEN Proceedings, 15*, 24-37. 10.18662/lumproc/gekos2021/3

Gigauri, I., Popescu, C., Panait, M., & Apostu, S. A. (2022). Integrating Sustainability Development Issues into University Curriculum. In E. Hysa & R. Foote (Eds.), *New Perspectives on Using Accreditation to Improve Higher Education* (pp. 69–95). IGI Global. doi:10.4018/978-1-6684-5195-3.ch004

Grigore, G., Molesworth, M., & Watkins, R. (2017). New Corporate Responsibilities in the Digital Economy. In A. Theofilou, G. Grigore, & A. Stancu (Eds.), *Corporate Social Responsibility in the Post-Financial Crisis Era*. Palgrave Studies in Governance, Leadership and Responsibility. Palgrave Macmillan. doi:10.1007/978-3-319-40096-9_3

Gunawan, S., Shieh, C., & Pei, Y. (2015). Effects of Crisis Communication Strategies and Media Report on Corporate Image in Catering Industry. *Acta Oeconomica, 65*(s2), 399–411. doi:10.1556/032.65.2015.s2.29

Herden, C. J., Alliu, E., Cakici, A., Cormier, T., Deguelle, C., Gambhir, S., Griffiths, C., Gupta, S., Kamani, S. R., Kiratli, Y.-S., Kispataki, M., Lange, G., Moles de Matos, L., Tripero Moreno, L., Betancourt Nunez, H. A., Pilla, V., Raj, B., Roe, J., Skoda, M., ... Edinger-Schons, L. M. (2021). "Corporate Digital Responsibility": New corporate responsibilities in the digital age. *NachhaltigkeitsManagementForum, 29*(1), 13–29. doi:10.100700550-020-00509-x

Hlioui, Z., & Yousfi, O. (2022). CSR and Innovation: Two Sides of the Same Coin. In B. Orlando (Ed.), *Corporate Social Responsibility*. doi:10.5772/intechopen.94344

Icheva, M., & Vasilev, V. (2021). The time for the next steps is here – from classic to modern paradigms in motivation. *International Journal of Social Science & Economic Research, 6*(3), 913–922. doi:10.46609/IJSSER.2021.v06i03.012

Institute of Public Administration. (2021). https://www.ipa.government.bg/bg/publications#cbp=/bg/sbornik-s-dobri-praktiki-2021

Karwowski, M., & Raulinajtys-Grzybek, M. (2021). The application of corporate social responsibility (CSR) actions for mitigation of environmental, social, corporate governance (ESG) and reputational risk in integrated reports. *Corporate Social Responsibility and Environmental Management, 28*(4), 1270–1284. doi:10.1002/csr.2137

Ministry of Labor and Social Policy of Bulgaria. (2019). *Strategy for Corporate Social Responsibility 2019-2023*. Retrieved March 21, 2023 from https://www.mlsp.government.bg/uploads/15/spitao/dokumenti/strategii/za-korporativna-sotsialna-otgovornost-2019-2023-g.pdf

Mochales, G., & Blanch, J. (2022). Unlocking the potential of CSR: An explanatory model to determine the strategic character of CSR activities. *Journal of Business Research*, 140, 310–323. doi:10.1016/j.jbusres.2021.11.002

MSCI. (n.d.). *MSCI KLD 400 Social Index*. https://www.msci.com/our-solutions/indexes/kld-400-social-index

Panait, M. C., Voica, M. C., Hysa, E., Siano, A., & Palazzo, M. (2022). The Bucharest Stock Exchange: A Starting Point in Structuring a Valuable CSR Index. *Journal of Risk and Financial Management*, 15(2), 94. doi:10.3390/jrfm15020094

Peterson, M., Minton, E. A., Liu, R. L., & Bartholomew, D. E. (2021). Sustainable Marketing and Consumer Support for Sustainable Businesses. *Sustainable Production and Consumption*, 27, 157–168. doi:10.1016/j.spc.2020.10.018

Porter, M. E., & Kramer, M. R. (2006). Strategy and Society: The link between competitive advantage and corporate social responsibility. *Harvard Business Review*, 84(12), 78–92. Retrieved February 2, 2023, from https://hbr.org/2006/12/strategy-and-society-the-link-between-competitive-advantage-and-corporate-social-responsibility PMID:17183795

Ramos-González, M. D. M., Rubio-Andrés, M., & Sastre-Castillo, M. Á. (2017). Building Corporate Reputation through Sustainable Entrepreneurship: The Mediating Effect of Ethical Behavior. *Sustainability (Basel)*, 9(9), 1663. doi:10.3390u9091663

Rodriguez-Gomez, S., Arco-Castro, M. L., Lopez-Perez, M. V., & Rodríguez-Ariza, L. (2020). Where Does CSR Come from and Where Does It Go? A Review of the State of the Art. *Administrative Sciences*, 10(3), 60. doi:10.3390/admsci10030060

Sen, S., & Bhattacharya, C. B. (2001). Does doing good always lead to doing better? Consumer reactions to corporate social responsibility. *JMR, Journal of Marketing Research*, 38(2), 225–243. doi:10.1509/jmkr.38.2.225.18838

Smith, N. C. (2003). Corporate social responsibility: Whether or how? *California Management Review*, 45(4), 52–76. doi:10.2307/41166188

Stoykov, S., & Vasilev, V. (2021). Prerequisites for efficiency of human resources management in crisis situations (from classic theories to a new vision). *Politics & Security*, 5(3), 15–21. doi:10.5281/zenodo.6402953

Szegedi, K., Fülöp, G., & Bereczk, Á. (2016). Relationships between social entrepreneurship, CSR and social innovation: In theory and practice. *International Journal of Social, Behavioral, Educational, Economic, Business and Industrial Engineering, 10*(5), 1402–1407.

UN. (2020). *United Nations Sustainable Development Goals.* United Nations. Retrieved February 3, 2023 from https://www.undp.org/content/undp/en/home/sustainable- development-goals.html

Valls Martínez, M., Martín-Cervantes, P. A., & Miralles-Quirós, M. M. (2022). Sustainable development and the limits of gender policies on corporate boards in Europe. A comparative analysis between developed and emerging markets. *European Research on Management and Business Economics, 28*(1), 100168. doi:10.1016/j.iedeen.2021.100168

VarnaUtre. (2013). https://varna.utre.bg/2013/09/02/184053-otvoriha_purvia_sotsialen_magazin

Vasilev, V., & Stefanova, D. (2021). Complex communication barriers in the organisation in a crisis context. *KNOWLEDGE - International Journal (Toronto, Ont.), 49*(1), 29–33. Retrieved March 20, 2023, from https://ikm.mk/ojs/index.php/kij/article/view/4617

Vial, G. (2019). Understanding digital transformation: A review and a research agenda. *The Journal of Strategic Information Systems, 28*(2), 118–144. doi:10.1016/j.jsis.2019.01.003

Wade, M. (2020). Corporate Responsibility in the Digital Era. *MIT Sloan Management Review.* Retrieved February 3, 2023 from https://sloanreview.mit.edu/article/corporate-responsibility-in-the-digital-era/

WCED. (1987). *Our Common Future: The World Commission on Environment and Development.* Oxford University Press.

Weber, M. (2008). The business case for corporate social responsibility: A company-level measurement approach for CSR. *European Management Journal, 26*(4), 247–261. doi:10.1016/j.emj.2008.01.006

Wei, A.-P., Peng, C.-L., Huang, H.-C., & Yeh, S.-P. (2020). Effects of Corporate Social Responsibility on Firm Performance: Does Customer Satisfaction Matter? *Sustainability (Basel), 12*(18), 7545. doi:10.3390u12187545

Wood, D. J. (1991). Corporate social performance revisited. *Academy of Management Review, 16*(4), 691–718. doi:10.2307/258977

Chapter 3
Toward Understanding the Underlying Causes of Scope Creep

Simon Cleveland
https://orcid.org/0000-0001-9293-3905
Purdue University Global, USA

Marisa Cleveland
Northeastern University, USA

ABSTRACT

Scope creep is an issue project managers must address across various industries. When scope creep is not addressed, the project becomes troubled or fails. Because scope creep appears to be a challenge for emerging and existing project managers, having an introductory understanding of the underlying causes of scope creep will add to the body of literature with particular focus on providing individuals new to projects a foundation to prevent being part of the problem. This includes new project managers, as well as new stakeholders and leaders who are unfamiliar with how projects operate and are best managed. This literature review provides a summation of an analysis of the underlying causes of scope creep and identifies a host of factors that contribute to it.

DOI: 10.4018/978-1-6684-8810-2.ch003

INTRODUCTION

Scope creep is a concept repeatedly used to rationalize why projects become troubled or fail. According to Larson & Larson (2009), scope creep is "adding additional features or functions of a new product, requirements, or work that is not authorized (i.e., beyond the agreed-upon scope)." The lack of scope creep management is "the main reason for project failure" (Komal et al, 2020). Because scope creep has the ability to impact projects in so many different ways, understanding the underlying cause of scope creep, and potentially identifying preventative solutions makes this topic important to investigate. As a result, this chapter addresses the following research question: What are the main causes of scope creep on construction and technology projects?

The practical importance and implication of scope creep to the general project management practices is that it offers a term for when a project's scope is not managed properly. Scope creep impacts projects across all industries, and the lack of scope creep management is "the main reason for project failure" (Komal et al, 2020, p. 125755). If projects do not have a defined scope at the beginning of the project, scope creep is more likely to add to a project's poor performance (Ajmal et al, 2021). Previous researchers have studied scope creep, including the causes and the impact, and the preliminary readings for this literature review are drawn from empirical studies that encompass projects within the following industries: construction and technology.

This literature review will draw on several peer-reviewed articles to leverage the concept of scope creep and the impact scope creep has for both emerging and established project managers. The remainder of the paper is structured as follows. First, an examination of the methodology is proposed. The focus is on the use of literature reviews to synthesize and create new knowledge. Next, the literature review is conducted, and results are distilled to highlight specific scope creep factors. This is followed by a summary and proposed future studies.

METHODOLOGY

Since scope creep can happen in small increments and without formal change processes in place, this research addresses the underlying factors for scope creep's ability to move undetected within a project until that project is troubled or failing. Since literature reviews examine "relevant literature on a research topic" (Machi & McEvoy, 2016, p. 2), this method was used to answer the research question for this study. This approach examines scope creep within two different industries: 1) Construction – this industry is known typically for large, complex projects that may favor the predictive project management methodology, such as Waterfall; and 2) Technology – these projects often focus on systems and software development and are known to use more adaptive methodology, such as Agile.

LITERATURE REVIEW

Scope Creep

Score creep has been defined in the literature as the accumulation of additional requirements and activities than originally planned on a project, with the overall result being to increased costs and change in the time estimates of a project (Madhuri et al, 2018). Wnuk and Kolly (2016) argued that scope creep is also defined as the expansion of the originally planned worked on a project with uncontrollable changes, which have been introduced once the approval of the original project plan has been received. Scope creep has been associated with project design instability and requirements volatility (Gullo, 2018), schedule delays (Turk, 2010), increase in project size and poor project quality (Thakurta, 2013), cost overruns (Amoatey & Anson, 2017), resource consumption (Nabet et al., 2017) and ultimately low project success (Komal et al., 2020).

Construction Projects

Construction projects focus on the creation of new buildings, roads, infrastructure, or other initiatives which provide long term benefits to large number of stakeholders in a variety of industries.

Ajmal et al (2021) conducted a detailed survey with construction stakeholders to examine the different scope creep factors within the construction industry. The researchers adopted a quantitative methodology to identify and validate five factors causing project scope creep: complexity/uncertainty, tasks/specifications, risk, communication, and customers (end-users).

Sindi (2018) conducted a survey among construction companies in Saudi Arabia to determine factors leading to scope creep and found that the pervasive ones were lack of clarity and precision of the specifications documents, unreasonable client demands, value added changes to the original scope as well as new regulations imposed by external agencies.

Nabet et al. (2017) conducted a quantitative study among 101 representatives of various construction companies in Egypt. Their study showed a host of factors leading to scope creep. They distilled the top five to: 1) poor scope definition, 2) client changes, 3) poor specifications, 4) inadequate government regulations, 5) selecting contractor bids with the lowest price.

Safapour and Kermanshachi (2019) conducted a survey among 37 construction project professionals to determine the key factors leading to scope creep on construction projects. They found that communication among owners, the number of oversight entities, and the project's location were reported as the most frequent causes.

In another study, Amoatey and Anson (2017) conducted a survey among Ghanian real estate development professionals, engineers, project managers and team members. The researchers found that the most pervasive causes of scope creep on projects include client scope changes, followed by unexpected risks finally poorly defined scope documents.

Furthermore, Teye et al (2017) investigated the causes and impact of scope creep on projects in the real estate development industry in Ghana, and their findings matched Ajmal et al's: client changes, unforeseen risks, and unclear scope.

Finally, Umuhoza et al (2021) investigated scope creep in D.R.Congo and Rwanda within the construction industry. In their research article, they mentioned a nationwide questionnaire survey in Ghana where out of seven causes of scope creep, "three were identified as significant" (p. 3): client change, unforeseen risk, unclear scope. The main causes in D.R.Congo included poor mitigation strategies, frequent change in stakeholders' needs, and poor estimations of activity resources and durations. The main causes identified in Rwanda were unskilled labor, poor estimations of activity resources and durations, and poor change control.

Technology Projects

Technology projects involve the use of software or systems to delivery products or services in a variety of industries.

Jain and Khurana (2015) showed an empirical comparison of information technology outsourcing models and validated the importance of clear scope, as well as a clear understanding of what is scope creep between clients and vendors.

According to Madhuri and Suma (2014), researchers studying scope creep on software projects, "Scope creep is deemed to be one of the several factors which influence the success of a project" (p. 1). In a case study, Madhuri and Suma (2014) aimed to research the ways in which scope creep impacted "project success critical factors such as time, cost, human personnel abilities, defect profile, technology, and domain of the application and so on" (p. 3).

Two other articles also explored the impact of scope creep on software projects, and an interesting finding is that the methodologies and approaches influenced the outcome of the projects (Madhuri et al, 2014; Aizaz et al, 2021). This suggests that the human component is the main factor in scope creep. Of note, by researching the factors which cause scope creep in software development, Aizas et al (2021) categorized scope creep into four factors:

1. People,
2. Process,
3. Project, and
4. Product.

Aizaz et al (2021) presented results and analysis consistent with the other case studies, but with one exception: "To overcome the shortcomings of the existing studies, we have validated the identified scope creep factors from practitioners (project managers) to legitimacy the obtained results" (p. 109172). Relatedly, according to Ajmal et al (2020), stakeholders reported communication among "the major causes of project scope creep" (p. 483). When analyzing the factors associated with the studies, every factor appears to be connected in some way to people and communication, and most specifically, to the project manager's ability to effectively receive and send information in a way that clarifies the limitations of the project.

In a study among Somaliland telecommunication project stakeholders, Fashina et al. (2020) found that factors contributing to scope creep on technology projects include poor communication (miscommunication), unrealistic timeline, scope changes, unsettled technical uncertainties and poor technical skills.

Davis et al. (2008) found scope creep in technology projects occurs due to changing software requirements. These changes typically arise from conflicting needs or lack of comprehension of what the project will deliver.

Finally, Komal et al. (2019) conducted a systematic literature review study of research on technology projects between 2010 and 2018. Their analysis revealed that time and budget constraints, as well as requirements management, stakeholders satisfaction, communication, resource allocation and project size were the most common factors leading to scope creep on software projects.

RESULTS

Findings of this literature review demonstrate a host of scope creep factors among construction and technology projects. The results are summarized in Table 1.

Table 1. Scope creep factors

Source	Project Type	Scope Creep Factors
Ajmal et al (2021)	Construction	complexity/uncertainty, tasks/specifications, risk, communication, and customers (end-users)
Sindi (2018)	Construction	lack of clarity and precision of the specification documents, unreasonable client demands, value added changes to the original scope, new regulations imposed by external agencies
Nabet et al. (2017)	Construction	poor scope definition, client changes, poor specifications, inadequate government regulations, selecting contractor bids with the lowest price
Safapour and Kermanshachi (2019)	Construction	communication among owners, the number of oversight entities, project's location
Amoatey and Anson (2017)	Construction	client scope changes, unexpected risks, poorly defined scope documents
Umuhoza et al (2021)	Construction	client changes, unforeseen risks, unclear scope documents; poor mitigation strategies, frequent change in stakeholders' needs, poor estimations of activity resources and durations; unskilled labor, and poor change control.
Aizaz et al (2021)	Technology	stakeholders reported communication
Fashina et al. (2020)	Technology	scope creep on technology projects include poor communication, unrealistic timeline, scope changes, unsettled technical uncertainties and poor technical skills.
Davis et al. (2008)	Technology	changing software requirements from conflicting needs or lack of comprehension on project objectives
Komal et al. (2019)	Technology	budget constraints, poor requirements management, low stakeholders' satisfaction, poor communication, resource allocation and project size

CONCLUSION

This study demonstrated that scope creep is caused by various factors. As Aizaz et al (2021) notes, "PMI's 2018 pulse of profession indicates that 52% of the projects experienced Scope Creep" (p. 109167). In evaluating the results, the primary cause of scope creep appears to be poor communication, whether it is due to unclear requirements, clarification of expectations among stakeholders, poorly defined scope document, or lack of understanding of the project goals brought on by poor communication processes between the project leaders and the customers.

In order to deepen the understanding of the underlying causes of scope creep, future studies must analyze how scope creep impacts projects, and moreover, they must examine who are the key individuals responsible for influencing scope creep. New project managers, as well as new stakeholders and leaders who are unfamiliar with how projects are best managed, need to first become aware of the concept of scope creep and then evaluate ways to avoid contributing to scope creep. Of note, Roy and Searle (2020) stated the potential for successful scope creep "when proper analysis is conducted to provide evidence that benefits could outweigh the cost and lost time" (p. 95), spotlighting that not all scope creep is negative.

REFERENCES

Aizaz, K., Khan, S. U. R., Khan, J. A., Inayat-Ur-Rehman, & Akhunzada, A. (2021). An Empirical Investigation of Factors Causing Scope Creep in Agile Global Software Development Context: A Conceptual Model for Project Managers. *IEEE Access : Practical Innovations, Open Solutions*, *9*, 109166–109195. doi:10.1109/ACCESS.2021.3100779

Ajmal, K., Khan, M., & Al-Yafei, H. (2020). Exploring factors behind project scope creep – stakeholders' perspective. *International Journal of Managing Projects in Business*, *13*(3), 483–504. doi:10.1108/IJMPB-10-2018-0228

Ajmal, M. M., Khan, M., Gunasekaran, A., & Helo, P. T. (2021). Managing project scope creep in construction industry. *Engineering, Construction, and Architectural Management*.

Amoatey, C. T., & Anson, B. A. (2017). Investigating the major causes of scope creep in real estate construction projects in Ghana. *Journal of Facilities Management*, *15*(4), 393–408. doi:10.1108/JFM-11-2016-0052

Amoatey, T. (2017). Investigating the major causes of scope creep in real estate construction projects in Ghana. *Journal of Facilities Management*, *15*(4), 393–408. doi:10.1108/JFM-11-2016-0052

Davis, A. M., Nurmuliani, N., Park, S., & Zowghi, D. (2008, July). Requirements change: What's the alternative? In *2008 32nd Annual IEEE International Computer Software and Applications Conference* (pp. 635-638). IEEE.

Fashina, A. A., Abdilahi, S. M., & Fakunle, F. F. (2020). Examining the challenges associated with the implementation of project scope management in telecommunication projects in Somaliland. *PM World Journal*, *9*(3), 1–16.

Gullo, L. J. (2018). Developing System Safety Requirements. *Design for Safety*, 87-114.

Komal, B., Janjua, U. I., Anwar, F., Madni, T. M., Cheema, M. F., Malik, M. N., & Shahid, A. R. (2020). The impact of scope creep on project success: An empirical investigation. *IEEE Access : Practical Innovations, Open Solutions*, *8*, 125755–125775. doi:10.1109/ACCESS.2020.3007098

Komal, B., Janjua, U. I., & Madni, T. M. (2019, April). Identification of scope creep factors and their impact on software project success. In *2019 International Conference on Computer and Information Sciences (ICCIS)* (pp. 1-5). IEEE. 10.1109/ICCISci.2019.8716390

Larson, R., & Larson, E. (2009). *Top five causes of scope creep ... and what to do about them.* Paper presented at PMI® Global Congress 2009—North America, Orlando, FL.

Machi, L., & McEvoy, B. (2016). *The literature review: Six steps to success* (3rd ed.). Corwin. doi:10.1093/obo/9780199756810-0169

Madhuri, K. L., Rao, J. J., & Suma, V. (2014). Effect of Scope Creep in Software Projects a [euro]" Its Bearing on Critical Success Factors. *International Journal of Computer Applications*, *106*(2).

Madhuri, K. L., & Suma, V. (2014, October). Influence of domain and technology upon scope creep in software projects. In *International Conference on Advances in Electronics Computers and Communications* (pp. 1-6). IEEE. 10.1109/ICAECC.2014.7002443

Madhuri, K. L., Suma, V., & Mokashi, U. M. (2018). A triangular perception of scope creep influencing the project success. *International Journal of Business Information Systems*, *27*(1), 69–85. doi:10.1504/IJBIS.2018.088571

Nabet, A. A., El-Dash, K. M., ElMohr, M. K., & Mohamed, M. A. (2017). Managing scope creep in construction projects in Egypt. *ERJ Faculty Eng Shoubra*, *33*(1), 1–16.

Psichogios, P. (n.d.). If you're not changing you're not growing. *Global Engagement Solutions.* https://www.globalengagementsolutions.com/blog/if-youre-not-changing-youre-not-growing/

Roy, & Searle, M. (2020). Scope Creep and Purposeful Pivots in Developmental Evaluation. *Canadian Journal of Program Evaluation*, *35*(1), 92–103.. doi:10.3138/cjpe.56898

Safapour, E., & Kermanshachi, S. (2019, June). Identifying manageable scope creep indicators and selecting best practice strategies for construction projects. In *Proceedings of the 7th CSCE International Construction Specialty Conference* (pp. 12-15). Academic Press.

Sindi, M. (2018). Scope creep in construction industry of Saudi Arabia. *Int. Res. J. Adv. Eng. Sci.*, *3*(2), 277–281.

Thakurta, R. (2013). Impact of Scope Creep on Software Project Quality. Vilakshan: The XIMB. *Journal of Management*, *10*(1).

Turk, W. (2010). Scope creep horror. *Defense AT&L, 39*(2), 53-55.

Umuhoza, B. F., & An, S.-H. (2021). Causes and preventive strategies of scope creep for building construction projects in democratic republic of Congo and Rwanda. *International Journal of Construction Management*, 1–12. . doi:10.1080/15623599.2021.1967576

Wnuk, K., & Kollu, R. K. (2016, June). A systematic mapping study on requirements scoping. In *Proceedings of the 20th International Conference on Evaluation and Assessment in Software Engineering* (pp. 1-11). 10.1145/2915970.2915985

Chapter 4

Does Financial Globalization Have a Benign or Malignant Effect on Development and Growth?

Fatma Taşdemir
https://orcid.org/0000-0001-8706-7942
Sinop University, Turkey

ABSTRACT

Globalization with trade and financial linkages is beneficial for countries, as indicated by theory. The literature often finds that these are less clear for financial globalization. This chapter examines the association amongst financial globalization, growth, sectoral value added, and employment in emerging market and developing economies. Accordingly, financial globalization tends to lower growth, based on the main descriptive analysis. Financial globalization encourages industrialization in Asian economies while it leads to de-industrialization in African and Latin American countries. The services sector is positively associated with financial globalization in all regional country groupings. The analysis in this chapter indicates that financial globalization directs the allocation of resources across and within sectors. A strategic and systematic industrial policy that channels selective foreign savings into the finance of critical industrial projects also contributes to Sustainable Development Goals by minimizing the side effects of financial globalization.

DOI: 10.4018/978-1-6684-8810-2.ch004

1. INTRODUCTION

Globalization is a process that leads countries to integrate with trade and financial linkages. For instance, trade globalization allows households to purchase not only domestically produced goods and services, but also foreign-produced ones. Financial globalization, on the other hand, enables investors to partner with foreign firms by purchasing stocks and treasury bills. Globalization has gained momentum with the phasing out of trade and financial restrictions since the beginning of the 1970s. Mishkin (2006) points out that trade globalization has increased substantially "from a little over $1 trillion (at current prices) in 1960 to over $15 trillion today" (p. 2), and financial globalization has increased by "more than eightfold" (p. 2). In this context, the investigation of whether globalization is benign or malignant for growth and development is a crucially important topic.

Openness to trade and international financial flows is beneficial for economies, as indicated by theory. Accordingly, trade globalization tends to encourage competition, which raises static and dynamic productivity in output and allocation, advocates technological change, and leads to increasing returns to scale and specialization based on comparative and competitive advantages (Gupta and Choudhry, 1997). The direct and indirect theoretical benefits of financial globalization are to increase economic growth, as explained by Prasad et al. (2007). From the perspective of direct effects, financial globalization stimulates savings, mitigates the cost of capital, enables technology transfer, and enhances the financial sector. The indirect impacts of financial globalization are to augment specialization and encourage better macroeconomic policies.

Gupta and Choudhry (1997) note that several studies in the literature find the growth-enhancing effect of trade globalization, while some maintain that trade globalization causes developing economies to specialize in low-technology-embedded economic activities, which impede growth. The seminal contributions by Frankel and Romer (1999) suggest that trade leads to higher income. Heimberger (2022) reports that the growth-augmenting effect of globalization is related to trade integration. Prasad et al. (2007) report that the impacts of financial globalization on growth are inconclusive. The literature, including Schmukler (2004) and Obstfeld (2009), emphasizes that financial globalization increases vulnerability to external shocks and the spread of "financial fear" by contagion. In this context, the investigation of the growth and development impacts of financial globalization has become much more important, and this chapter aims to examine this important issue.

Financial globalization can be measured based on *de facto* and *de jure* measures. *De facto* financial globalization can be represented by international financial integration (IFI), which is measured as the gross stocks of financial assets and liabilities in GDP. The data for IFI have been constructed based on the international investment position and are available for a large sample of countries over the 1970-2021 period (Lane and Milesi-Ferretti, 2018). The *de jure* financial globalization, Chinn-Ito index, is a measure of the openness of a country to international financial flows and investments. It is based on the IMF's Annual Report on Exchange Arrangements and Exchange Restrictions (AREAER), which provides information on the policies and regulations for capital flows. Chinn and Ito (2008) provide capital account index data for 182 countries during the 1970-2020 period. An increase in both *de facto* and *de jure* measures indicates that a country is becoming more integrated into the global financial system.

Kose et al. (2009) argue that *de facto* IFI is a better measure of financial globalization than *de jure* Chinn-Ito index because it measures the actual flow of capital across borders, rather than the policies and regulations that govern capital flows. In addition, Edison et al. (2002) suggest the use of *de facto* financial globalization since this measure does not oscillate much in response to changes in macroeconomic policies. All these arguments imply that *de facto* IFI is a better measure than *de jure* capital account openness index. *De facto* IFI also allows us to differentiate the financial investment decisions of foreign and domestic residents. In this context, financial investment decisions of foreign residents can be represented by capital inflows (gross financial liabilities), while financial investment decisions of domestic residents can be represented by capital outflows (gross financial assets). The literature often maintains that the effect of financial globalization on growth may change with respect to the composition. In this context, international financial integration can be decomposed as foreign direct investment (FDI) and non-FDI (sum of portfolio equity and banking flows) integration. In the literature, some studies (Romer, 1990 and Grossman and Helpman, 1991) indicate that FDI enhances domestic investment by introducing new products and production processes, along with worker training. Albuquerque (2003) suggests that non-FDI flows are more volatile and less stable than FDI flows. Many studies find that the growth-augmenting effect of financial globalization is due to FDI integration. In this vein, Neto and Veiga (2013) remark that integration with FDI linkages is associated with better growth.

To examine the impact of *de facto* IFI on growth and development, we consider the Economic Transformation Data (de Vries et al., 2021) for emerging market and developing economies during the 1990-2018 period. The data provides the value added in constant prices and employment in 12 sectors (agriculture, construction, mining, utilities, manufacturing, business services, financial services, government services, trade services, transport services, real estate services, and other services) by considering the International Standard Industrial Classification (ISIC, Revision 4). By using the disaggregated data, we can examine the effect of financial globalization on sectoral value added and employment.

Recent literature, including Benigno et al. (2015), finds that financial globalization tends to allocate resources out of the manufacturing sector. According to Kaldor (1966), manufacturing is the main driving force of growth. Considering the remark by Benigno et al. (2015), we can maintain that financial globalization may impede growth by mitigating the manufacturing industry. The conventional wisdom on the development stages of economies indicates that mitigation of the manufacturing sector corresponds to the increase in the services sector. Therefore, we can suggest that financial globalization tends to allocate resources from manufacturing to the services sector.

Rodrik (2016) notes that deindustrialization, which is the decline in the manufacturing share, can be measured based on output and employment. The Economic Transformation database and IFI allow us to examine the validity of output and employment de-industrialization at the sectoral level. Before delving into the investigation of this important topic, this chapter first aims to investigate the evolution of financial globalization, which can be decomposed into gross capital inflows and outflows. We also decompose financial globalization into FDI and non-FDI integration. Then, we examine the evolution of value added and employment in 12 sectors. Following these useful exercises, we aim to examine the association between financial globalization and sectoral value added and employment by scatter plots, main descriptive statistics, and correlation tables. Considering the Kaldorian argument that maintains the manufacturing sector is the main driving force of growth, we are able to connect the link amongst financial globalization, development, and growth.

This chapter is planned to structure as follows. Section 2 provides an evaluation of *de facto* IFI across different country groupings including advanced, emerging market and developing economies. Section 3 presents the evolution of value added and employment in 12 sectors over the 1990-2018 period. Section 4 examines the impact of *de facto* IFI on sectoral value added and employment by scatter plots, and correlations. We provide a summary of the chapter and some policy implications in Section 5.

2. FINANCIAL GLOBALIZATION

This section aims to examine the evolution of financial globalization in advanced[1], emerging market and developing[2] economies during the 1970-2020 period. We also disaggregate emerging market and developing economies according to the regions including Africa[3], Asia[4] and Latin America[5]. We first consider the *de jure* measure of financial globalization which is the capital account openness index (Chinn and Ito, 2008). It is based on the IMF's Annual Report on Exchange Arrangements and

Exchange Restrictions (AREAER), which provides information on the policies and regulations for capital flows. Capital account openness ranges from 0 to 1, with higher values indicating more financial globalization.

Figure 1 represents the evolution of the mean *de jure* financial globalization index during the 1970-2020 period. In advanced economies, financial globalization tends to increase over the years, albeit it slightly decreases during the 2008-2009 global financial crisis period. Financial globalization appears to exhibit an increasing trend in the sample of emerging market and developing economies, except for the 1980s and 2010s. These exceptional periods appear to be held in Latin American economies. The debt crisis in the 1980s and deterioration in economic indicators in the 2010s have led to the movement of capital out of Latin American economies and a slowdown in financial globalization. The mean of financial globalization is almost stable in Asian economies. As compared to the 1970-1990 period, the mean of financial globalization has almost doubled in African economies during the rest of the sample period. Figure 1 clearly indicates that the level of financial globalization is substantially higher in advanced economies than in emerging market and developing economies.

Figure 1. The evolution of de jure financial globalization

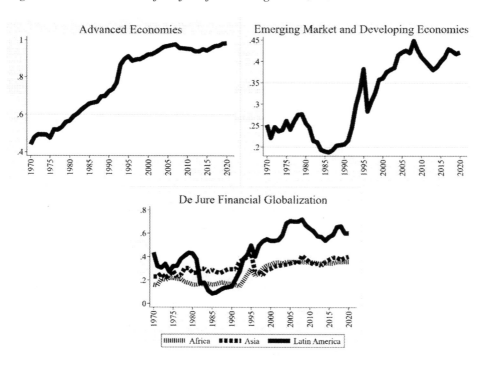

We now consider the evolution of the *de facto* measure of financial globalization, which is international financial integration. The data for international financial integration are from the External Wealth of Nations database provided by Lane and Milesi-Ferretti (2018). The level of international financial integration can be determined by calculating the total value of financial assets and liabilities as a proportion of the GDP. Higher values of international financial integration represent higher financial globalization.

Figure 2 shows the evolution of the mean international financial integration during the 1970-2020 period. In advanced economies, international financial integration tends to increase over the years, albeit the rate of increase is relatively stable during the 2010s. International financial integration also appears to increase in emerging market and developing economies, except for the 2003-2010 period. This exceptional period is due to diminishing international financial integration in African and Latin American economies. The countries in these regions tend to have an increasing trend in international financial integration up to 2003, a decreasing trend until 2010, and then an increasing trend during the rest of the sample period. The mean international financial integration increases in Asian economies. In a similar vein to Figure 1, Figure 2 clearly indicates that advanced economies are more financially globalized than emerging market and developing economies.

Figure 2. The evolution of De Facto financial globalization

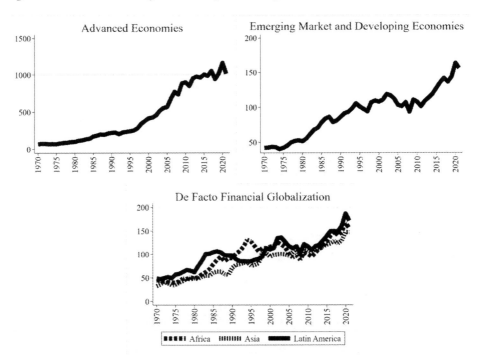

Table 1 reports the main descriptive statistics for *de jure* and *de facto* measures of financial globalization. The mean and median of *de jure* financial globalization are, respectively, 0.79 and 1 in advanced economies, and 0.32 and 0.16 in emerging market and developing economies. The mean and median values are much higher in advanced economies, although the standard deviation is the same in both country groupings. The mean and median of *de facto* financial globalization are, respectively, 447.3 and 226.9 in advanced economies, and 93.6 and 79.1 in emerging market and developing economies. As compared to advanced economies, the mean, median, and standard deviation of *de facto* financial globalization are noticeably much smaller in emerging market and developing countries.

We can disaggregate the sample of emerging market and developing economies with respect to the regions, including Latin America, Asia, and Africa. According to the mean and median values, *de jure* financial globalization is relatively much higher in Latin American economies. This appears to be the case for *de facto* measure of financial globalization. The standard deviation of *de jure* measure is slightly higher in the sample of Latin American economies, while the standard deviation of *de facto* measure is relatively higher in African economies. Considering the remarks by Edison et al. (2002) and Kose et al. (2009), which recommend that *de facto* financial globalization better measures the actual financial openness level of economies in practice, we consider international financial integration (IFI) as the measure of financial globalization for the rest of the chapter.

Figure 3 shows the evolution of *de facto* financial globalization disaggregated into the direction as assets and liability flows. Asset flows represent gross stocks of foreign financial asset purchases by domestic residents (as a percentage of GDP). Liability flows, on the other hand, illustrate gross stocks of domestic financial asset purchases by foreign residents in GDP. Liability and asset flows tend to move together in advanced economies. Liability flows are much higher than asset flows in emerging market and developing economies. This can indicate that international financial integration is mainly driven by liability flows in these economies. The difference between liability and asset flows tends to increase up to the beginning of the 2000s. Up to the mid-2000s, the difference seems to decrease, and this is driven by the mitigation of liability flows, although asset flows remain almost the same. After the global financial crisis, the difference between liability and asset flows again increases in emerging market and developing economies. This appears to be the case in African economies, while the difference tends to mitigate in Asian and Latin American countries after the global financial crisis.

Milesi-Ferretti and Tille (2011), Broner et al. (2013), Davis and van Wincoop (2018), and Eichengreen et al. (2018) point out that non-resident driven capital flows, i.e., liability flows, are much larger, fickle, and have a crucial importance for financial stability. According to Figure 3, liability flows are much larger than asset

Table 1. *The main descriptive statistics for financial globalization*

	De Jure Financial Globalization	*De Facto* Financial Globalization
	Advanced Economies	
Mean	0.79	447.28
Median	1	226.93
Standard Deviation	0.29	701.29
	Emerging Market and Developing Economies	
Mean	0.32	93.61
Median	0.16	79.06
Standard Deviation	0.29	63.77
	Latin American Economies	
Mean	0.44	101.90
Median	0.42	95.01
Standard Deviation	0.33	52.11
	Asian Economies	
Mean	0.32	84.87
Median	0.16	72.66
Standard Deviation	0.27	57.47
	African Economies	
Mean	0.27	94.46
Median	0.16	77.14
Standard Deviation	0.26	72.11

flows in emerging market and developing economies. Therefore, we can indicate that the undesirable properties of liability flows and financial stability concerns matter especially for this group of economies.

The External Wealth of Nations database enables the disaggregation of international financial integration based on its components. Conventional literature often maintains that foreign direct investment (FDI) flows are more beneficial than other flows. Romer (1990) and Grossman and Helpman (1991) find that FDI can increase domestic investment by three main arguments. First, foreign firms may bring new technologies and production processes to the host country, which can help to stimulate innovation and productivity growth. Second, foreign firms may provide training to local workers, which can help to improve the skills of the workforce and make it more attractive to other foreign investors. Third, foreign firms may create linkages with local suppliers and producers, which can help to boost domestic demand and investment. Based on these arguments, we disaggregate the international financial

Figure 3. The direction of financial globalization

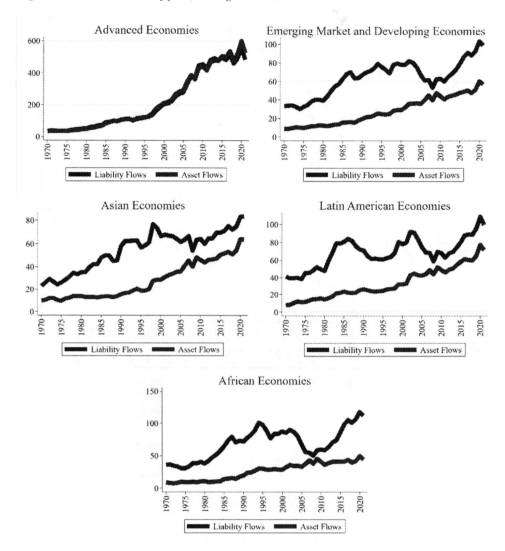

integration into FDI and non-FDI integration. FDI integration can be measured as the sum of gross stocks of FDI assets and liabilities as a percentage of GDP. Non-FDI integration can be calculated as the difference between international financial integration and FDI integration.

Figure 4 shows the evolution of FDI and non-FDI integration during the 1970-2020 period. Accordingly, international financial integration is mainly driven by non-FDI integration in both advanced and emerging market and developing economies. The gap between FDI and non-FDI integration appears to be stable in the sample

Figure 4. The evolution of FDI and non-FDI integration

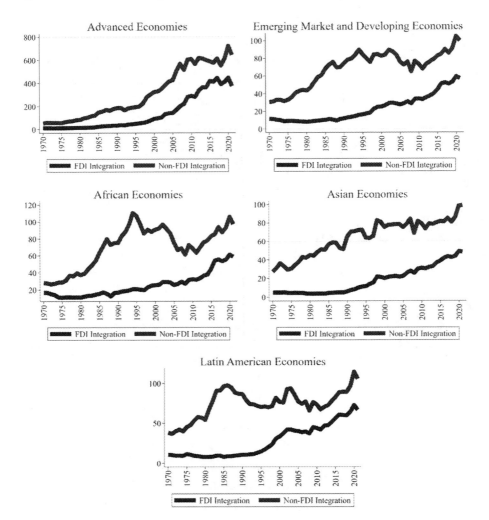

of advanced economies. However, the gap increased up to the mid-1990s and then decreased in emerging market and developing economies. This seems to be the case in African and Latin American economies. The difference between non-FDI and FDI integration is almost stable in Asian economies.

The first stylized fact in this section indicates that the level of financial globalization is substantially much higher in advanced economies than in emerging market and developing economies. The second stylized fact suggests that financial globalization is mainly driven by liability flows in emerging market and developing economies. The third stylized fact reveals that financial globalization is driven by non-FDI integration both in advanced and emerging market and developing economies.

3. SECTORAL VALUE ADDED AND EMPLOYMENT

This section aims to investigate the main properties of sectoral value added and employment. We consider the Economic Transformation database (de Vries et al., 2021), which is available for emerging market and developing economies. The database disaggregates the sectors according to the International Standard Industrial Classification (ISIC, Revision 4). Accordingly, the industrial sector includes the economic activities in the mining, manufacturing, construction, and utilities (electricity, gas, steam, and air conditioning supply; water supply; sewerage, waste management, and remediation activities) subsectors. The services sector, on the other hand, contains the economic activities in trade (wholesale and retail trade; repair of motor vehicles and motorcycles; accommodation and food service activities), government (public administration and defense; compulsory social security; education; human health and social work activities), real estate, transport (transportation and storage), financial (financial and insurance activities), business (information and communication; professional, scientific, and technical activities; administrative and support service activities), and other services (arts, entertainment, and recreation; other service activities; activities of households as employers; undifferentiated goods- and services-producing activities of households for own use; activities of extraterritorial organizations and bodies).

Table 2 reports the main descriptive statistics for sectoral value added share in constant prices. The values in parentheses are sectoral employment shares. According to the mean values, 18%, 29%, and 53% of total value added are, respectively, from agriculture, industry, and services sectors. The mean employment share in agriculture, industry, and services sectors are, correspondingly, 44%, 17%, and 39%. Considering that value added per employment represents productivity per labor, we can indicate that agriculture is the least productive sector. Almost half of the value added and employment in the industrial sector is due to manufacturing. Mining is the most productive sector within the industrial sector. The sum of the mean value added (employment) shares of trade and government services contributes almost half of the value added (employment) within the services sector. Real estate is the most productive sector in the services sector. Agriculture is the most volatile sector in emerging market and developing economies.

The sectoral value added and employment shares across the regions are almost the same as the main descriptive statistics for the sample of emerging market and developing economies. However, there are some differences in regional country groupings. For instance, the mean agricultural value added and employment shares, along with the volatility of the agricultural sector, are much lower in Latin American economies. The main statistics for the mining sector indicate that Asian economies are relatively resource-poor economies compared to Latin American and African

Table 2. Sectoral value added (employment) shares

	Agriculture	Industry				Services						
		Mining	Manufacturing	Construction	Utilities	Trade	Government	Real Estate	Transport	Financial	Business	Other Services
Emerging Market and Developing Economies												
Mean	18.13 (43.50)	5.89 (0.79)	15.35 (10.50)	5.65 (5.12)	2.22 (0.54)	14.57 (15.07)	13.15 (9.86)	6.01 (0.23)	5.33 (3.60)	3.94 (0.89)	6.21 (3.40)	3.54 (6.52)
Median	14.57 (41.25)	3.35 (0.50)	15.04 (10.87)	15.04 (5.32)	2.07 (0.40)	14.34 (15.14)	13.03 (7.98)	5.84 (0.12)	4.84 (3.60)	3.74 (0.68)	5.78 (2.22)	2.69 (5.00)
St. Dev.	13.21 (24.09)	6.68 (0.93)	6.16 (5.22)	6.16 (3.00)	1.29 (0.43)	3.73 (6.05)	5.49 (6.50)	3.54 (0.32)	2.57 (2.06)	1.98 (0.84)	3.47 (3.33)	3.14 (4.49)
Asian Economies												
Mean	19.17 (41.83)	3.87 (0.48)	18.03 (13.35)	6.24 (5.51)	2.04 (0.50)	15.22 (15.44)	10.34 (9.79)	5.11 (0.34)	6.25 (3.99)	4.19 (1.15)	5.85 (3.26)	3.69 (4.38)
Median	16.12 (42.98)	2.28 (0.44)	17.50 (13.15)	6.11 (5.59)	2.04 (0.43)	14.82 (15.26)	9.21 (7.94)	4.86 (0.20)	5.21 (4.02)	4.00 (0.84)	5.50 (1.76)	2.50 (4.14)
St. Dev.	12.66 (21.32)	4.45 (0.37)	6.51 (5.07)	2.41 (2.57)	0.99 (0.31)	3.91 (5.61)	4.72 (6.48)	4.07 (0.45)	2.89 (1.46)	2.16 (0.96)	3.73 (3.69)	3.71 (1.84)
Latin American Economies												
Mean	7.40 (20.32)	6.22 (0.85)	17.53 (12.01)	6.50 (6.59)	2.37 (0.74)	14.49 (20.70)	15.86 (13.68)	7.17 (0.30)	5.75 (5.80)	3.75 (1.24)	8.48 (6.18)	4.48 (11.60)
Median	6.81 (19.34)	5.92 (0.59)	16.72 (11.40)	6.24 (6.60)	2.36 (0.55)	14.59 (20.80)	15.59 (14.07)	8.18 (0.30)	5.44 (5.69)	3.64 (1.06)	8.30 (6.07)	3.32 (11.11)
St. Dev.	3.38 (11.14)	3.79 (0.70)	4.82 (3.26)	2.02 (1.38)	1.02 (0.57)	2.79 (3.79)	5.15 (5.26)	2.81 (0.25)	1.47 (1.76)	1.46 (0.82)	3.08 (2.88)	3.18 (4.48)
African Economies												
Mean	22.14 (55.26)	7.35 (1.01)	12.22 (7.55)	4.79 (4.14)	2.29 (0.47)	14.10 (12.24)	14.19 (8.20)	6.21 (0.11)	4.42 (2.30)	3.83 (0.52)	5.48 (2.26)	2.99 (5.95)
Median	19.15 (57.05)	4.25 (0.50)	12.02 (6.32)	4.23 (2.61)	1.97 (0.35)	13.86 (12.48)	14.32 (5.51)	6.11 (0.05)	4.02 (2.02)	3.48 (0.31)	4.87 (1.41)	2.12 (4.61)
St. Dev.	13.82 (22.48)	8.53 (1.23)	4.86 (4.47)	2.67 (3.48)	1.58 (0.41)	3.87 (5.33)	5.23 (6.31)	3.19 (0.14)	2.36 (1.56)	2.03 (0.56)	2.96 (2.34)	2.43 (4.24)

countries. The shares of manufacturing value added and employment are relatively much lower in the sample of African economies. Tregenna (2015) dubs the low level of manufacturing value added and employment in African economies as "pre-industrialization deindustrialization". Considering the main Kaldorian argument indicating manufacturing is the engine of growth, we can suggest that growth is lower in this country grouping.

The structural change argument maintains that employment and value added in sectors reallocate first from agriculture to manufacturing, and then from manufacturing to services, as indicated by Kuznets (1971). Thus, the employment and value added in the agricultural sector decrease as a natural consequence of the structural change postulate. In this vein, it is much more important to investigate the pattern in the industrial and services sectors.

Figure 5. Disaggregated sectoral value added

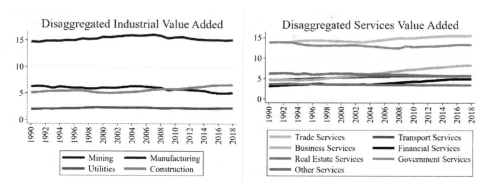

Figure 5 represents the evolution of disaggregated industrial and services value added (as a percentage of total value added) in emerging market and developing economies. Accordingly, manufacturing value added contains almost 15% of the total value added. Considering that deindustrialization represents a lower manufacturing value added share, this figure does not provide support to the output deindustrialization argument in our sample of emerging market and developing economies. The pattern in disaggregated industrial value added indicates that the share of construction tends to increase, while the share of mining seems to decrease after the 2008-2009 global financial crisis. This implies that the relative importance of mining has decreased, and construction has increased during the last decade. The figure for the disaggregated services value added indicates that the shares of business, trade, and financial services tend to increase, while the shares of government services and real estate services seem to decrease, especially in the mid-2000s and beyond. This indicates that the relative importance of government and real estate services has decreased and that of business, trade, and financial services has increased.

Figure 6 shows the evolution of disaggregated employment shares in industrial and services sectors (as a percentage of total employment). The employment share in manufacturing and construction tends to increase during the last decade, while that of mining and utilities remains almost stable over the years. The pattern for manufacturing employment also does not provide convincing evidence for the employment deindustrialization argument in our sample of emerging market and developing economies. The employment share in trade services, transport services, and business services appears to increase, while the employment share in other services tends to decrease over the years. The relative importance of employment in construction, manufacturing, trade, transport, and business services has increased within the industrial and services sectors, respectively.

Figure 6. Disaggregated employment shares in industrial and services sectors

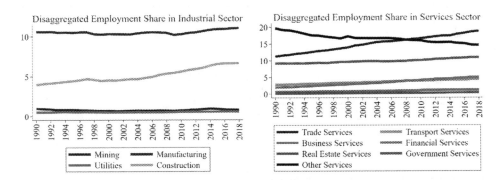

The fourth stylized fact based on the figures in this section suggests that the relative importance of the construction sector has increased within the industrial sector and that of trade, transport, and business services has raised within the services sector. A similar pattern appears to be the case for the share of employment. The fifth stylized fact suggests that neither output deindustrialization nor employment deindustrialization appears to be the case for our sample of emerging market and developing economies.

4. GROWTH, SECTORAL VALUE ADDED, SECTORAL EMPLOYMENT, AND FINANCIAL GLOBALIZATION

This section aims to first examine the relationship between financial globalization and growth, and then the association between financial globalization and sectoral value added and employment. The literature, including Obstfeld (1998) and Kose et al. (2010), suggests that financial globalization increases growth by supporting efficient capital allocation, risk sharing, and financial development. On the other hand, Schmukler (2004) and Obstfeld (2009) maintain that financial globalization leads to the spread of "financial fear" by contagion and exposes the economies to external shocks. To examine the association between growth and the *de facto* measure of financial globalization (international financial integration, IFI), we use the scatterplot of these variables.

Figure 7 shows the scatterplot of mean growth and mean international financial integration in emerging market and developing economies and their regional subgroups. Our measure of growth is the log difference of the total value added in constant prices. Accordingly, there is a negative relationship between international financial integration and growth. This pattern seems to hold in African, Asian, and Latin American economies.

Figure 7. Financial globalization and growth

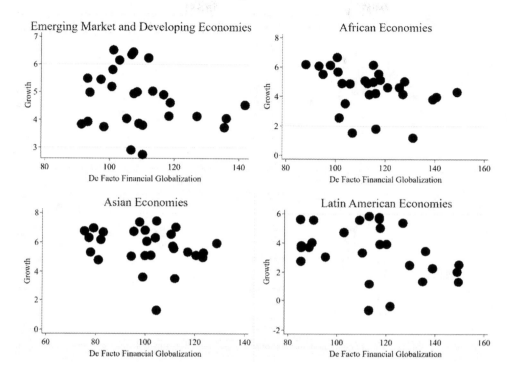

In emerging market and developing economies, the correlation of growth with IFI is -0.08, and it is statistically significant at the 1% level. The correlation coefficients are -0.02, -0.06, and -0.15, respectively, in the samples of African, Latin American, and Asian economies, although it is statistically significant only for the latter sample. The negative correlation between IFI and growth is consistent with the recent literature, including Taşdemir (2023), which suggests that "too much" international financial integration tends to lower growth. In this context, a recently published policy report by the IMF proposes the use of capital flow management measures, including capital controls, to provide financial and macroeconomic stability caused by high levels of financial globalization (Pasricha and Nier, 2022).

We now investigate the association between financial globalization and sectoral value added. Recent literature often maintains that financial globalization affects the allocation of resources across sectors. In this context, Rodrik (2016) remarks that financial globalization may lower manufacturing value added. This is briefly explained by Rodrik and Subramanian (2009). Accordingly, financial globalization leads to the appreciation of the domestic currency, diminishes the profitability in the tradable manufacturing industry, and lowers the investment motivation. In this

Figure 8. Industrial value added and financial globalization

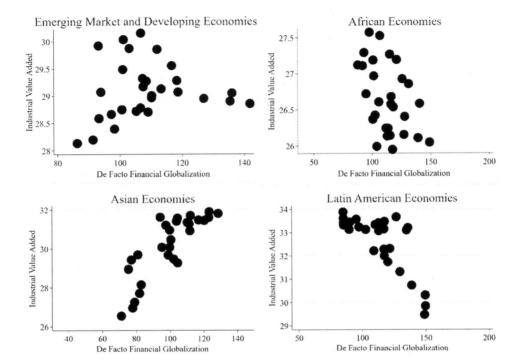

vein, Benigno et al. (2015) remark that financial globalization causes the movement of resources out of manufacturing industry. In another study, Benigno et al. (2020) find that financial globalization leads to global financial resource curse.

Figure 8 represents the scatter plot of mean industrial value added and mean de facto financial globalization in emerging market and developing economies during the 1990-2018 period. Accordingly, international financial integration tends to enhance industrial value added when the level of international financial integration is below almost 100. Beyond this level, international financial integration appears to diminish the industrial sector. In this context, the relationship between international financial integration and industrial value added appears to exhibit an inverted-U shaped pattern. The relationship between industrial value added and IFI tends to change with the regional country classification. IFI leads to lower industrial value added in African and Latin American economies. However, IFI increases industrial value added in Asian economies.

Table 3 shows the correlation of disaggregated industrial sector value added with international financial integration. IFI is positively correlated with the value added in the mining sector. This correlation is much higher in the sample of Latin

Table 3. Correlations of industrial sub-sector value added and IFI

	Mining_VA	Manufacturing_VA	Utilities_VA	Construction_VA
	Emerging Market and Developing Economies			
IFI	0.25*** (0.00)	0.02 (0.59)	0.25*** (0.00)	-0.08*** (0.00)
	Asian Economies			
IFI	0.14*** (0.00)	0.20*** (0.00)	0.10** (0.03)	-0.19*** (0.00)
	Latin American Economies			
IFI	0.40*** (0.00)	-0.15** (0.01)	0.15** (0.02)	-0.13** (0.04)
	African Economies			
IFI	0.25*** (0.00)	0.01 (0.89)	0.33*** (0.00)	0.01 (0.74)

Note: The numbers in parenthesis are p-values. ***<1%, **<5%.

American economies. The positive correlation between mining and IFI is consistent with the argument by Dunning (1980). Accordingly, the location-specific mining sector attracts capital flows by providing location advantages to investor economies. The correlation of IFI with manufacturing is positive but statistically insignificant in the sample of emerging market and developing economies. This appears to be the case for African economies. IFI tends to increase manufacturing in Asian economies, while it diminishes manufacturing in Latin American economies. The correlation for Asian economies is consistent with the theoretical benefits of financial globalization, which suggest that financial flows lead to a higher manufacturing industry. The case for Latin American economies is in accord with the findings by Rodrik (2016), which indicate that financial globalization is amongst the important determinants of deindustrialization. The value added in the utilities sub-sector is positively correlated with IFI. This is because financial globalization can finance new infrastructure projects, including water, gas, and electricity facilities, enhance the efficiency of existing utilities, and improve the quality of utilities by leading to competition. IFI is negatively correlated with the construction sub-sector, except the sample of African economies. This negative correlation could imply that financial globalization mitigates the profitability in construction sub-sector by appreciating the domestic currency.

The correlation coefficients in Table 3 indicate that financial globalization leads to the allocation of resources within the industrial sector for the sample of Asian and Latin American economies. In this context, financial globalization causes the allocation of resources from construction to the mining, manufacturing, and utilities

Figure 9. Services value added and financial globalization

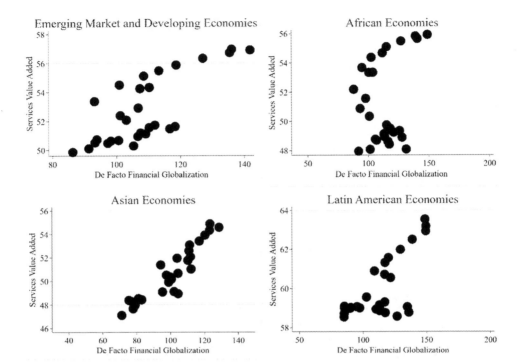

sub-sectors in Asian economies. In Latin American economies, financial globalization appears to allocate the resources from construction and manufacturing to the mining and utilities sub-sectors. The findings by Benigno et al. (2015), which suggest that financial globalization causes the movement of resources out of manufacturing, appear to be the case for Latin American economies.

Figure 9 shows the scatterplot of mean services value added and mean *de facto* financial globalization. Accordingly, IFI appears to increase services value added in emerging market and developing economies. This seems to hold also for African, Asian, and Latin American economies. The positive relationship between these variables may not be surprising because financial globalization leads to an enhanced financial sector within the services sector.

Table 4 shows the correlation of disaggregated services value added and IFI. There is a significant and positive correlation between trade services and IFI in Asian economies. The correlation between these variables is negative and significant in Latin American economies. Financial globalization tends to increase trade services in Asian economies while it lowers trade services in Latin American economies. This is closely associated with the correlation coefficients for the tradable manufacturing industry and IFI reported in Table 3. Accordingly, financial globalization leads to higher trade services by enhancing the tradable manufacturing industry in Asian economies while it mitigates trade services by decelerating the tradable sector in Latin American economies.

The correlation between transport services and IFI is negative and significant in emerging market and developing economies and Asian economies while it is positive and significant in Latin American and African economies. These correlations may indicate that financial globalization enhances large-scale transport infrastructure projects and transportation services in Latin American and African countries. Kotschwar (2012) remarks that Asian countries encourage intra-regional trade. The mitigation in distance for trade may have caused a negative correlation between transportation sector and financial globalization.

The correlation between business services and IFI is positive and statistically significant in emerging market and developing economies, Asian and Latin American economies. This correlation is positive but not significant in African economies. The positive association between business services and IFI indicates that financial globalization encourages the information and communication sub-sector. There is also a positive and significant correlation between financial services and IFI in all country groupings. This is consistent with the theoretical benefits of financial globalization as indicated by Prasad et al. (2007). Accordingly, financial globalization mitigates information asymmetry and encourages technology transfer and the financial sector.

Real estate services, on the other hand, are negative and significantly correlated with IFI. This may indicate that the non-tradable real estate sector, which is relatively inelastic, volatile, and has the potential for bubble effects, is subject to the side effects of financial globalization (Bardhan and Kroll, 2007).

The correlation between government services and IFI is positively significant in emerging market and developing economies and African economies, albeit they are correlated negatively and significantly in the sample of Latin American economies. By definition, government services include defense, compulsory social security, education, and health expenditures. Considering the main descriptive statistics in Table 2, mean government services is relatively higher in Latin American economies. This may cause a negative correlation of government services with IFI in this sample. High levels of financial globalization, on the other hand, tend to finance government services in African economies which are relatively low. Other services which include mainly cultural and other activities tend to mitigate with financial globalization in Asian economies while they increase with IFI in Latin American countries.

The correlation coefficients in Table 4 suggest that financial globalization leads to the allocation of resources within the services sector. In this context, high levels of financial globalization tend to allocate resources from transport and real estate to business, financial, and government services.

Table 4. Correlations of services sub-sector value added and IFI

	Emerging Market and Developing Economies	Asian Economies	Latin American Economies	African Economies
Trade_Services_VA	-0.03 (0.35)	0.17*** (0.00)	-0.35*** (0.00)	-0.06 (0.17)
Transport_Services_VA	-0.08*** (0.00)	-0.38*** (0.00)	0.26*** (0.00)	0.13*** (0.00)
Business_Services_VA	0.14*** (0.00)	0.30*** (0.00)	0.20*** (0.00)	0.01 (0.83)
Financial_Services_VA	0.25*** (0.00)	0.24*** (0.00)	0.21*** (0.00)	0.30*** (0.00)
Real_Estate_Services_VA	-0.13*** (0.00)	-0.11** (0.01)	-0.15** (0.02)	-0.19*** (0.00)
Government_Services_VA	0.14*** (0.00)	0.09 (0.07)	-0.46*** (0.00)	0.30*** (0.00)
Other_Services_VA	0.01 (0.62)	-0.24*** (0.00)	0.57*** (0.00)	0.05 (0.25)

Note: The numbers in parenthesis are p-values. ***<1%, **<5%.

Figure 10. Industrial employment and financial globalization

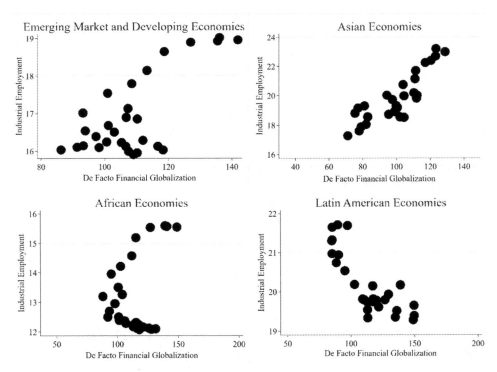

Figure 10 shows the scatter plot of sectoral employment with international financial integration. Accordingly, financial globalization tends to increase industrial employment in emerging market and developing economies. Figure 8 indicates that industrial value added declines with financial globalization when the level of international financial integration is 100 and beyond. Rethinking Figures 8 and 10 jointly, we can conclude that the labor productivity in the industrial sector appears to diminish when the level of financial globalization is higher than 100. The positive relationship between financial globalization and industrial employment appears to be the case for the sample of Asian and African economies. Financial globalization, on the other hand, leads to lower industrial employment in Latin American economies.

Figure 11 shows the scatterplot of financial globalization with services employment. The pattern for the whole sample suggests that financial globalization increases services employment. The positive relationship between these variables appears to hold in Asian and Latin American economies. Services employment first increases, then decreases, and afterwards increases with financial globalization in African economies.

Figure 11. Services employment and financial globalization

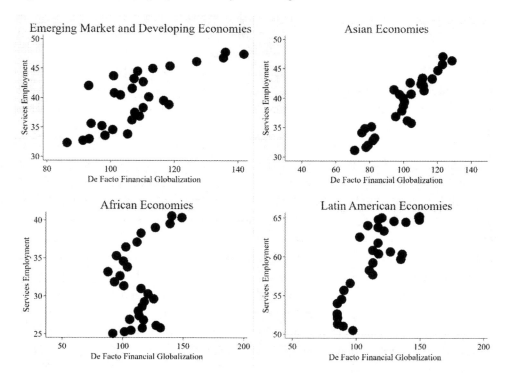

The sixth stylized fact suggests that financial globalization lowers growth in emerging market and developing economies. The seventh stylized fact indicates that financial globalization mitigates industrial value added in African and Latin American economies, although it encourages in Asian economies. Financial globalization, on the other hand, tends to enhance the services sector in all country groupings. Financial globalization also leads to the movement of resources within the sectors. Accordingly, resources are allocated from construction to mining and utilities sub-sectors within the industrial sector and from transport and real estate to business, financial, and government sub-sectors within the services sector. Considering the results by Rodrik (2016), output and employment de-industrialization arguments seem to hold in Latin American economies. However, Asian economies tend to industrialize with financial globalization.

5. CONCLUDING REMARKS

Conventional theory indicates that openness to trade and financial flows provides many benefits to countries, including higher productivity, efficient resource allocation, technological development, specialization based on comparative and competitive advantages, promotion of savings, financial development, and better macroeconomic policies. The literature, however, suggests that these beneficial effects often appear to be the case for trade openness, while these beneficial effects are less clear for the openness to financial flows, i.e., financial globalization. This chapter aims to investigate the relationship between financial globalization, growth, sectoral value added and employment in a sample of emerging market and developing economies during the 1990-2018 period.

Our measure of financial globalization is international financial integration, which represents the actual financial openness level of the economies in practice, as suggested by the literature. The main descriptive statistics indicate that advanced economies are more financially globalized than emerging market and developing economies. The disaggregation of financial globalization into the directions, i.e., resident-driven gross capital outflows (asset flows) and non-resident-driven gross capital inflows (liability flows), provides a different picture for advanced and emerging market and developing economies. Financial globalization is driven by the joint and equal impacts of gross capital inflows and outflows in advanced economies, while it is mainly driven by gross capital inflows in emerging market and developing economies. The recent literature often suggests that gross capital inflows are fickle, volatile, and crucially important for financial stability. Cavallo et al. (2018) find that growth is much lower when countries finance their investment with liability flows.

These arguments may imply that macroeconomic and financial stability concerns are higher in emerging market and developing economies.

The disaggregation of financial globalization into its components shows that advanced and emerging market and developing economies are mainly integrated with non-FDI flows, rather than FDI flows. However, the difference between non-FDI and FDI flows is much lower in advanced economies than in emerging market and developing economies. The literature often suggests the beneficial effects of globalization with FDI integration, because non-FDI integration is short-term, reversible, and more volatile. Considering that emerging market and developing economies are mainly integrated with gross capital inflows, the side effects of financial globalization matter especially for this group of economies. Therefore, we focus on the association amongst financial globalization, growth, sectoral value added and employment for this sample.

The literature, including Rodrik (2016), suggests that financial globalization is one of the most important determinants of de-industrialization. In this vein, Benigno et al. (2015) report that financial globalization allocates resources from manufacturing to services. In another paper, Benigno et al. (2020) find that financial globalization causes global financial resource curse. In emerging market and developing economies, the relative contribution of construction has increased within the industrial sector and the relative contribution of trade, financial, and business services has enhanced within the services sector during the 1990-2018 period. In this context, the time evolution of manufacturing value added and employment shares do not show the presence of the deindustrialization argument in our sample.

Then, we investigate the association between financial globalization and growth. The theory claims that financial globalization increases growth by providing efficient capital allocation, financial development and risk sharing. On the other hand, the literature finds that financial globalization can mitigate growth by exposing economies to external shocks and spreading financial fear through contagion. Financial globalization appears to lower growth in our sample of emerging market and developing economies. We disaggregate the whole sample into the regions, including Asian, African, and Latin American economies. The negative relationship between growth and financial globalization appears to be the case also for different regional country groupings. This may be related to the argument suggested by Rodrik and Subramanian (2009). Accordingly, financial globalization appreciates exchange rates, mitigates profitability in investment and leads to lower growth. The negative effect of financial globalization on growth may also be the natural consequence of integration with non-FDI flows which are easily reversible, short-term and fickle. This reminds the recent suggestions by the IMF, which indicate that financial and macroeconomic stability may be provided via pre-emptive capital flow management measures (Pasricha and Nier, 2022).

The association between sectoral value added and financial globalization varies with respect to the sectors. Accordingly, financial globalization tends to increase industrial value added up to a certain level of financial globalization, while "too much" financial globalization diminishes industrial value added. This suggests an inverted-U shaped relationship between these variables. The positive relationship between financial globalization and the industrial sector seems to hold in Asian economies. However, financial globalization mitigates industrial value added in African and Latin American economies. The services sector is positively associated with financial globalization in all country groupings. The mitigation in the industrial sector and enhancement in the services sector may be interpreted as the movement of resources from the industrial sector to the services sector with financial globalization.

Benigno et al. (2015) find that financial globalization leads to the movement of resources across the sectors. This study reports that financial globalization also changes the resource allocation within the sectors. In this vein, financial globalization tends to allocate resources from construction to mining and utilities within the industrial sector, and from transport and real estate to business, financial, and government sub-sectors within the services sector. Resource allocation within the sectors is consistent with the remarks by Rodrik and Subramanian (2009), which indicate that financial openness lowers profitability in some sectors. These sectors are the construction, transport, and real estate sub-sectors.

The Kaldorian argument maintains the crucial importance of manufacturing for growth. Financial globalization, on the other hand, increases manufacturing in Asian economies but mitigates it in Latin American economies. In the context of the Kaldorian argument, we may suggest that growth is much lower in Latin American economies, although it is much higher in Asian economies. The positive impact of financial globalization on manufacturing in Asian economies may be related to favorable structural domestic conditions, including high saving rates. In addition, the strategic industrial policies in Asian economies allow them to pave the way for developing competitive and technologically upgraded industrial bases, which also contributes to obtain the beneficial effects of financial globalization. The pre-emptive and effective policies on capital and foreign exchange controls, and selectively integration of domestic and foreign savings into the investment projects, contribute much to the success of Asian economies, as suggested by Storm (2017). The adaptation and adjustment of these policies, consistent with country-specific circumstances, are expected to be able to obtain the benefits of financial globalization for African and Latin American economies.

Considering that capital flows are fickle and foreign direct investment (FDI) flows are the most beneficial types of capital flows, countries can reap the potential benefits of financial globalization by changing the direction and composition of financial globalization through pre-emptive and effective capital flow management measures.

Given that foreign savings are fickle, the use of domestic savings in investment projects which have critical importance is expected to contribute to the sustainability of growth. A strategic and systematic industrial policy that channels selective foreign savings into the finance of critical industrial projects also contributes to sustainable development goals by minimizing the side effects of financial globalization.

REFERENCES

Albuquerque, R. (2003). The composition of international capital flows: Risk sharing through foreign direct investment. *Journal of International Economics, 61*(2), 353–383. doi:10.1016/S0022-1996(03)00013-8

Bardhan, A., & Kroll, C. A. (2007). *Globalization and the real estate industry: Issues, implications, opportunities.* http://web.mit.edu/sis07/www/kroll.pdf

Benigno, G., Converse, N., & Fornaro, L. (2015). Large capital inflows, sectoral allocation, and economic performance. *Journal of International Money and Finance, 55*, 60–87. doi:10.1016/j.jimonfin.2015.02.015

Benigno, G., Fornaro, L., & Wolf, M. (2020). *The global financial resource curse.* FRB of New York Staff Report No. 915.

Broner, F., Didier, T., Erce, A., & Schmukler, S. L. (2013). Gross capital flows: Dynamics and crises. *Journal of Monetary Economics, 60*(1), 113–133. doi:10.1016/j.jmoneco.2012.12.004

Cavallo, E., Eichengreen, B., & Panizza, U. (2018). Can countries rely on foreign saving for investment and economic development? *Review of World Economics, 154*(2), 277–306. doi:10.100710290-017-0301-5

Chinn, M. D., & Ito, H. (2008). A new measure of financial openness. *Journal of Comparative Policy Analysis, 10*(3), 309–322. doi:10.1080/13876980802231123

Davis, J. S., & Van Wincoop, E. (2018). Globalization and the increasing correlation between capital inflows and outflows. *Journal of Monetary Economics, 100*, 83–100. doi:10.1016/j.jmoneco.2018.07.009

de Vries, G., Arfelt, L., Drees, D., Godemann, M., Hamilton, C., Jessen-Thiesen, B., Ihsan Kaya, A., Kruse, H., Mensah, E., & Woltjer, P. (2021). *The economic transformation database (ETD): Content, sources, and methods. WIDER Technical Note 2021/2.* UNU-WIDER. doi:10.35188/UNU-WIDER/WTN/2021-2

Dunning, J. H. (1980). Toward an eclectic theory of international production: Some empirical tests. *Journal of International Business Studies*, *11*(1), 9–31. doi:10.1057/palgrave.jibs.8490593

Edison, H. J., Levine, R., Ricci, L., & Sløk, T. (2002). International financial integration and economic growth. *Journal of International Money and Finance*, *21*(6), 749–776. doi:10.1016/S0261-5606(02)00021-9

Eichengreen, B., Gupta, P., & Masetti, O. (2018). Are capital flows fickle? Increasingly? And does the answer still depend on type? *Asian Economic Papers*, *17*(1), 22–41. doi:10.1162/asep_a_00583

Frankel, J. A., & Romer, D. (1999). Does Trade Cause Growth? *The American Economic Review*, *89*(3), 379–399. doi:10.1257/aer.89.3.379

Grossman, G. M., & Helpman, D. (1991). *Innovation and Growth in the Global Economy*. MIT Press.

Gupta, S. D., & Choudhry, N. K. (1997). Globalization, growth and sustainability: An introduction. *Globalization, Growth and Sustainability*, 1-13.

Heimberger, P. (2022). Does economic globalisation promote economic growth? A meta- analysis. *World Economy*, *45*(6), 1690–1712. doi:10.1111/twec.13235

Kaldor, N. (1966). *Causes of the Slow Rate of Growth of the United Kingdom. An Inaugural Lecture*. Cambridge University Press.

Kose, M. A., Prasad, E., Rogoff, K., & Wei, S. J. (2009). Financial globalization: A reappraisal. *IMF Staff Papers*, *56*(1), 8–62. doi:10.1057/imfsp.2008.36

Kose, M. A., Prasad, E., Rogoff, K., & Wei, S. J. (2010). Financial globalization and economic policies. In D. Rodrik, & M. Rosenzweig (Eds.), Handbook of development economics (vol. 5, pp. 4283–4359). Elsevier. doi:10.1016/B978-0-444-52944-2.00003-3

Kotschwar, B. R. (2012). *Transportation and communication infrastructure in Latin America: lessons from Asia*. Peterson Institute for International Economics Working Paper No. 12-6.

Kuznets, S. (1971). *Economic growth of nations: Total output and production structure*. Harvard University Press. doi:10.4159/harvard.9780674493490

Lane, P. R., & Milesi-Ferretti, G. M. (2018). The external wealth of nations revisited: International financial integration in the aftermath of the global financial crisis. *IMF Economic Review*, *66*(1), 189–222. doi:10.105741308-017-0048-y

Milesi-Ferretti, G. M., & Tille, C. (2011). The great retrenchment: International capital flows during the global financial crisis. *Economic Policy*, *26*(66), 289–346. doi:10.1111/j.1468-0327.2011.00263.x

Mishkin, F. S. (2006). *The Next Great Globalization: How Disadvantaged Nations Can Harness Their Financial Systems to Get Rich*. Princeton University Press. doi:10.1515/9781400829446

Neto, D. G., & Veiga, F. J. (2013). Financial globalization, convergence and growth: The role of foreign direct investment. *Journal of International Money and Finance*, *37*, 161–186. doi:10.1016/j.jimonfin.2013.04.005

Obstfeld, M. (1998). The global capital market: Benefactor or menace? *The Journal of Economic Perspectives*, *12*(4), 9–30. doi:10.1257/jep.12.4.9

Obstfeld, M. (2009). International finance and growth in developing countries: What have we learned? *IMF Staff Papers*, *56*(1), 63–111. doi:10.1057/imfsp.2008.32

Pasricha, G. K., & Nier, E. (2022). *Review of The Institutional View on The Liberalization and Management of Capital Flows—Background Note on Capital Flows and Capital Flow Management Measures—Benefits and Costs (Policy Papers No. 2022/009)*. International Monetary Fund.

Prasad, E. S., Rajan, R. G., & Subramanian, A. (2007). Foreign capital and economic growth. *Brookings Papers on Economic Activity*, *2007*(1), 153–230. doi:10.1353/eca.2007.0016

Rodrik, D. (2016). Premature deindustrialization. *Journal of Economic Growth*, *21*(1), 1–33. doi:10.100710887-015-9122-3

Rodrik, D., & Subramanian, A. (2009). Why did financial globalization disappoint? *IMF Staff Papers*, *56*(1), 112–138. doi:10.1057/imfsp.2008.29

Romer, P. M. (1990). Endogenous technological change. *Journal of Political Economy*, *98*(5, Part 2), 71–102. doi:10.1086/261725

Schmukler, S. L. (2004). Financial globalization: Gain and pain for developing countries. *Federal Reserve Bank of Atlanta Economic Review*, *89*(2), 39–66.

Storm, S. (2017). *The political economy of industrialization: Introduction to Development and Change*. Academic Press.

Taşdemir, F. (2023). International financial integration: Too much? *Borsa Istanbul Review*, *23*(2), 402–411. doi:10.1016/j.bir.2022.11.005

Tregenna, F. (2015). *Deindustrialization, structural change and sustainable economic growth*. Inclusive and Sustainable Industrial Development Working Paper Series, Working Paper 02–2015.

ENDNOTES

[1] Advanced economies are Australia, Austria, Belgium, Canada, Cyprus, Denmark, Finland, France, Germany, Greece, Hong Kong, Iceland, Ireland, Italy, Japan, Netherlands, New Zealand, Norway, Portugal, Singapore, Slovenia, Spain, Sweden, Switzerland, United Kingdom, and United States.

[2] Emerging market and developing economies are Argentina, Bangladesh, Bolivia, Botswana, Brazil, Burkina Faso, Cambodia, Cameroon, Chile, China, Colombia, Costa Rica, Ecuador, Egypt, Ethiopia, Ghana, India, Indonesia, Israel, Kenya, Korea, Lesotho, Malawi, Malaysia, Mexico, Morocco, Mozambique, Myanmar, Namibia, Nepal, Nigeria, Pakistan, Peru, Philippines, Rwanda, Senegal, South Africa, Sri Lanka, Tanzania, Thailand, Tunisia, Türkiye, Uganda, Vietnam, and Zambia.

[3] African economies are Botswana, Burkina Faso, Cameroon, Egypt, Ethiopia, Ghana, Kenya, Lesotho, Malawi, Morocco, Mozambique, Namibia, Nigeria, Rwanda, Senegal, South Africa, Tanzania, Tunisia, Uganda and Zambia.

[4] Asian economies are Bangladesh, Cambodia, China, India, Indonesia, Israel, Korea, Malaysia, Myanmar, Nepal, Pakistan, Philippines, Sri Lanka, Thailand, Türkiye, and Vietnam.

[5] Latin American economies are Argentina, Bolivia, Brazil, Chile, Colombia, Costa Rica, Ecuador, Mexico, and Peru.

Chapter 5
Tourism Is an Essential Trade:
VR and AR Technologies Make It Profitable

C. V. Suresh Babu
 https://orcid.org/0000-0002-8474-2882
Hindustan Institute of Technolgy and Science, India

T. Jeyavasan
Hindustan Institute of Technology and Science, India

ABSTRACT

This chapter aims to present a sustainable growth solution for the tourism industry by utilizing virtual reality (VR) technology. The chapter focuses on creating a platform similar to a VR metaverse that offers users an immersive and compelling tourism experience of well-known tourist attractions worldwide. The platform aims to enable sustainable growth for the tourism industry while also promoting global social development. The chapter discusses the importance of such a platform, addressing key issues in VR tourism and providing recommendations for its effective implementation. The proposed solution offers a viable alternative to traditional tourism that has a significant environmental impact, such as carbon emissions and overcrowding. Through the VR-based platform, tourists can travel virtually, reducing the need for physical travel while still enjoying the beauty and culture of different locations worldwide. Overall, this chapter aims to present a solution that can promote sustainable tourism while simultaneously contributing to global social development.

DOI: 10.4018/978-1-6684-8810-2.ch005

1. INTRODUCTION

Tourism is a significant driver of economic growth and development in many countries worldwide. However, traditional tourism practices have a significant environmental impact, contributing to problems such as carbon emissions and overcrowding. In recent years, the tourism industry has increasingly focused on sustainability and environmentally friendly practices. In this chapter, we propose a solution that utilizes Virtual Reality (VR) and Augmented Reality (AR) technology to promote sustainable growth in the tourism industry.

The proposed solution involves creating a VR-based platform that offers an immersive and compelling tourism experience of well-known tourist attractions worldwide. This platform aims to enable sustainable growth for the tourism industry while also promoting global social development. By reducing the need for physical travel, the platform can significantly reduce the environmental impact of tourism while still allowing tourists to experience the beauty and culture of different locations worldwide.

This chapter will discuss the importance of such a platform, addressing key issues in VR tourism, and providing recommendations for its effective implementation. We will also explore the potential economic and social benefits of a VR-based tourism industry, including increased accessibility for individuals with disabilities and those living in remote areas.

Overall, this chapter aims to present a solution that can promote sustainable tourism while simultaneously contributing to global social development. Through the implementation of VR and AR technology, the tourism industry can embrace a more sustainable and environmentally-friendly approach, ensuring the preservation of natural and cultural resources for generations to come.

2. RELATED WORK

2.1 Define the Problem

The problem addressed by the proposed chapter is the negative impact of traditional tourism practices on the environment and local communities, and the need for sustainable solutions in the tourism industry. As stated in (Gössling et al., 2013), tourism is a major contributor to greenhouse gas emissions, with transportation accounting for the majority of these emissions. In addition, tourism can also have negative impacts on local communities, including cultural erosion and displacement of locals.

Although there has been an increasing focus on sustainability in the tourism industry, traditional approaches to sustainable tourism, such as ecotourism, have not taken hold due to factors such as high costs and limited accessibility. As noted in (Hall & Gössling, 2016), innovative and accessible solutions are needed to promote sustainable growth in the tourism industry.

The proposed solution, which uses VR and AR technology to create a VR-based tourism platform, addresses these issues. As stated in (Neuhofer et al., 2015), by reducing the need to physically travel, the platform can significantly reduce the environmental impact of tourism while allowing tourists to experience the beauty and culture of different places around the world. In addition, the platform can improve accessibility for people with disabilities and people living in remote areas. This solution offers a viable alternative to traditional tourism practices, promoting the sustainable growth of the industry while contributing to global social development.

Overall, the problem of unsustainable tourism practices and the need for sustainable solutions is an urgent issue, and the proposed solution of a VR-based tourism platform using VR and AR technology offers a promising solution to address this challenge.

2.2 Literature Searching

There are some studies that have investigated the use of virtual reality technologies (VR) in the tourism industry and their potential to promote sustainable growth (Amaranggana, 2019; Buhalis & Neuhofer, 2018; Jung & tom Dieck, 2018; Lee & Xiang, 2019). A study published in the Journal of Sustainable Tourism discusses the potential of VR technology to provide tourists with an immersive and environmentally friendly alternative to traditional tourism (Amaranggana, 2019; Buhalis & Neuhofer, 2018). The study suggests that VR-based tourism could reduce carbon emissions, reduce destination overcrowding, and promote sustainable growth in the industry (Amaranggana, 2019; Buhalis & Neuhofer, 2018). Another study published in the Journal of Travel Research concluded that the use of VR technology in the tourism industry could improve tourists' experiences and encourage them to visit destinations they might not otherwise have considered (Lee & Xiang, 2019).

In addition, a study published in the Journal of Hospitality and Tourism Technology suggests that implementing VR technology in the tourism industry requires careful planning and consideration of user needs (Jung & tom Dieck, 2018). The study emphasizes the importance of creating a user-friendly platform that provides a high-quality and seamless VR experience to drive user engagement and satisfaction (Jung & tom Dieck, 2018).

Overall, the literature suggests that the use of VR technology in the tourism industry has the potential to drive sustainable growth and improve tourist experiences.

However, careful consideration and planning are required to ensure effective implementation and user satisfaction.

2.3 Summarizing

The proposed chapter suggests using virtual reality technology (VR) to create a sustainable growth solution for the tourism industry. The chapter focuses on creating a VR -based platform that provides an immersive and engaging tourism experience of popular tourist attractions worldwide while promoting global social development. This platform can be created using Unity Engine and Oculus Reality to create an interactive and engaging experience for users. The proposed solution aims to provide an eco-friendly alternative to traditional tourism that can reduce carbon emissions and overcrowding in popular destinations. The chapter also emphasizes the importance of careful planning and consideration of user needs to ensure effective implementation and user satisfaction. Overall, the chapter aims to present a solution that can promote sustainable tourism while improving tourists' experiences and contributing to global social development.

2.4 Defining the Argument

1. Accessibility for users: the proposed platform requires that users have access to VR hardware, which may limit the accessibility of the platform for those who cannot afford or do not have access to the necessary equipment.
2. Development costs: developing a high-quality platform based on VR requires significant investment in terms of development resources and time, which could be challenging for organizations with limited resources.
3. Technical expertise: Developing a VR -based platform requires specialized technical expertise, particularly in the areas of 3D modeling and programming, which may be challenging for some developers.
4. Compatibility issues: There are several VR platforms on the market, and compatibility issues could arise if the platform is designed to work on multiple devices and platforms.
5. Internet connectivity: A platform based on VR that provides high-quality and immersive experiences requires a high-bandwidth Internet connection, which may limit accessibility in areas with poor Internet connectivity.
6. User acceptance: The success of the platform based on VR depends on user acceptance, and it may take some time for users to become familiar with the new technology and the idea of virtual tourism.

2.5 Detailed Argument

The proposed chapter proposes to leverage virtual reality technology (VR) to create a platform resembling a VR metaverse that provides users with an immersive and engaging tourism experience of famous tourist attractions worldwide. The platform is designed to enable sustainable growth of the tourism industry while promoting global social development. The solution offers a viable alternative to traditional tourism, which has significant environmental impacts such as carbon emissions and overcrowding. Through the platform based on VR, tourists can travel virtually, reducing the need for physical travel while enjoying the beauty and culture of different places around the world. The use of VR technology in education and training has been shown to improve understanding, critical thinking, and problem-solving skills, which can also be applied to the tourism industry. Technical barriers such as hardware and software limitations need to be addressed, and extensive research and development is required to ensure the platform's success. Despite potential setbacks, the proposed solution can promote sustainable tourism while contributing to global social development.

2.6 Drafting

The tourism industry is a significant contributor to the global economy, but it also has a considerable environmental impact, such as carbon emissions and overcrowding. Therefore, there is a need for sustainable growth solutions that can promote the industry's development while also protecting the environment. In this context, Virtual Reality (VR) technology has emerged as a viable alternative to traditional tourism that can significantly reduce the industry's carbon footprint. A VR-based platform, similar to a metaverse, can offer tourists an immersive and compelling experience of well-known tourist attractions worldwide, thereby reducing the need for physical travel.

This proposed chapter aims to present such a sustainable growth solution for the tourism industry by utilizing VR technology. The proposed platform can promote sustainable tourism while simultaneously contributing to global social development. The chapter highlights the importance of this platform and provides recommendations for its effective implementation.

The literature suggests that the incorporation of data analysis tools in economics education can provide significant benefits for students, including improved understanding of economic concepts, enhanced data analysis skills, and improved academic performance (Al-Amin & Saidy, 2020; Bohdanowicz & Zientara, 2020; Mottaleb et al., 2020; Pal, 2020). Similarly, the use of VR technology in tourism can have significant positive impacts on the industry and the environment (Bohdanowicz

& Zientara, 2020). However, there are technical setbacks that need to be addressed, such as the cost of developing VR content and the need for high-performance hardware (Buhalis & Neuhofer, 2018). Additionally, there may be potential setbacks related to the overall project, such as limited access to VR hardware and the possibility of the technology being perceived as a replacement for physical travel (Mottaleb et al., 2020).

3. METHODOLOGY

- **Gathering the Requirements:** The first step is to gather and analyze the requirements for the platform based on VR and AR. This includes identifying the types of tourist attractions to be featured, the specific features and functions needed, and any technical or user-friendliness considerations.
- **User Interface Design:** once requirements are identified, the next step is to design the user interface for the platform based on VR and AR. This involves creating wireframes or mockups that show how the user interface will look and function. The design should be captivating, user-friendly, and visually appealing.
- **Selecting Development Tools VR and AR:** The next step is to select the appropriate VR and AR development tools to be used to build the platform. This may include software development kits such as Unity or Unreal Engine or specialized VR and AR development tools such as Vuforia or ARCore.
- **Integration of VR and AR Development Tools:** Once the user interface design and the VR and AR development tools have been selected, the next step is to integrate the VR and AR development tools into the user interface. This involves programming the application using appropriate programming languages and frameworks, and integrating the VR and AR development tools into the application.
- **Testing and Quality Assurance:** Once the platform based on VR and AR is developed, it must be thoroughly tested to ensure that it works correctly and meets requirements. This includes both functional testing to ensure that the application works as expected and quality assurance testing to ensure that it is reliable and secure.
- **Deployment and Maintenance:** Deploying the VR and AR based platform to its intended users and maintaining it over the long term. This includes ongoing monitoring and support to ensure that the application continues to function correctly and to provide updates and enhancements as needed.

3.1 Design and Development of the Application

Step 1: Determine the Scope and Requirements

The first step is to define the scope of the tourism platform based on VR and AR and the specific requirements it must meet. This includes identifying the types of tourism data that will be analyzed by the platform, the specific features and functionalities that are required, and any technical or security considerations related to the VR and AR components.

Step 2: Design of the User Interface

Once the requirements are defined, the next step is to design the user interface of the platform. This involves creating wireframes or mockups of the VR and AR -based application that show how the user interface will look and function in a 3D environment. The design should be intuitive, user-friendly, and visually appealing to enhance the user experience.

Step 3: Select the Appropriate VR and AR Development Tools

The next step is to select the appropriate VR and AR development tools that will be used to create the immersive 3D environment for tourism data visualization. This may include specialized VR and AR development platforms such as Unity or Unreal Engine, as well as other 3D modeling and animation software.

Step 4: Development of the VR and AR-Based Platform

After the requirements, user interface, and VR and AR development tools are determined, the next step is to develop the VR and AR -based platform. This involves programming the application using appropriate programming languages and frameworks, and integrating the VR and AR components into the platform.

Step 5: Testing and Quality Assurance

Once the platform is developed, it must be thoroughly tested to ensure that it functions correctly and meets requirements. This includes both functional testing to ensure that the application works as expected in the 3D environment and quality assurance testing to ensure that it is reliable and secure.

Step 6: Deployment and Maintenance

The final step is to deploy the platform to its intended users and maintain it over time. This includes ongoing monitoring and support to ensure that the platform continues to function correctly and updates and enhancements are made as needed, as well as ensuring that the components of VR and AR are compatible with the latest hardware and software updates.

Overall, the design and development of a VR and AR -based platform for tourism involves a unique set of steps that require expertise in both software development and data analysis and VR /AR development. By taking a structured approach and using appropriate tools and frameworks, it is possible to develop a robust and effective platform that enhances the tourism experience for users in a variety of contexts.

3.2 Technical Stack

Programming Languages

The most commonly used programming languages for developing VR and AR based applications are C#, C++, and UnityScript (Unity's scripting language). These languages have powerful libraries and frameworks for game development, 3D modeling, and simulation.

3D Modelling and Simulation Software

To create realistic 3D models and simulations, software like Unity, Unreal Engine, and Blender can be used. These software provide a wide range of tools for modeling, animation, and visual effects.

Augmented Reality (AR) and Virtual Reality (VR) SDKs

For developing AR and VR based applications, SDKs like Vuforia, ARKit, ARCore, and Oculus SDK can be used. These SDKs provide tools for motion tracking, image recognition, and spatial mapping.

Cloud Platforms

Cloud platforms like AWS, Azure, and Google Cloud can be used for deploying and scaling VR and AR based applications. These platforms offer a range of services for data storage, processing, and analysis.

Web Frameworks

To develop web-based VR and AR applications, web frameworks like A-Frame, React 360, and Babylon.js can be used. These frameworks provide tools for building interactive web applications and visualizations.

3.3 The Following Are the Tools Features and Functionalities

- **Unity:** The platform will be created using the well-known game engine Unity, which facilitates the creation of VR and AR applications. 3D modelling, animation, and physics simulations are just a few of the capabilities Unity offers for making immersive experiences.
- **Vuforia:** This platform for developing augmented reality experiences will be used to build augmented reality experiences. It offers features for tracking, picture identification, and augmented reality effects.
- **Oculus SDK:** To integrate the platform with the Oculus reality glasses, use the Oculus SDK. It gives users access to tools for creating VR applications and integrating them with Oculus gear.
- **Integration with maps:** To give users instructions and location-based information, the platform will interact with mapping APIs like Google Maps.
- **User authentication:** In order to secure user data and enable customised experiences, the platform will contain user authentication capability.
- **Social media integration:** To enable users to share their experiences and communicate with one another, the platform will interface with social media websites like Facebook and Twitter.
- **Analytics:** To track user behaviour and learn more about platform usage, analytics solutions like Google Analytics will be employed (Suresh Babu, 2023).
- **CMS:** A content management system (CMS) will be utilised to manage platform content and make platform upgrades and modifications simple.
- **Payment Gateway:** To enable transactions for booking tours and activities, the platform will integrate with a payment gateway like PayPal or Stripe.
- **Customer Support:** The platform will contain a customer support feature that will let users seek assistance with any problems or queries they might have.

4. EVOLUTION OF VR AND AR TECHNOLOGY AND FUTURISTIC EXPECTATIONS:

Virtual reality (VR) and augmented reality (AR) technologies have come a long way since their inception. VR has been around for several decades, but only in recent years has it been made available to the general public. AR, on the other hand, is a relatively new field that is still in development. Both technologies have the potential to revolutionize the way we interact with the world around us.

VR technology has gone through several stages of development over the years. The first generation of VR technology was characterized by large, bulky, expensive, and difficult-to-use headsets. With the second generation of VR technology, more compact and affordable headsets were developed that were easier to use. With the third generation of VR technology that we are currently using, even more compact and affordable headsets have been developed that offer higher resolution and better performance.

AR technology, on the other hand, is still in the early stages of its development. The first generation of AR technology was characterized by simple mobile apps that overlaid digital information on top of the real world. The second generation of AR technology we are currently in is characterized by more advanced mobile apps and wearable devices that provide a more immersive experience. The future of AR technology is expected to be even more exciting, with the development of smart glasses that offer a completely hands-free AR experience.

The potential applications of VR and AR technology are diverse and extensive. In the entertainment sector, the VR and AR technologies can be used to create immersive gaming experiences, virtual theme parks and interactive movies. In education, VR and AR technologies can be used to create interactive learning experiences that engage students and help them understand complex concepts. In healthcare, the VR and AR technologies can be used to create virtual simulations for medical education and therapy.

It is expected that the VR and AR technologies will have an even greater impact on our lives in the future. As more advanced and affordable hardware is developed and software and content continue to evolve, the VR and AR technologies will become more mainstream and accessible to the general public. This will open up new opportunities for companies to create immersive experiences that engage and delight their customers. It will also open up new opportunities for individuals to explore and interact with the world in ways previously unimaginable.

Figure 1. Evolution of AR and VR since 2000

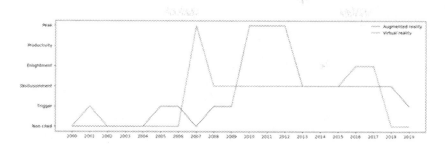

5. RESULT

1. Based on VR and AR, the platform has the potential to revolutionize the tourism industry by providing travellers with immersive and interactive experiences.
2. By showcasing a destination's cultural and natural heritage in a virtual environment, the platform can attract more tourists and generate economic growth.
3. The platform can provide a safer and more sustainable way of tourism by reducing the carbon footprint of travel and lowering the risk of accidents.
4. Leveraging the technologies of VR and AR can improve the hospitality industry by providing guests with personalized experiences, increasing customer satisfaction and boosting loyalty.
5. The platform can also benefit the local community by creating new employment opportunities in the technology and tourism industries.
6. The use of virtual and augmented reality can also help preserve cultural and natural heritage sites by reducing physical traffic and preventing destruction.
7. The platform can promote sustainable tourism by educating travelers about environmental and cultural conservation and encouraging responsible tourism practices.
8. The immersive experiences offered by the platform can increase visitor engagement and help create memorable and meaningful experiences.
9. The platform can also increase accessibility for people with disabilities, allowing them to experience travel in a new and inclusive way.
10. The platform can appeal to a broader audience, including younger generations who are more willing to engage with new technologies and experiences.
11. The use of VR and AR technologies in tourism can create a unique competitive advantage for destinations and hospitality businesses, attracting more customers and generating revenue.

12. Overall, the platform based on VR and AR has the potential to drive sustainable economic growth in the tourism and hospitality industry while promoting cultural and environmental preservation.

5.1 Effect of VR and AR-Based Tourism on Economics

- Three interconnected industries—tourism, virtual reality, and augmented reality—can all significantly boost economic growth. Here is a full analysis of how each of these areas might contribute to the expansion of the economy:
- Over the past few decades, one of the areas of the world economy with the quickest growth has been tourism. The World Tourism Organisation (UNWTO) reports that there were 25 million foreign visitors in 1950 and over 1.4 billion in 2018. Particularly in developing nations, tourism can generate large foreign exchange profits and job possibilities.
- The tourism sector has the potential to undergo a transformation thanks to virtual reality (VR) and augmented reality (AR) technologies, which offer immersive experiences that let travellers examine places and attractions before they travel. As a result, local companies and governments may see an increase in revenue. This may also lengthen visitors' stays.
- By delivering interesting and interactive experiences that are not achievable with conventional tourism methods, augmented reality and virtual reality technology can also improve the entire tourist experience. Visitors can view 3D representations of attractions or learn about the history of a monument, for instance, using AR-capable devices.
- The detrimental effects of tourism on the environment can be lessened through the employment of VR and AR technologies. For instance, using virtual tours can cut down on the amount of people visiting delicate habitats, protecting natural resources.
- The hotel sector can benefit from VR and AR by giving visitors immersive experiences. For instance, hotels can deploy augmented reality (AR)-enabled devices to give visitors interactive room service menus or virtual tours of their spaces.
- By giving potential visitors virtual tours of locations and attractions, VR and AR technology can also aid in destination marketing. As a result, the number of travellers to a location may increase, boosting the tourist sector.
- By raising the demand for regional goods and services, tourism, virtual reality, and augmented reality can help boost the local economy. This could enhance local businesses' profits and open up new job opportunities for locals.
- A new industry and set of business models may also emerge as a result of the application of VR and AR technology in the tourism sector. For instance, the

introduction of VR-compatible travel apps or VR/AR travel content can open up new business prospects.
- The expense of tourism might also be decreased with the aid of VR and AR technologies. VR-enabled tours, for instance, can cut the cost of travel, lodging, and other expenses related to conventional tourism.
- The safety and security of tourists can be increased through the employment of VR and AR technologies. Virtual tours, for instance, can assist guests in navigating unfamiliar settings without getting lost or running into peril.

5.2 Results of User Testing

User testing can be done to test the VR and AR-based tourism platform as a proof of concept. In user testing, a group of people are invited to utilise the platform and then give comments on it. The platform can then be further improved using the feedback.

User testing for the VR and AR-based tourism platform can be done in the following ways:

- Usability testing examines how simple it is to utilise the platform. The platform will be used by users to complete specific activities, and their interactions will be watched and recorded. The data gathered can be used to pinpoint platform components that can benefit from improvement.
- A/B testing entails comparing the performance of two different iterations of the platform. One platform version will be randomly given to users, and those users' interactions will be recorded. The gathered information can be used to assess which platform version is most efficient.
- Focus Groups: This entails requesting input from a number of users on the platform. The platform's users will be questioned about their experiences with it, and their answers will be recorded. The data gathered can be used to pinpoint platform components that can benefit from improvement.
- The comments gathered from the user testing can be used to enhance the platform. Based on user feedback, the platform could be improved in the following ways:
- User Interface: The user interface can be made more user-friendly and intuitive.
- Content: The platform's content can be enhanced to make it more interesting and educational.
- Performance: The platform's performance might be enhanced to make it quicker and more responsive.
- In order to expand accessibility, the platform can be modified to work with a greater variety of gadgets.

- Features: To improve the user experience, further features can be added to the platform.
- The platform may be optimised for optimal effectiveness and user happiness by consistently testing and enhancing it.

5.3 Comparing VR and AR-Based Tourism With Traditional Tourism

Both conventional tourism and VR/AR-based tourism have specific benefits and drawbacks. Here is a contrast between the two:

Advantages of Conventional Tourism

Physical presence: Visiting a location, mingling with the inhabitants, and learning about the local culture and history directly are some of the main benefits of traditional tourism.

Authenticity: Travellers can experience a place's true character, including its sights, sounds, and smells, through traditional tourism.

Socialisation: Traditional tourism offers the chance to interact with locals and other tourists, which makes it a richer experience.

Drawbacks to Conventional Tourism

Cost: The costs of travel, lodging, and activities can make traditional tourism prohibitively expensive.

Limited accessibility: Some places may be hard to get to or take a long time to get to, making it challenging for some travellers to visit.

Crowds: Popular tourist destinations may become too crowded, resulting in extended lineups, congested streets, and less pleasurable activities.

Benefits of VR/AR-Based Travel

Convenience: VR/AR-based tourism makes travel more accessible and convenient by allowing consumers to experience a destination without having to leave their house.

Customization: VR/AR-based tourism lets visitors tailor their experience by selecting particular excursions and sites to see.

Safety: VR/AR-based tourism does away with traditional tourist's safety worries, such as travel-related mishaps and natural calamities.

Cons of Tourism Based on VR/AR

Physical experience is constrained since VR/AR-based tourism cannot perfectly simulate the sensation of being in a place, which could reduce the entire experience.

Technical problems: VR/AR-based tourism may face technical problems, such as connectivity problems or broken technology, which could ruin the user experience.

Lack of socialisation: VR/AR-based tourism does not offer the chance to interact with locals or other tourists, which can have an adverse effect on the whole experience.

In conclusion, traditional tourism as well as VR/AR-based tourism each have specific benefits and drawbacks. VR/AR-based tourism offers ease, customisation, and safety while traditional tourism delivers the actual, true experience of visiting a place. The decision between the two ultimately comes down to personal preferences and environmental factors.

6. FUTURE RESEARCH

Future research can be conducted in a number of areas to enhance and broaden the usage of VR and AR in the tourism sector as these technologies continue to develop and become more widely available.

User Experience: Future study might concentrate on enhancing the entire VR and AR-based tourism platform user experience. This can entail looking into and creating more clear and user-friendly interfaces as well as looking into how to tailor the VR and AR experience for various user types.

Personalization: A different field of study might concentrate on tailoring each user's VR and AR experience. This can entail creating algorithms that adapt the user experience to their interests by taking into consideration the user's preferences and prior experiences.

Accessibility: As VR and AR technology is embraced more broadly, it is crucial to make sure that all users, including those with disabilities, can utilise it. Future studies might concentrate on creating inclusive and approachable VR and AR experiences.

Integration With AI and Machine Learning: To develop more intelligent and individualised travel experiences, VR and AR technologies can be combined with AI and machine learning algorithms. AI algorithms might be used, for instance, to recommend tailored vacation plans based on a user's interests and preferences.

Ethics: As VR and AR technology advances, it will be crucial to think about the ethical ramifications of its application in the tourism sector. Future studies should look into the ethical difficulties surrounding the usage of VR and AR technologies in tourism, such as concerns about data security, privacy, and cultural sensitivity.

Impact on Sustainability: The sustainability implications of VR and AR-based tourism platforms could be the subject of additional future research. The use of VR and AR to promote eco-friendly tourism practises and lessen the damaging effects of conventional tourism could be the subject of future research.

Future research in this area will, in general, be crucial to developing the application of VR and AR technology in the tourism sector and enhancing the overall user experience.

7. CONCLUSION

In conclusion, the VR and AR-based travel platform has enormous potential to completely transform the travel sector. The platform may give consumers immersive and interesting experiences, giving them a special method to discover places and attractions. By minimising the negative effects of travel on the environment and boosting economic advantages to nearby communities, this platform has the potential to increase the overall sustainability of the tourism industry.

The project demonstrated that the platform could be successfully created and executed, and users responded favourably. The goal of future research might be to advance the technology and increase the platform's functionality, either by introducing artificial intelligence or increasing the level of involvement with virtual worlds.

VR and AR-based tourism has many benefits over conventional tourism, including lower costs, access to inaccessible or isolated destinations, and improved safety. It does have drawbacks, too, namely the absence of direct contact with the environment and the requirement for specialised gear.

Overall, the VR and AR-based tourism platform has the power to revolutionise the travel and tourism sector, opening up fresh prospects for long-term economic growth and fostering cross-cultural interaction. This platform has the potential to keep enhancing and bettering the travel experience for users all around the world with additional study and development.

7.1 Implications of the Idea

- By offering engaging and immersive experiences, the VR and AR-based tourism platform can significantly improve guests' travel experiences.
- The platform may lead to more tourists visiting tourist sites, which would enhance local businesses' and economies' bottom lines.
- By lessening the damaging effects of tourism on the ecosystem, the platform can also aid in the development of sustainable tourist practises.
- The usage of VR and AR in the tourism industry may create new prospects for the promotion of travel destinations.
- The platform can offer insightful information on the preferences and behaviour of visitors, which can be leveraged to further enhance the travel experience.
- The platform may offer employment chances for those with expertise in VR and AR development and may help the tech sector expand.
- The platform can also promote remote travel, enabling people to digitally explore destinations from any location in the world and so extending access to travel-related experiences.
- If this initiative is a success, there is a chance that VR and AR-based tourism may undergo additional innovation and development, which will eventually change the tourism sector as a whole.

REFERENCES

Al-Amin, A. Q., & Saidy, C. (2020). Data Analysis Tools in Economics Education: Evidence, Promises, and Challenges. *Journal of Economic Surveys, 34*(5), 1018–1046.

Amaranggana, A. (2019). Smart tourism destinations enhancing tourism experience through personalisation of services. In *Information and communication technologies in tourism 2019* (pp. 377–389). Springer.

Bohdanowicz, P., & Zientara, P. (2020). Virtual Reality Applications in Tourism—A Review. *Sustainability, 12*(7), 2936.

Buhalis, D. (2000). Marketing the competitive destination of the future. *Tourism Management, 21*(1), 97–116. doi:10.1016/S0261-5177(99)00095-3

Buhalis, D., & Neuhofer, B. (2018). Augmented reality and virtual reality: Redefining tourism experiences. *Journal of Destination Marketing & Management, 8,* 1–3.

Di Pietro, L., Di Virgilio, F., & Pantano, E. (2020). Augmented reality for enhancing customer experiences: Advances and future challenges. *Journal of Business Research*, *109*, 267–276.

Gössling, S., Scott, D., & Hall, C. M. (2013). *Tourism and water: Interactions, impacts, and challenges*. Channel View Publications.

Hall, C. M., & Gössling, S. (2016). Tourism and water: Interactions, impacts and challenges: An introduction. In *Tourism and Water* (pp. 1–12). Channel View Publications.

Jolly, D., & Grabowski, M. (2018). Virtual and augmented reality in education. *Education and Information Technologies*, *23*(4), 1515–1520.

Jung, T. H., & tom Dieck, M. C. (2018). The potential of virtual reality for tourism. In *Information and communication technologies in tourism 2018* (pp. 737–749). Springer.

Lai, C. H., Yang, J. C., Chen, F. C., Ho, C. W., & Chan, T. W. (2007). Affordances of mobile technologies for experiential learning: The interplay of technology and pedagogical practices. *Journal of Computer Assisted Learning*, *23*(4), 326–337. doi:10.1111/j.1365-2729.2007.00237.x

Lee, M. J., & Xiang, Z. (2019). An empirical investigation of augmented reality and destination marketing. *Journal of Travel Research*, *58*(8), 1289–1307.

Mottaleb, K. A., Raheem, R. A., & Ayeh, J. K. (2020). Virtual Reality Tourism: An Effective Way to Promote Tourist Destinations. *Journal of Destination Marketing & Management*, *16*, 100409.

Neuhofer, B., Buhalis, D., & Ladkin, A. (2015). Technology as a catalyst of change: Enablers and barriers of the tourist experience and their consequences. The Routledge Handbook of Transport Economics, 45-58.

Pal, S. (2020). Does an Application of Data Analysis Tool Enhance Students' Performance in Macroeconomics? *The Journal of Economic Education*, *51*(2), 163–176.

Ryan, C., & Page, S. J. (Eds.). (2016). *The Routledge handbook of transport economics*. Routledge.

Suresh Babu, C. V. (2023). *Introduction to Data Science*. Anniyappa Publications.

Chapter 6
Distribution of Mechanization by Regions and Areas in the Republic of Serbia

Irina Marina
https://orcid.org/0000-0002-5894-363X
Institute of Agricultural Economics, Beilgrade, Serbia

Biljana Grujić Vučkovski
https://orcid.org/0000-0003-2588-4888
Institute of Agricultural Economics, Belgrade, Serbia

Marijana Jovanović Todorović
https://orcid.org/0000-0003-2048-0411
Institute of Agricultural Economics, Belgrade, Serbia

ABSTRACT

The goal of writing the chapter is to analyze the distribution of agricultural mechanization, which is the most common in the Republic of Serbia (single-axle tractors, two-axle tractors, universal combine harvesters). The purpose of this chapter is to analyze the used mechanization by regions and areas in Serbia during 2012 and 2018, as well as by the number of holdings at its disposal. Principal component analysis (PCA) was used in the research, and the results were presented both tabularly and graphically (loading plot and biplot). The results of the PCA method showed that the situation has not changed in the observed years when it comes to the distribution of mechanization by regions. The PCA method was also applied to mechanization that were used at the level of 25 areas in Serbia only in 2012 because the Statistical Office of the Republic of Serbia (SORS) does not have data for 2018. Based on the biplot presentation, the authors concluded the dominant representation of certain types of mechanization in certain regions and areas of Serbia.

DOI: 10.4018/978-1-6684-8810-2.ch006

THE SCENARIO

The term "agricultural mechanization" in the broadest sense of the word includes tools, work tools, agricultural tractors, various combine harvesters, as well as attachment machines. Also, agricultural mechanization can include machines used in the processing of agricultural products, regardless of whether they are of plant or animal origin. Agricultural mechanization also includes machines that facilitate the manipulation of forage or livestock products. Nowadays, dealing with agricultural production is simplified, and modern equipment and mechanization have become easy to handle (Grujić Vučkovski, 2022). Therefore, in our chapter we will analyze the distribution of agricultural mechanization, which is most often represented in the regions and areas of the Republic of Serbia. The necessity of agro-mechanization on agricultural holdings can be explained through two methods. First, it contributes to agrotechnical measures being carried out in optimal terms. The second method follow up the first, and represents the result of performing agrotechnical operations in an adequate period, which contributes to a higher yield. The advantage of using mechanization for land cultivation is reflected in the increase in labor productivity, as it contributes to the cultivation of a larger land surface in a shorter time. Apart from the usual application of mechanization that we encounter every day, it is important to mention the increasing application of modern agricultural systems such as agrodrones, which would replace certain agricultural operations. The use of agricultural mechanization is the basis for agricultural production. Agricultural operations carried out with the timely application of mechanization play a significant role in the implementation of optimal measures aimed at increasing the intensity of agricultural production (Milovanović, 2017). Also, agricultural mechanization affects the sustainability of agricultural and food systems, in terms of various economic and social aspects, such as: labor productivity, poverty reduction, food security, etc. (Daum, 2023). Scientists are looking for technological solutions to ensure sustainable intensification of global agriculture based on the model of increasing yields *"produce more with less"* (Popović et al., 2012).

Agricultural producers in the Republic of Serbia deal with significantly higher mechanization costs than producers in developed countries. The main reason is insufficiently used mechanization and the high average age of the machines. Such machines are prone to frequent breakdowns, so machine repairings are more frequent, which further increases maintenance costs. In the continuation of the text, it will be commented on single-axle tractors, two-axle tractors and universal combine harvesters, as already mentioned at the beginning.

The following mechanization is analyzed in this chapter: single-axle tractors, two-axle tractors and combine harvesters.

Distribution of Mechanization by Regions and Areas in Serbia

Single-axle tractors are small and lightweight tractors designed for use on smaller agricultural holdings or for performing simpler operations such as mowing (Nikolić et al., 2005). Such tractors have smaller dimensions compared to standard two-axle tractors. One of the main advantages of single-axle tractors is their affordability. This is especially important in Serbia, where most farmers operate on small parcels of land. In addition to affordability, single-axle tractors are also more economical than larger tractors. Their engines are smaller, so fuel that is used for operation is less used, thus reducing the operating costs of farmers. Considering the situation in the Republic of Serbia and unstable fuel prices, this characteristic of single-axle tractors is very important.Another advantage of single-axle tractors is their maneuverability. Given that a significant number of single-axle tractors are still in use in the Republic of Serbia, especially in rural areas, hilly and uneven terrain, the use of such tractors enables easier maneuvering in narrow scopes and on uneven terrains. (Mileusnic et al., 2005). However, there are also challenges related to the use of single-axle tractors in Serbia. One of the main challenges is their limited power, which is not suitable for larger holdings or complex operations. Also, these tractors are not as fast and efficient as larger tractors, which can limit productivity and increase operating costs.

Two-axle tractors are the basic machines used in the agricultural sector of Serbia (Milovanović, 2017). These tractors are utilized in a wide range of operations, so two-axle tractors are the most commonly used type of tractor in Serbia. These tractors are larger and more powerful than single-axle tractors, making them suitable for larger holdings and more complex operations. One of the main advantages of two-axle tractors is their power. They are also more efficient and can cover larger areas in less time, reducing labor costs and increasing productivity. Another advantage of two-axle tractors is their durability and dependability. Their construction allows durability for many years, so they are a long-term investment for farmers. Often, the conditions for production are very unfavorable, so this is a very important characteristic of mechanization. Two-axle tractors are also compatible with a wide range of attachments, such as plows, cultivators and seed drills, making them versatile and flexible tools for farmers. In addition to this, these tractors provide the operators with better working conditions, primarily in terms of safety but also comfort. One of the main problems farmers encounter when purchasing these tractors is the higher prices compared to single-axle tractors. They are more expensive to purchase and maintain, which can be a barrier for small and medium farmers. Farmers in mountainous areas and small, narrow plots have another problem, and it is related to the size and weight of the tractor. These two characteristics can affect the limitation of the maneuverability of these tractors.

Universal Combine Harvesters are the main assets of harvesting, used to harvest crops such as wheat, corn, sunflower and other grains. One of the main advantages of using a combine harvester in the Republic of Serbia is the increased efficiency and productivity it offers to farmers. Combine harvesters are capable of processing large areas quickly and accurately, reducing the need for manual labor while allowing much larger areas to be harvested in a shorter period of time. This can lead to savings of both time and money. Another advantage of using a combine harvester is the improved quality of the harvest. Along with these advantages, there are also challenges related to the use of combine harvesters in Serbia. The main problem, as with the purchase of two-axle tractors, is the high cost of purchase and maintenance of harvesters. Therefore, manufacturers decide to buy used harvesters (Koprivica et al., 2009). Combine harvesters are expensive machines and require regular maintenance and repairs to operate efficiently. This can be a significant obstacle for small and medium-sized farmers. Also, such complex mechanisms that make up each harvester require skilled and trained operators to operate the machines.

STRUCTURE OF AGRICULTURAL LAND IN THE REPUBLIC OF SERBIA

Agriculture is the most important branch of economy in Serbia, and sustainable agriculture is a priority for the nation and the world (Grujić Vučkovski et al., 2022). Considering that agricultural production combines agrotechnics and economics, agricultural production connected in this way can also be called agro-industrial complex or agrobusiness (Joksimović et al., 2018). For that purpose in the chapter we analyzed the state of agricultural mechanization in Serbia.

According to the data of the Farm Structure Survey (FSS) in 2018 (SORS, 2019), the area of used agricultural land is 3,476,788 ha, which represents an increase of 1.1% compared to the data obtained in 2012, when the area of used land was 3,437,423 ha. In 2018 (Figure 1), there was an increase in area in all categories, except for homesteads where there was a 0.06% decrease in area. According to the categories of used agricultural land (UAL), the largest share is occupied by arable land and pastures. The largest increase in area was recorded in the category of arable land and garden (0.86%). by categories of use in 2012 and 2018 (expressed in %)

According to the methodology of SORS (2019), agricultural holdings are classified into three groups:

- Small (up to 5 ha)
- Medium (5-20 ha)
- Large (over 20 ha)

Distribution of Mechanization by Regions and Areas in Serbia

Figure 1. FSS by categories of used agricultural land in 2012 and 2018 (expressed in %)
Source: Calculation based on SORS (2013, 2019)

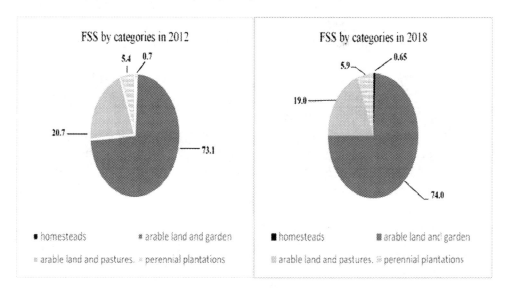

Figure 2. Ownership structure of family farms by region of Serbia (in %), in 2012 and 2018
Source: Calculation based on SORS (2013, 2019)

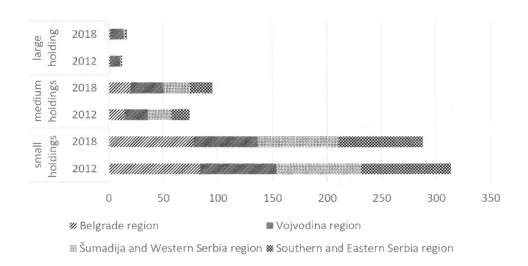

On the Figure 2 is showed the ownership structure of family agricultural holdings by regions, according to the Agricultural Census 2012, where a significantly higher share of small agricultural holdings can be observed in all four statistical regions (the Belgrade region, the Vojvodina region, the Šumadija and Western Serbia region, and the Southern and Eastern Serbia region). Small agricultural holdings also include holdings that do not own agricultural land.

Compared to other regions, the Belgrade region is characterized by the largest share of small agricultural holdings (83.71%), then 15.06% is occupied by holdings that own 5-20 ha, while the share of large holdings is 1.27%.

Compared to other regions, the Vojvodina region is the region with the most large holdings (9.32% of the total number of holdings in this region) and the fewest holdings with less than 5 ha (69.75%). The Western Serbia region is characterized by the largest number of medium holdings (21.49%). The Southern and Eastern Serbia region is distinguished by the smallest share of large holdings (0.97%).

A similar situation was observed in terms of the structure recorded in 2018, where small agricultural holdings also dominate, but with a smaller percentage share compared to the data from 2012. The region that in its structure has the largest number of holdings with an area of up to 5 ha is the Belgrade region (77.91%), in terms of large holdings, the same comparison is made by regions, but in this case, the participation of large holdings in the overall structure of each region is greater. The Vojvodina region also stands out for the number of medium holdings (29.96%).

The Republic of Serbia is a country dominated by small plots of land. Small agricultural holdings confront many challenges, including limited access to finance, lack of modern equipment and difficulty competing with larger competitors in the global market. According to authors Simonović et al., (2017) the reasons that affect small plots of land are primarily influences that include the ageing in villages, migration and globalization. Agricultural land in Serbia has been used irrationally for decades, which is confirmed by the high prevalence of small fragmented plots of land (47% of agricultural holdings in the Republic of Serbia cultivate up to 2 hectares of land (Jandrić et al., 2021).

By strategically improving the level of agricultural mechanization, regional production could be effectively improved (Liu & Li, 2023). Primarily considering diverse politics and support programs to small agricultural holdings. These include providing access to finance and credit, investing in rural infrastructure and providing training and technical assistance to farmers.

MATERIALS AND METHODS

For statistical analysis in 2012 were used empirical data from the database of the SORS, and for 2018 year were used data from *Farm Structure Survey (FSS) 2018* of the publisher mentioned above. There are four regions in Serbia (the Belgrade region, the Vojvodina region, the Šumadija and Western Serbia region, the Southern and Eastern Serbia region) and 25 areas (excluding Kosovo and Metohija). The last Agricultural Census was in 2012 and after that *Farm Structure Survey (FSS) 2018* was conducted, and as SORS announces, the Republic of Serbia expects a large Agricultural Census, which will include used agricultural land, as well as used agricultural mechanization, equipment and tools. The Agricultural Census will be conducted from October 1 to December 15, 2023, and preliminary results are expected by January 31, 2024 at the latest. In this way, continuity in data collection will be ensured (SORS, 2023) and 680,000 households, legal entities and entrepreneurs engaged in agricultural production will be covered. The Agricultural Census is expected to provide an overview of the basic characteristics of national agriculture, thus creating a database, as well as a basic statistical register of agricultural holdings that provides a framework for research. On the basis of the new data, it is possible to carry out almost the same analysis and compare it with the current data, which will result in an overview of the trend of growth or decline in the number of agricultural mechanization by regions or in more detail by areas of the Republic of Serbia.

As already mentioned, agricultural mechanization included: single-axle tractors, two-axle tractors and universal combine harvesters. These data are supplemented by the number of agricultural holdings for the analyzed years.

The statistical analysis used is Principal components analysis (PCA), which aims to reduce the number of variables to a smaller number of new variables. (Fatima et al., 2022). With this method, the largest possible part of the variance of the original variables is explained by a smaller number of principal components. In this way, it is enabled to understand the data more easily (Abdi & Williams 2010).

The basic task of the PCA method is to construct a linear combination of the original variables, but under the condition that they include as much of the variance of the original set of variables as possible. The second task is based on the fact that, apart from determining several linear combinations of the original components, which have the maximum variance, they should be mutually uncorrelated, in order to lose as little information as possible from the initial set (Abdi & Williams 2010).

In case that set has n variables $X_1, X_2 \ldots X_n$, which are characteristic for each unit, new variables can be formed in the form of the following form (equation 1) (Đoković, 2013):

$$Y_1 = \alpha_{11}X_1 + \alpha_{12}X_2 + \ldots + \alpha_{1n}X_n \tag{1}$$

where α_{11}, α_{12} ...α_{1n} are linear correlation coefficients, while Y_1 represents the first principal component. If it is necessary to determine more than one linear combination, the second linear combination (equation 2) has the form:

$$Y_2 = \alpha_{21}X_1 + \alpha_{22}X_2 + \ldots \alpha_{2n}X_n \tag{2}$$

where the coefficients α_{21}, α_{22} ...α_{2n} represent the coefficients of the second linear correlation, and Y_2 the second main component, with the condition that the covariance Y_1 i Y_2 is equal to zero. In this way, it is possible to determine all the principal components. There are as many principal components as there are different characteristic square roots of the covariance matrix. The first principal component explains most of the original variance, and each subsequent principal component explains less. Therefore, it is necessary to determine the number of principal components.

For the purposes of determining the number of principal components required for the analysis, the Kaiser criterion is used, which requires at least 80% of the variation. In addition, the eigenvalues of the principal components must be greater than or equal to 1 (de Almeida et al., 2022; de Almeida et al., 2019).

Principal component analysis does not consider the dependent variable, but only deals with space transformations. When conducting PCA analysis, there are several types of graphs that can be used to interpret the results. Loading plot and biplot graph were used to write the chapter. A loading plot is a graph that shows the relationship between variables and principal components. It can be used to identify which variables contribute most to each principal component. Trygg et al., (2007). In a loading plot, each variable is represented by a vector, and the length and direction of the vector represent the correlation between the variable and the principal component. Simply put, the longer the vector, the higher the correlation between the variable and the principal component.

In addition to this graph, a biplot graph was also used, which is a graphical representation of the correlation between variables and observations in the first two or three principal components (Graffelman & Tuft, 2004; Graffelman & Aluja-Banet, 2003) It is a commonly used tool for visualizing the results of PCA analysis. For example, if two variables have vectors pointing in the same direction, they are positively correlated. Conversely, if two variables have vectors pointing in opposite directions, they are negatively correlated.

The collected data were processed using the SPSS 25 software package, and graphical representations in the form of loading plots and biplots were obtained using the XLSTAT package.

RESEARCH RESULTS

Using the method of descriptive statistics, we observed that in 2018 compared to 2012. the number of agricultural holdings decreased by 10.61% (Figure 3), and the largest decrease was recorded in the Vojvodina Region.

Based on the total number of single-axle tractors, it can be concluded that the number of single-axle tractors decreased by 16,404 (8.78%). A significant difference is observed in the Šumadija and Western Serbia region, where the number of single-axle tractors (Figure 3) increased by 4,695. While the largest decrease in the number of single-axle tractors was recorded for the Southern and Eastern Serbia region, the number of these tractors decreased by 14,982, which represents a decrease of 15.75%. The decline in this type of tractors can be linked to the growing trend of using larger, more efficient tractors for agricultural operations.

Figure 3. Number of agricultural holdings by region of Serbia in 2012 and 2018
Source: Calculation based on SORS (2013, 2019)

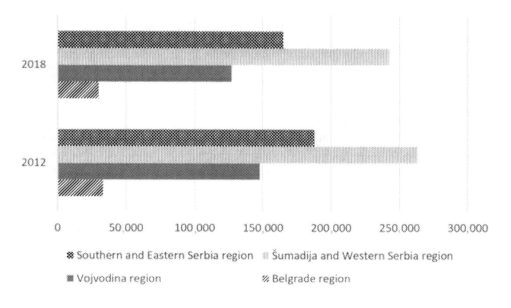

Figure 4. Number of single-axle tractors, two-axle tractors and harvesters in 2012 and 2018
Source: Calculation based on SORS (2013, 2019)

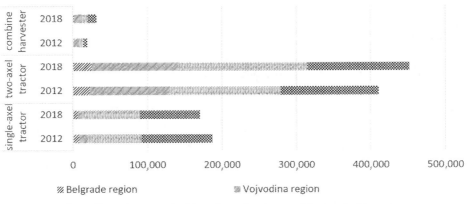

Figure 4 shows the structure of two-axle tractors. The number of two-axle tractors on the territory of the Republic of Serbia for this period increased by 41,089 tractors, which represents a 9.09% increase. The largest increase in two-axle tractors was observed in the Šumadija and Western Serbia region by 24,455, i.e. by 14.07%. While the smallest increase was observed in the Southern and Eastern Serbia region and that number is 5,507, the more precise increase is by 4.03%. This increase can be attributed to the growing trend of using larger and more efficient tractors for agricultural production.

The same figure (Figure 4) also shows the combine harvesters used in 2012 and 2018. Compared to the rest of the analyzed mechanization, the largest percentage increase is for combine harvesters, where in 2018 there were 38.86% more combine harvesters. The largest increase in the number of used combine harvesters in 2018 was achieved in the Southern and Eastern Serbia region, where the increase was 51.34%, i.e. by 5,770 combine harvesters. Despite all the challenges encountered by producers, the use of combine harvesters in Serbia is increasing. Many farmers recognize the advances in technology that make combines more efficient, durable and easier to operate. In this way, some of the obstacles to the adoption and application of such systems are being overcome.

The area cultivated by the average agricultural holding in 2012 was 5.4 ha, while in 2018 this area amounted to 6 ha. During 2012 one single-axle tractor cultivated 18.4 ha, one two-axle 8.37 ha, while one universal combine harvester was used for an area of 176.51 ha. Condition of agricultural mechanization in 2018 showed that

Table 1. Correlation matrix of observed variables for 2012 (number)

		Agricultural Holdings	Two-axle Tractors	Single-axle Tractors	Used Harvesters
Correlation	Agricultural holdings	1.000	0.973	0.738	0.565
	Two-axle tractors	0.973	1.000	0.742	0.705
	Single-axle tractors	0.738	0.742	1.000	0.164
	Used harvesters	0.565	0.705	0.164	1.000

Source: Calculation of the authors. Output from the *SPSS* program.

one single-axle tractor was used for 20.16 ha, one two-axle tractor for 7.6 ha, and one universal combine for an area of 107.92 ha.

Based on the analysis of the principal components, a very similar situation was observed for both years of the research. The Šumadija and Western Serbia region and the Southern and Eastern Serbia region are very similar regarding all four variables (number of agricultural holdings and used mechanization). The correlation ratio of observed variables for 2012 is shown in the following table (Table 1).

The strongest correlation between the observed variables in 2012 was observed between the number of holdings and the number of two-axle tractors and is 0.973. The weakest correlation was between the number of combines and single-axle tractors (0.164).

In order to explain the variability of the data for 2012 the first two components, which account for 96.27% of the total observed variability, were sufficient (Table 2). This indicates that out of 100% of the variation, the first principal component (PC1) explains 75.15%, and the second (PC2) explains 21.12% of the variability.

Of the four Eigenvalues that were obtained, only the first one has a value greater than 1 and is 3.006. Considering that the two-dimensional graphic representation

Table 2. PCA of observed variables for 2012

Component	Initial Eigenvalues			Extraction Sums of Squared Loadings		
	Total	% of Variance	Cumulative %	Total	% of Variance	Cumulative %
1	3.006	75.146	75.146	3.006	75.146	75.146
2	0.845	21.123	96.269	0.845	21.123	96.269
3	0.149	3.731	100.000			
4	-4.326E-17	-1.082E-15	100.000			

Source: Calculation of the authors. Output from the *SPSS* program.

Figure 5. Loading plot of observed variables for 2012 (number)
Source: Calculation of the authors. Output from the XLSTAT program.

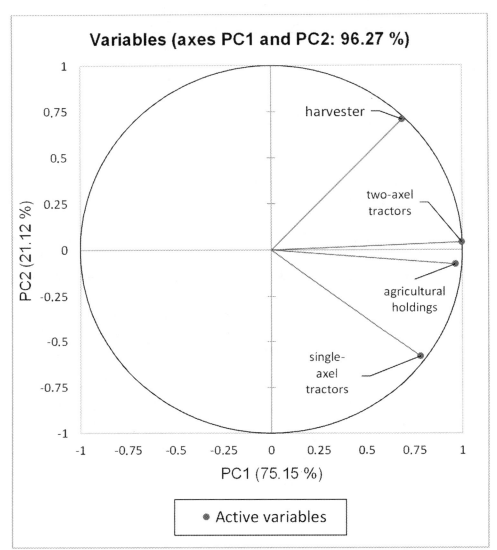

follows, we keep these two Eigenvalues so that along the "X" axis they represent the first "principal" component of PC1, and on the "Y" axis the variations of the PC2 component (Figure 5).

In this loading plot, the previous statement that there is a strong correlation between the number of holdings and two-axle tractors is confirmed, because an acute angle between these variables is clearly observed. Also, this loading plot confirmed the previous conclusion that there is the smallest dependence of variables between

Figure 6. Biplot observed variables for 2012
Source: Calculation of the authors. Output from the XLSTAT program.

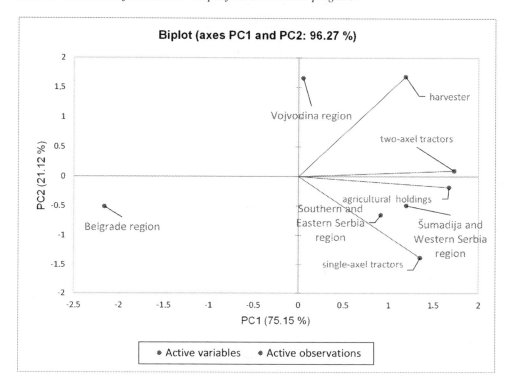

the number of universal combines and single-axle tractors, considering the angle they form.

On this loading plot, no vectors forming an angle of 180° were observed, which proves that there is no negative correlation between the analyzed variables. Variable changes by regions are graphically represented by Biplot (Figure 6). A biplot allows us to visualize the relationships between observation variables and principal components in a single graph. This biplot shows that the Southern and Eastern Serbia region is similar to the Šimadija and Western Serbia region.

We graphically presented the manner variables change by region with a Biplot. This biplot shows that the Southern and Eastern Serbia region is similar to the Šumadija and Western Serbia region.

The angle between two vectors represents the correlation between variables, while the distance between two points represents the similarity between observations. Specifically, the length of the vector representing a variable is proportional to the contribution of that variable to the principal component, while the projection of an observation toward the vector represents the result of that observation on that variable.

Table 3. Correlation matrix of observed variables for 2018 (number)

		Agricultural Holdings	Two-axle Tractors	Single-axle Tractors	Used Harvesters
Correlation	Agricultural holdings	1.000	0.982	0.808	0.616
	Two-axle tractors	0.982	1.000	0.765	0.752
	Single-axle tractors	0.808	0.765	1.000	0.421
	Used harvesters	0.616	0.752	0.421	1.000

Source: Calculation of the authors. Output from the *SPSS* program.

What is further observed is the distance of the Belgrade region from the other regions as well as the variables, which confirms the smallest number of mechanization and the biggest difference from the other regions. Consequently, we can conclude that the Belgrade region has a negative impact on PC2 because of a lack of mechanization.

In the continuation of the chapter, the results of the PCA analysis of the available agricultural mechanization, which were realized in 2018, are given. At the very beginning, the results of the correlation matrix are shown (Table 3). The obtained results show the same correlation and connection between variables as in 2012.

During 2018, as in 2012, the strongest correlation was between two-axle tractors and the number of holdings (0.982), and the weakest with the number of universal combine harvesters and single-axle tractors (0.421), whereby this value is slightly higher compared to the data from 2012.

To interpret data variability in 2018. the first two components accounting for 95.1% of the total observed variability were sufficient, with PC1 explaining 80.03% and PC2 15.08% of the variability (Table 4).

Of the four Eigenvalues obtained, only the first one has a value greater than 1 and is 3.201. Considering that the two-dimensional graphic representation follows, we keep the first two Eigenvalues so that along the X axis we present the variations of the PC1 component, and on the Y axis the variations of the PC2 component (Figure 7).

In this loading plot, the previous statement that there is a strong correlation between the number of holdings and two-axle tractors is confirmed, because a sharp angle between these variables is clearly observed. Also, in this loading plot, the previous conclusion was confirmed that there is the smallest dependence of variables between the number of universal combine harvesters and single-axle tractors, regarding the angle they form. No vectors forming an angle of 180° were observed on this loading plot, which proves that there is no negative correlation between the analyzed variables.

The changes between the variables that occur when observing the level of the region are shown graphically by Biplot (Figure 8). This biplot shows that the

Distribution of Mechanization by Regions and Areas in Serbia

Table 4. PCA of observed variables for 2018

Component	Initial Eigenvalues			Extraction Sums of Squared Loadings		
	Total	% of Variance	Cumulative %	Total	% of Variance	Cumulative %
1	3.201	80.027	80.027	3.201	80.027	80.027
2	0.603	15.075	95.102	0.603	15.075	95.102
3	0.196	4.898	100.000			
4	4.458E-17	1.114E-15	100.000			

Source: Calculation of the authors. Output from the *SPSS* program.

Figure 7. Loading plot observed variables for 2018 (number)
Source: Calculation of the authors. Output from the XLSTAT program.

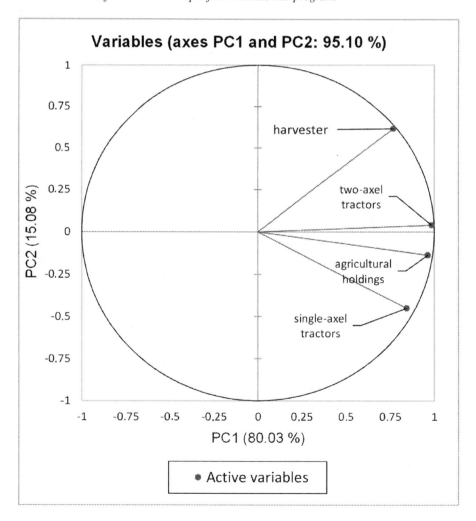

Figure 8. Biplot observed variables for 2018
Source: Calculation of the authors. Output from the XLSTAT program.

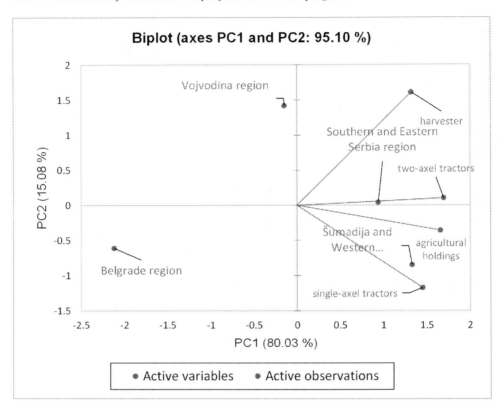

Table 5. Correlation matrix of observed variables for 25 areas in Serbia in 2012 (number)

		Agricultural Holdings	Two-Axle Tractors	Single-Axle Tractors	Used Harvesters
Correlation	Agricultural holdings	1.000	0.700	0.274	0.81
	Two-axle tractors	0.700	1.000	0.336	0.602
	Single-axle tractors	0,274	0,336	1.000	-0,292
	Used harvesters	0.081	0.602	-0,081	1.000

Source: Calculation of the authors. Output from the *SPSS* program.

Southern and Eastern Serbia region is similar to the Šumadija and Western Serbia region, which was also observed in 2012.

We conclude that in 2018, as well as in 2012, the Belgrade region had a negative impact on PC2, which is proven by the lowest number of used agricultural machinery.

The authors intended to apply the PCA method to the area level in Serbia, but there are no corresponding data collected by the SORS for the observed variables. More precisely, SORS does not have data on the number of observed mechanization for 2018. Accordingly, if we conclude that there were no changes in the observed variables at the level of regions in these two years, then there will be no changes at the areas level either. Therefore, the PCA method with observed variables will be analyzed by regions of Serbia in 2012.

According to the available data, for 25 regions in Serbia (Table 5), the strongest correlation is between the number of holdings and two-axle tractors (0.7), and the weakest is between the number of holdings and universal combine harvesters (0.081).

By the same analysis, we observed a negative correlation between single-axle tractors and universal combine harvesters (-0.292).

In order to explain the data variability, the first two components which account for 84.26% of the total observed variability, were sufficient. PC1 explained 50.79% and PC2 explained 33.47% of the variability (Table 6).

Regarding that we have already shown the loading plot for 2012 and 2018 by regions of Serbia, we start from the assumption that the loading plot by areas would give the same results when it comes to correlations between variables. Therefore, we present a biplot representation according to the defined areas of Serbia in 2012 (Figure 9). The biplot graph is presented in two-dimensional space, which explains a total of 84.26% of the variations.

A certain similarity between the regions was observed, whereby the Mačva area stands out in terms of the number of agricultural holdings. Observing the number of used agricultural mechanization, single-axle tractors are the most numerous in the Rasina area, two-axle tractors are the most represented in the Braničevo area, while universal combines are the most numerous in the Southern Bačka area.

According to the biplot with a clear representation of the vector representing the number of single-axle tractors, the largest number of them is located in Rasina and Niš areas. Most combine harvesters are expressed in the Southern Banat and Southern Bačka areas, two-axle tractors in the Mačva and Rasina areas. The largest number of agricultural holdings was observed in Mačva and Zlatibor area. Based on this, it can be concluded that the connection between areas is not the same according to each variable (number of holdings and mechanization) and that it varies depending on their number.

Table 6. PCA of observed variables for areas in Serbia in 2012

Component	Initial Eigenvalues			Extraction Sums of Squared Loadings		
	Total	% of Variance	Cumulative %	Total	% of Variance	Cumulative %
1	2.032	50.793	50.793	2.032	50.793	50.793
2	1.339	33.471	84.264	1.339	33.471	84.264
3	.583	14.567	98.831			
4	.047	1.169	100.000			

Source: Calculation of the authors. Output from the *SPSS* program.

Figure 9. Biplot according to areas of Serbia
Source: Calculation of the authors. Output from the XLSTAT program

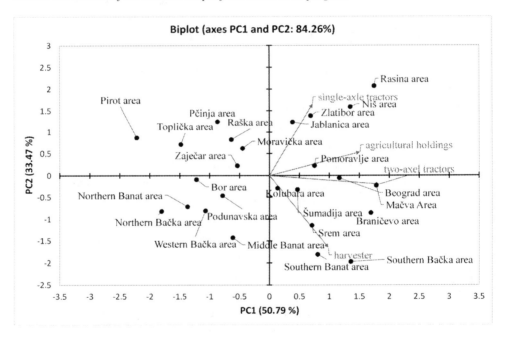

CURRENT PROBLEMS OF USING AGRICULTURAL MACHINERY

Agricultural strength can be defined as power consisting of manual labor, agricultural tools, draft animals, tractors, tools, equipment and machinery (Rijk, 2005), whereby in developed countries there is an effort to replace human labor with certain machines (Clarke, 2000).

In almost every system of agricultural production, the annual cost of a farm's power, whether for human labor, or fuel consumption and depreciation of machinery, exceeds the cost of other inputs such as agrochemicals and reproductive material in the form of seeds. Insufficient food supply in many developed countries is associated with reduced farm labor use, low productivity or labor shortage. Agricultural mechanization is an important part of any plan related to the modernization and improvement of agricultural practices. However, in Serbia, agricultural mechanization faces several problems that negatively affect its effective application. In the following text, some of the main problems faced by agricultural mechanization in Serbia are presented in detail.

- Old agricultural machinery

In the first place, the biggest challenge faced by agricultural producers is old machinery. Most of the agricultural equipment used in Serbia is outdated and in poor condition, which makes it difficult for farmers to use it efficiently. Outdated equipment has a lower efficiency compared to modern machinery, because it takes more time and energy to perform operations than using more modern systems. Also, high maintenance costs (Nikolić et al., 2006) represent another of the link that old mechanization carries with it. This type of machinery, with many operating hours, requires more frequent maintenance. Very often parts fail and need to be replaced, which leads to a decrease in the profitability of the agricultural manufacturer. The profitability of the manufacturer is also affected by the much higher fuel consumption of older machines (Vasiljević et al., 2008). Old agricultural mechanization requires skilled labor in order to operate it efficiently, but most young people are not interested in working with this type of mechanization, and therefore the production that uses old mechanization involves an older workforce with experience.

- Lack of investments to invest in machinery

Another significant problem faced by producers during the use of agricultural machinery in Serbia is the lack of funds to invest in the purchase of new machinery or the improvement of existing machinery. In this way, many farmers are unable to expand and improve their production. According to the authors Tepavac & Brzaković (2013) for producers who use over 86% of the land tractor prices are too high.

- Inadequate agricultural infrastructure

This primarily refers to bad roads, a smaller number of storage facilities, as well as inadequate field electrification. All this affects the safe transport of agricultural products and the efficient handling of machines.

- Small agricultural holdings farms

An obstacle for the development of the usage of mechanization in Serbia is represented by small agricultural holdings, which according to the structure in Serbia are the majority (Nikolić et al., 2006). Although such farms play a very important role in providing food both for their own needs and for needs at the local level, it is much more difficult for small farms to raise the funds to invest in the equipment and machinery itself.

- Lack of awareness and education

Many farmers in Serbia are not aware of the advantages provided by the adequate application of agricultural mechanization or do not have the knowledge to operate modern equipment. Lack of education is also a major obstacle to agriculture (Akdemir, 2013).

CONCLUSION

The use of mechanization on agricultural holdings is the basis for efficient production. Therefore, tractors and combine harvesters have an important part in the production chain of agriculture. Regarding the satisfactory number of mechanization on agricultural holdings, Serbia is not at an enviable level. Despite the still significant number of single-axle tractors in use in the country, the trend is towards larger and more efficient two-axle tractors. The number of combine harvesters in use in Serbia has been relatively stable in recent years, although there is a trend towards using more modern, more efficient combine harvesters. As Serbia continues to modernize its agricultural sector, there is probability that the number of single-axle tractors in use will continue to decrease, while the number of two-axle tractors and modern combine harvesters will increase. Also, the replacement of outdated mechanization is another step of modernization. This will enable farmers to increase their productivity, reduce their operating costs and remain competitive in the global market.

Agricultural mechanization is an important part of any plan related to the modernization and improvement of agricultural practices. However, in Serbia, agricultural mechanization encounters several problems that negatively affect its effective application. Some of those problems are certainly represented by outdated agricultural mechanization that requires high maintenance costs, while the efficiency is much lower compared to newer machinery, because it takes more time and energy to perform operations. Although we know that complete agricultural mechanization can be used in the entire production cycle, we believe that this investment requires large financial allocations for most farmers in Serbia. This leads to another significant problem, which is the lack of funds to invest in the purchase of new mechanization or the improvement of existing mechanization. An obstacle to the development of the application of mechanization in Serbia is represented by small agricultural holdings, which according to the structure are the most in Serbia. In order for the application of agricultural mechanization to be more successful, it is necessary to implement several solutions, the first of which is certainly the provision of greater benefits when purchasing mechanization. This refers to the establishment of a credit system that would provide favorable loans to farmers for the purchase of new agricultural mechanization, such as loans with low interest rates and longer repayment terms, thus enabling farmers to purchase appropriate equipment. Then, by increasing the level of education of farmers by providing an adequate training and education, it is crucial to promote mechanization. As well as supporting small producers.

The correlation of the region during 2012 and 2018 proved that the situation in terms of mechanization has not changed. The applied PCA method on the availability of mechanization according to the regions in both observed years showed that the strongest correlation was between the number of agricultural holdings and two-axle tractors, and the weakest between the number of combine harvesters and single-axle tractors, which was also confirmed by the graphical representation using the loading plot. Changes in variables by regions were shown using a biplot, which showed us that in both analyzed years similarities were observed between variables in the Southern and Eastern Serbia region with the Šumadija and Western Serbia region, while the Belgrade region has a negative impact because of the least amount of agricultural mechanization.

The authors applied the PCA method to the used agricultural mechanization (variables) in 25 areas in Serbia only in 2012, because SORS does not have the number of mechanization in 2018 by areas. Consequently, the strongest correlation coefficient was achieved between the number of agricultural holdings and two-axle tractors, and the weakest between the number of agricultural holdings and universal combine harvesters. A negative correlation was also observed between single-axle tractors and universal combine harvesters. Based on the biplot display, the authors concluded that a certain type of mechanization is dominant in certain areas. For example. it is mostly harvesters in the Southern Bačka area, two-axle tractors in the Mačva area, and single-axle tractors in the Rasina area.

Using the PCA method, the authors explained the similarities between regions and areas based on the available types of mechanization.

We believe that the correlation between information technologies and agricultural mechanization is increasingly intense and that machines classified under the term "precision agriculture" are increasingly necessary for successful agricultural production. Therefore, future research should include this type of mechanization.

ACKNOWLEDGMENT

Paper is a part of research financed by the Ministry of Science, Technological Development and Innovation of the Republic of Serbia and agreed in decision no. 451-03-47/2023-01/200009 from 03.02.2023 and research results on project U 01/2023 Green economy in the era of digitization, Faculty of Finance, Banking, and Auditing, Alpha BK University in Belgrade, Republic of Serbia.

REFERENCES

Abdi, H., & Williams, J. L. (2010). Computational statistics: Principal component analysis. *Wiley Interdisciplinary Reviews: Computational Statistics*, 2(4), 433–459. doi:10.1002/wics.101

Akdemir, B. (2013). Agricultural mechanization in Turkey. *IERI Procedia*, 5, 41–44. doi:10.1016/j.ieri.2013.11.067

Clarke, L. J. (2000). *Strategies for Agricultural Mechanization Development: The roles of the private sectore and the Government*. https://hdl.handle.net/1813/10216

Daum, T. (2023). Mechanization and sustainable agri-food system transformation in the Global South. A review. *Agronomy for Sustainable Development*, 43(1), 16. doi:10.100713593-023-00868-x

de Almeida, F. A., Gomes, G. F., & Gaudêncio, J. H. D. (2019). A new multivariate approach based on weighted factor scores and confidence ellipses to precision evaluation of textured fiber bobbins measurement system. *Precision Engineering*, 60, 520–534. doi:10.1016/j.precisioneng.2019.09.010

de Almeida, F. A., Santos, A. C. O., de Paiva, A. P., Gomes, G. F., & Gomes, J. H. D. F. (2022). Multivariate Taguchi loss function optimization based on principal components analysis and normal boundary intersection. *Engineering with Computers*, 38(2), 1–17. doi:10.100700366-020-01122-8

Đoković, A. (2013). *Strukturna korelaciona analiza u interpretaciji vektorskih koeficijenata korelacije* [Structural correlation analysis in the interpretation of vector correlation coefficients] [Doctoral dissertation]. University of Belgrade. https://nardus.mpn.gov.rs/handle/123456789/3059

Fatima, S. U., Khan, M. A., Siddiqui, F., Mahmood, N., Salman, N., Alamgir, A., & Shaukat, S. S. (2022). Geospatial assessment of water quality using principal components analysis (PCA) and water quality index (WQI) in Basho Valley, Gilgit Baltistan (Northern Areas of Pakistan). *Environmental Monitoring and Assessment*, *194*(3), 151. doi:10.100710661-022-09845-5 PMID:35129685

Graffelman, J., & Aluja-Banet, T. (2003). Optimal representation of supplementary variables in biplots from principal component analysis and correspondence analysis. *Biometrical Journal. Biometrische Zeitschrift*, *45*(4), 491–509. doi:10.1002/bimj.200390027

Graffelman, J., & Tuft, R. (2004). Site scores and conditional biplots in canonical correspondence analysis. *Environmetrics: The Official Journal of the International Environmetrics Society*, *15*(1), 67-80. doi:10.1002/env.629

Grujić Vučkovski, B. (2022): *Analiza oblika finansiranja poljoprivrede Republike Srbije, Monografija* [Analysis of forms of financing agriculture in the Republic of Serbia, Monograph]. Institut za ekonomiku poljoprivrede, Beograd. https://www.iep.bg.ac.rs/images/2022/Analiza%20oblika%20finansiranja%20FIN.pdf

Grujić Vučkovski, B., Simonović, Z., Ćurčić, N., & Miletić, V. (2022). The role of agriculture in the economic structure of Serbia and budget support for rural development of Kladovo municipality. *Ekonomika Poljoprivrede*, *69*(3), 863–876. doi:10.5937/ekoPolj2203863G

Jandrić, M., Hadrović, S., Rakonjac, L., & Ćosić, M. Posedovna struktura zemljišta Jugozapadnog dela Srbije [Land ownership structure of the Southwestern part of Serbia]. *Akademski pregled*, 59-65. doi:10.7251/AP2102059J

Joksimović, M., Grujić, B., & Joksimović, D. (2018). Correlation and regression analysis of the impact of leasing on agricultural production in Republic of Serbia. *Ekonomika Poljoprivrede*, *65*(2), 583–600. doi:10.5937/ekoPolj1802583J

Koprivica, R., Veljković, B., Stanimirović, N., & Topisirović, G. Eksplatacione karakteristike kombajna john deere 5820 u pripremi kukuruzne silaže za muzne krave na porodičnim farmama [Silage harvester zmaj 350 productivity in harvesting and chopping of maize silage for dairy cows on a commercial farm]. *Poljoprivredna tehnika*, *34*(3), 23-30. https://scindeks.ceon.rs/article.aspx?artid=0554-55870903023K

Liu, X., & Li, X. (2023). The Influence of Agricultural Production Mechanization on Grain Production Capacity and Efficiency. *Processes (Basel, Switzerland), 11*(2), 487. doi:10.3390/pr11020487

Mileusnic, Z., Djevic, M., Miodragovic, R., & Petrovic, D. (2005). On the Applicabillity of the Single-Shaft Tractors Motocultivators in Serbia. *Poljoprivredna tehnika, 30*(1), 17-25. http://arhiva.nara.ac.rs/handle/123456789/140

Milovanović, Ž. (2017). Primena ELECTRA metode u nabavci poljoprivredne mehanizacij. [Aplication of the ELECTRA method in the purchase of agricultural mechanization]. *Ekonomski signali, 12*(2), 11-21. doi:10.5937/ekonsig1702011M

Nikolic, R., Savin, L., Furman, T., Tomic, M., & Gligoric Radojka, S. M. (2006). Istraživanje podloga i razvoj traktora za poljoprivredu [The advancement of production and development of tractors]. *Letopis naučnih radova strana*, 28-37. https://scindeks.ceon.rs/article.aspx?artid=0350-29530304137N

Nikolić, R., Savin, L., Furman, T., Tomić, M., Simikić, M., & Gligorić, R. (2005). Pogonske mašine i traktori u poljoprivredi [Power machines and tractors in agriculture]. *Savremena poljoprivredna tehnika, 31*(1-2), 15-23. https://scindeks.ceon.rs/article.aspx?artid=0350-29530502015N

Popović, V., Sarić, R., & Jovanović, M. (2012). Sustainability of agriculture in Danube basin area. *Economics of Agriculture, 59*(1), 73-87. https://scindeks.ceon.rs/article.aspx?artid=0352-34621201073P

Republički zavod za statistiku [Statistical Office of the Republic of Serbia]. (2013). *Popis poljoprivrede 2012 Knjiga 1*. Republički zavod za statistiku (RZS).

Republički zavod za statistiku [Statistical Office of the Republic of Serbia]. (2019). *Anketa o stukturi poljoprivrednih gazdinstava 2018*. Author.

Republički zavod za statstiku [Statistical Office of the Republic of Serbia]. (2023). *Metodološko uputstvo: Popis poljoprivrede Republički zavod za statistiku (RZS)*. Academic Press.

Rijk, A. G. (2005). *Agricultural mechanization strategy*. https://www.un-csam.org/sites/default/files/2020-10/CIGR_APCAEM_Website_0.pdf

Simonović, Z., Mihailović, B., & Ćurčić, N. (2017). Struktura poljoprivrednih gazdinstava u Republici Srbiji prema površini poljoprivrednog zemljišta [Structure of agricultural distributions in the Republic of Serbia, by the surface of agricultural land]. *Poslovna ekonomija: časopis za poslovnu ekonomiju, preduzetništvo i finansije, 11*(2), 247-259. doi:10.5937/poseko12-15416

Tepavac, R., & Brzaković, T. (2013). Suffering of wild animals in hunting-grounds from application of agricultural mechanization and pesticides. *Sustainable agriculture and rural development in terms of the republic of Serbia strategic goals realization within the Danube region. Achieving regional competitiveness*, 539-556. https://mpra.ub.uni-muenchen.de/52472/1/MPRA_paper_52472.pdf

Trygg, J., Holmes, E., & Lundstedt, T. (2007). Chemometrics in metabonomics. *Journal of Proteome Research, 6*(2), 469–479. doi:10.1021/pr060594q PMID:17269704

Vasiljević, Z., Todorović, S., & Popović, N. (2008). Uticaj promene cene goriva na optimizaciju ukupnih troškova upotrebe poljoprivredne mehanizacije za obradu zemljišta [An influence of the fuel price change on optimization of total operating costs of the tillage agricultural machinery]. *Poljoprivredna tehnika, 33*(4), 69-77. https://scindeks.ceon.rs/article.aspx?artid=0554-55870804069V

Chapter 7

Impact of Financial Literacy on the Risk Tolerance Behavior of Females Working in the Unorganized Sector

Anushree Srivastava
https://orcid.org/0000-0002-0902-9104
Dr. A.P.J. Abdul Kalam Technical University, India

Neha Yadav
https://orcid.org/0000-0003-2688-3051
Babu Banarasi Das University, India

Anuradha Maurya
https://orcid.org/0000-0003-0751-8198
Babu Banarasi Das University, India

ABSTRACT

Risk and return are the two terms which are used while making investments. Financial literacy is an important indicator of measuring risk tolerance level as it helps in making sound financial decisions and planned investment choices. Financial literacy not only broadens the scope of investment choices and financial planning but also helps in the process of rotating money and diversification of funds. This study helps to explore the impact of financial literacy on risk tolerance behavior of females. Risk tolerance is an important indicator which helps in looking at the amount of surplus funds with the people, the preferred tool of investment, and how well they are managing and diversifying funds. As per the authors, 200 females working in the unorganized sector were surveyed in Uttar Pradesh region. Data was collected through a questionnaire which was designed to test the financial literacy, financial prudence, and investment pattern of females and how the access to financial products, services, and wealth impacts the confidence and risk-taking aptitude of females.

DOI: 10.4018/978-1-6684-8810-2.ch007

INTRODUCTION

Financial literacy is the combination of financial skills, knowledge, attitude, awareness. It helps in the long-term financial planning, investment, asset building and wealth creation (Tamimi and Kalli, 2009) Lack of financial literacy leads to conditions of extreme poverty, debt defaulters, dependence on others for financial matters and inability to utilize funds. Risk is an important factor which needs to be concerned while making wise investment choices. It is therefore seen that the investor considers the relationship between the rate of return and risk level of the financial investment tools. The financial risk tolerance of individual investors influences their choice of financial products and services and the use of their wisdom in financial markets. By Financial risk tolerance we mean the maximum amount of uncertainty faced by the investors while making a sound financial decision. Individual financial risk tolerance gets impacted by the social, ethical, financial, cultural, physical factors.

Financial literacy is an important factor to assess financial risk tolerance. Financial literacy uses financial skills, knowledge and education so as to be financially viable and sound. Various new schemes of investment are available in the market for providing investment opportunities to the investor so that they can plan their future requirements and can also better utilize its savings by generating more returns. Financial literacy has always proved to be a significant factor for making sound financial decisions by the investors (NSFE, 2012). I. This study has been done to find out the financial literacy level of females working in the unorganized sector. Women working in the unorganized sector due to shortage and instability of money seriously affects retirement planning, saving and other crucial decisions. This study is conducted to explore the impact of financial literacy on the risk tolerance behavior of females. Many investors are only investing in secured investment tools to avoid loss and a situation of extreme debt and poverty.

A very small segment of investors invests in capital market instruments due to lack of financial literacy and risk intolerance. Financial literacy not only broadens the scope of investment choices and financial planning but also helps in the process of rotating money and diversification of funds. This study helps to explore the impact of financial literacy on risk tolerance behavior of females. Risk tolerance is an important indicator which helps in looking at the amount of surplus funds with the people, the preferred tool of investment and how well they are managing and diversifying funds.

According to the survey done by IIM Ahmedabad and Citi Foundation in 2011 on financial literacy it was found that men have higher financial knowledge than women among both employees and the retired. This is due to the relatively greater exposure of adult men to personal and household finances and also due to decision making autonomy. According to OECD/INFE Policy Guidance on addressing Women's and Girl's Needs for Financial Awareness and Education it has been found that there are significant gender differences in financial literacy, financial attitude and savings behavior. Women also exhibit lower confidence than men in their financial knowledge and skills. As it has been explored through previous researches that the financial literacy of men and women significantly differ. Women lack financial knowledge, financial prudence, financial aptitude to take risks. This also affects their ability to invest in capital markets, rotating money, taking calculated risks to expand and diversify money. It has been seen that women depend on their male counterparts for major financial decisions to make financial choices. It has a major impact on women as due to greater longevity it is up to women to look after herself after the death of spouse (Ramtohul, 2020). Conditions have been seen where women have suffered extreme losses due to lack in financial literacy, financial knowledge and financial risk tolerance. Unorganized sector is the sector where due to lack of unwritten regulations and guidelines employees suffer the most. Risk and return are the two terms which are used while making investments along with lock in period. Financial literacy is an important indicator of measuring risk tolerance level as it helps in making sound financial decisions and planned investment choices. As per the authors 200 females working in the unorganized sector were surveyed in Uttar Pradesh region. Females were taken in the sampling frame as there have been few studies done to assess their financial literacy and financial risk tolerance behavior. Unorganized sector is the sector which employs people but has no set regulations and guidelines for the employees. They neither have proper rules regarding socials security benefits, remuneration benefits, maternity rules. Due to a woman's primary role of care giver they are induced to work in a set up where less time is consumed but monetary benefits are also less.

Since they lack social security benefits, proper increment plans and lack of funds employees are left with no choice but to keep money in liquid form the most. As it is evident from the reports and survey studies that women due to career breaks and care giver roles are mostly employed in unorganized sector, it needs to be found out whether lack of financial risk tolerance is due to paucity of funds and lower levels of financial literacy (Bhushan and Medury 2014). The Government, stakeholders and institutions need to focus on the conditions of people working in the unorganized sector and tailor-made products should be introduced in the financial market to cater the needs of such consumers.

LITERATURE REVIEW

Women experience difficulties in selecting the right investment avenues due to lack of financial literacy and dependency on others (Lusardi and Mitchell 2008).

Financial literacy would help women to become independent and confident enough to speak up for themselves (Arora Bhaskar and et al. 2018). They further insisted that women should be made capable of investing in financial instruments in order to generate income, and secure their future, practice of proactive money management and financial planning to secure their future. Women have to take more career breaks as compared to their male counterparts which makes them work in unorganized sector and plan lesser retirement benefits and investment opportunities (Ranjani KS, Chopra, 2011; Qiao X, 2012)

Although most professional women have a basic understanding of finance, they are still unable to manage their money effectively or make sound financial decisions along with taking moderate risk (Sebastian T. and Raju Middi A. 2016).It was reported that the biggest hurdle in the way of achieving financial goals for women was low income (Lown JM. 2010). Risk as a fundamental factor has been studies to understand the behavior of people behaving differently (Bucciol & Zarri, 2015). Decisions about a household's portfolio are heavily influenced by risk tolerance, which measures how eager a person is to incur risks (Sung & Hanna, 1996) and has consequences for both individuals and financial service providers (Hallahan, Faff, & McKenzie, 2004). Women lack interest in financial matters which makes it more difficult for them to invest in capital market(Luotonen N. 2009) Financial risk tolerance is the amount of discomfort a person is ready to put up with when risking their existing wealth in order to increase it in the future (Gibson, Michayluk, & Van de Venter, 2013).It is the maximum amount of uncertainty someone is willing to endure while making a sound financial decision (Grable 2000).Risk taking is an integral component of financial decision making influenced by sociodemographic, psychological, and environmental characteristics, and is mediated by risk perception, risk attitude, and risk propensity (Garling et al. 2009). Women are believed to own less wealth, save in fixed income rather than in capital markets (Neelakantan and Chang, 2010).

Demographic characteristics that are utilized to compare differences in financial risk tolerance are common denominators among earlier studies. Lack of financial knowledge and confidence to take risks in women, impact their financial ability (Chen and Volpe 2002). Women who make investments pause to consider the nature of the investment and the potential returns. Women prioritize safety and avoid making rash judgments when making investments (Yusof 2015). Women are more risk averse than men as they protect their capital while making financial decisions (Edward et al. 2006). It is found that women who are economic empowered influences household decision-making process by contributing income and being self-reliant (Brule and Gaikwad, 2021).

Grable and Lytton (1999) in their research found that age and gender were the most important variables influencing risk tolerance along with other characteristics such as marital status, occupation, self-employment, income, race and education. Chetna and Kumar Raj (2017) highlighted the urgent need to educate women about different investment avenues available in the market and risk and return associated with these financial products. Efficient financial system is needed for greater financial inclusion which also helps in women empowerment (Park and Mercado, 2015) It has been researched that risk tolerance increases with enhanced labels of financial literacy (Fisher & Yao, 2017; Mahdzan et al., 2017; Mishra & Mishra, 2016; Pinjisakikool, 2017; Rahmawati et al., 2015; Sharma et al., 2017; Weber, 2014; Yong & Tan, 2017).

RESEARCH GAP

According to theoretical background and subsequent review it has been observed that females are less willing to take financial risk as compared to males. It has also been observed that the males are more materialistic as compared to females, and are therefore more financial risk tolerant. If age as a variable is taken into consideration studies have shown that younger individuals are more risk averse as compared to older individuals. Future studies need to focus on exploring the nature of family as it has been observed that children are more influenced by their mothers therefore financial literacy of females need to be improved taking risk tolerance behavior as one of the variables. While current studies acknowledge that family plays a significant role in socializing its members to market economy and personal finances, parents don't have an understanding and knowledge of influencing financial behaviors of children there is significant research gap in finding out that how parents with limited income and assets can socialize their children to be well effective wealth builders by investing in financial instruments. This paper addresses the following objectives.

1. To assess the financial literacy of working women in the unorganized sector.
2. To study the relationship between financial literacy and risk tolerance behavior.
3. To extract the most important behavioral factor on the risk tolerance level of females.
4. To explore how demographic factors impacts the financial awareness and investment pattern of females.

RESEARCH MODEL AND HYPOTHESES DEVELOPMENT

This paper highlights the relationship of financial literacy with the risk tolerance level of females. It also reflects the role of demographic factors in assessing the

Figure 1. Conceptual model

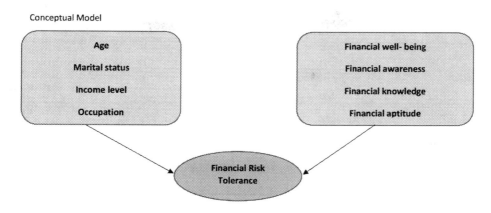

level of financial literacy and also how it impacts the risk tolerance level of females. Subsequently findings and statistical results would be discussed and probable solutions would be suggested in order to avoid situations of financial loss and tragedy. Based on theoretical assumptions and review of literature this study proposes a conceptual model and the following hypotheses.

H01: Demographic variables do not play a significant role in risk tolerance level of females working in an unorganized sector.
HA1: Demographic variables play a significant role in risk tolerance level of females working in an unorganized sector.
H02: There is no significant relationship between financial literacy and risk tolerance level of females working in an unorganized sector.
HA2: There is a significant relationship between financial literacy and risk tolerance level of females working in an unorganized sector.

Data Analysis and Results

The data was collected from primary source via questionnaire and secondary source by means of articles and journal. Convenience sampling technique is used to collect the responses.

Respondent's profile: Table 1 shows the demographic profile of respondents. Data has been collected from 200 women working in the unorganized sector of Uttar Pradesh. It is clearly evident from the table that maximum respondents lie in the age group of 25-35 years. It shows working women of 25-35 years age group

Table 1. Demographic profile

Demographic Factors	Classification	Total Respondents	Percentage
Age	25-35	88	43.8%
	36-45	59	29.4%
	>45	53	26.9%
Education	Intermediate/Diploma	41	20.4%
	Graduation	51	25.4%
	Post-graduation	66	32.8%
	Doctorate	42	21.4%
Marital Status	Married	107	53.2%
	Unmarried	93	46.8%
Occupation	Government contractual	62	30.8%
	Self- job	59	29.3%
	Private unorganized sector	79	39.9%
Income group	<180000	58	28.9%
	180000-250000	47	23.4%
	251000-320000	44	21.9%
	>320000	51	25.9%

are postgraduates. Around 53.2% of women are married and majority of women i.e. 39.9% working in the private unorganized sector.

RELIABILITY STATISTICS

Cronbach's Alpha coefficient was used to determine the reliability and internal consistency of the questionnaire testing the impact of financial literacy on risk tolerance behavior. According to Table 2. The results indicate that the scale has good reliability and internal consistency (@= 0.752) since Cronbach's alpha lies between 0.70-0.79 hence the reliability of the questionnaire is proved.

Table 2. Reliability statistics

Cronbach's Alpha	Cronbach's Alpha Based on Standardized Items	N of Items
.757	.752	10

Hypothesis Testing: A one-way independent sample analysis of variance (ANOVA) was conducted to investigate the impact of financial literacy, financial awareness, investment patterns and risk tolerance aptitude.

(1) It was found that there was a significant impact of demographic variables on risk tolerance of females working in an unorganized sector. $F(4,195) = 25.46$, $p<.001$. Hypothesis 1 is accepted.
(2) Financial literacy has a positive relationship with the risk tolerance level of females working in an unorganized sector. $F(4,195) = 11.155$, $p<.001$. Hypothesis 2 is accepted.

Exploratory Factor Analysis

5-point Likert scale was used to design the questionnaire and subsequently women's financial literacy, their risk tolerance behavior was checked. SPSS version 20 was used to analyze data and findings were reported. Factor analysis was performed which extracted maximum common variance from all variables and put them into a common score. Table 3. shows the result of KMO and Bartlett's Test. The typical assumption is that the KMO Sampling Adequacy should be larger than 0.5 for use with the Kaiser-Meyer-Olkin Measure of Sampling Adequacy (Malhotra and Das, 2010). It may be concluded from Table 3's KMO Sampling Adequacy value of .914 that "the sample size is sufficient enough to undertake factor analysis." The significant value for the Bartlett's Test of Sphericity is 0.000, which is less than 0.05 and shows that there is enough correlation between the variables. Therefore, it may be argued that the data is suitable for using in factor analysis.

Extraction Method: Principal Component Analysis.

Table 4 shows communalities values. Communalities refers to the degree to which one variable is correlated with the other variables. In Table 4 Communalities value for the entire variable is more than 0.4 which indicates "that the entire variables are appropriate for conducting factor analysis". The Eigenvalue refers to the variance

Table 3. KMO and Bartlett's test

Kaiser-Meyer-Olkin Measure of Sampling Adequacy.	.914
Approx. Chi-Square	2795.504
Bartlett's Test of Sphericity df	91
Sig.	.000

Table 4. Communalities

	Initial	Extraction
Financial services	1.000	.746
Financial awareness	1.000	.708
Financial planning	1.000	.825
Financial products	1.000	.775
Financial knowledge	1.000	.732
Financial aptitude	1.000	.825
Financial access	1.000	.758
Financial prudence	1.000	.634
Financial behavior	1.000	.692
Investment knowledge	1.000	.841
Financial well-being	1.000	.804
Financial planning confidence	1.000	.805
Access to assets	1.000	.491
Risk tolerance	1.000	.596

Table 5. Total variance explained

Component	Initial Eigenvalues			Extraction Sums of Squared Loadings		
	Total	% of Variance	Cumulative %	Total	% of Variance	Cumulative %
1	8.542	61.013	61.013	8.542	61.013	61.013
2	1.688	12.057	73.071	1.688	12.057	73.071
3	.905	6.463	79.533			
4	.635	4.535	84.068			
5	.499	3.566	87.634			
6	.341	2.434	90.068			
7	.295	2.104	92.172			
8	.261	1.862	94.034			
9	.201	1.435	95.469			
10	.177	1.265	96.734			
11	.158	1.128	97.862			
12	.125	.896	98.758			
13	.111	.794	99.552			
14	.063	.448	100.000			

Table 6. Component matrix

	Component	
	1	2
Financial planning	.638	.582
Financial awareness	.731	.417
Financial behavior	.662	.622
Financial products	.844	-.249
Financial knowledge	.642	.565
Financial aptitude	.874	-.245
Financial access	.844	-.216
Financial prudence	.795	.042
Financial services	.832	-.015
Investment knowledge	.882	-.251
Financial well-being	.892	-.091
Financial planning confidence	.883	-.158
Access to assets	-.636	.294
Risk tolerance	-.692	.342
Extraction Method: Principal Component Analysis. **2 components extracted**		

associated with the factor. 0.1 is the ideal Eigen value. Factors with an Eigen value more than 0.1 are considered, whereas those that have a value lower than 0.1 are not (Hair.et.al; 2014). In social science research, a cumulative variance solution of at least 60 percent is typically regarded as satisfactory (Hair.et.al; 2014). Figure 5. Two components were isolated with a cumulative variance of 73.071%, which is higher than the cutoff of 60%. The eigenvalue for factor 1 is 8.542 with a variance of 61.013 percent, and the eigenvalue for factor 2 is 1.688 with a variance of 12.057%.

In Table 6, Rotated Component Matrix has been performed using Principal Component Method of Factor Extraction and Varimax with Kaiser Normalization rotation method. Once the rotation of factors is done a factor loading point generally above 0.5 for each variable is selected (Malhotra and Dash, 2010). Here in Table 6 all the 14 variables factor loading is above 0.50 and are to be taken into consideration for two factors extracted.

Limitations and Scope for Further Research

1. The sample size collected for the study is small and data was also collected according to the convenience. It cannot be generalized for the entire population as the respondents were limited only to Uttar Pradesh.
2. Working women who were approached for the study were educated, employed in the private sector, Government sector and self-employed running a small shop. Inferences based on their opinion cannot be implied on uneducated and non-working women working in seasonal capacity, unpaid work.
3. It is limited to only a few selected demographic factors and behavioral factors and their association with financial literacy.
4. Future study can consider socio-cultural factors, psychological bias and personality traits to understand its effect on financial literacy. It can also focus on how financial literacy and personality type affects the risk tolerance level of working women.
5. This study is only limited to test the basic and secondary level of financial literacy. Further studies should also contribute to advanced level of financial literacy.
6. Comparative analysis should be made to compare and contrast between the levels of financial knowledge, behavior and prudence.

RECOMMENDATIONS AND CONCLUSION

Government, stakeholders, financial institutions, fintech bodies, academic collaborations should be made in future to impart training and awareness about financial products, services and markets. Since achieving gender equity is one of the goals of SDGs. Financial literacy alone would help in achieving most of the SDGs and would also help in empowerment, economic growth, nation building. It has been found out that women lack enough income generation opportunities due to which they are less financially risk tolerant. Due to working in the unorganized sector they were lacking timely and surplus funds to invest in capital markets. They were not in a position to take risk as they would be left in a position where they can even loose the principal amount also. Demographic and cultural norms also play an important role in impacting financial and investment patterns. Since women lack the temperament to make financial choices, they are not even involved in long term financial planning. In order to achieve financial and social inclusion women need to be empowered for which financial markets should be strong and their participation should be guaranteed. It will help in the process of financial inclusion, gender equity, nation building, economic growth, achieving sustainable development goals.

REFERENCES

Akshita, A. (2016). *Assessment of Financial literacy among working Indian Women.* https://www.researchgate.net/pubilcation/298790053

Allianz. (2017). *When will the penny drop? Money, financial literacy and risk in the digital age.* Retrieved from https://gflec.org/initiatives/money-finlit-risk/

Atkinson, A., & Messy, F. (2012). *Measuring financial literacy: results of the OECD/ international network on financial education (INFE) pilot study.* OECD Working Papers on Finance, Insurance and Private Pensions, No. 15. OECD Publishing. doi:10.1787/20797117

Atkinson, A., & Messy, F. A. (2011). Assessing financial literacy in 12 countries: An OECD/INFE international pilot exercise. *Journal of Pension Economics and Finance, 10*(4), 657–665. doi:10.1017/S1474747211000539

Bhaskar, A., Saurabh, S., & Manvinder, P. S. (2018). Empowering women through financial literacy in Rajasthan. *International Journal on Computer Science and Engineering, 6*(9), 20–22. Advance online publication. doi:10.26438/ijcse/v6si9.2022

Bucciol, A., & Zarri, L. (2015). The shadow of the past: Financial risk taking and negative life events. *Journal of Economic Psychology, 48,* 1–16. doi:10.1016/j.joep.2015.02.006

Census of India. (2011). *2011 Census Data.* Office of the Registrar General and Census Commissioner, India. Available at: https://censusindia.gov.in/2011-prov-results/data_files/mp/07Literacy.pdf

Chetna, S., & Raj, K. (2017). Study of Women's Financial Literacy- A case of BHU. *Pacific Business Review International, 10*(4), 128–136.

Drever, A. I., Odders-White, E., Kalish, C. W., Else-Quest, N. M., Hoagland, E. M., & Nelms, E. N. (2015). Foundations of financial well-being: Insights into the role of executive function, financial socialization, and experience-based learning in childhood and youth. *The Journal of Consumer Affairs, 49*(1), 13–38. doi:10.1111/joca.12068

Fisher, P. J., & Yao, R. (2017). Gender differences in financial risk tolerance. *Journal of Economic Psychology, 61,* 191–202. doi:10.1016/j.joep.2017.03.006

Ghosh, S., & Vinod, D. (2017). What constrains financial inclusion for women? Evidence from Indian micro data. *World Development, 92,* 60–81. doi:10.1016/j.worlddev.2016.11.011

Grable, J. E. (2000). Financial Risk Tolerance and Additional Factors That Affect Risk Taking in Everyday Money Matters. *Journal of Business and Psychology*, *14*(4), 625–630. doi:10.1023/A:1022994314982

Helms, B. (2006). *Access for all consultative group to assist the poor.* doi:10.1596/978-0-8213-6360-7

Hill, J., & Hill, J. (2018). *Fintech and Government Regulation*. FinTech and the Remaking of Financial Institutions. doi:10.1016/B978-0-12-813497-9.00015-9

Hung, A., Parker, A. M., & Yoong, J. (2009). *Defining and measuring financial literacy.* Working Paper No. WR-708, Rand Corporation. doi:10.2139/ssrn.1498674

Johnston, J. D. (2005). *Importance of financial literacy in the global economy.* The Financial Education Summit, Kuala Lumpur. https://www.oecd.org/general/35883324.pdf

Kadoya, Y., Khan, M. S. R., Hamada, T., & Dominguez, A. (2018). Financial literacy and anxiety about life in old age: Evidence from the USA. *Review of Economics of the Household*, *16*(3), 859–878. doi:10.100711150-017-9401-1

Kahlor, L. A. (2007). An augmented risk information seeking model: The case of global warming. *Media Psychology*, *10*(3), 414–435. doi:10.1080/15213260701532971

Kezar, A., & Yang, H. (2010). The importance of financial literacy. *About Campus*, *14*(6), 15–21. https://doi.org/.20004 doi:10.1002/abc

Kiliyanni, A. L., & Sivaraman, S. (2018). A predictive model for financial literacy among the educated youth in Kerala, India. *Journal of Social Service Research*, *44*(4), 537–547. doi:10.1080/01488376.2018.1477699

Lusardi A. And Mitchell, O. (2008). Planning and Financial Literacy: How do Women Fare. *The American Economic Review*, *98*(2), 413–417. doi:10.1257/aer.98.2.413

Morgan, P., & Trinh, L. (2019). Determinants and impacts of financial literacy in Cambodia and VietNam. *J Risk Financ Manag*, *12*(1), 19. doi:10.3390/jrfm12010019

Mottola, G. R. (2013). In our best interest: Women, financial literacy, and credit card behavior. *Numeracy*, *6*(2), 1–15. doi:10.5038/1936-4660.6.2.4

NCFE-FLIS. (2013). *Financial Literacy and Inclusion in India.* Final Report, National Institute of Securities Market (NISM), Mumbai. Available https://www.ncfe.org.in/images/pdfs/ nasionalsurveyy/NISM_Final%20Report%20%20All%20India.pdf

Sinha, S., Pandey, K. R., & Madan, N. (2018). Fintech and the demand side challenge in financial inclusion. *Enterprise Development & Microfinance, 29*(1), 94–98. doi:10.3362/1755-1986.17-00016

Stein, P. (2010). Towards universal access: financial inclusion: addressing the global challenge of financial inclusion. Korea-World Bank high level conference on post-crisis growth and development, 1–35.

Sun, H., Yuen, D. C. Y., Zhang, J., & Zhang, X. (2020). Is knowledge powerful? Evidence from financial education and earnings quality. *Research in International Business and Finance, 52*, 101179. doi:10.1016/j.ribaf.2019.101179

Sun, T. (2017). Balancing innovation and risks in digital financial inclusion-experiences of ant financial services group. In *Handbook of blockchain, digital finance, and inclusion* (1st ed., Vol. 2). Elsevier Inc. doi:10.1016/B978-0-12-812282-2.00002-4

SungJ.HannaS. D. (1996). *Factors Related to Risk Tolerance. Financial Counseling and Planning*. https://ssrn.com/abstract=8284

Thanvi & Appalla. (2016). A study on the financial literacy of Professional Women in the district of Ernakulum, Kerala. *International Journal of Technology Enhancements and Emerging Engineering Research, 4*(7), 4-8. https://www.coursehero.com/file/63540321/A-Study-On-The-Financial-Literacy-Of-Professional-Women-In-The-District-Of-Ernakulum-Keralapdf/

Thung. (2012). *Determinants of saving behavior among university students in Malaysia*. Final Year Project. UTAR. http://eprints.utar.edu.my/607/1/AC-2011-0907445.pdf

Urban, C., Schmeiser, M., Collins, J. M., & Brown, A. (2018). The effects of high school personal financial education policies on financial behavior. *Economics of Education Review*. https://www.sciencedirect.com/science/article/abs/pii/

Williams, O. J., & Satchell, S. E. (2011). Social welfare issues of financial literacy and their implications for regulation. *Journal of Regulatory Economics, 40*(1), 1–40. doi:10.100711149-011-9151-6

Worthington, A. C. (2016). Financial literacy and financial literacy programmes in Australia. *Finance Lit Limits Finance DecisMak, 18*, 281–301. doi:10.1007/978-3-319-30886-9_14

Zavolokina, L., Dolata, M., & Schwabe, G. (2016). The FinTech phenomenon: Antecedents of financial innovation perceived by the popular press. *Financial Innovation, 2*(1), 16. doi:10.118640854-016-0036-7

Chapter 8
Rural Tourism Destinations and the Sustainable Development of Tourism in the Republic of Serbia:
Analysis of Variables Affecting the Competitiveness

Predrag Miroslav Vuković
Institute of Agricultural Economics, Belgrade, Serbia

Natatasa Kljajic
Institute of Agricultural Economics, Belgrade, Serbia

ABSTRACT

The problem of rural development is present in a large number of countries. Rural areas today are characterized by negative trends of population migration to urban centers, depopulation, aging of the rural population, reduction of macro-economic indicators, etc. The aim of the chapter is to identify the variables that influence the current situation in the sector of rural tourism based on the theoretical analysis of the management of rural tourist destinations and the conducted empirical research on the perceptions of tourists as consumers and domestic stakeholders on the quality of tourist offers in rural destinations in Serbia and the potential offer of rural tourist destinations in Serbia to propose strategic directions for the development of rural destinations and to present a sustainable management model for improving the competitiveness of the rural tourist destinations.

DOI: 10.4018/978-1-6684-8810-2.ch008

INTRODUCTION

Tourism represent sector with huge potential for economic development, job creation and social revival of rural areas (Nicolaides, 2020). There are large spared opinions in scientific literature that rural tourism represent as some kind of booster economic strategy how to help to fix problems that burden life of local population in rural areas (Adamov et al., 2020). Rural tourism development is frequently focused on activities that have the potential to bring benefit to local communities such as economically, socially, cultural, etc. (Sima, 2019). Problem that affecting to successful developing rural tourist destinations is spread growing competition (Chee Hua Chin 2022). Researching rural competitiveness of rural tourist destination is nowadays very actual because at the market there are many of destinations with similarly or almost equal tourist offer.

LITERATURE REVIEW

Until to day there is no dominant definition of competition (Cronje, F., D. at al. 2020, Alexandros & Metaxas, 2016, etc.). Porter and Van der Linde (1995, p.97) argued that competitiveness results from "superior productivity, either in terms of lower costs than rivals or the ability to offer products with superior values that justifies premium price." This principle can be applied to the tourism industry even though tourism is not a physical product (Du Plessis et al., 2015).

Researching the competitiveness of tourist destinations it is noticeable that at the beginning of the 21st century there were numerous of authors who tried to give their own definitions, different concept of models tourist destination competitiveness, identified factors that influence the growth of competitiveness and analyzed different aspects of the competitiveness of tourist destinations (Enright and Newton 2004, Dwyer and Kim 2003, Ritchie and Crouch 2003, Heath 2003, Hassan 2000, etc.).

Retchie and Croach (2003) have so far given the most acceptable and comprehensive definition of the competitiveness of a tourist destination. According to them, "Essentially, what makes a destination competitive is the ability to increase tourist consumption in a way that animates tourists, so that they are satisfied with the offer and remain with positive experiences that they will remember for a long time and want to repeat. This must be done in a profitable manner. On the other hand, the well-being of the residents must be increased and natural and cultural resources must be preserved, so that they will be useful for future generations".

Zengeni (2015) noted that measuring the competitiveness of a tourist destination can be done through subjective and objectively measurable variables. He distinguished two types of data, primary and secondary. He suggested quantifiable data as more precise and accurate. As he notes, the qualitatively measurable can be collected as "soft measurable" which are measured on the basis of a survey of tourists' attitudes and "hard", as precisely determined by some relevant state institution. This kind of approach with the so-called hard" and "soft" data has The World Economic Forum when measuring the competitiveness of countries as tourist destinations through the Travel and Tourism competitiveness index, which it regularly publishes annually in its Report on the competitiveness of countries as tourist destinations.

In the Travel & Tourism Competitiveness Report (2019) it is shown which indicators are useful for measuring the sustainable development of tourism, which contributes to the tourist competitiveness of the destination. They are determined by the World Economic Forum and measured on a scale of 1 to 7, which is the most desirable outcome (Calderwood & Soshkin, 2019).

A certain number of authors (Eom, et al., 2019; Dangi et al., 2016; Forstner, 2004, etc.) state that due to difficult living conditions in rural areas, rural households cannot depend only on agricultural production as the only source of income, but emphasis must be placed on additional sources of income. In this sense, they suggest the inclusion of rural households in community-based tourism that enables the creation of additional sources of income and strengthens alternatives to survival in rural areas.

A large number of organizations that follow the development of rural tourism gave their own definition. Today, the definition of rural toursim which gave the World Tourism Organization is most often cited (UNWTO, 2017, p.15): "Rural tourism represent a type of tourism activity in which the visitor experience is linked to a wide range of products related to activities based on nature, agriculture, rural lifestyle, culture, hunting, fishing and sightseeing. Rural tourism activities take place in rural areas, i.e. not urban areas characterized by: 1) low population density; 2) landscapes and land use dominated by agriculture and forestry; and 3) traditional social structure, rural way of life".

Accelerated and exaggerated concentration of inhabitants in town centers and problems made by industrial production, have given assumptions for the appearance and growth of the need for the vacation in nature. (Vuković at al. 2013). Rural tourist destination attracted people for coming and rest (Vuković, et al. 2017).

Kotler P. et al. (2017) distinguished between macro and micro destinations and emphasizes the perception of what the destination represents. Bearing in mind this approach, depending on the management's perception, it could be micro location, entire regions, even countries, can be viewed as tourist destinations.

Vuković, P. (2019), defined a rural tourist destination:

- *"Represents a rural area that has physical and administrative boundaries, which are defined by the management;*
- *It has attractive natural and social/anthropogenic resources that are characteristic for the rural area and rural environment;*
- *Agricultural production is the dominant economic activity and represent the main source of income for the resident population. It provides an opportunity for tourists to become familiar with its specificities, direct and indirect impacts on the local social environment and natural environment;*
- *It has a developed tourist offer, that is, it has capacities for accommodation, rest, nutrition, recreation and entertainment for tourists;*
- *It has an appropriate traffic infrastructure which with its construction and architectural solutions, does not damage its ambience to a greater extent;*
- *The rural environment is preserved: ecologically, construction-urbanlly, spatial planning and cultural-historically.*
- *There is an appropriate level of marketing and management activities in order to animate and attract tourist demand to come and stay in the rural areas.*
- *The management constantly works to improving the quality and quantity of the tourist supply (boarding/pensions and non-boarding facilities), which strengthens its competitiveness and creates an own destinations image."*

MATERIALS AND METHODS

The target area of conducted research was the territory of Republic of Serbia, which with its natural and social specificities, possesses numerous respectable natural and social/anthropogenic resources suitable for the development of rural tourism.

Accepting the views expressed by Zodorov, A. V., (2009) on the phased development of rural tourism with appropriate features, it can be concluded that the development of rural tourism in Serbia has left the phase of independent establishment and has entered the phase of dedicated development. Namely, in 2006, the Ministry of Agriculture, Forestry and Water Management (Analysis of budget support for the development of rural tourism in Serbia and diversification of economic activities in the countryside, 2009) allocated about 1 million Euros for the development of rural tourism and the diversification of economic activities in to the village, which from a theoretical point of view can be marked as the beginning of the second phase in the development of rural tourism. Today, rural tourism is rapidly developing in Europe, so the question of Serbia's competitiveness on the rural tourism market is justifiably raised. Therefore, the subject of research in the paper is the competitiveness of rural tourist destinations in Serbia.

Bearing in mind the fact that rural tourism in the phase of independent establishment developed spontaneously, without an appropriate strategy, i.e. no strategy of differentiated marketing was applied, i.e. focus, which is insisted on in the literature, (Kotler P., et al., 2017, p.261-263) the research goals of chapter are logically set:

- Analysis of the current situation in the rural tourism sector;
- Assessment of the quality of all elements of the rural tourism offer that affect the current and potential future competitive position of rural tourism in Serbia.

This survey used a quantitative methodology that the authors implemented in the territory of the Republic of Serbia in the period from April, 01st to October 15th, 2022. The target area was the territory of Serbia, which with its natural and social specificities, possesses numerous respectable natural and social/anthropogenic resources suitable for the development of rural tourism. A total of 304 respondents were surveyed. The survey is considered a volunteer pilot survey. The sample could be much larger in relation to the number of villages and the number of inhabitants, but due to the existing limiting circumstances, the answers received can be considered representative, as it is a pilot study. It was necessary to spend up to 10 minutes on average for data collection per respondent. The research was conducted "on-line" at the level of the entire Republic, as well as directly by collecting data through a "face-to-face" survey on the ground.

The *first phase* of the research consisted of cabinet research, which was based on the analysis of existing literature, documents, development studies, as well as all other relevant sources that would serve as the basis of secondary research through comparative analysis. In the second phase, the direct collection, processing and analysis of data was started. Quantitative and qualitative research methods were used. As a tool for data collection, a survey questionnaire was used, which was structured with a combination of structured (Likert scale) and unstructured questions (open questions). After interviewing the interest groups (stakeholders), the obtained data were checked, followed by their electronic processing. In this way, it is possible to cross-reference data according to different bases and criteria (table, graph, etc.). In the last phase, final considerations were made, on the basis of which appropriate evaluations and recommendations were given for the complementary development of rural tourism.

The questionnaire consisted of two parts. In the first, respondents gave general evaluations of the rural tourism offer in Serbia, while in the second, the evaluation of elements tourist offer was carried out. The list of elements of the tourist offer was developed based on the most represented and well-known foreign professional literature related to the development of rural tourism, primarily taking into account the level of development of rural tourism in the developed countries of Western Europe.

The authors created a list of elements of the tourist supply, which was used to evaluate the quality elements of boarding and non-boarding/non-pension tourist services relevant for rural tourist destinations in Serbia. This synthetic list was created as a result of a combination of lists of tourism offers suggested by authors and organizations listed in the Literature Review section (Vanhove, N. 2022, Kotler et al. 2017, Roberts and Hall 2003, etc.) as well as a list of the World Economic Forum that measures competitiveness countries as tourist destinations each year, but also on the basis of personal research on actual state of development of rural tourism on the basis of research into the current situation in the tourism sector in the Republic of Serbia – (cabinet research of strategic and planning documents such as Strategy for development tourism in the Republic of Serbia for the period 2016 - 2025, Master plan for sustainable development rural tourism in Serbia 2011, etc.), the existing the Law on the Planning System (Official Gazette No. 30/2018), as well as the Law on Tourism (Official Gazette No. 17/2019) etc.

One of the aim in the research was to test the assumption about the perception of the tourist offer. The basic hypothesis that the conducted research aimed to examine was established.

H0: There is no difference in the overall scoring of the rural tourist supply when the perception of tourists is evaluated before and after the obtained individual scorings of all elements of the rural tourist offer, i.e. H0: $\mu d = 0$.

H1: There is difference in the overall scoring of the rural tourist offer when the perception of tourists is evaluated before and after the obtained individual scorings of all elements of the rural tourist offer, i.e. H1: $\mu d \neq 0$.

The statistical software "SPSS" (Statistical Program Software System) was used in the processing and analysis of the data, which made it possible to obtain the results that were the subject of the analysis with high reliability using the latest computer technology.

RESULTS AND DISCUSSIONS

Vuković et al. (2022) stated: "Numerous of countries that have lost the race in industrial development today are looking to realize their chance on economy development in tourism as economic brance. Their standpoint comes for the fact that they possess a numerous preserved natural and socio-cultural values as tourist attractions which can attract tourist to visit their potential destinations. In Serbia is not present conditions for develop mass types of tourism. The attitude is based on the fact that Serbia has no access to the seaside coast and it is present only one real ski resort (mountain Kopaonik). In order to enter the tourist market, Serbia should offer what it has at its disposal". Rural areas of Serbia make up more than 80% of its territory. About 43% of the total Serbian population lives in these areas. 7 national parks are located in rural areas of Serbia. Around 30 different nationalities lives in rural areas with characteristic cultural and historical heritage, foods and different customs, etc. There are 4,706 villages in Serbia, which, due to the accelerated process of industrialization after the Second World War, are today burdened with numerous problems, such as: the decline of macroeconomic indicators, unemployment, the process of accelerated aging of the population, population migration to urban centers, etc. (Vuković at. al 2009). These problems of rural areas are not only characteristic for the Republic of Serbia, but also characterize the other European countries.

In order to stop these negative trends, it is suggested that, in addition to primary agricultural production, development should also be focused on the rural non-agricultural economy In this sense, the development of rural tourism can be seen as one of the main drivers of the economic development of rural areas. For this reason, it is important to examine the elements of Serbia's rural tourism offer and to discover the strongest and weakest elements in the tourism supply chain in order to be able to act in a timely manner, that is, to increase the competitiveness of these tourist destinations. The authors conducted research, the results of which are presented. The total sample of respondents included in the conducted research according to gender, age, education and occupation is presented in Table 1.

As we can be seen from Table 1, the total sample included 304 respondents, of which 139 were male (45.7%) and 158 female (52.0%). The analysis of the age structure of the respondents showed that the most significant number of respondents belonged to the categories between 31 to 40 years of age (25,0%), followed by 41 to 50 years of age (24%), etc. We can conclude that these two categories of respondents make up ¾ of the respondents. The structure of respondents by education indicates that the largest number of respondents have a Universtity (59.5%) and High School education (34.9%). According to the occupational category, the respondents declared that they are clearks (44.4%), followed by workers (16.1%), while 4,9% of the respondents belong to the category of unemployed. The sample also included professors (4.3%), pensioners (6,9%), business people (6,6%) etc. Based on these data, we concluded that the respondents by education and profession were competent to make evaluations about the current rural tourist offer as well as contents related to the presence of non boarding/non pansions contents. The survey included the following categories of respondents: 1) tourists, those who have already stayed in one of the rural tourist destinations; 2) potential tourists, those who have never stayed but show interest in staying in one of the rural tourist destinations;

Table 1. Structure of the respondents according to the selected features (n=304)

Answer	Frequency	Percent	Valid Percent
a) Gender	**297**	**97,7**	**100**
Female	158	52,0	53,2
Male	139	45,7	46,8
b) Age	**302**	**99,3**	**100**
Up to 20	7	2,3	2,3
21-30	52	17,1	17,2
31-40	76	25,0	25,2
41-50	73	24,0	24,2
51-60	50	16,4	16,6
61 and more	44	14,5	14,6
c) Education	**299**	**98,4**	**100**
Primary Education	4	1,3	1,3
High school	106	34,9	35,3
University education	181	59,5	60,5
In progress (pupil, student)	7	2,3	2,3
Other	1	0,3	0,3
d) Place	**301**	**99,0**	**100**
Belgrade	96	31,6	31,9
Čačak	41	13,5	13,6
Kragujevac	50	16,4	16,6
Niš	54	17,8	17,9
Novi Sad	60	19,7	19,9
d) Profession	**294**	**96,7**	**100**
Worker	49	16,1	16,7
Clerk	135	44,4	45,9
Businessman	20	6,6	6,8
Pupil, student	17	5,6	5,8
Sportsman	2	0,7	0,7
Unemployed	15	4,9	5,1
Other	22	7,2	7,5
Professor	13	4,3	4,4
Pensioner	21	6,9	7,1

Source: Authors' research.

The structure of the respondents shows that 99% answered the question, of which 78.7% gave a positive answer, while 21.3% declared that they would not spend part of their vacation in one of the rural tourist destinations. It can be concluded that a high percentage of positive responses (78.7%) indicates that rural tourism is attractive and can attract a significant part of tourist demand from urban areas in Serbia. However, 21.3% of negative responses indicate that it is necessary to work additionally on the promotion of rural tourism and to improve the quality of the rural tourism offer.

In the further course of the research, the interest was to determine in which rural tourist destinations the respondents would spend their vacation. However, due to the large dispersion in the answers to this open question, it was not possible to statistically single out specific destinations. Namely, a large number of respondents mentioned villages, that is, rural areas near their cities, i.e. the places from which they came to the cities where they live and work. In this way, the answers to these questions were of a subjective nature, i.e. the motive of traveling to those places is to visit the homeland, relatives and friends, and not just vacation, which is not relevant for this research. Nevertheless, as attractive rural tourist destinations for which there is potentially the greatest tourist demand, the mountains Zlatibor, Mokra gora and Tara can be singled out, followed by farms in AP Vojvodina, as well as ethno-villages in Central and Western Serbia.

It was also important to investigate how many times the respondents spent their vacation in one of the rural tourist destinations. The results showed that the largest number of respondents who answered the question rested in one of the rural tourist destinations, 53.5%, i.e. 161 respondents. A large number of respondents (20.9% to be exact) never spent a vacation or part of their vacation in rural tourist destinations, while 15.3% stayed once.

Given that more than half of the respondents declared that they had spent their vacation in one of the rural tourist destinations more than twice, it can be concluded that they were satisfied with the quality of the tourist offer. Also, the high percentage of respondents (20.9%) who did not stay points to the conclusion that marketing and management efforts must be strengthened in order to further animate this segment of tourist demand to visit rural areas.

Respondents were also asked to indicate which rural tourist destinations they had heard of so far. This was done in a targeted manner in order to determine which of the destinations have a good promotional policy and built image. The results of the research showed a large dispersion in the answers received. Namely, the respondents mentioned a very large number of different rural tourist destinations. This can be illustrated by the fact that one destination is mentioned by at most 10% of respondents, then there are more than 50 tourist destinations that are mentioned by only one respondent. Therefore, the answers received are not representative.

However, as rural tourist destinations that tourists have heard of, the following are most often mentioned: mountain Zlatibor (ethno-village Sirogojno), the village of Guča in the Dragačevo region known for the "Sabor trubača u Guča" event, the village of Borač in the municipality of Knić, the National Park "Kopaonik", Mokra gora with the ethno-village "Drvengrad", Stara Planina, National Park "Fruška gora", farms in AP Vojvodina, "Đavolja varoš" located on the Radan mountain near Kuršumlija and Lake Palić with accompanying facilities, etc.

Out of a total of 304 respondents, 272 respondents or 89.5% answered the question. There are 32 missing answers or 10.5%. It was observed that more than 2/3 of the respondents (86.8%) independently organize vacations in rural tourist destinations. This answer corresponds to the answer in which only 7.6% of respondents mentioned the agency as a source of information about rural tourist destinations, that is, only 10.3% answered through a travel agency. Based on the answers received, it can be concluded that there is little involvement of domestic travel agencies in the development of rural tourism in Serbia, which is also a criticism of their work.

Bearing in mind the quality of the transport infrastructure in Serbia, as well as its importance for the development of rural tourism, the survey respondents answered the questions about which means of transport they use to go to rural tourist destinations. Car as a means of transport was circled by 221 respondents, which is almost 80% (79.8%) of those surveyed. Bus as a means of transport was circled by 63 respondents or 22.7%. The results obtained in the research are in accordance with the theoretical views on the importance of road traffic for the development of rural tourist destinations. Bearing in mind the poor condition of the railway infrastructure and the conditions for traveling by railway in Serbia, it is clear why only 3.6% of respondents mentioned the train as a means of transport.

Of all respondents who answered this question, 36.9% (107) would spend 2-3 days in rural destinations. 19% of respondents would spend 4 to 6 days, while approximately the same number of respondents chose 7 days and more than 7 days (17.6% or 51 respondents, or 15.5% or 45 respondents). Given that the largest number of respondents stayed 2-3 days in rural tourist destinations, it can be assumed that weekend vacations, i.e. short vacations are very popular, which is in agreement with theoretical views on rural tourism as a type of tourism primarily intended for that segment of tourist demand interested in short vacations. Each of the element of the tourist supply affects the creation of the overall tourist experience.

It often happens that the perception of the overall tourist offer is different from the perception of individual elements, that is why in the paper, data was collected through a survey on the assessment of the overall tourist offer in Serbia (Table 2)

Table 2. Score of total tourist supply in Serbia

	Answer	Frequency	Percent	Valid Percent	Cumulative Percent
Valid	Insufficient (socre 1).	13	4,3	4,4	4,4
	Sufficient (socre 2).	60	19,7	20,1	24,5
	Good (score 3).	128	42,1	43,0	67,4
	Very good (score 4).	66	21,7	22,1	89,6
	Excellent (score 5).	31	10,2	10,4	100,0
	Total	298	98,0	100,0	
Missing	System	6	2,0		
	Total	304	100,0		

Source: Authors research.

Table 3. Descriptive statistics

	N	Minimum	Maximum	Mean	Std. Deviation
Total score	301	1,31	4,46	3,0048	0,56988
Valid N (list wise)	301				

Source: Authors research.

Table 4. Paired samples statistics

		Mean	N	Std. Deviation	Std. Error Mean
Pair 1	Please, score the overall rural tourism supply	3,1414	297	1,00010	0,05803
	Total score	3,0032	297	0,56137	0,03257

Source: Authors research.

and on the assessment of individual elements of the rural tourism offer in Serbia (Table 6).

The research showed that the largest number of respondents, 43%, gave a score of good 3, while approximately the same percentage, around 20% of respondents, gave score of sufficient 2 and very good 4. Only 4.4% of respondents gave the score insufficient. The average rating of the total rural tourist offer is 3.0048.

H0: There is no difference in the overall scoring of the rural tourist supply when the perception of tourists is evaluated before and after the obtained individual scorings of all elements of the rural tourist offer, i.e. H0: $\mu d = 0$.

Table 5. Paired samples test

	Paired Differences					t	df	Sig. (2-Tailed)
	Mean	Std. Dev.	Std. Error Mean	95% Confidence Interval of the Difference				
				Lower	Upper			
Pair 1	0,13818	0,96429	0,05595	0,02807	0,24830	2,47	296	0,014

p = 0,014 < α = 0, 05

H1: There is difference in the overall scoring of the rural tourist offer when the perception of tourists is evaluated before and after the obtained individual scorings of all elements of the rural tourist offer, i.e. H1: μd ≠ 0.

The average score of the total tourist supply is 3.1414. Also, individual evaluations were analyzed for each component of the rural tourism offer. When the evaluation of the total offer is determined based on the evaluations of individual components, a value of 3.0032 is obtained. When statistically testing whether these two ratings are the same, the result is that they are not, that is, with a confidence of 95%, the null hypothesis can be rejected.

Table 6. Assessment of individual elements of the rural tourism offer in Serbia

Elements of Rural Tourist Supply	N	Mean		Std. Deviation
		Statistic	Std. Error	
Natural attractions	300	4,3533	0,05178	0,89694
Silence and peace	299	4,3010	0,05328	0,92124
Possibility of excursions and stay in nature	298	4,0604	0,05850	1,00991
Personal and material safety and security	296	4,0507	0,05375	0,92469
Cultural-historic heritage	299	3,9431	0,05381	0,93053
Hospitality	300	3,9133	0,05895	1,02109
Food in the accommodation facility	298	3,7617	0,05585	0,96414
Farms	291	3,7491	0,05969	1,01826
Ecological preservation	296	3,7061	0,06469	1,11299
Food in restaurants	298	3,6812	0,05510	0,95119
Ethno-villages	297	3,5859	0,06164	1,06235
The possibility of playing sports	295	3,5831	0,06404	1,09996
National parks	297	3,5421	0,06343	1,09317
Rural accommodation facilities (houses)	300	3,5233	0,05733	0,99301

continued on following page

Table 6. Continued

Elements of Rural Tourist Supply	N	Mean		Std. Deviation
		Statistic	Std. Error	
Natural reserves	294	3,3810	0,06601	1,13181
Service in restaurants	297	3,3266	0,05816	1,00223
Archaeological sites	298	3,3054	0,06631	1,14476
Apartments, villas, camps	299	3,2809	0,05997	1,03691
Cultural manifestations and events	294	3,1565	0,06363	1,09108
Terms for entertainment	298	3,0101	0,06457	1,11460
Postal services	294	2,9762	0,05929	1,01664
Hygiene	297	2,9495	0,05726	0,98681
Health services	294	2,9150	0,05871	1,00659
Hotels	296	2,8514	0,05953	1,02421
Possibilities for village fairs	289	2,8201	0,06379	1,08436
The possibility of holding symposiums and business meetings	291	2,7457	0,06578	1,12216
Price level	294	2,7245	0,05522	0,94685
Motels	297	2,6397	0,06368	1,09737
Museums and galleries	297	2,5993	0,06807	1,17306
Bus lines	295	2,5797	0,05821	0,99979
Services of travel agencies	293	2,5597	0,06194	1,06018
Tourist Organizations	294	2,5442	0,05910	1,01343
Condition for purchase (shopping)	294	2,5340	0,06182	1,05991
The possibility of changing foreign currency	294	2,4864	0,06071	1,04088
Camping	293	2,4539	0,06582	1,12662
Local transport	294	2,3980	0,05477	0,93917
Tourist information centers	295	2,3966	0,06412	1,10132
Tourist signage	294	2,3946	0,06679	1,14515
The possibility of using the Internet	290	2,3448	0,06990	1,19038
Tourist associations	286	2,3112	0,06395	1,08143
Taxi services	292	2,3014	0,06450	1,10214
State policy and institutional mechanisms for the development of rural tourism in Serbia	291	2,2474	0,06121	1,04417
Botanical gardens	293	2,1570	0,06996	1,19757
Thematic parks	296	2,0946	0,06626	1,13995
Road quality	300	2,0833	0,05373	0,93056
Rent-a-car	291	1,9141	0,06204	1,05839
Railway quality	296	1,7939	0,05291	0,91026

Source: Authors research.

The perception of the quality of the offer of rural tourist destinations (3.1414) is higher than that when all components of the rural tourist offer are partially assessed (3.0032), Certain components are important to the respondents to varying degrees, that is, the respondents individually rated the more "important" elements of the offer with "higher" ratings, i.e. "lower" depending on the "overall tourist experience" and their "individual importance" during the stay.

An important part of the research was the examination of the attitudes of the respondents on how to rate individual elements of the tourist offer of rural tourist destinations in Serbia. Namely, they were asked to rate each of the elements of rural torust supply on a Likert scale from 1 to 5. This was done with the aim of identifying the weakest links in the chain of tourist supply, so that they could be removed with appropriate preventive action, i.e. improve the weakest links in the tourist supply chain. The list of obtained scores is shown in Table 6.

The purpose of the conducted research was to assess the quality of elements of rural tourism supply in Rural areas in the Republic of Serbia. The conducted research gave the following results from which appropriate conclusions can be extracted:

- It was determined that the respondents gave the highest average score to the element of rural tourist offer of natural attractiveness, 4.35; in second place is silence and peace with an average score of 4.3; the possibility for excursions and spending time in nature was scored with 4.06; while personal and material safety and security was rated 4.05; etc. This order of ratings is in favor of the generally accepted views on the tourist offer, what's more, the elements of the offer that actually represent the biggest limiting factors in the development of rural tourism, railway quality 1.79, which can be interpreted as the current situation in Serbian Railways, received the lowest ratings. It can be concluded that this outcome is expected, followed by Rent-a-car 1.91. The assumption is that the respondents started from the fact that in urban centers it is possible to rent cars that would be used as transportation to certain rural tourist destinations. However, the problem is that there are no such services in rural destinations in Serbia. Road quality is rated 2,083, etc. (Table 6).
- The perception of the quality of the offer of rural tourist destinations (3.14) is higher than that when all elements of the rural tourist offer are partially evaluated (3.00). Certain elements are important to the respondents to varying degrees, that is, the respondents individually rated the more "important" elements of the offer as "higher", i.e., "lower" grades depending on the "overall tourist experience" during the stay.
- 53% of respondents expressed the intention to recommend to their relatives and friends a trip to one of the rural tourist destinations. More than 1/3 (33.2%) were undecided, while only 13.2% gave negative answers. In order

- to increase the competitiveness of rural tourist destinations, it is necessary to work additionally on improving the quality of the offer, that is, those elements that were evaluated by the respondents with the lowest marks.
- Rural tourism is attractive for residents of Serbia's largest cities, as evidenced by 78.7% of positive responses received. However, 21.3% of negative responses lead to the conclusion that it is necessary to make further investments in the quality of the rural tourist offer, i.e. it is necessary to invest additionally in promotion, i.e. development and distribution of means of promotional mix, in order to additionally animate those segments of the market that have a negative attitude towards rural tourism.
- The mountains Zlatibor, Mokra gora, Tara, farms in AP Vojvodina well known as "salash" and ethno-villages located in Central and Western Serbia, stand out as attractive rural tourist destinations for which there is potentially the greatest tourist demand.
- There is a large disproportion in the sources of information about rural tourist destinations. The survey showed that the most common source of information is television (52.2%), followed by friends and relatives (35.9%), etc. What is encouraging is that the Internet is in fourth place (32.2%), which shows that the population's information literacy is increasing over time.
- 74.3% of the respondents prefer vacation and recreation as a reason why they would spend their vacation/holidays in one of the rural tourist destinations.
- The fact that 53.5% of those surveyed have rested in one of the rural tourist destinations more than once indicates that they are satisfied with the quality of services, that is, the rural tourist offer of Serbia. A high percentage of those surveyed (20.9%) who did not stay in rural tourist destinations points to the conclusion that marketing and management efforts must be further strengthened in order to further animate this segment of tourist demand.
- The large percentage of respondents (86.6%) who independently organize vacations in rural tourist destinations corresponds to the low involvement of domestic travel agencies in the development of rural tourism.
- The research confirmed the importance of road traffic for the development of rural tourism. Namely, about 80% (79.8%) of the respondents mentioned the car as a means of transport used by the respondents to go to rural destinations, the bus in a much smaller percentage, 22.7%, etc.
- Tourists between the ages of 21 and 30 stay in a statistically higher percentage for less than 7 days, while tourists who are 61 and older in a statistically significantly higher percentage stay for 7 days or longer.
- Respondents' associations with rural tourist destinations in Serbia are very different, as evidenced by the large dispersion in the answers received. Positive experiences mostly relate to the preserved natural environment, the

quality and variety of domestic cuisine (organically produced food, quality of agricultural food products, domestic drinks - alcoholic and non-alcoholic), while in the opinion of respondents, poor rural infrastructure stands out as a limiting factor in the development of rural tourism. That is, poor road quality and poor rural hygiene.
- Propaganda messages about rural tourism in Serbia were not noticed by 35.8% of respondents, which points to the conclusion that it is necessary to additionally animate this segment of tourist demand with the means of the promotional mix and inform potential tourists about Serbia's rural tourism offer, i.e., that additional investments in propaganda are necessary and promotional mix assets.
- The results of the research show that 74.9% of the respondents mentioned television as the media through which they get information about rural tourist destinations in Serbia. In second place are daily newspapers and magazines with 34.4%, while the Internet is in third place with 24.6%, which is encouraging data, primarily considering the importance of IT literacy among the population. The lowest percentage, 6%, was given to tourist agencies, which confirms the already stated critical attitude about the work of domestic agencies and their attitude towards the development of rural, i.e., development of receptive tourism.

Based on the knowledge obtained through primary research, the recommendations for future research on the competitiveness of rural tourist destinations in the Republic of Serbia refer to the following:

- The reason for future research may be in the function of obtaining information related to the behavior of potential tourists (consumers) when choosing certain rural tourist destinations, i.e. obtaining information about the preferences of tourists about those elements of the tourist product that are important when choosing a destination in order to appropriate future strategic and planning activities.
- Given that rural tourism is attractive for foreign tourists as well, research can be conducted with the aim of obtaining information about the segments of foreign tourist demand and its characteristics and preferences in relation to the rural tourism offer in Serbia.
- Special emphasis should be placed on combining the obtained results with qualitative research methods.
- The reason for the research may be the implementation of the multivariate analysis procedure, which could be used to extract the competitiveness factors of rural tourist destinations in Serbia.

- It would be useful to conduct the same research after a certain period of time, in order to compare the results obtained.

The limitations of the conducted research were: the sample was convenient and not simple random; The Statistical Office of the Republic of Serbia (RZS) does not monitor tourists by type of tourism, as well as by the places from which they come from, so the data obtained from the survey cannot be compared with the official data of the Statistical Office of the Republic of Serbia; answers of a subjective nature; open questions; response errors; etc.

CONCLUSION

Tourism represents one of the economic branches with the most dynamic growth in the last five decades. It has become an economic, political, sociological, ecological factor that brings major changes to the environment in which it develops. In its strategic documents and official announcements, the Government of Serbia emphasizes the importance of tourism as an economic branch that, with its synergistic effect, can positively influence the development of related activities. It is expected that tourism could help solve a large number of problems that burden the Serbian economy and rural areas.

The process of diversification of tourist products, which is immanent in the tourist market today, favors the development of tourism in Serbia, given the limited conditions for the development of mass forms of tourism, i.e. the small number of winter ski centers and the lack of a natural-geographic exit of the Serbian territory to the sea coast.

Rural tourism is one of the products for which there are resource opportunities for intensive development.

An essential issue in the development of rural tourist destinations is the way to gain and preserve competitiveness.

The conducted research on the quality of the offer of rural tourist destinations in Serbia showed that the perception of the quality of the offer of rural tourist destinations is higher than when all the elements of the rural tourist offer are partially assessed. Certain elements are important to the respondents to varying degrees, that is, the respondents individually rated the more "important" elements of the offer as "higher", i.e., "lower" grades depending on the "overall tourist experience" during the stay. The results of the research showed that the following elements of the rural tourism offer have the highest average rating: natural attractiveness 4.35; silence and peace 4.3; possibility for excursions and stay in nature 4.06; personal and material safety and security 4.05; etc.

The order of the received ratings corresponds with the other received answers, that is, it supports the generally accepted views on the quality of the elements of the rural tourism offer in Serbia. The lowest scores were given to those elements that represent the biggest limiting factors of development, namely: the quality of railways (1.79), rent-a-car services (1.91), the quality of roads (2.08), etc.

Empirical research confirmed the hypothesis: there is difference in the overall scoring of the rural tourist offer when the perception of tourists is evaluated before and after the obtained individual scorings of all elements of the rural tourist offer.

Based on the obtained results of the primary research, as well as on the basis of insight into the prepared development studies, strategic documents and literature, it can be concluded that the elements of the offer that should be given the greatest attention in the development of rural tourist destinations are: attractiveness; receptive capacities; development of the service system through personnel development; availability of rural tourist destinations; tourist mediation; sector of destination organization. If these elements of the tourist offer were to be improved, the expectations are that the competitiveness of rural tourist destinations would increase significantly, that is, rural tourism would become more attractive on the market.

Based on the above, it can be concluded that there are great potentials for the development of rural tourism in Serbia. In order to make better use of the available resources for development, it is necessary to constantly work on education, raising the awareness of the local population, and greater involvement of stakeholders. It is necessary that the approach to the development of rural tourism receives equal treatment in the overall tourism offer of Serbia, considering that the Tourism Development Strategy emphasizes that it does not belong to the so-called group. "quick win" products.

Based on the knowledge obtained through primary research, recommendations for future research and opportunities for improving the development of sports and recreational tourism in the area of AP Vojvodina refer to the following:

- The reason for the future research may be in the function of obtaining information related to the behavior of potential tourists when choosing certain rural tourist destinations, i.e. obtaining information about the preferences of tourists about those elements of the tourist product that are important when choosing a destination for the purpose of appropriate future strategic and planning activities.
- Bearing in mind that rural tourism are also attractive for foreign tourists, research can be conducted with the aim of obtaining information about segments of foreign tourist demand and its characteristics and preferences.
- Special emphasis should be placed on combining the obtained results with qualitative research methods.

- The reason for the research may be the implementation of the multivariate analysis procedure with which the competitiveness factors of rural tourist destinations could be extracted.
- It would be useful to conduct the same research after a certain period of time, in order to compare the results obtained.

ACKNOWLEDGMENT

Paper is a part of research financed by the MSTDI RS and agreed in decision no. 451-03-47/2023-01/200009 from 03.02.2023.

REFERENCES

Adamov, T., Ciolac, R., Iancu, T., Brad, I., Pet, E., Popescu, G., & Smuleac, L. (2020). Sustainability of agritourism activity. Initiatives and challenges in Romanian mountain rural regions. *Sustainability (Basel)*, *12*(6), 1–23. doi:10.3390u12062502

Alexandros, P. N., & Metaxas, T. (2016). "Porter vs. Krugman": History, analysis and critique of regional competitiveness. *Journal of Economics & Political Economy*, *3*(1), 65–80. doi:10.1453/jepe.v3i1.657

Analysis of budget support for the development of rural tourism in Serbia and diversification of economic activities in the countryside. (2009). Ministry of Agriculture, Forestry and Water Management of the Republic of Serbia.

Calderwood, L. U., & Soshkin, M. (2019). *The travel & tourism competitiveness report 2019*. The World Economic Forum. https://www3.weforum.org/docs/WEF_TTCR_2019.pdf

Census. (2022). *Republic of Serbia*. https://popis2022.stat.gov.rs/sr-Latn/

Chee Hua Chin (2022). Empirical research on the competitiveness of rural tourism destinations: a practical plan for rural tourism industry post–COVID-19. *Consumer Behaviour in Tourism and Hospitality, 17*(2), 211-231.

Cronje, F. D., & du Plessis, E. (2020). A review on tourism destination competitiveness. *Journal of Hospitality and Tourism Management*, *45*, 256–265. doi:10.1016/j.jhtm.2020.06.012

Dangi, T. B., & Jamal, T. (2016). An Integrated approach to Sustainable community based tourism, journal. *Sustainability (Basel)*, *2016*(8), 2–32. doi:10.3390u8050475

Du Plessis, E., Saayman, M., & van der Merwe, A. (2015). What makes South African tourism competitive? *African Journal of Hospitality, Tourism and Leisure*, *4*(2), 1–14. https://doaj.org/article/f47353129d7046d3bb772d0535eada2e

Dwyer, L., & Kim, C. (2003). Destination competitiveness: Determinants and indicators. *Current Issues in Tourism*, *6*(5), 369–414. doi:10.1080/13683500308667962

Enright, M. J., & Newton, J. (2004). Tourism destination competitiveness: A quantitative approach. *Tourism Management*, *25*(6), 777–788. doi:10.1016/j.tourman.2004.06.008

Eom, T., & Han, H. (2019). Community-based tourism (TourDure) experience program: A theoretical approach, pp. 956-968. *Journal of Travel & Tourism Marketing*, *36*(8), 956–968. doi:10.1080/10548408.2019.1665611

Forstner, K. (2004). Community Ventures and Access to Markets: The Role of Intermediaries in Marketing Rural Tourism Products. *Development Policy Review*, *22*(5), 497–514. doi:10.1111/j.1467-7679.2004.00262.x

Hassan, S. S. (2000). Determinants of market competitiveness in an environmentally sustainable tourism industry. *Journal of Travel Research*, *38*(3), 239–245. doi:10.1177/004728750003800305

Kotler, P., Bowen, J. T., Makens, J. T., & Baloglu, S. (2017). Marketing for Hospitality and Tourism (7th ed.). Pearson Education Limited.

Master plan for sustainable development rural tourism in Serbia. (2011). UNWTO, Tourism & Leisure Advisory Services.

National program for renewal villages of Serbia – State, problems and priorities. (2020). Academia Board for Villages, SANU (Serbian Academy of Science and Arts), Ministry for Regional Development. Institute of Agricultural Economics.

Nicolaides, A. (2020). Sustainable ethical tourism (SET) and rural community involvement. *African Journal of Hospitality, Tourism and Leisure*, *9*(1), 1–16.

Porter, M. E., & Van der Linde, C. (1995). Toward a new conception of the environmentcompetitiveness relationship. *The Journal of Economic Perspectives*, *9*(4), 97–118. doi:10.1257/jep.9.4.97

Ritchie, J. R. B., & Crouch, G. I. (2003). *The competitive destination: A sustainable tourism perspective.* CABI Publishing. doi:10.1079/9780851996646.0000

Roberts, L., & Hall, D. (2003). Rural Tourism and Recreation: principles to practice. In Leisure and Tourism Management Department. CABI Publishing.

Sima, E. (2019). Economic, social and environmental impact of Romanian rural tourism. *Agricultural Economics and Rural Development, 16*(1), 137–146.

Strategy for development tourism in the Republic of Serbia for the period 2016 – 2025 (Official Gazete, RS, No. 98, 08th December 2016).

UN WTO. (2017). *Report of Secretary-General.* A/22/10(I) rev.1, Madrid, 01st September 2017, General Assembly, Twenty-Second Sessions, Chengdu, China.

Vanhove, N. (2022). The Economics of Tourism Destinations – Theory and Practice (4th ed.). Routledge.

Vuković, P, (2017). Character and dynamics of development rural tourism in the Republic of Serbia. *Ekonomika/Economics, 63*(4), 53 – 60.

Vuković, P. (2019). *Competitiveness of rural tourist destinations in area of the Lower Danube region in the Republic of Serbia. Institute of Agricultural Economics.* Serbia.

Vuković, P., & Kljajić, N. (2013). Education and training employees and local residents as presumption to develop rural tourism. In *International Scientific Conference Sustainable Agriculture and Rural Development in Terms of the Republic of Serbia Strategic Goals Realization within the Danube Region: Achieving Regional Competitiveness*. Institute of Agricultural Economics.

Vuković, P., Kljajić, N., & Roljević, S. (2009). Strategic determinations of tourism development in the process of transition in the Republic of Serbia. *Ekonomika/Economic, 3-4*, 168–177.

Vuković, P., Kljajić, N., & Sredojević, Z. (2022). The future of development rural tourism in the Republic of Serbia. Agro*ekonomika/Agroeconomic, 63*(4).

Zdorov, A. B. (2009). Comprehensive Development of Tourism in the Countryside. Studies on Russian Economic Development, 20(4), 453–455.

Zengeni, T. (2015). *The Competitiveness and performance of the Zimbabwe poultry industry* [MA dissertation]. University of the Witwatersrand.

Chapter 9
Short Food Supply Chains for Achieving Sustainable Growth in Central and Eastern European Countries

Vesna Paraušić
 https://orcid.org/0000-0001-6193-5297
Institute of Agricultural Economics, Belgrade, Serbia

Vlado Kovačević
Institute of Agricultural Economics, Belgrade, Serbia

ABSTRACT

Traditional types of short food supply chains have represented a significant part of food systems in most Central and Eastern European countries for centuries. In these countries, direct sales are the result of the dominance of small-scale family farms with subsistence and semi-subsistence farming, and their insufficient market integration in global food supply chains. The literature highlights that "short supply circuits" have undeniably contributed to reaching the sustainable growth of local communities and securing sustainable income of farmers. However, the authors' clear and critical opinion is that the positive contribution of short food supply chains to sustainable growth should not be generalised or excessively glorified. This attitude relies on the fact that the contribution of short food supply chains to all sustainability dimensions is determined by numerous factors and assumptions, and that the combination of different marketing channels is frequently required to maximise their total contribution to sustainable growth.

DOI: 10.4018/978-1-6684-8810-2.ch009

INTRODUCTION

Short food supply chains (abbr. SFSCs) or *"short supply circuits"* have long been constituents of the concepts of sustainability, rural development, diversification of rural economy and value-added agriculture in many European countries (Marsden, Banks & Bristow, 2000; Van der Ploeg et al., 2000; Renting, Marsden & Banks, 2003; EU, 2013; Kneafsey et al., 2013). In all countries of the world their importance is growing with the rise of consumers' awareness of and concern about the environmental, social, ethical, and health issues related to the food that is produced and consumed.

These supply chains are an alternative or a response to global food systems and long conventional supply chains (mostly led by supermarkets and hypermarkets, as well as by large traders and buyers of agricultural products). Small-scale farmers often have low bargaining power and an inferior position in long chains, while consumers have insufficient or inexistent knowledge about the product's manufacturer, origin or production method (Renting, Marsden & Banks, 2003; Kneafsey, et al., 2013; Augère-Granier, 2016; Gneiting & Sonenshine, 2018; Djordjević Milošević et al., 2021).

SFSCs are characterised by the decreased physical distance and social and cultural distance between farmers and direct food consumers, i.e. by the minimised number of intermediaries in food trade (Marsden, Banks & Bristow, 2000; Galli & Brunori, 2013; Kneafsey et al., 2013; UNIDO, 2020). The focus is not placed on the geographical distance between farmers and consumers, but rather on connection, closeness, trust, exchange of information about the product and its production method, as well as elimination or reduction of the number of intermediaries (Marsden, Banks & Bristow, 2000; Galli & Brunori, 2013; Kneafsey et al., 2013).

The European Commission (abbr. EC) supports shorter supply chains and local markets in order to: (a) strengthen small-scale farmers' position and their integration in food supply and value chains, (b) encourage farmers' sustainable income and competitiveness; (c) contribute to the realization of environmental goals; and (d) build fair, strong and resilient food systems in all member countries (EU, 2013; EC, 2020; EU, 2021).

Direct farmer-consumer sales of agricultural products are traditionally and widely represented in food systems in all Central and Eastern European countries (abbr. CEECs). This concept is gradually being acknowledged in literature, i.e. in the papers that underline their contribution to the economic empowerment of farmers and sustainable rural development (Goszczyński & Knieć, 2011; Borychowski et al., 2020; FAO, 2020; Brumă et al., 2021; Djordjević Milošević et al., 2021).

Shortening of supply chains is beneficial for all farmers, although it is mainly regarded as a solution for securing sustainable income of small-scale and medium-scale farmers (Marsden, Banks & Bristow, 2000; Kneafsey et al., 2013; Djordjević

Milošević et al., 2021). These farmers are the most prevalent in the agriculture of the European Union (abbr. EU), particularly in CEECs and Western Balkan countries (abbr. WBCs). In these group of countries, they have a key role in food systems and supply chains (Kotevska et al., 2015; Gneiting & Sonenshine, 2018; Guiomar et al., 2018; Hanf & Gagalyuk, 2018; Borychowski et al., 2020; FAO, 2020; Djordjević Milošević et al., 2021; Šūmane et al., 2021). Therefore, the promotion and institutional development of the SFSC concept is exceptionally significant for the sustainable rural development of all CEECs, for strengthening the competitiveness of small and medium-scale family farms and integrating them more efficiently in the market.

In this chapter, the authors focus on analysing the factors which determine the "traditional" prevalence of "traditional" types of SFSCs in almost all CEECs. In addition, they offer a thorough literature review confirming the positive contribution of these supply chains to sustainable growth dimensions, as well as a critical analysis which questions their glorification and contribution to sustainability (in all dimensions and at all levels of analysis).

DEFINITION AND TYPES OF SHORT FOOD SUPPLY CHAINS

Supply chains are identified as distribution channels and defined throughout the literature as a "set of three or more entities (organizations or individuals) directly involved in the upstream and downstream flows of products, services, finances, and/or information from a source to a customer" (Mentzer et al., 2001, p. 4). They regulate the framework for performing several important activities during the product flow from producers to end users, such as "physical flow and product ownership flow, payment flow, information flow, product promotion flow, and other" (Kovačević & Jeločnik, 2022, p. 169).

SFSCs are part of the supply chain concept and they represent one of dimensions which are opposed to long, global, commercial or conventional supply chains. According to Marsden, Banks & Bristow (2000) and Renting, Marsden & Banks (2003), in order to define SFSCs, there needs to be a specific relationship between food producers and consumers based on their direct contact (close relations), mutual trust and provision of information regarding food (its origin, quality, safety) to consumers by producers. This is further manifested through the possibility of creating a new, higher value of products and price premiums if the information and products are considered significant and valuable by consumers (Marsden, Banks & Bristow, 2000; Renting, Marsden & Banks, 2003).

All SFSCs rely on the same principles which assume the following: "i) the distance between producer and consumer (proximity) should be as short as possible; ii) the number of intermediaries involved in the supply chain should be as few as possible,

Table 1. Types of SFSCs and marketing channels by types

Types of SFSCs	SFSCs' Initiatives/Marketing Channels
Direct on-farm and off-farm sales (direct transaction between farmers and consumers)	On-farm selling: shops owned by farmers; On-farm selling through a selling scheme, such as: (a) *"Pick Your Own"*; (b) *"Grow Your Own"*; (c) *Farm-based hospitality* or (d) simple selling of products to individual consumers; Farmers' (green) markets (off-farm sales); Basket (box) schemes: farm direct deliveries or home deliveries (sales at a distance). For example, a veg box for consumers in urban and peri-urban areas; Roadside selling; Selling at local food festivals or fairs (off-farm sales); Selling to small retail outlets, with the maximum of one intermediary; Online (Internet) sales;
Collective direct sales (farmers' cooperation in selling local products)	Sales through farmers' owned shops (retail outlets) or in local outlets (local retail facilities with the maximum of one intermediary); Sales through farmers' and/or consumers' cooperatives; Direct sales to public institutions through public procurement. For example, participation of producer organisations in public (collective) procurement: supplying schools, hospitals, etc.;
Partnerships between local farmers and consumers	*"Community Supported Agriculture"*: partners are bound by a written agreement; consumers cover a proportional share of agricultural production costs, while in return they obtain a regularly arranged or agreed quantity of agricultural products; Various social movements for promoting local food and its sustainability mainly organised and supported by urban population.

Source: The authors' presentation based on: EU, 2012; Kneafsey et al., 2013; Galli & Brunori, 2013; Augère-Granier, 2016; Malak-Rawlikowska et al., 2019; UNIDO, 2020.

and; iii) understanding and communication between the producer and consumer should also be promoted as much as possible since recognising the 'story' behind the product adds value to the consumers' purchase, and develops a long-term loyalty to and relationship with the products" (EU, 2012, p. 5).

According to the EU's common agricultural policy (abbr. CAP), these marketing channels involve "a limited number of economic operators, committed to co-operation, local economic development, and close geographical and social relations between producers, processors and consumers" (EU, 2013, p. 499). The Commission Delegated Regulation makes precise that "support for the establishment and development of short supply chains, as referred to in Article 35(2)(d) of Regulation (EU) No 1305/2013 shall cover only supply chains involving no more than one intermediary between farmer and consumer" (EC, 2014, p. 9).

In practice, there are a large number of different SFSC types involving different methods of product marketing and different relationships between farmers and consumers. However, they all tend to connect the places of food production and food consumption, i.e. food producers and direct users, by means of geographical, economic and social relations (UNIDO, 2020). Basically, marketing channels within SFSCs differ significantly between countries (according to the sociohistorical and economic heritage of the country). They depend on the type of traded products and nature of production, as well as on farmers' economic and social characteristics, consumers' habits and numerous other factors (Galli & Brunori, 2013; Kneafsey et al., 2013). For the needs of this chapter, the authors have classified SFSCs into three broad groups based on the review of comprehensive literature (Table 1).

The literature includes an approach that classifies SFSCs into two categories - traditional and neo-traditional (Augère-Granier, 2016). The first group mainly involves direct on-farm and off-farm sales (direct transaction between farmers and consumers). The main links in these supply chains are small-scale family farms (Table 1). This category is traditionally widely represented in food supply chains of most CEECs and almost all Mediterranean countries (Gordon, Salvioni & Hubbard, 2014; Augère-Granier, 2016; Borowska, 2016; FAO, 2020; Djordjević Milošević et al., 2021). The second category, i.e. neo-traditional SFSCs, encompasses more modern, complex and innovative approaches to local food, which do not compromise food quality, sustainability and application of environmental and traditional agricultural practices (Augère-Granier, 2016). This category might involve *"community supported agriculture"* as a collectively owned food system led and supported by a network of farmers, consumers and local institutions, as well as various social movements, mainly in cities promoting local food and alike (Sylla, Olszewska & Świąder, 2017; Augère-Granier, 2016).

SHORT FOOD SUPPLY CHAINS IN CEECs

Academic and professional circles, as well as, the general public in CEECs are not familiar with the notions of SFSCs or *"short supply chain circuits"*. Nevertheless, traditional types of these supply chains have been significantly represented in food systems of most CEECs for centuries and they have had an undeniable contribution to reaching the sustainable growth of local communities and to securing farmers' sustainable income (Gorton, Salvioni & Hubbard, 2014; Borowska, 2016; Malak-Rawlikowska et al., 2019; Pilař et al., 2019; FAO, 2020; Brumă et al., 2021; Djordjević Milošević et al., 2021).

For instance, in Romania there is a growing market of dairy products distributed directly from producers. Consumers are becoming increasingly aware of the health benefits of fresh and high-quality food and they demand innovative and modernised development of SFSCs through digitalisation (Brumă et al., 2021). Also, Hungarian consumers believe that SFSCs *"could help the livelihood of farmers"* (Gorton, Salvioni & Hubbard, 2014, p. 16).

Traditional food products are one of the typical products placed through SFSCs. A group of authors (Balogh et al., 2016) conducted a study on the willingness of consumers to pay the price premium for a Hungarian traditional food product (*"Hungarian mangalitza salami"*). They showed that, among other factors (retail price, quality certification, origin or type of the raw material – meat), the appropriate selection of retail channels significantly affected consumers' decision to buy this product and pay the price premium for it. The authors stated that marketing this product through butchers' offer and farmers' markets secured a higher selling price and greater farmers' share than its marketing through hyper- and supermarkets. They also found that a larger number of intermediaries provided opportunities for greater sales but lower price premiums (Balogh et al., 2016).

In addition, products which can be successfully marketed through SFSCs involve those within various quality schemes. Borowska (2016) conducted a study on producers of different types of regional honey with the geographical indication in Poland and highlighted the significance of direct sales and outdoor markets for the efficient marketing of these products. WBCs are still not sufficiently successful in protecting and marketing products within geographical indication schemes, although they have favourable agro-environmental conditions for producing these products and a reputation for producing traditional products (Kovačević et al., 2022). The production of these products in WBCs might improve if the legal framework is additionally adapted to the EU and a stimulating environment for producers is created (Kovačević et al., 2022).

It is common to sell agricultural products at farmers' markets in WBCs (which belong to CEECs). Roadside sales are very frequent in some countries, particularly when it comes to non-wood forest products (Zivkov, 2013; Barjolle et al., 2015; FAO, 2020; Djordjević Milošević et al., 2021). Forms of collective direct sales are underdeveloped, since farmers are disunited and lack horizontal and vertical arrangements and contractual relationships (Zivkov, 2013; FAO, 2020; Djordjević Milošević et al., 2021).

Neo-traditional SFSC types are mainly present in high income EU countries. However, the example of Poland shows that groups within *"community supported agriculture"* are also growing fast in CEECs (Sylla, Olszewska & Świąder, 2017). Namely, as in highly developed EU countries, these groups in Poland are characterised by the following elements: they are active in large cities; and consumers pay farmers in advance (at the beginning of vegetation) for the production and delivery of high-quality, fresh and/or organic food (Sylla, Olszewska & Świąder, 2017; Kovačević & Jeločnik, 2022).

In economically developed EU countries, SFSCs and local markets are part of value-added agriculture, which secures farmers with a greater share in the food value chain and consequently leads to higher farm income (EU, 2013). On the other hand, the presence of direct sales (on-farm and off-farm selling) in CEECs is a result of completely different factors, the most significant being the following:

1. Dominance of small-scale family farms with subsistence and semi-subsistence farming and their insufficient integration in commercial or global food supply chains (Gorton, Salvioni & Hubbard, 2014; Kotevska et al., 2015; Malak-Rawlikowska et al., 2019; FAO, 2020; Djordjević Milošević et al., 2021). Due to having small production volume (lack of the effect of economies of scale) and low productivity (Key, 2019; Čechura, Kroupová & Lekešová, 2022), and due to not applying food safety and quality assurance standards, a large number of small-scale farmers, particularly in WBCs, trade in (semi) informal channels of direct selling and do not manage to ensure sustainable farm income (Gorton, Salvioni & Hubbard, 2014; Kotevska et al., 2015; FAO, 2020; Djordjević Milošević et al., 2021);
2. Farmers' associations, vertical coordination and unions of interest of market participants, cluster associations, cooperatives, production contracting, organised buying up, collective sales, strong local initiatives – all represent the missing links in the food systems of most CEECs and almost all WBCs (Zivkov, 2013; Kotevska et al., 2015; Paraušić, Domazet & Simeunović, 2017; Paraušić & Domazet, 2018; Zakić, Nikolić & Kovačević, 2018; Paraušić, Kostić & Subić, 2023; FAO, 2020; Djordjević Milošević et al., 2021). As a result, farmers, particularly small-scale ones, take part in traditional SFSC types, and frequently face high transaction costs of production and marketing. This consequently results in low productivity and high risks (FAO, 2020);
3. Existence of consumers' traditional preferences for buying domestic food and food of local origin at farmers' markets, built trust between consumers and small food producers, and an increasing consumer interest in healthy products obtained in sustainable production systems (Pilař et al., 2019; Hanus, 2020; Brumă et al., 2021; Haas et al., 2021; Djordjević Milošević et al., 2021);
4. A long-standing tradition of small-scale farmers selling their products at open markets, with higher margins than in other sales channels (Zivkov, 2013; Gorton, Salvioni & Hubbard, 2014; FAO, 2020).

ROLE OF SFSCs IN SUSTAINABLE GROWTH IN CEECs

Numerous studies highlight the positive contribution of SFSCs and the related concept of local food to rural development and to economic, environmental and social dimensions of sustainability. This contribution is present both at the level of the involved agricultural producers (farm level) and consumers, as well as at

Table 2. SFSCs' contribution to sustainable growth: literature review

Sustainability Dimensions	Role of SFSCs
Economic	Integrating small-scale farmers in local food markets; Higher bargaining power of farmers in comparison to long supply chains; Improving farmers' position in the income distribution through supply and value chains; Higher farmgate prices than in long supply chains, as a result of consumers' willingness to pay price premiums for local products distributed through SFSCs; Higher farm revenue and income than in long supply chains; Stable and sustainable farm income; Decreasing farmers' exposure to price fluctuations; Strengthening the value-added agriculture concept; Developing the local food market; Diversification of activities and income on agricultural holdings; Diversification of marketing channels and greater resilience of food systems; Supporting the development of family agriculture and strengthening of rural economy; Supporting the survival and development of family farms with small production and processing capacities; Creating conditions for additional employment in local rural communities; Stimulating local rural development by means of the bottom-up approach;

Sustainability dimensions	Role of SFSCs
Social	Social cohesion in local communities; Promoting the farmer-consumer relationship based on closeness, trust, honesty, understanding, solidarity and mutual values; Strengthening social capital and sense of community; Promoting the local identity of rural areas; Social recognition of local food producers: they are acknowledged and respected by consumers and local community; Fair trade and equality between the actors in the supply chain; Consumer benefit is realised by the availability of high-quality and fresh food to low-income consumers, since the food placed through SFSCs is cheaper than organic food;
Environmental	Promoting sustainable production systems by applying extensive production methods (production without pesticides, less intensive farming); Promoting the production and consumption of healthy, fresh, seasonal and high-quality food which is safe and traceable; Short product transport distances resulting in energy savings and reducing greenhouse gas emissions; Activating the peri-urban agricultural land; Protecting local agrobiodiversity; Using local natural resources more efficiently; Lowering food waste;

the level of local communities, regions and countries regardless of their economic development level. Therefore, it was not necessary to consider this segment of the analysis exclusively for the CEEC group.

In this section, the authors analyse the contribution of SFSCs to all three dimensions of sustainable growth: the economic, social and environmental dimension (Table 2). The authors analyse comprehensive literature which undeniably indicates that these supply chains satisfy the sustainable growth aims of the United Nations defined in *"2030 Agenda for Sustainable growth"* (United Nations, 2015). Thus, their promotion should stimulate local food producers and consumers to participate in various SFSCs' initiatives.

The authors' presentation based on: Goszczyński & Knieć, 2011; Galli & Brunori, 2013; Kneafsey et al., 2013; Feldmann & Hamm, 2015; Augère-Granier, 2016; Kiss, Ruszkai & Takács-György, 2019; Malak-Rawlikowska et al, 2019; Zhang, Qing, & Yu, 2019; Borychowski et al., 2020; Jarzębowski, Bourlakis & Bezat-Jarzębowska, 2020; UNIDO, 2020; Stein & Santini, 2021; Bui et al., 2021; Djordjević Milošević, et al, 2021.

The results presented in Table 2 should be interpreted having in mind the fact that the positive contribution of SFSCs should not be generalised. This contribution is defined by numerous factors and assumptions (heterogeneity of producers, products, different locations and organisational forms of SFSCs), while a combination of different marketing channels is frequently required to maximise the total contribution of SFSCs to sustainable growth (Ilbery & Maye, 2005; Galli & Brunori, 2013; Kiss, Ruszkai & Takács-György, 2019; Vittersø et al., 2019; Chiffoleau & Dourian, 2020; Stein & Santini, 2021).

Furthermore, numerous sustainability indicators are still not measurable (Brunori et al., 2016), particularly in WBCs (Radukić, Petrović-Ranđelović & Kostić, 2019), and many studies examine the SFSC sustainability only to a certain degree. Therefore, one should be very cautious when giving advantage to short over long distribution channels. This is particularly important when making conclusions and business decisions.

CAUTION IN GLORIFYING SFSCs

Numerous authors are cautious when interpreting different aspects of sustainability of SFSCs and related local food systems. They do not glorify them, and they do not define them as a priori good, fair and sustainable practices. Stein & Santini (2021) indicate that local food markets and marketing through SFSCs cannot be easily and simply equalised with the sustainable growth principles (bearing in mind that sustainability is defined by numerous factors). It is only possible to estimate their contribution to sustainability for each case separately.

The authors agree only on the position that the SFSCs' contribution to sustainable growth is evident in the social dimension of sustainability (Kiss, Ruszkai & Takács-György, 2019; Vittersø et al., 2019; Chiffoleau & Dourian, 2020; Stein & Santini, 2021). The SFSCs' contribution to the economic and environmental dimension of sustainable development is debatable, particularly in the following analysis contexts:

- Comparison with long, global and commercialised supply chains, which are rationally and efficiently organised;
- Comparison of small and medium-scale farmers' production (with high production costs due to the lack of effects of economies of scale) with the large-scale farmers with intensive farming methods;
- Consumers' willingness to buy and pay price premiums for local products distributed directly by producers.

The following text provides the arguments of a number of authors expressing doubts or stating decisively that SFSCs do not contribute to the sustainable growth aims in the economic and environmental dimension.

I Questionable contribution of SFSCs to the economic dimension of sustainable growth:
- Producers involved in SFSCs are mainly small and medium-scale farmers who do not achieve the advantages of economies of scale (Augère-Granier, 2016; Bayir et al., 2022). They have limited productive, financial, marketing and logistic capacities and skills. Along with the lack of workforce and underdeveloped rural infrastructure, this frequently causes inefficient and expensive distribution of products (Kneafsey et al., 2013; Augère-Granier, 2016; Bayir et al., 2022).
- The prerequisites of economic sustainability are strong farmers' competences for participating in direct sales, such as: free time for marketing and travel, skills required for preserving communication with buyers, available workforce on the holding, developed logistic services and infrastructure, and alike (Gorton, Salvioni & Hubbard, 2014; Jarzębowski, Bourlakis & Bezat-Jarzębowska, 2020; Rucabado-Palomar & Cuéllar-Padilla, 2020; Bayir et al., 2022). According to the report of UNIDO (2020), economic sustainability of SFSCs is significantly higher for producers whose farms are located in the vicinity of cities and/or tourist destinations, for farmers having the required competences and skills, for those who have sufficient family workforce and possibilities of investing in the equipment for processing, transport and selling;
- A study conducted by a group of authors Kneafsey et al. (2013) showed that consumers did not always know how to reach local producers, and they did not have sufficient time or transportation means to reach the sales points, particularly if they were based on farms.
- A significant factor determining the contribution of SFSCs to the economic dimension of sustainability is the fact that the price represents the key determinant for most buyers when purchasing food. Other

significant determinants are the benefits and product range offered by supermarkets (Weatherell et al., 2003; Gorton, Salvioni & Hubbard, 2014; Jarzębowski, Bourlakis & Bezat-Jarzębowska, 2020);
- The stereotype of the SFSC economic sustainability is additionally shattered by the fact that a large number of agricultural producers simultaneously participate in both long and short supply chains (Malak-Rawlikowska et al., 2019; Stein & Santini, 2021), and that in practice the differences between these channels are minor and not striking (Ilbery & Maye, 2005). For example, Malak-Rawlikowska et al. (2019) states that a number of farmers believe that hypermarket chains are their reliable and trustworthy business partners that offer a possibility of purchasing large quantities of products at accessible prices and that pay at a regular basis.

II Questionable contribution of SFSCs to the environmental dimension of sustainable growth:
- Studies show that transport distance is an indicator of the environmental impact which is not sufficient for estimating the ecological feasibility of short supply chains. Transportation can be even less environmentally efficient in SFSCs due to possible deconcentration (lack of economies of scale in transportation), i.e. a large number of small orders, travelling longer distances for supplying individual buyers, etc. (Kiss, Ruszkai & Takács-György; 2019; Majewski et al., 2020; Stein & Santini, 2021). On average, long food supply chains can generate fewer negative impacts on the environment in comparison to short chains (in terms of consumption of fossil fuel energy, pollution and greenhouse gas emissions) per kg of a given product (Majewski et al., 2020);
- Authors increasingly believe that the environmental sustainability of SFSCs is much more dependent on the manner of land use, production efficiency, supply chain infrastructure, and not only on the geographical distance between producers and consumers (Majewski et al., 2020; Stein & Santini, 2021);
- The UNIDO report (2020) also states that in terms of environmental sustainability, SFSCs are not more acceptable than conventional supply chains. It also underlines that it is important to consider the effects of methods of production, packing, distribution or waste in each supply chain. Basically, if producers do not use extensive production methods or if their system of production and/or distribution is not focused on environmental sustainability, SFSCs will not contribute to the sustainability of this dimension (Kiss, Ruszkai & Takács-György, 2019; UNIDO, 2020).

When it comes to CEECs, the following factors additionally strengthen doubts regarding the SFSCs' contribution to the sustainable growth dimensions:

- The initial assumptions which direct ("push") small-scale farmers into SFSCs. This involves the first two factors determining the representation of direct sales in CEECs presented in the section "Short food supply chains in CEECs";
- In these countries, the complete business environment in which farmers work does not acknowledge SFSCs on a "healthy" or high-quality basis. The business environment is characterised by the unstable agricultural market, increased land fragmentation, low technical efficiency of agriculture and productivity, particularly on small-scale farms, as well as by the limited access to the financial market, workforce and agricultural product market (Kotevska et al., 2015; Ciaian et al., 2018; FAO, 2020; Horvat et al., 2020; Djordjević Milošević et al., 2021; Čechura, Kroupová & Lekešová, 2022);
- The market of products placed through direct marketing channels in WBCs is still not institutionally arranged to a sufficient degree. It fails to be mature and subject to sales tax. In addition, sales through (semi)informal channels should be reduced (FAO, 2020; Brumă, et al., 2021; Djordjević Milošević et al., 2021). Furthermore, WBCs do not have a sufficiently developed institutional framework related to the safety and quality of locally produced food. Therefore, it must be strengthened in the future period following the best methods from the EU countries (Haas et al., 2021);
- There is a strong motivation for the consumption of traditional food marketed mainly through SFSCs. However, a study on the consumers' perceptions and habits regarding this food in WBCs showed that there were several obstacles to a higher consumption of these products, and thus indirectly to the acknowledgement of direct sales (Barjolle et al., 2015). These factors are primarily: product price (low and medium-income consumers in WBCs are very price sensitive), product availability, uncertainty regarding the correct production method or product character, etc. (Barjolle et al., 2015);
- Group of authors Gorton, Salvioni & Hubbard (2014) underlined some of the difficulties of applying direct marketing in Hungary. They believed that similar problems were also present in Romania. Namely, less than one half of the respondents in the Hungarian sample responded that they were willing to pay the price premium for local products and consequently improve local farmers' life (Gorton, Salvioni & Hubbard, 2014). An additional problem was perceived in the low purchasing power of consumers, i.e. low market potential, reflected in a small number of strong consumers interested in buying local products (Gorton, Salvioni & Hubbard, 2014). Also, there is

often a discrepancy between farmers in need of assistance (when marketing their products by premium pricing), who are mainly situated in remote rural areas, and market potential. This is confirmed by the fact that *"the most successful farmers' markets, in terms of raising sale prices, have been in Budapest, amongst middle-class 'concerned consumers"* (Gorton, Salvioni & Hubbard, 2014, p. 16).

CONCLUSION AND RECOMMENDATIONS

This chapter presents the basic elements of the concept and typology of short food supply chains, as well as their development and representation in CEECs. It was concluded that traditional types of these supply chains has existed as a significant part of food systems in most CEECs for centuries.

In economically developed EU countries, SFSCs and local markets are part of value-added agriculture. In contrast, in most CEECs the existence of direct sales (on-farm or off-farm selling) is the result of completely different factors, the most significant being: (a) dominance of small-scale family farms with subsistence and semi-subsistence farming; (b) a low level of market integration of small and medium-scale family farms in commercial or global food supply chains, which makes them trade frequently in (semi)informal channels of direct selling; (c) associations of farmers, vertical coordination and unions of interest of market participants, cluster associations, and cooperatives representing the missing links of food systems in most CEECs and almost all WBCs, (d) existence of traditional consumers' preferences for buying domestic food and food of local origin at farmers' markets, built trust between consumers and small food producers, and an increasing consumer interest in healthy products obtained in sustainable production systems, and (i) a long-standing tradition of small-scale farmers selling their products at open markets, with higher margins compared to other types of sales.

The literature highlights that SFSCs have undeniably contributed to reaching the sustainable growth of local communities and securing the sustainable income of farmers in CEECs. This contribution is additionally emphasized having in mind the developmental problems of small and medium-scale farms (Gneiting & Sonenshine, 2018; Key, 2019; FAO, 2020; Čechura, Kroupová & Lekešová, 2022) and general underdevelopment of rural areas characterised by unfavourable demographic transitions, underdeveloped social and physical infrastructure and similar limitations (Kotevska et al., 2015; EC, 2021; EU, 2021).

However, the comprehensive analysis showed that the contribution of these distribution channels to sustainability dimensions (particularly the economic and environmental one) is often questionable, having in mind the following: (1) comparison with long, global or commercialised supply chains, (2) comparison of the low production volume of small and medium-scale farmers (with higher production risks due to the lack of effects of economies of scale) with large production volume and intensive farming methods applied on large farms, and (3) consumers' willingness to buy through these supply channels and pay price premiums for local products.

These doubts are even greater in CEECs, bearing in mind the factors initiating the centuries-long existence of direct trade in these countries, lack of institutional framework (which would conduct the development of direct trade in compliance with the law, quality standards and food safety), as well as the inexistence of efficient public policies adjusted to small-scale farmers' needs.

The authors believe that the positive contribution of SFSCs to sustainable growth should not be generalised and that these supply channels should not be excessively glorified. This attitude relies on the fact that the contribution of SFSCs is determined by numerous factors and assumptions, and that the combination of different marketing channels is frequently required to maximise their total contribution to sustainable growth.

Finally, it should be underlined that if SFSCs are developed on a "healthy basis" (fair exchange, social inclusion, environmental protection), they can definitely contribute to all dimensions of sustainable growth in CEECs. The conditions for creating stable and high-quality "pillars" of development of these supply channels involve: (a) constant science – policy interface and development of public policies supporting small farm productivity; in this manner they would become more profitable and economically sustainable, which would consequently slow down the consolidation rate and abandoning of farming in these countries; b) increasing production volume and market integration of small-scale famers, while strengthening consumers' environmental awareness based on the principles of healthy nutrition, environmental protection and supporting local communities and food producers; (c) encouraging small-scale farmers to participate in SFSCs in WBCs according to the aims of the EU's CAP, by means of traditional support measures and/or the EU instrument for pre-accession assistance for rural development. In addition, we would like to emphasize the agreement with the opinion of the group of authors related to the future development of SFSCs in all countries that reads *"from the farming point of view, if younger generations are not engaged, valuable knowledge, skills and heritage could be lost"* (Kneafsey et al., 2013, p. 113).

FUNDING ACKNOWLEDGMENT STATEMENT

This chapter was financially supported by the Ministry of Science, Technological Development and Innovation of the Republic of Serbia, Contract No. 451-03-47/2023-01//200009 dated February 3rd, 2023.

REFERENCES

Augère-Granier, M.-L. (2016). *Short food supply chains and local food systems in the EU*. Briefing – September 2016, European Parliamentary Research Service. Retrieved from https://www.europarl.europa.eu/RegData/etudes/BRIE/2016/586650/EPRS_BRI(2016)586650_EN.pdf

Balogh, P., Békési, D., Gorton, M., Popp, J., & Lengyel, P. (2016). Consumer willingness to pay for traditional food products. *Food Policy, 61*, 176–184. doi:10.1016/j.foodpol.2016.03.005

Barjolle, D., Brecic, R., Cerjak, M., & Giraud, G. (2015). Traditional Food in Western Balkan Countries Consumers' Perceptions and Habits. *Intellectual Property Rights for Geographical Indications: What is at Stake in the TTIP?*, 3-15.

Bayir, B., Charles, A., Sekhari, A., & Ouzrout, Y. (2022). Issues and Challenges in Short Food Supply Chains: A Systematic Literature Review. *Sustainability (Basel), 14*(5), 3029. doi:10.3390u14053029

Borowska, A. (2016). The role of outdoor markets in the food supply chain of regional food in Poland. *Handel Wewnętrzny, 362*(3), 50-62. https://www.ceeol.com/search/journal-detail?id=1801

Borychowski, M., Stępień, S., Polcyn, J., Tošović-Stevanović, A., Ćalović, D., Lalić, G., & Žuža, M. (2020). Socio-economic determinants of small family farms' resilience in selected Central and Eastern European countries. *Sustainability (Basel), 12*(24), 10362. doi:10.3390u122410362

Brumă, I. S., Vasiliu, C. D., Rodino, S., Butu, M., Tanasă, L., Doboş, S., Butu, A., Coca, O., & Stefan, G. (2021). The behavior of dairy consumers in short food supply chains during COVID-19 pandemic in Suceava area, Romania. *Sustainability (Basel), 13*(6), 3072. doi:10.3390u13063072

Brunori, G., Galli, F., Barjolle, D., Van Broekhuizen, R., Colombo, L., Giampietro, M., Kirwan, J., Lang, T., Mathijs, E., Maye, D., de Roest, K., Rougoor, C., Schwarz, J., Schmitt, E., Smith, J., Stojanovic, Z., Tisenkopfs, T., & Touzard, J. M. (2016). Are local food chains more sustainable than global food chains? Considerations for assessment. *Sustainability (Basel)*, *8*(5), 449. doi:10.3390u8050449

Bui, T. N., Nguyen, A. H., Le, T. T. H., Nguyen, V. P., Le, T. T. H., Tran, T. T. H., Nguyen, N. M., Le, T. K. O., Nguyen, T. K. O., Nguyen, T. T. T., Dao, H. V., Doan, T. N. T., Vu, T. H. N., Bui, V. H., Hoa, H. C., & Lebailly, P. (2021). Can a Short Food Supply Chain Create Sustainable Benefits for Small Farmers in Developing Countries? An Exploratory Study of Vietnam. *Sustainability (Basel)*, *13*(5), 2443. doi:10.3390u13052443

Čechura, L., Kroupová, Z. Ž., & Lekešová, M. (2022). Productivity and efficiency in Czech agriculture: Does farm size matter? *Zemedelská Ekonomika*, *68*(1), 1–10. doi:10.17221/384/2021-AGRICECON

Chiffoleau, Y., & Dourian, T. (2020). Sustainable food supply chains: Is shortening the answer? A literature review for a research and innovation agenda. *Sustainability (Basel)*, *12*(23), 9831. doi:10.3390u12239831

Ciaian, P., Guri, F., Rajcaniova, M., Drabik, D., & Paloma, S. G. (2018). Land fragmentation and production diversification: A case study from rural Albania. *Land Use Policy*, *76*, 589–599. doi:10.1016/j.landusepol.2018.02.039

Djordjević Milošević, S., Möllers, J., Marcantonio, F., & Di., & Ciaian, P. (2021). *The best practices and potential of smallholders' participation in short value chains in the Western Balkans and Turkey* (No. JRC125555). JRC Technical Report. Luxembourg. *Publications Office of the European Union*. Advance online publication. doi:10.2760/921512

EC. (2014). Commission delegated regulation (EU) No 807/2014 of 11 March 2014 supplementing Regulation (EU) No 1305/2013 of the European Parliament and of the Council on support for rural development by the European Agricultural Fund for Rural Development (EAFRD) and introducing transitional provisions. *Official Journal of the European Union, L, 227*. https://eur-lex.europa.eu/legal-content/en/ALL/?uri=CELEX:32014R0807

EC. (2020). *A Farm to Fork Strategy for a fair, healthy and environmentally-friendly food system*. Brussels, 20.05.2020. COM(2020) 381 final. Retrieved from https://food.ec.europa.eu/system/files/2020-05/f2f_action-plan_2020_strategy-info_en.pdf

EC. (2021). *A long-term Vision for the EU's Rural Areas – Towards stronger, connected, resilient and prosperous rural areas by 2040.* Brussels, 30.6.2021. COM(2021) 345 final. Retrieved from https://eur-lex.europa.eu/legal-content/EN/TXT/DOC/?uri=CELEX:52021DC0345

EU. (2012). *Local Food and Short Supply Chains.* EU Rural Review. No 12, Summer 2012. Retrieved from https://enrd.ec.europa.eu/sites/default/files/E8F24E08-0A45-F272-33FB-A6309E3AD601.pdf

EU. (2013). Regulation (EU) No 1305/2013 of the European Parliament and of the Council of 17 December 2013 on support for rural development by the European Agricultural Fund for Rural Development (EAFRD) and repealing Council Regulation (EC) No 1698/2005. *Official Journal of the European Union, L, 347.* https://eur-lex.europa.eu/legal-content/EN/TXT/PDF/?uri=CELEX:32013R1305

EU. (2021, December). Regulation (EU) 2021/2115 of the European Parliament and of the Council of 2 December 2021establishing rules on support for strategic plans to be drawn up by Member States under the common agricultural policy (CAP Strategic Plans) and financed by the European Agricultural Guarantee Fund (EAGF) and by the European Agricultural Fund for Rural Development (EAFRD) and repealing Regulations (EU) No 1305/2013 and (EU) No 1307/2013. *Official Journal of the European Union, L, 435*, 6. https://eur-lex.europa.eu/legal-content/EN/TXT/?uri=CELEX%3A32021R2115

FAO. (2020). *Empowering Smallholders and Family Farms in Europe and Central Asia. Regional Synthesis Report 2019 based on country studies in eight countries in Europe and Central and Asia.* Food and Agriculture Organization of the United Nations., doi:10.4060/ca9586en

Feldmann, C., & Hamm, U. (2015). Consumers' perceptions and preferences for local food: A review. *Food Quality and Preference, 40,* 152–164. doi:10.1016/j.foodqual.2014.09.014

Galli, F., & Brunori, G. (Eds.). (2013). *Short Food Supply Chains as drivers of sustainable development.* Document developed in the framework of the FP7 project FOODLINKS (GA No. 265287). Laboratorio di studi rurali Sismondi. Retrieved from https://www.foodlinkscommunity.net/fileadmin/documents_organicresearch/foodlinks/CoPs/evidence-document-sfsc-cop.pdf

Gneiting, U., & Sonenshine, J. (2018). A living income for small-scale farmers: tackling unequal risks and market power. *Oxfam Discussion Papers,* 1–24. Retrieved from https://oxfamilibrary.openrepository.com/bitstream/handle/10546/620596/dp-living-income-smallscale-farmers-151118-en.pdf

Gorton, M., Salvioni, C., & Hubbard, C. (2014). Semi-subsistence farms and alternative food supply chains. *EuroChoices (Uckfield)*, *13*(1), 15–19. doi:10.1111/1746-692X.12045

Goszczyński, W., & Knieć, W. (2011). Strengthening alternative agro-food networks in the Eastern European Countryside. *Eastern European Countryside*, *17*(2011), 5–20. doi:10.2478/v10130-011-0001-4

Guiomar, N., Godinho, S., Pinto-Correia, T., Almeida, M., Bartolini, F., Bezák, P., Biró, M., Bjørkhaug, H., Bojnec, Š., Brunori, G., Corazzin, M., Czekaj, M., Davidova, S., Kania, J., Kristensen, S., Marraccini, E., Molnár, Z., Niedermayr, J., O'Rourke, E., ... Wästfelt, A. (2018). Typology and distribution of small farms in Europe: Towards a better picture. *Land Use Policy*, *75*, 784–798. doi:10.1016/j.landusepol.2018.04.012

Haas, R., Imami, D., Miftari, I., Ymeri, P., Grunert, K., & Meixner, O. (2021). Consumer perception of food quality and safety in Western Balkan Countries: Evidence from Albania and Kosovo. *Foods*, *10*(1), 160. doi:10.3390/foods10010160 PMID:33466641

Hanf, J. H., & Gagalyuk, T. (2018). Integration of Small Farmers into Value Chains: Evidence from Eastern Europe and Central Asia. In G. Egilmez (Ed.), *Agricultural Value Chain* (pp. 181–197). IntechOpen. doi:10.5772/intechopen.73191

Hanus, G. (2020). Ethnocentrism in polish consumer food behaviour as a determinant of short supply chain development. *European Journal of Sustainable Development*, *9*(4), 169–169. doi:10.14207/ejsd.2020.v9n4p169

Horvat, A. M., Matkovski, B., Zekić, S., & Radovanov, B. (2020). Technical efficiency of agriculture in Western Balkan countries undergoing the process of EU integration. *Agricultural Economics – Czech*, *66*(2), 65-73. . doi:10.17221/224/2019-AGRICECON

Ilbery, B., & Maye, D. (2005). Alternative (shorter) food supply chains and specialist livestock products in the Scottish–English borders. *Environment & Planning A*, *37*(5), 823–844. doi:10.1068/a3717

Jarzębowski, S., Bourlakis, M., & Bezat-Jarzębowska, A. (2020). Short food supply chains (SFSC) as local and sustainable systems. *Sustainability (Basel)*, *12*(11), 4715. doi:10.3390u12114715

Key, N. (2019). Farm size and productivity growth in the United States Corn Belt. *Food Policy*, *84*, 186–195. doi:10.1016/j.foodpol.2018.03.017

Kiss, K., Ruszkai, C., & Takács-György, K. (2019). Examination of Short Supply Chains Based on Circular Economy and Sustainability Aspects. *Resources*, *8*(4), 161. doi:10.3390/resources8040161

Kneafsey M., Venn, L., Schmutz, U., Balázs, B., Trenchard, L., Eyden-Wood, T., ...Blackett, M. (2013). Short Food Supply Chains and Local Food Systems in the EU. A State of Play of their Socio-Economic Characteristics. In *JRC Scientific and policy reports*. Luxembourg: Publications Office of the European Union. doi:10.2791/88784

Kotevska, A., Bogdanov, N., Nikolić, A., Dimitrievski, D., Gjoshevski, D., Georgiev, N., & Martinovska Stojcheska, A. (2015). Consulisons and recommendations. In A. Kotevska & A. Martinovska Stojcheska (Eds.), *The Impact of Socio-Economic Structure of Rural Population on Success of Rural Development Policy* (pp. 117–124). Association of Agricultural Economists of Republic of Macedonia. Retrieved from https://publicpolicy.rs/publikacije/d16435796b8009eb918aa100c03cfbba0d5423f3.pdf

Kovačević, V., Brenjo, D., Cvetković, S., & Rainović, L. (2022). Comparative analyse of foodstuff geographical indications in the Western Balkans. *Ekonomika Poljoprivrede*, *69*(1), 163–178. doi:10.5937/ekoPolj2201163K

Kovačević, V., & Jeločnik, M. (2022). *Tržište i trgovanje poljoprivrednim proizvodima/ Market and trading of agricultural products*. Beograd: Institut za ekonomiku poljoprivrede, Begrad, 2022. Retrieved from https://www.iep.bg.ac.rs/images/stories/izdanja/Monografije/Trziste%20i%20trgovanje%20PP%20LQ.pdf

Majewski, E., Komerska, A., Kwiatkowski, J., Malak-Rawlikowska, A., Wąs, A., Sulewski, P., Gołaś, M., Pogodzińska, K., Lecoeur, J.-L., Tocco, B., Török, Á., Donati, M., & Vittersø, G. (2020). Are short food supply chains more environmentally sustainable than long chains? A life cycle assessment (LCA) of the eco-efficiency of food chains in selected EU countries. *Energies*, *13*(18), 4853. doi:10.3390/en13184853

Malak-Rawlikowska, A., Majewski, E., Wąs, A., Borgen, S. O., Csillag, P., Donati, M., Freeman, R., Hoàng, V., Lecoeur, J.-L., Mancini, M. C., Nguyen, A., Saïdi, M., Tocco, B., Török, Á., Veneziani, M., Vittersø, G., & Wavresky, P. (2019). Measuring the economic, environmental, and social sustainability of short food supply chains. *Sustainability (Basel)*, *11*(15), 4004. doi:10.3390u11154004

Marsden, T., Banks, J., & Bristow, G. (2000). Food supply chain approaches: Exploring their role in rural development. *Sociologia Ruralis*, *40*(4), 424–438. doi:10.1111/1467-9523.00158

Mentzer, J. T., DeWitt, W., Keebler, J. S., Min, S., Nix, N. W., Smith, C. D., & Zacharia, Z. G. (2001). Defining supply chain management. *Journal of Business Logistics*, *22*(2), 1–25. doi:10.1002/j.2158-1592.2001.tb00001.x

Paraušić, V., & Domazet, I. (2018). Cluster development and innovative potential in Serbian agriculture. *Ekonomika Poljoprivrede*, *65*(3), 1159–1170. doi:10.5937/ekoPolj1803159P

Paraušić, V., Domazet, I., & Simeunović, I. (2017). Analysis of the Relationship Between the Stage of Economic Development and the State of Cluster Development. *Argumenta Oeconomica*, *39*(2), 279–305. doi:10.15611/aoe.2017.2.12

Paraušić, V., Kostić, Z., & Subić, J. (2023). Local development initiatives in Serbia's rural communities as rerequisite for the Leader implementation: Agricultural advisors' perceptions. *Ekonomika Poljoprivrede*, *70*(1), 117–130. doi:10.59267/ekoPolj2301117P

Pilař, L., Stanislavská, L. K., Moulis, P., Kvasnička, R., Rojík, S., & Tichá, I. (2019). Who spends the most money at farmers' markets? *Zemedelská Ekonomika*, *65*(11), 491–498. doi:10.17221/69/2019-AGRICECON

Radukić, S., Petrović-Ranđelović, M., & Kostić, Z. (2019). Sustainability-based goals and and achieved results in Western Balkan countries. *Economics of Sustainable Development*, *3*(1), 9–18. doi:10.5937/ESD1901009R

Renting, H., Marsden, T. K., & Banks, J. (2003). Understanding alternative food networks: Exploring the role of short food supply chains in rural development. *Environment & Planning A*, *35*(3), 393–411. doi:10.1068/a3510

Rucabado-Palomar, T., & Cuéllar-Padilla, M. (2020). Short food supply chains for local food: A difficult path. *Renewable Agriculture and Food Systems*, *35*(2), 182–191. doi:10.1017/S174217051800039X

Stein, A. J., & Santini, F. (2021). The sustainability of "local" food: A review for policy-makers. *Review of Agricultural, Food and Environmental Studies*, 1–13. doi:10.100741130-021-00148-w

Šūmane, S., Miranda, D. O., Pinto-Correia, T., Czekaj, M., Duckett, D., Galli, F., ... Tsiligiridis, T. (2021). Supporting the role of small farms in the European regional food systems: What role for the science-policy interface? *Global Food Security*, *28*, 100433. doi:10.1016/j.gfs.2020.100433

Sylla, M., Olszewska, J., & Świąder, M. (2017). Status and possibilities of the development of community supported agriculture in Poland as an example of short food supply chain. *Journal of Agribusiness and Rural Development, 43*(1), 201–207. doi:10.17306/J.JARD.2017.00266

UNIDO. (2020). *Short food supply chains for promoting local food on local markets.* UNIDO. Retrieved from https://suster.org/wp-content/uploads/2020/06/SHORT-FOOD-SUPPLY-CHAINS.pdf

United Nations. (2015). *Transforming our world: the 2030 Agenda for Sustainable Development.* General Assembly. United Nations, 21 October 2015, A/RES/70/1. Retrieved from https://www.un.org/ga/search/view_doc.asp?symbol=A/RES/70/1&Lang=E

Van der Ploeg, J. D., Renting, H., Brunori, G., Knickel, K., Mannion, J., Marsden, T., de Roest, K., Sevilla-Guzman, E., & Ventura, F. (2000). Rural development: From practices and policies towards theory. *Sociologia Ruralis, 40*(4), 391–408. doi:10.1111/1467-9523.00156

Vittersø, G., Torjusen, H., Laitala, K., Tocco, B., Biasini, B., Csillag, P., de Labarre, M. D., Lecoeur, J.-L., Maj, A., Majewski, E., Malak-Rawlikowska, A., Menozzi, D., Török, Á., & Wavresky, P. (2019). Short food supply chains and their contributions to sustainability: Participants' views and perceptions from 12 European cases. *Sustainability (Basel), 11*(17), 4800. doi:10.3390u11174800

Weatherell, C., Tregear, A., & Allinson, J. (2003). In search of the concerned consumer: UK public perceptions of food, farming and buying local. *Journal of Rural Studies, 19*(2), 233–244. doi:10.1016/S0743-0167(02)00083-9

Zakić, V., Nikolić, M., & Kovačević, V. (2018). International experiences in cooperative audit and lessons for Serbia. *Ekonomika Poljoprivrede, 65*(3), 1111–1122. doi:10.5937/ekoPolj1803111Z

Zhang, X., Qing, P., & Yu, X. (2019). Short supply chain participation and market performance for vegetable farmers in China. *The Australian Journal of Agricultural and Resource Economics, 63*(2), 282–306. doi:10.1111/1467-8489.12299

Zivkov, G. (2013). *Association of farmers in the Western Balkan countries.* Policy Studies on Rural Transition (No 2013-1). FAO Regional Office for Europe and Central Asia. Retrieved from https://www.fao.org/3/ar592e/ar592e.pdf

ADDITIONAL READING

Aggestam, V., Fleiß, E., & Posch, A. (2017). Scaling-up short food supply chains? A survey study on the drivers behind the intention of food producers. *Journal of Rural Studies, 51*, 64–72. doi:10.1016/j.jrurstud.2017.02.003

Clark, J. K., Jablonski, B. B., Inwood, S., Irish, A., & Freedgood, J. (2021). A contemporary concept of the value (s)-added food and agriculture sector and rural development. *Community Development (Columbus, Ohio), 52*(2), 186–204. doi:10.1080/15575330.2020.1854804

Cruz, J. L., Puigdueta, I., Sanz-Cobena, A., & Gonzalez-Azcarate, M. (2021). Short Food Supply Chains: Rebuilding consumers' trust. *New Medit, 20*(4), 33–47. doi:10.30682/nm2104c

Elghannam, A., & Mesias, F. (2019). Short food supply chains from a social media marketing perspective: A consumer-oriented study in Spain. *New Medit, 18*(1), 79–90. doi:10.30682/nm1901g

Elghannam, A., Mesias, F. J., Escribano, M., Fouad, L., Horrillo, A., & Escribano, A. J. (2020). Consumers' perspectives on alternative short food supply chains based on social media: A focus group study in Spain. *Foods, 9*(1), 22. doi:10.3390/foods9010022 PMID:31878255

KEY TERMS AND DEFINITIONS

Caution in Glorifying SFSCs: The contribution of SFSCs to sustainability dimensions (particularly the economic and environmental one) is often questionable in literature and in practice. Positive contribution of SFSCs to sustainable growth should not be generalised and these supply channels should not be excessively glorified. This attitude relies on the fact that the contribution of SFSCs is determined by numerous factors and assumptions, and that the combination of different marketing channels is frequently required to maximise their total contribution to sustainable growth.

Characteristics of SFSCs: They are characterised by the decreased physical distance and social and cultural distance between farmers and direct food consumers, i.e. by the minimised number of intermediaries in food trade. The focus is not placed on the geographical distance between farmers and consumers, but rather on their direct connection, closeness, trust, exchange of information about the product and its production method, as well as on elimination or reduction of the number of intermediaries in trade.

Importance of SFSCs for Sustainable Rural Development in Central and Eastern European Countries: Shortening of supply chains is beneficial for all farmers, although it is mainly regarded as a solution for securing sustainable income of small-scale and medium-scale farmers. These farmers are the most prevalent in the agriculture of the Central and Eastern European countries, where have a key role in food systems. The promotion and institutional development of the SFSC concept is exceptionally significant for the sustainable rural development of all CEECs, for strengthening the competitiveness of small and medium-scale family farms and integrating them more efficiently in the market.

Neo-Traditional Type of SFSCs: This type encompasses modern, complex and innovative approaches to local food, which do not compromise food quality, sustainability and application of environmental and traditional agricultural practices. This category might involve "community supported agriculture" as a collectively owned food system led and supported by a network of farmers, consumers and local institutions, as well as various social movements, mainly in cities promoting local food.

SFSCs as a Part of Value-Added Agriculture: Relations between farmers and consumers are manifested through the possibility of creating a new, higher value of products and price premiums if the received information regarding to products (its quality and food safety) are considered significant and valuable by consumers.

Short vs. Global Food Supply Chains: Short food supply chains (abbr. SFSCs) are part of the supply chain concept and they represent one of dimensions which are opposed to long, global, commercial or conventional supply chains, mostly led by supermarkets and hypermarkets, as well as by large traders and buyers of agricultural products. In all countries of the world the importance of SFSCs is growing with the rise of consumers' awareness of and concern about the environmental, social, ethical, and health issues related to the food that is produced and consumed.

Traditional Type of SFSCs: This type mainly involves direct on-farm and off-farm sales (direct transaction between farmers and consumers). The main links in these supply chains are small-scale family farms. This category is traditionally widely represented in food supply chains of most CEECs and almost all Mediterranean countries.

Chapter 10
The Analysis of the Relationship Between Renewable Energy and Human Development

Mustafa Batuhan Tufaner
https://orcid.org/0000-0003-0415-4368
Beykent University, Turkey

ABSTRACT

As in all areas of human life, energy plays a vital role in these areas as well. However, reasons such as the risk of depletion of traditional energy sources, damage to the environment, and supply shocks have led to more discussion of renewable energy sources. The aim of the study is to analyze the relationship between renewable energy and human development for 37 OECD countries for the period 1990-2018. For this purpose, Gengenbach, Urbain, and Westerlund panel cointegration test and Dumitrescu-Hurlin panel causality tests were applied. Empirical results reveal that the increase in the rate of renewable energy consumption in total energy consumption positively affects human development. Also, the Dumitrescu-Hurlin panel causality test shows that there is no causality between human development and renewable energy consumption. These results will help policy makers and government officials in OECD countries better understand the role of renewable energy in the human development process.

1. INTRODUCTION

Human development (HD) is accepted as one of the most important indicators showing the level of development of a country. One of the most accepted indicators to measure HD in the literature is the human development index (HDI). HDI was published in the United Nations Development Program in 1990 (Arisman, 2018). The HDI is evaluated under three sub-headings: health, education and standard of living. The health dimension is formulated by life expectancy at birth, the education dimension by average years of schooling and expected years of schooling, and the standard of living by gross national income per capita (Wang et al., 2021). Although the HDI is criticized for its deficiencies, it can be stated that it is a good indicator for evaluating the development of countries.

Energy has a direct impact on all dimensions of HD, including health, education and standard of living. Therefore, it does not seem possible for HD to take place without energy (Sadorsky, 2009). The fact that hospitals can effectively maintain their functions such as patient treatments or newborn units reveals the health dimension of energy. The Covid-19 pandemic has revealed the role of energy in health, especially intubated patients. On the other hand, the transition to distance education due to the Covid-19 pandemic has revealed the role of energy in education. Energy can be defined as a production factor in terms of economy. Sustainable energy is an indispensable element in terms of employment, agriculture, industry, transportation and economic development. The use of traditional energy sources has an important share in most economies today. However, it has been argued that although the use of traditional energy sources contributes in the short term, it will negatively affect economic growth and development in the long run (Zhao et al., 2018). Because excessive use of traditional energy sources can increase the emission of harmful gases. It is thought that substituting traditional energy sources with renewable energy (RENE) sources will contribute to sustainable development and HD (Kazar and Kazar, 2014).

The issue of RENE has gained importance recently for various reasons. Researchers have recently focused on RENE and examined it from different perspectives (Wu et al., 2010; Bello, 2015; Soukiazis et al., 2017; Sung and Park, 2018). The risk of depletion of traditional energy sources and their damage to the environment reveal the economic and social reasons for RENE. In addition, the Russia-Ukraine war in 2022 has increased the concerns of world countries about energy supply security. Supply shocks in traditional energy sources (oil and natural gas) have pushed countries to seek alternative energy, especially RENE sources (Sari Hassoun and Mekidiche, 2018). The orientation to RENE sources such as solar, wind, and hydroelectricity has increased in recent years due to the gaining weight of sustainable policies and the decrease in their costs. The rate of RENE consumption in total energy consumption reached 19% in 2015. (REN21 Renewables, 2017). According to an estimate from the International Renewable Energy Agency (IREA), this rate could rise to 60% or more by 2050 (REN21 Renewables, 2007). On the other hand, both the World Bank and the United Nations Development Program financed projects supporting RENE sources. UNDP has determined 17 basic articles for the sustainable development goals. In the subtitle of the accessible and clean energy target, it is stated that investment in various RENE sources should be made to ensure that everyone has access to energy by 2030 (UNDP, 2020).

Given the importance that RENE consumption will play in meeting future energy needs, the scarcity of studies investigating the relationship between RENE consumption and HD is surprising. Previous studies have mostly addressed the relationship between RENE and carbon emissions and economic growth. A limited number of studies have been conducted on the effects of RENE use on HD. Researches on the relationship between RENE and HD also yield inconsistent results. While some studies indicate that the use of RENE improves HD (Pirlogea, 2012), others show the opposite result (Wang et al., 2018).

The contribution of the study to the literature is that it is an innovative research into the existing literature that measures the relationship between RENE consumption and HD. It also provides policymakers with a knowledge base in policy-making regarding the use of RENE and promotes HD. Another contribution is the inclusion of all 37 OECD countries in the analysis and the use of up-to-date data. The purpose of this article is to analyze the impact of RENE on HD for 37 OECD countries during the period 1990-2018. Panel data analysis will be used to investigate the dynamic relationship between variables. This study is divided into 5 parts: introduction, literature review, data and methodology, empirical results and discussion, and conclusion.

2. LITERATURE REVIEW

The relationship between RENE and HD is a topic that has attracted attention recently. Various econometric models have been used in studies on the subject and different results have been obtained. While some studies indicate that the use of RENE increases HD (Pirlogea, 2012; Hassoun and Ayad, 2020; Sasmaz et al., 2020; Cerqueira et al., 2021), others show the opposite result (Wang et al., 2018; Adekoya et al., 2021). In some of these studies, a bidirectional causality relationship was found between RENE and HD in the short run (Kazar and Kazar, 2014; Hassoun and Ayad, 2020; Wang et al., 2021). The number of studies analyzing OECD countries on this subject is limited (Hassoun and Ayad, 2020; Sasmaz et al., 2020; Cerqueira et al., 2021).

Pirlogea (2012) researched the relationship between RENE consumption and HD in EU member countries for the period 1997-2008. As a result of the regression analysis, it was concluded that there is a relationship between RENE consumption and HD. Hassoun and Ayad (2020) analyzed the relationship between RENE and economic development in 17 OECD countries for the period 1990-2017. Random effect and ARDL cointegration model were applied in the study and it was found that RENE positively affects sustainable development in the long run. In addition, it has been determined that there is a bidirectional causality relationship between the two variables. Sasmaz et al. (2020) investigated the relationship between RENE and HD in OECD countries for the period 1990-2017. As a result of cointegration and causality analysis, it was determined that RENE positively affects HD and there is a bidirectional causality between the variables. Cerqueira et al. (2021) examined the relationship between RENE and sustainable development on 28 OECD countries and for the period 2000-2016. As a result of the GLS analysis, it was revealed that RENE is a driving force of sustainable development. Wang et al. (2021) analyzed the relationship between RENE consumption and HD in terms of public debt. In this context, the BRICS countries were examined for the period 1990-2016 and a bidirectional causality relationship was determined between HD and RENE.

Kazar and Kazar (2014) examined the relationship between RENE production and economic development on 154 countries for the period 1980-2010. Granger causality test was used and a bidirectional causality relationship was found between RENE and economic development in the short run. However, it has been observed that the causality relationship between economic development and RENE production varies depending on the HD level of countries both in the short and long term. Wang et al. (2018) investigated the relationship among RENE consumption, economic growth and HD in Pakistan for the period 1990-2014. In the study using the Two-Stage Least Square (2SLS) method, it was found that the increase in RENE does not improve HD. Adekoya et al. (2021) researched the relationship among RENE, carbon emissions and HD for the period 2000-2014. In the study, 126 countries were divided into 8 regions and regression analysis was performed. It has been concluded that RENE has a negative impact on HD in MENA and Central America&Caribbean, while it has a positive impact on Europe.

3. DATA AND METHODOLOGY

While previous studies examine the energy-development relationship using diverse econometric models, in recent studies the use of panel cointegration estimation has increased (Ouedraogo, 2013; Caraballo and Garcia, 2017; Satrovic, 2018; Hassoun and Ayad, 2020; Sasmaz et al., 2020; Wang et al., 2021). Panel data analysis is interesting because it has more freedom and efficiency than individual time series analysis. This study uses the panel cointegration method to examine the relationship between RENE consumption and HD in a sample of OECD countries.

In order to determine cointegration tests to be applied in the model, cross-sectional dependence and homogeneity should be tested first. Testing the cross-sectional dependence is also important for the selection of the panel unit root test. If there is a cross-sectional dependence in the series, second-generation panel unit root tests are performed. It is appropriate to use the Pesaran CD (2004) test since the number of samples included in our analysis is greater than the number of years (N>T). The hypotheses of the Pesaran CD test are as follows;

$H_0: p_{ij} = 0$
$H_0: p_{ij} \neq 0$

The statistics of the Pesaran CD test is as follows;

$$CD = \sqrt{\frac{2T}{N(N-1)}} (\sum_{i=1}^{N-1}\sum_{j=i+1}^{N} \hat{p}_{ij}) \qquad (1)$$

$\hat{p}_{ij}$ is defined as follows;

$$\hat{p}_{ij} = \hat{p}_{ji} = \frac{\sum_{t=1}^{T} e_{it}e_{jt}}{(\sum_{t=1}^{T} e_{it}^2)^{1/2}(\sum_{t=1}^{T} e_{it}^2)^{1/2}} \qquad (2)$$

e_{it} is the residuals estimated from each unit by the appropriate method. T_{ij} is correlation coefficient calculated number of observations. If the probability of Pesaran CD statistical is less than 0.05, there is a cross-sectional dependence.

The Swamy S test will be used to test for homogeneity. To test the RCM, we look at the difference between the OLS estimators and the weighted average matrices of WE. The statistics of the S test developed by Swamy (1971) are defined as follows;

$$\hat{S} =^2_{k(N-1)} = \sum_{i=1}^{N} (\hat{\beta}_i - \overline{\beta}^*)' \hat{V}_i^{-1} (\hat{\beta}_i - \overline{\beta}^*) \qquad (3)$$

$\hat{\beta}_i$ represents the OLS estimators determined from regressions by units, $\overline{\beta}^*$ the weighted WE estimator, and $\hat{V}_i$ represents the difference between the variances of the two estimators. The test statistic has χ^2 distribution with k(n-1) degrees of freedom. If the test statistic is greater than the critical value, the parameters are homogeneous.

In order to reveal a consistent relationship between the variables, the stationary of the series should be tested If the series contains cross-sectional dependence, first-generation panel unit root tests are insufficient and therefore second generation panel unit root tests are applied. Pesaran (2007) proposed the CIPS statistics, which is a cross-section expanded type of IPS test, to eliminate cross-sectional dependence;

$$CIPS^*(N,T) = \frac{1}{N}\sum_{i=1}^{N} t_i^*(N,T) \qquad (4)$$

The degree of extension can be selected by information criteria or sequential tests. The combined asymptotic limit of the CIPS statistic is not standard. Also, critical values were calculated for various T and N pairs.

The existence of a long-term relationship between non-stationary variables can be determined with the panel cointegration test. Panel cointegration tests are derived based on residual or error correction models. For heterogeneous panels allowing the cointegration pattern to vary by unit, the asymptotics depends on unit-specific outcomes. In the case of cross-sectional dependence, first-generation panel cointegration tests are weak. For this reason, Gengenbach, Urbain, and Westerlund (2016) panel cointegration test, which is among the second generation panel cointegration tests, will be applied.

Gengenbach, Urbain, and Westerlund (2016) derived an error correction-based panel cointegration test using a common factor structure. In the first stage of the test, the OLS estimation is obtained for each unit and the null hypothesis is tested with the help of the panel t-test. The t statistic is defined as follows;

$$\bar{t}_c = \frac{1}{N}\sum_{i=1}^{N} t_{c_i} \qquad (5)$$

While $H_0: \alpha_{yi} = \ldots = \alpha_{yx} = 0$, $H_1: \alpha_{yi} < 0$ for at least one i. Rejecting the null hypothesis means that there is a cointegration relationship between the variables.

If there is a cointegration relationship between the variables, the long-run relationship needs to be estimated. Pedroni (2001) uses the following model in the dynamic ordinary least squares mean group (DOLSMG) estimator;

$$Y_{it} = \mu_i + \beta_i X_{it} + u_{it} \qquad i = 1,\ldots,N \qquad t = 1,\ldots,T$$

It shows that the cointegration model is heterogeneous on the basis of units. Adding the leading values and lags of X's to the DOLSMG estimator ensures that feedback effects and endogeneity are eliminated.

In the first step, dynamic ordinary least squares (DOLS) are estimated for each unit. Then the results are combined with the Pesaran and Smith (1995) mean group (MG) estimator for the entire panel;

$$\hat{\beta}_{DOLSMG} = N^{-1} \left[\sum_{i=1}^{N} \left(\sum_{t=1}^{T} Z_{it} Z_{it}^* \right)^{-1} \left(\sum_{t=1}^{T} (Z_{it} \bar{Y}_{it}) \right) \right] \qquad (6)$$

The DOLSMG estimator is obtained by taking the mean of the DOLS estimators obtained for each unit. The t statistic is also obtained by taking the mean.

$$t_{\hat{\beta}_{DOLSMG}} = N^{-1} \sum_{t=1}^{T} t_{\hat{\beta}_{DOLS,i}} \qquad (7)$$

The panel causality test measures whether the variables provide useful information in predicting their future values. There are many tests that investigate the causality relationship between variables. In this research, Dumitrescu and Hurlin (2012) panel causality test was applied. The D-H test takes into account the cross-sectional dependence on the panel. The test is explained with the help of the linear model given below;

$$Y_{it} = \alpha_i + \sum_{k=1}^{K} \gamma_i^{(k)} \gamma_{it-k} + \sum_{k=1}^{K} \beta_i^{(k)} X_{it-k} + e_{it} \qquad (8)$$

K represents the lag length, β_i represent ($\beta^{(1)}_i,..., \beta^{(K)}_i$). The null hypothesis is "all βs equal zero" and states that there is no causality from X to Y for the entire panel.

4. EMPIRICAL RESULTS AND DISCUSSION

Empirical results investigate the relationship between RENE consumption and HD for the full sample of 37 OECD countries. The REC variable represents the share of RENE consumption in total energy consumption, and the HDI variable represents the human development index. The REC variable was taken from the World Bank dataset and the HDI variable was taken from the UNDP dataset.

Table 1. Cross-sectional dependence test results

Variable	CD-test	p-value
REC	59.37	0.000
HDI	134.97	0.000

In the study, cross-sectional dependence was tested with the Pesaran CD test, which gave better results when N>T. The results of the cross-sectional dependence test are given in the Table below. The test results show that there is a cross-sectional dependence for both variables. In other words, a shock to occurs in one of the OECD countries may affect other OECD countries as well.

The Swamy S test was used to test whether the parameter was homogeneous. The basic hypothesis in the Swamy S test is "H_0: There is no parameter heterogeneity/ parameters are homogeneous". According to the test results in the table, the H_0 hypothesis is rejected at the 5% significance level. The parameters of the model examined have characteristics specific to the units that are statistically significant. Therefore, estimators which assume that the slope parameters are homogeneous for all units are insufficient at this stage.

In case of cross-sectional dependence problem in series, second-generation unit root tests are applied. Thus, reliable and consistent results are obtained from the unit root test. Maxlag and bglag were chosen as one. The results of the Pesaran CIPS unit root test are shown in Table. Unit root test results show that the series are not stationary at level. When the first differences of the series are taken, they become stationary at the 1% and 5% significance levels.

Gengenbach, Urbain and Westerlund panel cointegration estimates are reported in Table. The lag length is chosen heterogeneous, it varies according to the units. According to the cointegration test result, H0 hypothesis cannot be rejected since it is (p-value<=0.05). There is a cointegration relationship between REC and HDI variables.

Second-generation heterogeneous estimators should be used because there is a cross-sectional dependence problem between the variables and the units are heterogeneous. For long-term coefficient estimation, the Mean Group Dynamic Least

Table 2. Swamy S homogeneity test results

chi2(72)	Prob > chi2
12374.31	0.000

Table 3. Panel unit root test results

Variable	CIPS	Critical Values		
		10%	5%	1%
REC	-2.16	-2.08	-2.16	-2.3
ΔREC	-5.166	-2.08	-2.16	-2.3
HDI	-2.12	-2.08	-2.16	-2.3
ΔHDI	-4.297	-2.08	-2.16	-2.3

Table 4. Panel cointegration test results

d.y	Coefficient	T-bar	p-value
y(t-1)	-0.414	-2.590	<=0.05

Table 5. Long-term coefficient test results

Variables	Beta	t-stat
REC_td	0.118	8.184*

Table 6. Panel causality test results

Causality	W-bar	Z-bar tilde
ΔREC does not Granger-cause ΔHDI	11.9735	0.6810
ΔHDI does not Granger-cause ΔREC	12.5290	0.9376

Squares (DOLSMG) estimator was used. The lag length is chosen as one. DOLSMG panel cointegration estimates are reported in Table. The estimated value of 1.187 is the long-term parameter for the entire panel. The t-stat of the long-term coefficient is significant (at the 5% significance level, the t table value is 1.96), which shows that RENE consumption positively affects HD in the long run. A 1% increase in RENE consumption in total energy consumption increases the HDI by 0.118%.

The table reports the Dumitrescu-Hurlin panel causality results. The number of lag lengths for variables in each equation was set at seven as determined by the

Akaike information criteria. P-values computed using 100 bootstrap replications. According to the test results, there is no causality between REC and HDI.

5. CONCLUSION

The HDI is an important indicator for monitoring the development levels of countries. HD, which is based on health, education and living standards, is improving with developments in these areas. As in all areas of human life, energy plays a vital role in these areas as well. However, reasons such as the risk of depletion of traditional energy sources, damage to the environment and supply shocks have led to more discussion of RENE sources.

This study investigates the impact of RENE consumption on HD in the sample of OECD countries from 1990 to 2018. Empirical analysis has demonstrated the importance of the relationship between RENE consumption and the HDI, using econometric techniques that can take into account heterogeneity and the cross-sectional dependence problem. The increase in the rate of RENE consumption in total energy consumption positively affects HD. Also, the Dumitrescu-Hurlin panel causality test shows that there is no causality between HD and RENE consumption.

The empirical findings suggest some policy implications for OECD countries. The results show that the use of RENE advances HD. Therefore, governments in OECD countries should develop policies to promote the positive effects of RENE on HD. Governments should also design policies that will increase the proportion of RENE in energy consumption by substituting traditional energy sources with RENE sources. Governments in OECD countries should limit the use of traditional energy sources and accelerate the transition to RENE sources. It is necessary to raise awareness about RENE, to give incentives to the private sector and individuals for the use of RENE, to increase investments in the RENE sector and to provide support financing for clean energy projects.

In this study, the relationship between RENE consumption and HD was investigated in the example of OECD countries Future studies may examine the countries in the sample by subdividing them according to different HD thresholds. In addition, the relationship between RENE consumption and HD can be analyzed with different econometric methods. In addition, evaluating the impact of each RENE source group on HD by dividing renewable energy sources into subgroups may be a suggestion for future researchers.

REFERENCES

Adekoya, O., Olabode, J., & Rafi, S. (2021). Renewable energy consumption, carbon emissions and human development: Empirical comparison of the trajectories of world regions. *Renewable Energy, 179*, 1836–1848. doi:10.1016/j.renene.2021.08.019

Arisman, A. (2018). Determinant of human development index in ASEAN countries. *Jurnal Ilmu Ekonomi, 7*, 113–122.

Bello, M. (2015). Renewable energy for sustainable socio-economic development in developing countries: A case study of Sub-saharan Africa. *Advanced Materials Research, 1116*, 33–44. doi:10.4028/www.scientific.net/AMR.1116.33

Caraballo, M., & Garcia, S. (2017). Renewable energy and economic development: An analysis for Spain and the biggest European economies. *El Trimestre Economico, 84*, 571–609.

Cerqueira, P., Soukiazis, S., & Proença, S. (2021). Assessing the linkages between recycling, renewable energy and sustainable development: Evidence from the OECD countries. *Environment, Development and Sustainability, 23*(7), 9766–9791. doi:10.100710668-020-00780-4

Dumitrescu, E., & Hurlin, C. (2012). Testing for Granger non-causality in heterogeneous panels. *Economic Modelling, 29*(4), 1450–1460. doi:10.1016/j.econmod.2012.02.014

Gengenbach, C., Urbain, J., & Westerlund, J. (2016). Error correction testing in panels with common sthocastic trends. *Journal of Applied Econometrics, 31*(6), 982–1004. doi:10.1002/jae.2475

Hassoun, S., & Ayad, H. (2020). Renewable energy and sustainable development: Evidence from 17 OECD countries. *International Journal of Economics, Business and Politics, 4*, 41–60.

Kazar, G., & Kazar, A. (2014). The renewable energy production-economic development nexus. *International Journal of Energy Economics and Policy, 4*, 312–319.

Ouedraogo, N. (2013). Energy consumption and human development: Evidence from a panel cointegration and error correction model. *Energy, 63*, 28–41. doi:10.1016/j.energy.2013.09.067

Pedroni, P. (2001). Purchasing power parity tests in cointegrated panels. *The Review of Economics and Statistics, 83*(4), 727–731. doi:10.1162/003465301753237803

Pesaran, H. (2004). *General diagnostic tests for cross-section dependence in panels.* Cambridge University Press. doi:10.2139srn.572504

Pesaran, H. (2007). A simple panel unit root test in the presence of cross-section dependence. *Journal of Applied Econometrics, 22*(2), 265–312. doi:10.1002/jae.951

Pesaran, H., & Smith, P. (1995). Estimating long-run relationships from dynamic heterogeneous panels. *Journal of Econometrics, 68*(1), 79–113. doi:10.1016/0304-4076(94)01644-F

Pirlogea, C.Panel Data Evidence. (2012). The human development relies on energy: Panel data evidence. *Procedia Economics and Finance, 3,* 496–501. doi:10.1016/S2212-5671(12)00186-4

REN21. (2007). *Renewables, global status report.* Available at: https://www.ren21.net/wp-content/uploads/2019/05/GSR2007_Full-Report_English.pdf

REN21. (2017). *Renewables, global status report.* Available at: https://www.ren21.net/wp-content/uploads/2019/05/GSR2017_Full-Report_English.pdf

Sadorsky, P. (2009). Renewable energy consumption and income in emerging economies. *Energy Policy, 37*(10), 4021–2028. doi:10.1016/j.enpol.2009.05.003

Sari Hassoun, S., & Mekidiche, M. (2018). Does renewable energy affect the economic growth in Algeria. *Journal of Applied Quantitative Methods,* 13.

Sasmaz, M., Sakar, E., Yayla, E., & Akkucuk, U. (2020). The relationship between renewable energy and human development in OECD countries: A panel data analysis. *Sustainability (Basel), 12*(18), 1–16. doi:10.3390u12187450

Satrovic, E. (2018). The human development relies on renewable energy: evidence from Turkey. *Proceedings of the 3rd International Energy & Engineering,* 19-27.

Soukiazis, E., Proença, S., & Cerqueira, P. (2017). The interconnections between renewable energy, *Economic development and environmental pollution: A simultaneous equation system approach. Centre for Business and Economics Research, 10,* 1–26.

Sung, B., & Park, D. (2018). Who drives the transition to a renewable-energy economy? multi-actor perspective on social innovation. *Sustainability (Basel), 10*(2), 1–32. doi:10.3390u10020448

Swamy, P. (1971). *Statistical inference in random coefficient regression models.* Springer. Available at: https://www.tr.undp.org/content/turkey/tr/home/sustainable-development-goals.html

Wang, Z., Bui, Q., Zhang, C., Nawarathna, C., & Mombeuil, C. (2021). The nexus between renewable energy consumption and human development in BRICS countries: The moderating role of public debt. *Renewable Energy*, *165*, 381–390. doi:10.1016/j.renene.2020.10.144

Wang, Z., Danish, B., Zhang, B., & Wang, B. (2018). Renewable energy consumption, economic growth and human development index in Pakistan: Evidence form simultaneous equation model. *Journal of Cleaner Production*, *184*, 1081–1090. doi:10.1016/j.jclepro.2018.02.260

Wu, Q., Masyluk, S., & Clulow, V. (2010). *Energy consumption transition and human development.* Monash University Press.

Zhao, H., Guo, S., & Zhao, H. (2018). Impacts of gdp, fossil fuel energy consumption, energy consumption intensity, and economic structure on SO2 emissions: A multivariate panel data model analysis on selected Chinese provinces. *Sustainability (Basel)*, *10*(3), 1–20. doi:10.3390u10030657

Chapter 11
The Complementary Effect of Network Capability and Learning Orientation on Firm Performance:
Evidence From SMEs in Türkiye

Pelin Karaca Kalkan
Ankara Science University, Turkey

Nilay Aluftekin Sakarya
Genta Pty., Turkey

ABSTRACT

It is widely accepted that network capability (NC) and learning orientation (LO) directly enhance small and medium-sized enterprises' (SMEs) performance. Yet relatively little attention has been paid to the study of the complementary effects of internal and external capabilities on innovation and firm performance. Drawing on the dynamic capabilities theory, this study investigates the complementary effect of NC and LO on SME performance. Moreover, this research examines how product and process innovation capability mediates the complementary effect of NC and LO on SME performance. The hypotheses were tested on 309 high-technology manufacturing SMEs in Türkiye. Empirical results revealed that NC and LO jointly influence product innovation capability. The results also suggested that only process innovation capability performs a mediating role in the complementary effect of NC and LO on firm performance. This study contributes to the literature by providing a comprehensive analysis of the relationships between NC, LO, innovation capabilities, and SME performance.

DOI: 10.4018/978-1-6684-8810-2.ch011

INTRODUCTION

Since SMEs have a significant impact on economic advancement in developing countries, identifying the factors that drive SMEs' success is crucial (Akman & Yilmaz, 2008) in the context of innovation-based competitiveness on a global scale (Teece, 2014). The literature suggests that SME innovation and performance are highly influenced by both internal and external resources and capabilities (see, e.g., Caloghirou et al., 2004; Salavou et al., 2004). Since small firms have been confronted resource scarcity, which potentially hinders their innovation activities, they need to develop internal and external capabilities to mitigate the repercussions of scarce resources (Parida & Örtqvist, 2015). Emerging market in Türkiye is known for its uncertainty and dynamism, and firms operating in this environment strive to increase their capacity for innovation (Bouguerra et al., 2022). Therefore, improving SMEs' innovative capabilities has been one of the main priorities for Türkiye's SME policy (Cakar & Erturk, 2010).

This study focuses on the complementary effect of an external and an internal capability on SMEs' innovation capabilities and firm performance. More specifically, this study suggests that SMEs' success can be collectively influenced by their external capability, such as Network Capability (NC), as well as their internal capability, like Learning Orientation (LO). Individual direct effects of NC and LO on innovation capability and firm performance have been previously suggested (see, e.g., Alegre & Chiva, 2013; Xie & Zheng, 2020), however, there are no empirical research that have investigated the complementary effect of NC and LO on SME performance in an emerging market.

The arguments of this study are built on dynamic capabilities theory (Teece, 2007) which is an extension of Resource-Based View (RBV) of the firm (Barney, 1991). This theory addresses the integration of internal and external resources and capabilities to gain competitive advantage (Teece et al., 1997). Moreover, dynamic capability theory complements RBV of the firm by suggesting the evolutionary nature of organizational resources and capabilities in dynamic environmental contexts to explain differences in firm performance (Wang & Ahmed, 2007). Therefore, dynamic capability approach builds an appropriate theoretical foundation to elucidate the development of NC and LO which enable SMEs' improved performance (Mu et al., 2017).

According to the dynamic capability framework, the mechanisms that link the dynamic capabilities to firm performance needs to be understood comprehensively (Chen et al., 2021). Dynamic capabilities influence organizational outcomes indirectly through an effect on other capabilities (Baker et al., 2022). Firms with a strong LO which is complemented by NC are generally in a better position to develop specific capabilities that ultimately affect firm performance (Calantone et al., 2002). In this sense, innovation capabilities seem to be a crucial link between other capabilities and firm performance (Hult et al., 2004). Therefore, this study suggests that NC and LO collectively contribute to the firm performance through their effect on product and process innovation capabilities.

THEORETICAL FRAMEWORK AND RESEARCH HYPOTHESES

Dynamic Capabilities Theory

As research has been conducted, RBV has evolved in such a way that it now encompasses capabilities in addition to resources (Helfat & Peteraf, 2003). The first definition of dynamic capabilities refers to "the firm's ability to integrate, build and reconfigure internal and external competencies to address rapidly changing environments" (Teece et al., 1997, p. 516). Dynamic capabilities theory focuses on how businesses obtain new knowledge, produce it, decide which investments to make, and undergo the necessary organizational changes. Therefore, this perspective inherently requires comprehension of both organizational and technological change (Augier & Teece, 2009).

Market dynamism (Zahra et al., 2006), strategic orientations (Zahoor & Lew, 2022), knowledge resources about customers and competitors (Chien & Tsai, 2012), organizational learning (Zollo & Winter, 2002) are some of the important factors that influence the development of dynamic capabilities. Firms with strong dynamic capabilities are not only adaptive to external environment, but they also shape the environment through innovative activities and networking (Teece, 2007). Therefore, firms should incorporate external resources and knowledge in addition to internal ones to enhance their technological and innovation capabilities (Mu & Di Benedetto, 2012).

Concerning the relationship between dynamic capabilities and performance outcomes, three perspectives have been offered. The first one proposes that there is a direct relationship between dynamic capabilities and organizational performance. According to second perspective, dynamic capabilities do not necessarily result in successive outcomes, and performance results might be dependent upon the features of the consequent new resource configurations or upon how managers employ dynamic capabilities. The last perspective argues that dynamic capabilities and organizational performance have an indirect relationship (Barreto, 2010). Dynamic capabilities have an impact on a wide range of performance indicators from competitive advantage (Ferreira et al., 2020) to SME performance (Arend, 2014).

Network Capability, Learning Orientation, and Innovation Capabilities

The ability of a firm to create, use, manage, and terminate relationships with other organizations within their network becomes of utmost significance, because firms are embedded in networks of relations with other entities (Ritter & Gemünden, 2003). As the innovation landscape continues to expand, collaboration with outside partners is becoming an increasingly important method for businesses to access crucial resources from the outside while improving their capacity for innovation (Kittilaksanawong & Ren, 2013). The research on businesses' network management should concentrate on how relationships are initiated and leveraged rather than the structure of relations (Mu & Di Benedetto, 2012). Therefore, this study focuses on NC rather than network structural characteristics such as density/centrality, direct and indirect ties, since NC of the firm is one of the most significant factors that might contribute to the innovation capabilities (Mitrega et al., 2017). NC is conceptualized as "a firm's abilities to develop and utilize inter-organizational relationships to gain access to various resources held by other actors" (Walter et al., 2006, p. 542). Walter et al. (2006) initially conceptualized NC as a four-dimensional construct comprising coordination, relational skills, partner knowledge, and internal communication. However, Parida et al. (2017) proposed a new dimension entitled as building new relations because the current NC construct has overlooked a crucial element that encompasses the function of network construction.

One of the most important dimensions of dynamic capabilities is learning, which is strongly tied to understanding customers' needs and expectations, exploring different applications for new technologies, and questioning the value of ongoing operations and the business model (Teece, 2014). LO is defined as the "set of organizational values that influence the propensity of the firm to create and use knowledge" (Sinkula et al., 1997, p. 309). Calantone et al. (2002) proposed that LO is a second-order construct, and its first-order dimensions are commitment to learning, shared vision, open-mindedness and intraorganizational knowledge sharing.

Firms with high levels of LO frequently question widely held beliefs about forces in their external environment like competitors, customers etc. (Baker & Sinkula, 1999). Moreover, firms with strong LO scan their environment for changes, and then make the necessary adjustments (Calantone et al., 2002). LO has significant implications for various organizational outcomes. For instance, LO is positively related to the overall performance of the business, new product success, and change in relative market share (Baker & Sinkula, 1999), and innovative outcomes (Sinkula et al., 1997).

Because of the recent, rapid shifts in technology, consumer tastes and preferences, and general market dynamics, today's organizations' ability to innovate is essential to their survival and success (Iddris, 2016). It is crucial for firms to adopt innovative activities to achieve superior performance in a market where buyer preferences always changing, customers are continually looking for new items, and new buyers are regularly entering to the market (Hult et al., 2004).

Innovation capability is defined as "the ability to continuously transform knowledge and ideas into new products, processes and systems for the benefit of the firm and its stakeholders" (Lawson & Samson, 2001, p. 384). Innovation capability has been subjected into different categorizations in the respective academic studies: product, process, marketing, service, and administrative innovation (Lin et al., 2010). This research focuses on product and process innovation capabilities. O'Cass and Sok (2014) defined product innovation capability as "bundles of interrelated routines used to undertake specified product innovation related activities in areas such as developing new products and improving existing product quality" (p. 999). Product innovation capability can be thought of as continuous, cross-functional process that incorporates an increasing range of different capabilities from both inside and outside the company (Kafetzopoulos & Psomas, 2015). Process innovation capability offers firms more efficient and effective manufacturing processes compared to current operations (Liao et al., 2007). Moreover, process innovations aim to improve quality and flexibility of operations while reducing unit costs of production and lead times for deliveries (Kafetzopoulos & Psomas, 2015).

Complementary Effect of NC and LO on Innovation Capabilities

Innovation entails a complementary approach, which is based on the notion that a firm need to NC to access external information and knowledge as well as its own resources and capabilities for creating a new value (Caloghirou et al., 2004). "Collaboration with different external actors such as suppliers, customers, competitors, and research organizations (e.g. universities or government laboratories) improves both knowledge sharing and market knowledge acquisition by the firm, resulting in expansion of the firm's existing knowledge base, which in turn advances a firm's innovation capability" (Najafi-Tavani et al., 2018, p. 193). Firms can use NC to anticipate new opportunities and, thus they can improve product and process innovation capabilities by gathering their resources with external partners (Fitjar et al., 2013).

NC and LO are strongly linked to innovation and may help firms succeed and survive by developing new products and processes (Fitjar et al., 2013). Baker et al. (2022) stated that LO influences the growth of other capabilities in a synergistic way, which enhances innovation and performance outcomes. In this sense, NC might be particularly beneficial as interactions with network partners complement the learning process by providing missing inputs such as unknown information about market and technology (Romijn & Albaladejo, 2002). The implication of complementary perspective for this research is that firm performance would be increased by joint influence of its internal and external capabilities. Therefore, firms that are learning oriented are more likely be aware about reaching knowledge emanates from partners in their networks. Therefore, the followings are hypothesized:

Hypotheses 1a: NC and LO jointly has a positive effect on product innovation capability.

Hypotheses 1b: NC and LO jointly has a positive effect on process innovation capability.

Product and Process Innovation Capability and Firm Performance

In emerging countries, innovation capabilities have become a significant aspect for SMEs, because they generate competitive advantage for the company (Ferreira et al., 2020). Innovation capability is the most important aspect in determining the success of an innovation (Akman & Yilmaz, 2008). Innovation capability is positively related to long-term corporate growth (Yang, 2012), product quality and operational performance (Kafetzopoulos & Psomas, 2015).

Product and process innovation capabilities have long been recognized as distinct constructs that enhance organizational performance and competitiveness (Damanpour, 2010). Gupta and Gupta (2019) examined the impacts of product innovation, process innovation and innovation culture on firm performance, and they found that only process innovation affects firm performance significantly. In contrast, Ar and Baki (2011) found that, compared to process innovation, product innovation showed a stronger direct correlation with firm performance. Several research examined the moderating role of innovation capabilities to shed light on performance impacts of innovation capabilities with other factors in a holistic way. For instance, O'Cass and Sok (2014) found that SME growth was significantly related to the synergistic effect of product innovation capability and intellectual resources. Based on arguments above, following hypotheses are proposed:

Hypothesis 2a: Product innovation capability has a positive effect on firm performance.

Hypothesis 2b: Process innovation capability has a positive effect on firm performance.

The Mediating Role of Innovation Capabilities

Innovation, specifically technological innovation, can be an important mediating mechanism in the relationships between dynamic capabilities and firm performance (Zhou et al., 2019). For instance, Gronum et al. (2012) suggested that in the relationship between networking and firm performance, innovation should be considered as an intermediate mechanism. The literature also suggests that innovation capabilities mediate the relationship between organizational learning and firm performance (Jiménez-Jiménez & Sanz-Valle, 2011). Specifically, LO influences firm performance indirectly through innovation instead of affecting directly (Calantone et al., 2002).

Several studies have investigated the mediating role of innovation capabilities by addressing different dimensions. For instance, Anning-Dorson (2018) found product and process innovation mediates the relationship between firm-level customer involvement capability and firm performance. Camisón and Villar-López (2010) showed that the impact of manufacturing flexibility on firm performance was mediated by product, process and organizational innovations. The literature supports that capabilities of a firm are more likely to have an indirect relationship with firm performance. That is, external and internal capabilities jointly enhance product and process innovation capabilities that can improve SME performance. Therefore, following hypotheses are proposed:

Hypothesis 3a: Product innovation capability mediates the interactive effect of NC and LO on firm performance.

Hypothesis 3b: Process innovation capability mediates the interactive effect of NC and LO on firm performance.

Figure 1. Research model

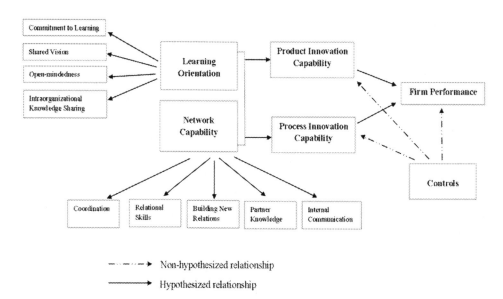

METHODOLOGY

Research Setting

Small firms need to be innovative, because they can move forward with novel and ambitious ideas more rapidly, have an organizational structure that is less bureaucratic and more adaptable, and struggle less to embrace and implement change (Damanpour, 2010). High-technology sector was chosen for this study, because this context is deemed as highly relevant for testing the proposed research model. High-technology manufacturing SMEs are substantially engaging in innovation in terms of producing innovative, tangible products (Cenamor et al., 2019), and thus innovation capability is an essential requirement, especially for high-technology SMEs in emergent countries (Akman & Yilmaz, 2008; Yang, 2012). According to Parida et al. (2017), all industries need to the capability to build, nurture, and maintain new relationships, but those that deal with high technology can benefit from this capability most. Additionally, firms in high-technology industry also need strong LO to enhance performance (D'Angelo & Presutti, 2019). In conclusion, all the capabilities included in this study's theoretical model are critical in the high-technology manufacturing sector.

Sampling and Data Collection

A survey methodology was employed for the data collection. In this sense, purposive sampling, often referred to as subjective or perceptual sampling in the literature, was used. This research follows the classification of technology intensity based on NACE Rev.2. According to Turkish Statistical Institute (TurkStat) (2020), high-technology includes: manufacture of basic pharmaceutical products and pharmaceutical preparations (21), manufacture of computer, electronic and optical products (26), manufacture of air and spacecraft and related machinery (30.3). There were 2.442 manufacturing SMEs operated in high-technology industry in Türkiye in the year of 2020.

Manufacturing SMEs in high-technology sector in Ankara were selected to test hypotheses. Ankara province can be characterized as a significant number of high-technology firms with strong innovation capabilities and a highly effective competitive presence in domestic and international markets. The most comprehensive list based on the technology intensity classification obtained in the website of Ankara Chamber of Commerce. According the Ankara Chamber of Commerce data, there are 172 firms registered in the manufacture of basic pharmaceutical products and pharmaceutical preparations category, 623 firms registered in the manufacture of computer, electronic and optical products category, and lastly 141 firms registered in the manufacture of air and spacecraft and related machinery category. Of the 936 potential respondents, 657 firms were contacted via telephone or e-mail to ask them if they participate the study. Of these 657 firms, 321 questionnaires were returned, including 12 invalid questionnaires, yielding a sample size of 309 or a 47 percent usable response rate. According to Hair et al. (2014), researchers should strive to have at least five observations for each indicator variable. The sample size is considered to be sufficient with 59 indicators because it is 309, which is higher than the minimum required sample size.

The measures were adapted from prior studies. Since the questionnaire was originally developed in English, the items were translated into Turkish with back-translation (Brislin, 1970). The survey items were translated into Turkish by an academic proofreader, then back translated into English by another native proofreader in order to ensure conceptual equivalence. Two academicians in the field of management and organization assessed measurement scales in terms of clarity and understandability, and gave valuable feedback regarding the wording of some survey items and capturing the construct domains. Moreover, a sample of twelve senior managers in high-technology firms pretested the questionnaire items for face and construct validity prior to the fieldwork. The survey was completed on site through personal appointments or via online survey with the key informants (founder, senior or middle level managers) based on their preference, due to Covid-19 pandemic concerns. Interviews were conducted with founders, top managers or middle level managers who were knowledgeable about organization's strategic posture and innovative activities.

Personal characteristics in this study are summarized in Table 1. Of the 309 participants, 129 are female and 180 are female. The majority of the respondents (80.6%) are senior or middle-level managers. Regarding educational status, 61.4% of the respondents are university graduates followed by 31.5% that have master's degree.

Firm characteristics of the sample are depicted in Table 2. Regarding firm size, approximately 85% of the respondent firms are small and medium sized firms. Majority of the firms' age (133) are in between one to ten years, which can be stated as newly established firms.

Table 1. Personal characteristics of the study sample

Personal Characteristics		Frequency	Percent
Participant status	Senior or middle level manager	249	80,6
	Founder	60	19,4
Gender	Female	129	41,7
	Male	180	58,3
Age	$20 \leq x \leq 29$	82	26,5
	$30 \leq x \leq 39$	136	44,0
	$40 \leq x \leq 49$	63	20,4
	> 50	28	9,10
Years of employment	≤ 4 years	58	18,8
	$5 \leq x \leq 9$	71	23,0
	$10 \leq x \leq 19$	101	32,7
	≥ 20 years	79	25,6
Years of employment in the firm	< 2 years	69	22,3
	$2 \leq x \leq 4$	105	34,0
	$5 \leq x \leq 9$	76	24,6
	≥ 10 years	59	19,1
Educational status	High school	13	4,2
	Graduate	189	61,4
	Master degree	97	31,5
	Doctoral degree	9	2,9
	Total	309	100,0

Table 2. Firm characteristics of the study sample

Firm Characteristics		Frequency	Percent
Firm size	≤ 10 employees	47	15,2
	$11 \leq x \leq 50$ employees	120	38,8
	$51 \leq x \leq 250$ employees	142	46,0
Firm age	$1 \leq x \leq 10$ years	133	43,0
	$11 \leq x \leq 25$ years	86	27,8
	$26 \leq x \leq 50$ years	65	21,0
	> 50 years	25	8,1
Sector	Manufacture of basic pharmaceutical products and pharmaceutical preparations	87	28,2
	Manufacture of air and spacecraft and related machinery	99	32,0
	Manufacture of computer, electronic and optical products	123	39,8
	Total	309	100

Variables and Measures

Network Capability

The authors adopted Parida and Örtqvist's (2015) scale to measure NC. In several studies (see, e.g., Walter et al., 2006; Zacca et al., 2015) NC is treated as a second-order construct comprises four components: Coordination, Relational Skills, Partner Knowledge, and Internal Communication. However, in a recent study Parida et al. (2017) proposed a new dimension pertaining to building new relationships. Included building new relations as a new component, NC was measured with five dimensions.

Learning Orientation

LO is conceived as a second-order construct (Sinkula et al., 1997) constituted by four dimensions: Commitment to Learning, Shared Vision, Open-mindedness, Intraorganizational Knowledge Sharing. This study utilized Calantone et al.'s (2002) scale to measure LO.

Product Innovation Capability and Process Innovation Capability

In order to measure product and process innovation capability, the authors used scales adapted and validated by Camisón and Villar-López (2014). Product innovation capability scale consists of five items, process innovation capability was measured with eleven items.

SME Performance

Small business performance is a multidimensional construct, and the integration of different dimensions of performance is important in revealing different aspects of it (Wiklund & Shepherd, 2005). Since SME managers are reluctant to divulge financial information, gathering objective financial data to measure SME performance is difficult (Altinay et al., 2016). However, objective and subjective measurements of firm performance have been shown to have a high correlation and concurrent validity in the literature (see, e.g., Venkatraman & Ramanujan, 1987). Therefore, managers were asked to evaluate their firm's performance indicators in comparison with competitors in their firm's sector over the last three years on a five-point Likert scale from 1 (much worse than competitors) to 5 (much higher than competitors).

Control Variables

The size of a firm has long been recognized as an important variable affecting firm performance, and thus it is included as a control variable. Firm size was measured by the number of employees. Firm age also strongly influences firm performance and thus, it was adopted as a second control variable. Firm age refers to the years that the firm has been in business. According to dynamic capabilities theory, firm performance is prone to be affected by environmental factors, thereby these factors should be taken into account to clearly specify dynamic capability- performance relationship (Wilden et al., 2016). Therefore, environmental turbulence was included as a control variable. Jaworski and Kohli (1993) proposed that environmental turbulence involves technological turbulence, market turbulence, and competitive intensity and hence, they were considered as the last three control variables.

Common Method Variance

Since this study collected data from single respondents, common method bias may cause problems. The Harman single-factor test, possibly the most well-known and extensively used method for evaluating common method variance (Podsakoff & Organ, 1986), was performed to address common method bias. Basically, exploratory factor analysis is used to all of the study's factors. Common method variance is presumed to exist, "either a) a single factor will emerge from the factor analysis, or b) one general factor will account for the majority of the covariance in the independent and criterion variables" (Podsakoff & Organ, 1986, p. 536). According to the results, a single factor explained 30.2% variance, which means that no single factor was discernible in the unrotated factor structure.

DATA ANALYSIS AND FINDINGS

Exploratory Factor Analysis

Exploratory factor analysis (EFA) was performed to examine the construct validity of the scales used in the study. As can be seen in Table 3 above, EFA of product and process innovation capabilities indicates that KMO (Kaiser-Meyer-Olkin) value of 0.90 means that sample size is sufficient for factor analysis. Significant Bartlett's test of sphericity ($\chi 2= 2075,55$; $p< 0.01$) purports that the data has a factorable structure. In interpreting practical significance of factor loadings, the concept of statistical power, which indicates that significance level of factor loadings is evaluated based on sample sizes was used. Hair et al. (2014) suggested that factor loadings of 0.35

Table 3. Results of exploratory factor analysis of product and process innovation capability

Product and Process Innovation Capability Scales	Factor Loadings
Product Innovation Capability	
My firm is able to replace obsolete products.	0,657
My firm is able to extend the range of products.	0,721
My firm is able to develop environmentally friendly products.	0,45
My firm is able to improve product design.	0,664
My firm is able to reduce the time to develop a new product until its launch in the market.	0,625
Process Innovation Capability	
My firm is able to create and manage a portfolio of interrelated technologies.	0,662
My firm is able to master and absorb the basic and key technologies of business.	0,62
My firm continually develops programs to reduce production costs.	0,451
My firm has valuable knowledge for innovating manufacturing and technological processes.	0,497
My firm has valuable knowledge on the best processes and systems for work organization.	0,754
My firm organizes its production efficiently.	0,833
My firm assigns resources to the production department efficiently.	0,751
My firm is able to maintain a low level of stock without impairing service.	0,562
My firm manages production organization efficiently.	0,612
My firm is able to offer environmentally friendly processes.	0,854
My firm is able to integrate production management activities.	0,775
Total Variance Explained: 50.41; KMO: 0.90; Bartlett's Test: 2075,55; df=120; p= 0.000	

and above are considered significant, since the sample size is bigger than 250. All facor loadings in Table 3 are bigger than the cutoff value 0.35 and thus, they are considered significant in a sample of 309 respondents.

As indicated in Table 4, KMO value of the NC is 0.87, which means the data structure is suitable for factor analysis in terms of sample size. Bartlett's test of sphericity ($\chi2= 2330,65$; $p< 0.01$) is statistically significant.

KMO value of the LO is 0.93 and Bartlett's test of sphericity ($\chi2= 2657,50$; $p< 0.01$) is significant. Additionally, the four factors represented 64.87% of the variance of the 17 items, considered sufficient in terms of total variance explained (Table 5).

EFA results of firm performance demonstrates that sample size is sufficient for factor analysis, since KMO value is 0.86. Bartlett's test of sphericity ($\chi2= 1515,08$;

Table 4. Results of exploratory factor analysis of network capability

Network Capability Scale	Factor Loadings
Coordination	
In our firms we analyze what we would like and desire to achieve with which partner.	0,719
In our firms we develop relationships with each partner based on what they can contribute.	0,809
In our firms we discuss regularly with our partners how we can support each other.	0,756
Relational skills	
In our firms we have the ability to build good personal relationships with our business partners.	0,745
In our firms we can deal flexibly with our partners.	0,641
In our firms we almost always solve problems constructively with our partners.	0,76
Building new relations	
In our firms we are constantly open to new relationships with new partners.	0,868
In our firms we have the ability to initiate a mutual relationship with new partners.	0,836
In our firms we have our eyes open to find new partners.	0,84
Partner knowledge	
In our firms we know our partners' markets.	0,833
In our firms we know our partners' products/procedures/services.	0,784
In our firms we know our partners' strengths and weaknesses.	0,802
Internal communication	
In our firms we have regular meetings for every project.	0,802
In our firms, employees develop informal contacts among themselves.	0,937
In our firms, managers and employees often give feedback to each other.	0,81
Total Variance Explained: 74.28; KMO: 0.87; Bartlett's Test: 2330,65; df=105; p= 0.000	

p< 0.01) is significant (Table 6). Firm performance is one-dimensional, and the single factor explains 58.96% of the total variance.

Scale Reliabilities and Validities

Descriptive statistics, correlations, reliabilities and discriminant validities of the variables are displayed in Table 7 below. The reliability of scale items is assessed by Cronbach's alpha. The rule of thumb is Cronbach's alpha coefficients of 0.70 or higher are considered acceptable (Nunnally & Bernstein, 1994). In this study, with two exceptions all the constructs have Cronbach's alpha values greater than 0.70.

Table 5. Results of exploratory factor analysis of learning orientation

Learning Orientation Scale	Factor Loadings
Commitment to learning	
Managers basically agree that our organization's ability to learn is the key to our competitive advantage.	0,72
The basic values of this organization include learning as key to improvement.	0,713
The sense around here is that employee learning is an investment, not an expense.	0,704
Learning in my organization is seen as a key commodity necessary to guarantee organizational survival.	0,776
Shared vision	
There is a commonality of purpose in my organization.	0,731
There is total agreement on our organizational vision across all levels, functions, and divisions.	0,739
All employees are committed to the goals of this organization.	0,727
Employees view themselves as partners in charting the direction of the organization.	0,72
Open-mindedness	
We are not afraid to reflect critically on the shared assumptions we have made about our customers.	0,641
Personnel in this enterprise realize that the very way they perceive the marketplace must be continually questioned.	0,668
We rarely collectively question our own bias about the way we interpret customer information.	0,683
We continually judge the quality of our decisions and activities taken over time.	0,739
Intraorganizational knowledge sharing	
There is a good deal of organizational conversation that keeps alive the lessons learned from history.	0,758
We always analyze unsuccessful organizational endeavors and communicate the lessons learned widely.	0,72
We have specific mechanisms for sharing lessons learned in organizational activities from department to department (unit to unit, team to team).	0,628
Top management repeatedly emphasizes the importance of knowledge sharing in our company.	0,686
We put little effort in sharing lessons and experiences.	0,657
Total Variance Explained: 64,87; KMO: 0,93; Bartlett's Test: 2657,50; df=136; p= 0,000	

The sub-dimension of LO, open-mindedness, has a Cronbach's alpha of 0.50, but the alpha value of second-order construct is 0.91, which is well above the recommended

Table 6. Results of exploratory factor analysis of firm performance

	Factor Loadings
Firm Performance	
Sales Revenue	0,828
Net Profitability	0,84
Return on Investment	0,789
Growth Rate	0,771
Market Share	0,764
Product Quality	0,695
Customer Satisfaction	0,685
Brand Image	0,757
Total Variance Explained: 58.96; KMO: 0.86 Bartlett's Test: 1515,08; df=25; p= 0.000	

cut-off. Another sub-dimension of NC, internal communication, has a reliability coefficient of 0.55. Still, the alpha value of second-order construct is 0.88, and above the minimum acceptable limit.

Regarding convergent validity of the scales, Average Variance Extracted (AVE) and Composite Reliability (CR) value were computed (Bagozzi & Yi, 1988). AVE is an assessment of a measurement model's validity because it shows how much of the variance in the indicators is explained by the latent constructs (Fornell & Larcker, 1981). Malhotra (2010) posited that:

An AVE of 0.5 or more indicates satisfactory convergent validity, as it means that the latent construct accounts for 50 percent or more of the variance in the observed variables, on the average. If AVE is less than 0.5, the variance due to measurement error is larger than the variance captured by the construct, and the validity of the individual indicators, as well as the construct, is questionable. Note that AVE is a more conservative measure than CR. On the basis of CR alone, the researcher may conclude that the convergent validity of the construct is adequate, even though more than 50 percent of the variance is due to error. (p. 702)

As indicated in the quote above and also recommended by Fornell and Larcker (1981), the authors relied on only CR values alone to conclude that the validity of all the constructs in this study is acceptable. Each construct's CR score exceeds the suggested cutoff point of 0.70 (Fornell & Larcker, 1981). Although all AVE values

The Complementary Effect of Network Capability

	Mean	Standard Deviation	(1)	(2)	(3)	(4)	(5)	(6)	(7)	(8)	(9)	(10)	(11)	(12)	(13)	(14)	(15)	(16)	(17)
(1) Firm size	2,31	0,72	1																
(2) Firm age	1,94	0,98	0,420**																
(3) Market turbulence	3	1,13	0,076	-0,021															
(4) Technological turbulence	3,74	1,09	-0,117*	-0,126	0,291**														
(5) Competitive intensity	4,25	0,84	-0,039	0,033	0,112*	0,314**													
(6) Product innovation capability	4,26	0,54	-0,111	-0,099	-0,039	0,115*	0,026	*0,63*											
(7) Process innovation capability	4,03	0,55	-0,077	-0,097	-0,052	0,133*	0,184**	0,553**	*0,68*										
(8) Commitment to learning	4,15	0,72	0,162**	-0,178**	-0,066	0,202**	0,134*	0,406**	0,600**	*0,72*									
(9) Shared vision	3,85	0,68	-0,191**	-0,157**	-0,002	0,169**	0,136*	0,348**	0,646**	0,701**	*0,72*								
(10) Open-mindedness	3,64	0,54	-0,192**	-0,159**	-0,120*	0,082	0,127	0,336**	0,573**	0,619**	0,670**	*0,68*							
(11) Intraorganizational knowledge sharing	3,58	0,76	-0,168**	-0,137*	-0,058	0,088	0,063	0,349**	0,627**	0,603**	0,710**	0,655**	*0,69*						
(12) Coordination	3,81	0,73	-0,232**	-0,133*	-0,006	0,191**	0,073	0,386**	0,560**	0,456**	0,610**	0,478**	0,601**	*0,76*					
(13) Relational skills	3,97	0,65	-0,231**	-0,129*	-0,075	0,148**	0,047	0,352**	0,492**	0,467**	0,544**	0,425**	0,549**	0,682**	*0,71*				
(14) Building new relations	4,01	0,74	-0,158**	-0,096	0,029	0,172**	0,01	0,276**	0,296**	0,252**	0,300**	0,271**	0,248**	0,303**	0,375**	*0,84*			
(15) Partner knowledge	3,91	0,69	-0,071	-0,053	-0,006	0,075	0,030	0,252**	0,243**	0,240**	0,308**	0,284**	0,350**	0,519**	0,506**	0,393**	*0,80*		
(16) Internal communication	4,11	0,49	-0,097	-0,109	-0,053	0,141*	0,150**	0,769**	0,958**	0,601**	0,615**	0,556**	0,601**	0,563**	0,498**	0,322**	0,274**	*0,85*	
(17) Firm performance	3,75	0,76	0,114*	0,129*	-0,040	0,092	0,079	0,254**	0,427**	0,334**	0,413**	0,393**	0,365**	0,336**	0,256**	0,135*	0,199**	0,415**	*0,76*
Cronbach's alpha								0,71	0,88	0,86	0,81	0,50	0,79	0,86	0,79	0,85	0,84	0,55	0,90
CR								0,76	0,94	0,81	0,81	0,77	0,82	0,80	0,75	0,88	0,84	0,88	0,91
AVE								0,40	0,46	0,53	0,53	0,46	0,47	0,58	0,51	0,71	0,65	0,72	0,58

Notes. ** Correlation is significant at the 0.01 level (2-tailed). * Correlation is significant at the 0.05 level (2-tailed). Diagonal elements (in italics) represent the square root of the AVE

do not exceed the threshold of 0.50, most of the AVE values of constructs are above the 0.50 level (Anderson & Gerbing, 1988) (Table 7).

The discriminant validity was evaluated by comparing the square root of the AVE with correlation values. As reported in Table 7, all diagonal elements reflecting the square root of the AVE are greater than the off-diagonal elements, indicating that all the constructs satisfy the criteria of discriminant validity (Fornell & Larcker, 1981).

Test of Hypotheses

Results of Direct Effects

Table 8 presents hierarchical regression analysis results of the complementary effects of NC and LO on product and process innovation capability. Model 1 shows that none of the control variables has an impact on product innovation capability. For direct effects, Model 2 reveals that NC ($\beta = 0.237$, t = 3.485) and LO ($\beta = 0.258$, t = 3.775) significantly affect product innovation capability. However, with the involvement of interaction term in Model 3, the direct effects of NC and LO on firm performance become insignificant. The coefficient of the interaction term of NC and LO is positive and significant at 0.05 level ($\beta = 1.197$, t = 2.295). Therefore, Hypothesis 1a is supported. Model 2 also shows that NC and LO prove to have significant and positive effects on process innovation capability. The former has a β value of 0.172 ($p< 0.01$) whereas the latter indicates 0.603 ($p< 0.001$) for its β value. As the interaction effect of NC and LO is insignificant in Model 3, Hypothesis 1b is rejected.

Table 9 depicts the independent effects of product and process innovation capability on firm performance. Control variables make significant contribution to the regression model [F = 2.717, $p< 0.05$]. As the independent variables entered into regression, it explains an additional 18.3% variance in firm performance and this change in the model is significant [F = 12.553, $p< 0.001$]. The effect of product innovation capability on firm performance is not significant. The regression coefficient of process innovation capability in Model 2 is significant and positive at 0.001 level ($\beta = 0.419$, t = 6.713), meaning that process innovation capability has a significant and positive impact on firm performance. Consequently, Hypothesis 2a is rejected while Hypothesis 2b is accepted.

Results of Mediating Effects

In order to investigate the mediating mechanisms posited in the conceptual model, the PROCESS procedure (version 4.1) through SPSS was utilized (Hayes, 2018). Mediation is tested by evaluating the indirect effect's magnitude and its confidence

Table 8. Results of the complementary effects of NC and LO on product and process innovation capability

	Product Innovation Capability						Process Innovation Capability					
	Model 1		Model 2		Model 3		Model 1		Model 2		Model 3	
	β	t-value	β	t-value	β	t-value	β	t-value	β	t-value	β	t-value
Controls												
Firm size	-0,068	-1,078	0,009	0,151	0,014	0,242	-0,015	-0,247	0,094*	2,111	0,096*	2,156
Firm age	-0,056	-0,898	-0,016	-0,285	-0,017	-0,300	-0,086	-1,392	-0,009	-0,195	-0,009	-0,202
Market turbulence	-0,070	-1,181	-0,036	-0,663	-0,053	-0,978	-0,099	-1,693	-0,030	-0,709	-0,036	-0,862
Technological turbulence	0,122	1,949	0,054	0,934	0,069	1,203	0,096	1,559	-0,006	-0,136	0,000	0,000
Competitive intensity	-0,005	-0,091	-0,039	-0,719	-0,047	-0,870	0,167**	2,837	0,102*	2,443	0,099*	2,364
Direct effects												
Learning orientation			0,258***	3,775	-0,042	-1,415			0,603***	11,529	0,331	1,375
Network capability			0,237**	3,485	-0,378	-1,369			0,172**	3,3	-0,067	-0,315
Interaction effects												
Learning orientation x Network capability					1,197*	2,295					0,465	1,156
Model R^2	0,030		0,212		0,225		0,058		0,536		0,538	
Adjusted R^2	0,014		0,193		0,204		0,043		0,525		0,526	
Change in R^2			0,182		0,014				0,478		0,002	
Model F	1,865		11,536***		10,895*		3,753**		49,706***		43,709	
Change in F			34,675		5,267				155,050		1,337	

*p< 0.05, **p< 0.01, ***p< 0.001

interval. If the confidence interval includes zero, a true mediation effect doesn't exist. If the confidence interval doesn't include zero, the mediation has taken place (Field, 2009).

The results of SPSS PROCESS Macro Regression are shown in Table 10. NC and LO jointly have a significant impact on product innovation capability, $b = 0.06$, $t = 8.57$, $p < 0.001$, with a 95% bootstrap confidence interval of 0.05 to 0.08. Furthermore, NC and LO jointly have a significant impact on process innovation capability, $b = 0.10$, $t = 16.76$, $p < 0.001$, with a 95% bootstrap confidence interval of 0.09 to 0.11. As indicated in Table 10 above NC and LO jointly has a significant impact on firm performance, $b = 0.05$, $t = 4.01$, $p < 0.001$, with a 95% bootstrap confidence interval of 0.03 to 0.09. Additionally, product innovation capability does not predict firm performance, $b = 0.01$, $t = 0.19$, $p = 0.84$, with a 95% bootstrap

Table 9. Results of the direct effects of product and process innovation capability on firm performance

	Model 1		Model 2	
	ß	t-Value	ß	t-Value
Controls				
Firm size	0,095	1,515	0,104	1,833
Firm age	0,102	1,628	0,140*	2,475
Market turbulence	-0,087	-1,473	-0,043	-0,800
Technological turbulence	0,126*	2,022	0,081	1,433
Competitive intensity	0,049	0,826	-0,021	-0,381
Direct effects				
Product innovation capability			0,037	0,595
Process innovation capability			0,419***	6,713
Model R^2	0,043		0,226	
Adjusted R^2	0,027		0,208	
Change in R^2			0,183	
Model F	2,717*		12,553***	
Change in F			35,592	

*p< 0.05, **p< 0.01, ***p< 0.001

Table 10. Results of SPSS PROCESS macro regression

Regression Type	b-Value	t-Value	p-Value	95% LLCI-ULCI
The complementary effect of NC and LO on product innovation capability	0.06	8.57	< 0.001	[0.05, 0.08]
The complementary effect of NC and LC on process innovation capability	0.10	16.76	< 0.001	[0.09, 0.08]
The complementary effect of NC and LO on firm performance	0.05	4.01	< 0.001	[0.03, 0.09]
The effect of product innovation capability on firm performance	0.02	0.19	0.84	[-0.15, 0.18]
The effect of process innovation capability on firm performance	0.32	3.07	< 0.01	[0.12, 0.53]

Note. Abbreviations: LLCI, lower limit confidence interval; ULCI, upper limit confidence interval.

Figure 2. Model of the mediating effects of product and process innovation capability

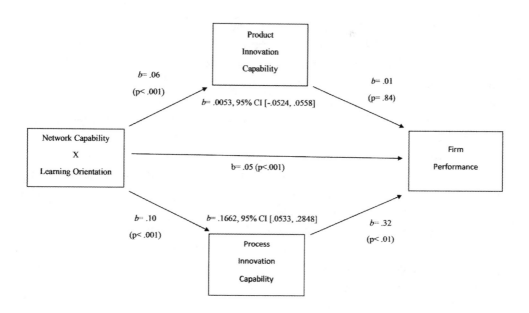

confidence interval of -0.15 to 0.18. Process innovation capability significantly predicts firm performance, $b = 0.32$, $t = 3.07$, $p < 0.01$, with a 95% bootstrap confidence interval of 0.12 to 0.53.

Hayes' PROCESS Macro produces bootstrap confidence intervals for the mediation analysis based on 5,000 bootstrap resamples. As indicated in Figure 5 below, there is insufficient evidence for the mediating effect of product innovation capability $b = 0.0053$, with 95% bootstrap confidence interval of -0.05 to 0.05. On the other hand, as evidenced by 95% bootstrap confidence intervals of 0.05 to 0.28, which do not include zero, the authors conclude that process innovation capability mediates the complementary effect of NC and LO on firm performance. Hypothesis 3a is rejected, whereas Hypothesis 3b is accepted.

DISCUSSION

Theoretical Contribution

This research enriches dynamic capability theory by demonstrating how having simultaneous NC and LO combinations improves SME performance. An internally focused innovation strategy that depends on a firm's own resources and capabilities can be considered as a conservative strategic choice, because the firm would be missing the dynamic influences of the interaction (Caloghirou et al., 2004). The results signified that NC and LO jointly has a positive effect on product innovation capability. Product innovation capability has an external, market-oriented approach, which enables firms to develop distinguishing products, and thus gain competitive advantage. Firms might have difficulties in meeting changing customer demands by only relying on their internal capabilities, they also need to build and nurture relationships with external partners to serve differentiated products to the market. For this reason, the collective influence of NC and LO might be reflected in product innovation capability. On the other hand, the complementary effect of NC and LO on process innovation capability was not supported. Process innovation focuses on processes and systems related to production and technologies internal to the firm. For this reason, manufacturing firms may not fully exploit the positive impacts of NC and LO in combination to improve process innovation capability. Instead, they might benefit from NC and LO in isolation to develop process innovation.

This study demonstrated that only process innovation capability had a significant positive impact on the level of firm performance within the context of high-technology manufacturing SMEs. The outcomes of this research are in line with those of Ar and Baki (2011), Gupta and Gupta (2019), Jiménez-Jiménez and Sanz-Valle (2011), and Kafetzopoulos and Psomas (2015). Therefore, this study supports the notion that manufacturing SMEs are more inclined to utilize process innovation compared to product innovation to improve firm performance (Laforet & Tann, 2006). It might also be that Turkish manufacturing SMEs focus on decreasing production costs and thus, they prioritize ways of working in the firm because of money concerns.

This research provides new insights concerning the mechanisms through which complementary capabilities affect firm performance of manufacturing SMEs. The mediating role of process innovation capability offers a more complete insight of how NC and LO interactively influence firm performance of SMEs and contribute to the extant literature focusing on the interaction of capabilities. Findings of this study empirically confirmed the notion that the effect of different capabilities on firm performance was realized through the development of other capabilities (Wang & Ahmed, 2007; Zahoor & Lew, 2022). Additionally, our results are in line with the literature posited that innovation capability should be considered as a critical intermediate outcome in the relationship between firm resources and capabilities, and performance (Gronum et al., 2012).

This research can be deemed as the first attempt to explore the role of NC and LO together in explaining SMEs' performance in Türkiye as a developing country. Since SMEs are catalyst for economic advancement in Türkiye, it is important to reveal the factors that affect innovation capabilities of SMEs, especially those operating in high-technology sector. Another contribution of this research pertains to the measurement of the scales used in this study. This research uses broad measures of LO, NC, innovation capability and firm performance. Specifically, NC was measured as a second-order construct comprises five dimensions, rather than a one-dimensional structure.

The requirement that dynamic capabilities lead competitive advantage has been indicated as a tautology in the literature, yet dynamic capabilities do not necessarily provide successful outcomes for firms (Di Stefano et al., 2010; Zahra et al., 2006). The distinct impact of the interactive effect of NC and LO only on product innovation capability as well as the mediating effect of process innovation capability on firm performance can be associated with the tautology issue of the dynamic capabilities theory, that is different dynamic capabilities are related to firm performance differently.

Managerial Implications

This study suggests several important implications for managers or founders of high-technology manufacturing SMEs. This research found that only process innovation capability enhances firm performance. Therefore, managers should improve their firms' process innovation capability by applying high-quality and flexible operations and incorporating efficient and effective manufacturing or technological processes to improve firm performance.

While building networks with external partners is crucial, managers/founders should also focus on improving internal capabilities such as LO. LO enables firms to generate and utilize knowledge emanates from inside the firm as well as from external actors. Hence, to be able to increase product and process innovation capabilities and consequently firm performance, managers or founders of SMEs in high-technology sector should simultaneously develop NC and LO capabilities. This study demonstrates the mediating role of process innovation capability in the joint impact of NC with LO on firm performance. In order to take advantage of the complementary benefit of NC and LO on firm performance, managers should utilize process innovation capability as a vehicle for increasing firm performance.

Limitations and Future Research Directions

There are a number of limitations in this study, which provide valuable directions for future research. Rather than using a totally random sample, a purposive sample of high-technology manufacturing SMEs was chosen in this study. Research findings quite likely are applicable to other developing countries. Therefore, research into the high-technology manufacturing industry of other emerging countries should be conducted in order to generalize the study's findings for this industry. Additionally, design of this research was cross-sectional in nature. Cross-sectional data may not be able to reflect the interactive effect of NC and LO on firm performance over time, due to the fact that NC and LO are dynamic constructs that require investments and develop over time. Future research therefore should adopt longitudinal and experimental approach to make causal inferences in a rigorous sense.

In this research, an adequate model for confirmatory factor analysis could not be developed. Subsequent analyses were conducted after performing only EFA, which is deemed as another empirical limitation of this study. Therefore, future studies may conduct confirmatory factor analysis to evaluate the reliability and validity of the scales and use structural equation modelling for hypotheses testing. This study collected self-reported, perceptual data on firm performance from a single informant. Even if the results of the Harman's one factor test indicated that common method bias is not a serious problem, this limitation must be taken into account when interpreting the results. In this respect, future research might adopt multi-informant approach, which is collecting data from different sources in the firm to alleviate common method bias.

A fruitful direction for future studies would be to explore interrelationships among different innovation capability types that improve firm performance. It would also be better to investigate the boundary conditions (i.e., organizational and environmental contingencies) that might influence the synergistic effect of different innovation capabilities on performance outcomes of firms. Future research might also address the role of contextual and situational factors. For instance, competitive market conditions, industry types, national cultural characteristics, managerial characteristics can be included as moderators in research models.

NOTE

The book chapter is based on the first author's doctoral dissertation.

REFERENCES

Akman, G., & Yilmaz, C. (2008). Innovative capability, innovation strategy and market orientation: An empirical analysis in Turkish software industry. *International Journal of Innovation Management*, *12*(1), 69–111. doi:10.1142/S1363919608001923

Alegre, J., & Chiva, R. (2013). Linking entrepreneurial orientation and firm performance: The role of organizational learning capability and innovation performance. *Journal of Small Business Management*, *51*(4), 491–507. doi:10.1111/jsbm.12005

Altinay, L., Madanoglu, M., De Vita, G., Arasli, H., & Ekinci, Y. (2016). The interface between organizational learning capability, entrepreneurial orientation, and SME growth. *Journal of Small Business Management*, *54*(3), 871–891. doi:10.1111/jsbm.12219

Anderson, J. C., & Gerbing, D. W. (1988). Structural equation modeling in practice: A review and recommended two-step approach. *Psychological Bulletin*, *103*(3), 411–423. https://doi.org/.3.411 doi:10.1037/0033-2909.103

Anning-Dorson, T. (2018). Customer involvement capability and service firm performance: The mediating role of innovation. *Journal of Business Research*, *86*, 269–280. doi:10.1016/j.jbusres.2017.07.015

Ar, I. M., & Baki, B. (2011). Antecedents and performance impacts of product versus process innovation: Empirical evidence from SMEs located in Turkish science and technology parks. *European Journal of Innovation Management*, *14*(2), 172–206. doi:10.1108/14601061111124885

Arend, R. J. (2014). Entrepreneurship and dynamic capabilities: How firm age and size affect the 'capability enhancement–SME performance' relationship. *Small Business Economics*, *42*(1), 33–57. doi:10.100711187-012-9461-9

Augier, M., & Teece, D. J. (2009). Dynamic capabilities and the role of managers in business strategy and economic performance. *Organization Science*, *20*(2), 410–421. doi:10.1287/orsc.1090.0424

Bagozzi, R. P., & Yi, Y. (1988). On the evaluation of structural equation models. *Journal of the Academy of Marketing Science*, *16*(1), 74–94. doi:10.1007/BF02723327

Baker, W. E., Mukherjee, D., & Perin, M. G. (2022). Learning orientation and competitive advantage: A critical synthesis and future directions. *Journal of Business Research*, *144*, 863–873. doi:10.1016/j.jbusres.2022.02.003

Baker, W. E., & Sinkula, J. M. (1999). The synergistic effect of market orientation and learning orientation on organizational performance. *Journal of the Academy of Marketing Science, 27*(4), 411–427. doi:10.1177/0092070399274002

Barney, J. B. (1991). Firm resources and sustained competitive advantage. *Journal of Management, 17*(1), 99–120. doi:10.1177/014920639101700108

Barreto, I. (2010). Dynamic capabilities: A review of past research and an agenda for the future. *Journal of Management, 36*(1), 256–280. doi:10.1177/0149206309350776

Bouguerra, A., Mellahi, K., Glaister, K., Sadeghi, A., Temouri, Y., & Tatoglu, E. (2022). Absorptive capacity and organizational performance in an emerging market context: Evidence from the banking industry in Turkey. *Journal of Business Research, 139*, 1575–1587. doi:10.1016/j.jbusres.2021.10.077

Brislin, R. W. (1970). Back-translation for cross-cultural research. *Journal of Cross-Cultural Psychology, 1*(3), 185–216. doi:10.1177/135910457000100301

Cakar, N. D., & Erturk, A. (2010). Comparing innovation capability of small and medium-sized enterprises: Examining the effects of organizational culture and empowerment. *Journal of Small Business Management, 48*(3), 325–359. doi:10.1111/j.1540-627X.2010.00297.x

Calantone, R. J., Cavusgil, S. T., & Zhao, Y. (2002). Learning orientation, firm innovation capability, and firm performance. *Industrial Marketing Management, 31*(6), 515–524. doi:10.1016/S0019-8501(01)00203-6

Caloghirou, Y., Kastelli, I., & Tsakanikas, A. (2004). Internal capabilities and external knowledge sources: Complements or substitutes for innovative performance? *Technovation, 24*(1), 29–39. doi:10.1016/S0166-4972(02)00051-2

Camisón, C., & Villar López, A. (2010). An examination of the relationship between manufacturing flexibility and firm performance: The mediating role of innovation. *International Journal of Operations & Production Management, 30*(8), 853–878. doi:10.1108/01443571011068199

Camisón, C., & Villar-López, A. (2014). Organizational innovation as an enabler of technological innovation capabilities and firm performance. *Journal of Business Research, 67*(1), 2891–2902. doi:10.1016/j.jbusres.2012.06.004

Cenamor, J., Parida, V., & Wincent, J. (2019). How entrepreneurial SMEs compete through digital platforms: The roles of digital platform capability, network capability and ambidexterity. *Journal of Business Research, 100*, 196–206. doi:10.1016/j.jbusres.2019.03.035

Chen, Y. K., Coviello, N., & Ranaweera, C. (2021). How does dynamic network capability operate? A moderated mediation analysis with NPD speed and firm age. *Journal of Business and Industrial Marketing*, *36*(2), 292–306. doi:10.1108/JBIM-01-2020-0050

Chien, S., & Tsai, C. (2012). Dynamic capability, knowledge, learning, and firm performance. *Journal of Organizational Change Management*, *25*(3), 434–444. doi:10.1108/09534811211228148

D'Angelo, A., & Presutti, M. (2019). SMEs international growth: The moderating role of experience on entrepreneurial and learning orientations. *International Business Review*, *28*(3), 613–624. doi:10.1016/j.ibusrev.2018.12.006

Damanpour, F. (2010). An integration of research findings of effects of firm size and market competition on product and process innovations. *British Journal of Management*, *21*(4), 996–1010. doi:10.1111/j.1467-8551.2009.00628.x

Di Stefano, G., Peteraf, M., & Verona, G. (2010). Dynamic capabilities deconstructed: A bibliographic investigation into the origins, development, and future directions of the research domain. *Industrial and Corporate Change*, *19*(4), 1187–1204. doi:10.1093/icc/dtq027

Ferreira, J., Coelho, A., & Moutinho, L. (2020). Dynamic capabilities, creativity and innovation capability and their impact on competitive advantage and firm performance: The moderating role of entrepreneurial orientation. *Technovation*, *92*, 102061. doi:10.1016/j.technovation.2018.11.004

Field, A. (2009). *Discovering statistics using SPSS*. Sage Publications.

Fitjar, R. D., Gjelsvik, M., & Rodríguez-Pose, A. (2013). The combined impact of managerial and relational capabilities on innovation in firms. *Entrepreneurship and Regional Development*, *25*(5-6), 500–520. doi:10.1080/08985626.2013.798353

Fornell, C., & Larcker, D. (1981). Evaluating structural equation models with unobservable variables and measurement error. *JMR, Journal of Marketing Research*, *18*(1), 39–50. doi:10.1177/002224378101800104

Gronum, S., Verreynne, M. L., & Kastelle, T. (2012). The role of networks in small and medium-sized enterprise innovation and firm performance. *Journal of Small Business Management*, *50*(2), 257–282. doi:10.1111/j.1540-627X.2012.00353.x

Gupta, A. K., & Gupta, N. (2019). Innovation and culture as a dynamic capability for firm performance: A study from emerging markets. *Global Journal of Flexible Systems Managment*, *20*(4), 323–336. doi:10.100740171-019-00218-5

Hair, J. F. Jr, Black, W. C., Babin, B. J., & Anderson, R. E. (2014). *Multivariate data analysis* (7th ed.). Pearson Education Limited.

Hayes, A. F. (2018). *Introduction to mediation, moderation, and conditional process analysis: A regression-based approach* (2nd ed.). The Guilford Press.

Helfat, C. E., & Peteraf, M. A. (2003). The dynamic resource-based view: Capability lifecycles. *Strategic Management Journal*, (24), 997–1010. doi:10.1002/smj.332

Hult, G. T. M., Hurley, R. F., & Knight, G. A. (2004). Innovativeness: Its antecedents and impact on business performance. *Industrial Marketing Management*, *33*(5), 429–438. doi:10.1016/j.indmarman.2003.08.015

Iddris, F. (2016). Innovation capability: A systematic review and research agenda. *Interdisciplinary Journal of Information, Knowledge, and Management*, *11*, 235–260. doi:10.28945/3571

Jaworski, B. J., & Kohli, A. K. (1993). Market orientation: Antecedents and consequences. *Journal of Marketing*, *57*(3), 53–70. doi:10.1177/002224299305700304

Jiménez-Jiménez, D., & Sanz-Valle, R. (2011). Innovation, organizational learning, and performance. *Journal of Business Research*, *64*(4), 408–417. doi:10.1016/j.jbusres.2010.09.010

Kafetzopoulos, D., & Psomas, E. (2015). The impact of innovation capability on the performance of manufacturing companies: The Greek case. *Journal of Manufacturing Technology Management*, *26*(1), 104–130. doi:10.1108/JMTM-12-2012-0117

Kittilaksanawong, W., & Ren, Z. (2013). Innovation capability building through intermediary organizations: Cases of manufacturing small-and medium-sized enterprises from China's Zhejiang province. *Asian Journal of Technology Innovation*, *21*(2), 62–79. doi:10.1080/19761597.2013.819247

Laforet, S., & Tann, J. (2006). Innovative characteristics of small manufacturing firms. *Journal of Small Business and Enterprise Development*, *13*(3), 363–380. doi:10.1108/14626000610680253

Lawson, B., & Samson, D. (2001). Developing innovation capability in organisations: A dynamic capabilities approach. *International Journal of Innovation Management*, *5*(3), 377–400. doi:10.1142/S1363919601000427

Liao, S. H., Fei, W. C., & Chen, C. C. (2007). Knowledge sharing, absorptive capacity, and innovation capability: An empirical study of Taiwan's knowledge-intensive industries. *Journal of Information Science*, *33*(3), 340–359. doi:10.1177/0165551506070739

Lin, R. J., Chen, R. H., & Chiu, K. K. S. (2010). Customer relationship management and innovation capability: An empirical study. *Industrial Management & Data Systems*, *110*(1), 111–133. doi:10.1108/02635571011008434

Malhotra, N. K. (2010). *Marketing research- An applied orientation* (6th ed.). Pearson Education, Inc.

Mitrega, M., Forkmann, S., Zaefarian, G., & Henneberg, S. C. (2017). Networking capability in supplier relationships and its impact on product innovation and firm performance. *International Journal of Operations & Production Management*, *37*(5), 577–606. doi:10.1108/IJOPM-11-2014-0517

Mu, J., & Di Benedetto, A. (2012). Networking capability and new product development. *IEEE Transactions on Engineering Management*, *59*(1), 4–19. doi:10.1109/TEM.2011.2146256

Najafi-Tavani, S., Najafi-Tavani, Z., Naudé, P., Oghazi, P., & Zeynaloo, E. (2018). How collaborative innovation networks affect new product performance: Product innovation capability, process innovation capability, and absorptive capacity. *Industrial Marketing Management*, *73*, 193–205. doi:10.1016/j.indmarman.2018.02.009

Nunnally, J. C., & Bernstein, I. H. (1994). *Psychometric theory* (3rd ed.). McGraw Hill.

O'Cass, A., & Sok, P. (2014). The role of intellectual resources, product innovation capability, reputational resources and marketing capability combinations in firm growth. *International Small Business Journal*, *32*(8), 996–1018. doi:10.1177/0266242613480225

Parida, V., & Örtqvist, D. (2015). Interactive effects of network capability, ICT capability, and financial slack on technology-based small firm innovation performance. *Journal of Small Business Management*, *53*(S1), 278–298. doi:10.1111/jsbm.12191

Parida, V., Pesämaa, O., Wincent, J., & Westerberg, M. (2017). Network capability, innovativeness, and performance: A multidimensional extension for entrepreneurship. *Entrepreneurship and Regional Development*, *29*(1-2), 94–115. doi:10.1080/08985626.2016.1255434

Podsakoff, P. M., & Organ, D. W. (1986). Self-reports in organizational research: Problems and prospects. *Journal of Management*, *12*(4), 531–544. doi:10.1177/014920638601200408

Ritter, T., & Gemünden, H. G. (2003). Network competence: Its impact on innovation success and its antecedents. *Journal of Business Research, 56*(9), 745–755. doi:10.1016/S0148-2963(01)00259-4

Romijn, H., & Albaladejo, M. (2002). Determinants of innovation capability in small electronics and software firms in southeast England. *Research Policy, 21*(7), 1053–1067. doi:10.1016/S0048-7333(01)00176-7

Salavou, H., Baltas, G., & Lioukas, S. (2004). Organisational innovation in SMEs: The importance of strategic orientation and competitive structure. *European Journal of Marketing, 38*(9/10), 1091–1112. doi:10.1108/03090560410548889

Sinkula, J. M., Baker, W. E., & Noordewier, T. (1997). A framework for market-based organizational learning: Linking values, knowledge and behavior. *Journal of the Academy of Marketing Science, 25*(4), 305–318. doi:10.1177/0092070397254003

Teece, D. J. (2007). Explicating dynamic capabilities: The nature and microfoundations of (sustainable) enterprise performance. *Strategic Management Journal, 28*(13), 1319–1350. doi:10.1002mj.640

Teece, D. J. (2014). The foundations of enterprise performance: Dynamic and ordinary capabilities in an (economic) theory of firms. *The Academy of Management Perspectives, 28*(4), 328–352. doi:10.5465/amp.2013.0116

Teece, D. J., Pisano, G., & Shuen, A. (1997). Dynamic capabilities and strategic management. *Strategic Management Journal, 18*(7), 509–533. doi:10.1002/(SICI)1097-0266(199708)18:7<509::AID-SMJ882>3.0.CO;2-Z

Venkatraman, N., & Ramanujan, V. (1987). Planning system success: A conceptualization and an operational model. *Management Science, 33*(6), 687–705. doi:10.1287/mnsc.33.6.687

Walter, A., Auer, M., & Ritter, T. (2006). The impact of network capabilities and entrepreneurial orientation on university spin-off performance. *Journal of Business Venturing, 21*(4), 541–567. doi:10.1016/j.jbusvent.2005.02.005

Wang, C. L., & Ahmed, P. K. (2007). Dynamic capabilities: A review and research agenda. *International Journal of Management Reviews, 9*(1), 31–51. doi:10.1111/j.1468-2370.2007.00201.x

Wiklund, J., & Shepherd, D. (2005). Entrepreneurial orientation and small business performance: A configurational approach. *Journal of Business Venturing, 20*(1), 71–91. doi:10.1016/j.jbusvent.2004.01.001

Wilden, R., Devinney, T. M., & Dowling, G. R. (2016). The architecture of dynamic capability research identifying the building blocks of a configurational approach. *The Academy of Management Annals, 10*(1), 997–1076. doi:10.5465/19416520.2016.1161966

Xie, Y., & Zheng, X. (2020). How does corporate learning orientation enhance industrial brand equity? The roles of firm capabilities and size. *Journal of Business and Industrial Marketing, 35*(2), 231–243. doi:10.1108/JBIM-10-2018-0320

Yang, J. (2012). Innovation capability and corporate growth: An empirical investigation in China. *Journal of Engineering and Technology Management, 29*(1), 34–46. doi:10.1016/j.jengtecman.2011.09.004

Zacca, R., Dayan, M., & Ahrens, T. (2015). Impact of network capability on small business performance. *Management Decision, 53*(1), 2–23. doi:10.1108/MD-11-2013-0587

Zahoor, N., & Lew, Y. K. (2022). Sustaining superior international performance: Strategic orientations and dynamic capability of environmentally concerned small- and medium-sized enterprises. *Business Strategy and the Environment, 31*(3), 1002–1017. doi:10.1002/bse.2931

Zahra, S. A., Sapienza, H. J., & Davidsson, P. (2006). Entrepreneurship and dynamic capabilities: A review, model and research agenda. *Journal of Management Studies, 43*(4), 917–955. doi:10.1111/j.1467-6486.2006.00616.x

Zhou, S. S., Zhou, A. J., Feng, J., & Jiang, S. (2019). Dynamic capabilities and organizational performance: The mediating role of innovation. *Journal of Management & Organization, 25*(5), 731–747. doi:10.1017/jmo.2017.20

Zollo, M., & Winter, S. G. (2002). Deliberate learning and the evolution of dynamic capabilities. *Organization Science, 13*(3), 339–351. doi:10.1287/orsc.13.3.339.2780

KEY TERMS AND DEFINITIONS

Emergent Economy: Countries that are developing their economies, which are frequently characterized by relatively strong economic growth and an increase of trade and investment flows.

High-Technology Sector: It is the industry comprises technology-oriented firms that focus on developing and producing high-added-value products to increase competitive advantage.

Learning Orientation: It is a cultural feature that highlights the process of creating and utilizing knowledge that may eventually affect organizational outcomes.

Network Capability: The firm's capabilities to build and leverage relationships with other entities that enable organizations to have access to various resources.

Process Innovation Capability: The firm's ability to apply more efficient and effective production processes compared to current operations.

Product Innovation Capability: The firm's ability to introduce novel or differentiated products or services for the benefit of the organization and its stakeholders.

Small and Medium Enterprises: Enterprises contribute to the economic development, which have less than 250 employees and annual net sales income or financial balances under 125 million Turkish Liras.

Chapter 12
Women Entrepreneurship in Multifunctional Agriculture for Rural Revival in Serbia

Vesna Popović
 https://orcid.org/0000-0003-1018-2461
Institute of Agricultural Economics, Belgrade, Serbia

Branko Mihailović
 https://orcid.org/0000-0002-2398-6568
Institute of Agricultural Economics, Belgrade, Serbia

ABSTRACT

The COVID-19 crisis has revealed the benefits of rural living and underlined the importance of strengthening local food systems and empowering family farming and women farmers given the crucial role they play in multifunctional agriculture, climate resilience, and recovery from the pandemic. Multifunctional agriculture is an effective framework for a set of business models that integrate economic, environmental, and socio-cultural impacts of agriculture and food production on sustainable rural development. Innovative business models in multifunctional agriculture give new opportunities for women farmers only if they enjoy gender equality and have access to work-life balance services. This chapter per the authors analyzes women entrepreneurship in Serbian agriculture using business model canvas analysis of a case study farm from the Homolje area (East Serbia). Research results, solutions, and recommendations aim to raise awareness of the role of women's multifunctional entrepreneurship and collaborative business strategies in rural revival within the new normal paradigm.

DOI: 10.4018/978-1-6684-8810-2.ch012

Copyright © 2023, IGI Global. Copying or distributing in print or electronic forms without written permission of IGI Global is prohibited.

INTRODUCTION

The interlinked climate change, COVID-19 pandemic and Russia-Ukraine conflict have raised serious food shortages, trade disruptions, price inflation and quality and safety challenges within international supply chains. Farmers, consumers, scientists and policy-makers worldwide are increasingly advocating more resilient and localized food systems, relied on diversified, shorter, fairer and cleaner values-based supply chains to buffer external shocks (De Schutter, 2019; Gaupp et al., 2020; Gomez et al., 2021; Zaremba et al., 2021; Gargano et al., 2021; USDA, 2022). Proclaiming 2019-2028 as the UN Decade of Family Farming, the United Nations emphasize the role of multifunctional agriculture, family farming and women farmers in achieving SDGs related to sustainable and inclusive food systems, gender equality and no poverty (FAO & IFAD, 2019). Rural areas, valued for food production, tourism and management of natural resources and climate risks but also faced with women and youth outflows, get new opportunities for comprehensive post-pandemic revival, based on the green and digital transition.

Multifunctionality allows farmers to act holistically on various aspects of sustainable development (FAO & IFAD, 2019). Multifunctional agriculture is a framework for a set of business models related to vertical integration and on-farm diversification that integrate economic performance of food production with environmental and socio-cultural issues within sustainable territorial development (Cadiou, 2018; Mihailović et al., 2020). Farm activities are deepening towards value addition (organic, place-based and high-quality food production and short food supply chains), broadening by diversification (e.g., agrotourism, nature & landscape management, care farming) and re-grounding by resource mobilization based on cost reduction and off-farm income (van der Ploeg & Roep, 2003). Carter (1998) linked farm pluriactivity to portfolio entrepreneurship, noting that "pluriactivity has always been an important and distinctive feature of the farm sector" (p. 17). For Tohidyan Far and Rezaei-Moghaddam (2019) entrepreneurship is the heart of multifunctional agriculture.

Lans et al. (2017) included farm women's affinity for new on-farm businesses among specifics of agricultural entrepreneurship, along with the farm location and business environment, and family farms' entrepreneurial tradition. Montagnoli (2020) pointed out that 32% of agricultural enterprises in Italy are female-led while among agritourism companies this share reaches 39%. Innovative business models, based on agroecology, food re-localization, collaboration, e-services and cultural and creative industries, provide new opportunities for rural women farmers and entrepreneurs, notably young, skilled and well-educated newcomers (Sutherland et al., 2015; Cadiou, 2018; Uvarova & Vitola, 2019; European Commission, 2021). These women are building new rurality with their insights, knowledge and skills, connections and participation in public life, and changing social norms concerning work–life balance (Baylina et al., 2017; Franić & Kovačićek, 2019). In its Resolution on women and their roles in rural areas, European Parliament (2017) stresses that women in rural areas can be agents of change in moving towards sustainable agriculture and green jobs. However, there is still a number of gender stereotypes and inequalities that prevent women from using their full potential to run a farm business successfully. Rural cultures and traditions affect female careers (Wiest, 2016). Women farmers often have fewer resources, incomes and assets, and therefore low decision-making power at home and in the community that, associated with poor provision of work-life balance services in rural areas (Franić & Kovačićek, 2019; Addati et al., 2018), limit their access to training, extension, technology, markets, credit and social networks (Brandth, 2002; FAO, 2011).

Serbia is not an exception on these issues. Women in Serbia participate with 87% in the category of part-time employees that indicate caring for children or disabled persons as the reason for working part-time. Compared to men, women work twice long time in the house and spend half the time working paid jobs (Statistical office of the RS, 2020). Prejudice and patriarchal mentality maintain the tradition in owning property and inheritance. In 2019, only 25% of real estate is owned by women while another 10% is jointly owned (Gender Equality Strategy, 2021). Although the law provides women with rights in inheritance, an analysis of the court decisions shows that 36% of women renounced inheritance, most often in favour of their brothers and sons (Beker, 2017). Women make up 19.4% of farm holders and 15.3% of farm managers, usually manage small farms and more than half of them belong to 65 and older age cohort (Statistical office of the RS, 2018). In spite of these challenges, there are inspiring stories of female entrepreneurship in multifunctional agriculture in Serbia. One of them is Milosava Grozdić from Homolje area in East Serbia, farm holder, president of the women's association "Homoljke" and member of the municipal assembly of Žagubica town. Under the slogan "Natural & Healthy," she has developed a range of food products and health remedies from fruits, vegetables and medicinal herbs, gathered in the surrounding mountain forests, meadows and pastures and, to a lesser extent cultivated on the farm.

Grozdić farm case study is based on the survey conducted with Mrs. Grozdić in January, 2019 within the "Taste of Region" project of Regional Development Agency "Braničevo-Podunavlje" (RDA BP) (2018-2019), and a number of articles about her farm business in national and regional press and portals. Data is elaborated using the Business Model Canvas methodology (Osterwalder & Pigneur, 2010). Research results aim to highlight the role of women farmers in sustainable agriculture and rural revival and to point out possible solutions for fostering women's entrepreneurship in multifunctional agriculture.

BACKGROUND

According to Osterwalder and Pigneur (2010), "a business model describes the rationale of how an organization creates, delivers, and captures value" (p. 14). The focus on business models and entrepreneurial skills fosters innovation in the food value chains (van der Schans et al., 2014). Multifunctional agriculture usually comprises various mix of differentiation and diversification business models, although the commons and experience models are also increasingly present. Differentiation includes production of high-quality niche food products and vertical integration outside long value chains. Diversification is a strategy of creating income by providing on-farm services (recreation, tourism, social and education services, nature and landscape maintenance, etc.) or diversifying into farming. A shared economy includes co-production and participatory farming while experience model is based on food experience as adding value to target audience (Pölling, 2018).

Consumer-oriented differentiation and diversification business strategies, such as health food production, short food supply chains and agro-environmental and tourism services can give the best results when applied on farms with location advantages, such as those close to protected areas and tourist resorts (Popović et al., 2012; Pölling & Mergenthaler, 2017; Popović & Mihailović, 2020). Sustainable use of agricultural land in and around protected areas should be based on traditional agriculture as an excellent ground for agroecological / organic farming that can create more economic opportunities and social benefits for women (Nikolić & Popović, 2010; Beck et al., 2016; Khadse, 2017). Agroecology is also highly relevant for mountain farming systems (Romeo et al., 2021). Artisanal production of differentiated food products on small farms located in high nature value (HNV) farmland area improves the image of a tourist destination (Schermer, 2018).

Altieri et al., (1987) defined peasant agroecosystems as a continuum of plant gathering and crop production, integrated and practiced using ethnobotanical knowledge contained in local cultural heritage. Howard (2003) reveals the crucial role of women in these activities, with emphasis on their high motivations for preservation of biological and cultural diversity and intergenerational knowledge transfer. Van der Ploeg (2010) argues that the reconstitution of the peasantry is of strategic importance for the world food security while van der Berg et al. (2021) pointed to agroecological peasant territories as a basis for emancipatory transformation. Studying a new generation of young farmers entrepreneurs in Italian rural areas, Milone & Ventura (2019) refer to them as "the vanguard of the new peasantry" (p. 43) and attribute the success of their business models to their creativity, cooperativeness, innovation and responsiveness to new societal demands regarding food and agriculture.

According to Shahraki (2022), multifunctional agriculture contains important identity features that encompass diverse orientations of rural people toward space, career and gender. Women often have a crucial role in multifunctional entrepreneurship on family farms, particularly in cultivation, processing and marketing of local quality and traditional foods and in diversification towards agrotourism, handicrafts and care farming (Lassithiotaki, 2011; Alonso & Trillo, 2014). Research conducted by Seuneke and Bock (2015) highlighted the key role of women in starting negotiation within the family regarding farm entrepreneurship, introducing new practices and providing new knowledge, skills and networks. According to Bock (2004), farm women start by adjusting new activities to existing farm and family duties, and then gradually build their professional identity by investments in new business, knowledge and skills. Van der Ploeg and Bruil (2020), saw farm redesign, a territorial ecosystems approach and innovative marketing as a reflection of "the way women move in and around the farm" (p. 17).

Women are generally seen as the promoters of social cohesion with their networking activities (Wiesinger, 2007). Rural women can organize operational groups and platforms for experiments, innovation and knowledge transfer in partnerships with research organizations and other stakeholders (Ragasa et al., 2014). Many innovative rural business models in the future could be linked to women farmers and entrepreneurs, if they enjoy gender equality and better access to resources, markets, knowledge, innovation and work-life balance services.

GROZDIĆ FARM CASE STUDY

Study Area

Homolje area is located in East Serbia, 125 km southeast of the capital, Belgrade and encompasses about 733 km^2 of two valleys separated by hills and bordered by Carpathian Mountains. This is the area of the rivers Mlava and Krupaja and their famous springs, four gorges and numerous other karst springs including thermal, sinking rivers and caves, sinkholes and pits. Mountains are covered with beech and oak forests and pastures and meadows rich in wild fruits, medicinal and aromatic herbs and mushrooms. The beauty of unspoiled nature is complemented by medieval monasteries, mystical customs and legends of natives, and a number of ethno festivals. A procedure of initiating the protection of the national park covering nearly half of the Homolje area in its southern part has recently been announced by the line ministry along with drafting of spatial planning documents for ski resort and a highway in its vicinity. According to preliminary results of the 2022 Census, Homolje area (Žagubica municipality) had 9,855 inhabitants (Statistical office of the RS, 2022a).

People are mostly oriented towards family agriculture. According to 2018 Farm structure survey data, 2,973 agricultural holdings managed 22,763 ha of utilized agricultural area, of which meadows and pastures amounted to 63%, arable land 34% and orchards 2% while 2,868 holdings also had 15,879 ha of forests. Natural grasslands are an excellent basis for extensive livestock grazing (0.43 LU/ha of UAA) and beekeeping, and production of high-quality cheese and honey of protected designation of origin as well as lamb, brandy with medicinal herbs and other healthy foods known across the country. Family farms controlled 96% of the UAA, and while livestock farms, apiaries, dairy and honey cooperatives and brandy distilleries are mostly run by men, on-farm processing of wild and cultivated food plants is most often in the hands of women. There were 1,127 holdings with other gainful activities, of which 42.5% were women-run farms (far above the national level of 17.6%). Half of those female farmers were 65 and older with a low standard output per farm (on average 4,400 euros in 2018), but the other half were more successful, especially those aged 35-54 (13,700 euros in the same year) (Statistical office of the RS, 2018). The 2011 Census of Population registered 2,847 people working abroad (Stanković, 2014) and their earnings are a significant source of funding for their family farm businesses. Planners advocate the development of organic agriculture, tourism and agri-environmental services. Tourist accommodation in modern family farm houses whose owners spend most of the year working abroad and catering services relying on high-quality food produced on-farm or in the immediate vicinity could improve local economy, attract returnees and newcomers and initiate overall rural revival.

However, relocation decisions largely depend on the availability of rural jobs, infrastructure and work-life balance services. The local administration expects financial support from the government for investments in these areas. The average monthly net salary in 2021 was at the level of 80.2% of the national average (Statistical office of the RS, 2022b). According to municipal Development plan (2021), local economy is dominated by small and micro enterprises in the trade, catering and timber production while entrepreneurs are mainly engaged in services. Underground coal mine is the only medium-sized employer, but it is about to close. Rural road and water supply network are of poor quality. The construction of a sewerage network and wastewater treatment plant is underway as well as broadband infrastructure. Preschool education covers 55% of children. There is no day care facility for handicapped children. Technical school educates economy and culinary technicians and cooks. Health Centre comprises 11 infirmaries, six specialist departments and five pharmacies. There is a lack of counselling and therapeutic services as well as home help services for the elderly and people with disabilities. Three women's associations take care of old crafts, gastronomic traditions and handicrafts.

Grozdić Farm Business Model

Grozdić farm (Žagubica town, Homolje) is focused on vertical integration to respond to societal needs for authentic food that promotes cultural heritage and social networking. The farm holder, Milosava Grozdić, makes traditional high-quality food products and homemade health remedies from wild plants gathered in the mountain forests, meadows and pastures and old plum variety and vegetables cultivated on the farm. She uses traditional receipts inherited from her grandmother, but also, experiments with new products in order to meet customer demands. For years, it was her hobby, in addition to their permanent job in a local water supply company. Healthy food products ended up on the table of her family, relatives, friends and

Table 1. Canvas business model for Grozdić farm

Key Partnerships	Key Activities	Value Propositions	Customer Relationships	Customer Segments
• Municipality of Žagubica. • Regional Chamber of Commerce. • Regional Development Agency. • Municipal tourist organization. • Women association "Homoljke". • Ingredient suppliers (honey, rakija, etc.). • Extension service. • Regional Institute of Public Health. • Line ministry.	• Wild herbs and forest fruit gathering. • Fruit and vegetable growing, including old plum variety. • Artisanal, on-farm processing and innovation in traditional foods. • Participation in ethnic food fairs and events with traditional local dishes.	• Close to forty homemade traditional, nutritious and healthy food products and health remedies (syrups, jams, compotes, sweets (slatko), liqueurs, fermented salads, teas and tinctures) of wild herbs, fruits and vegetables. • Product innovation. • Tailoring products to customer needs.	• Personal contact based on trust, competence, product benefit tips and consumer preferences: – on the farm, – at the food fairs and tourist events, – at the sale booth in tourist resorts and – via Facebook page.	• Food- and health-conscious people (especially families with kids, convalescents and the elderly) among: – neighbours working abroad, – weekend hikers from the capital and surrounding cities, – tourists from the country and abroad and – visitors of ethno food and tourism fairs and events.
	Key Resources • Nearby forests, pastures, meadows and hedgerows. • Orchard with old plum variety. • Kitchen garden. • Traditional receipts and equipment. • On-farm manufacturing and storage space. • Seasonal employees and volunteers.		**Channels** • Direct sale: on-farm, sale booth, food fairs and direct mail order selling. • Advertisement: Facebook page, regional e-market, local TV channel, newspapers, youtube, food fairs, tasting events and WOM marketing.	
Cost Structure • Cost of fruit and vegetable growing, equipment, ingredients, advisory, safety control, packaging, labelling, marketing; salary for seasonal workers; other running costs				**Revenue Streams** • Sale of food products.

Source: Authors' elaboration.

colleagues until Milosava applied and successfully completed entrepreneurial skill development training for women in agribusiness within the USAID Agribusiness project in Serbia in 2012. Then, she decided to start production for the market. She is now retired and enjoys this creative on-farm job that allows her to be in contact with nature and tradition, but also with youth, tourists, business people, product innovation and e-marketing. She wants to pass on her knowledge to young women from the women association she chairs, and especially to her grandchildren who like to join her both in the woods and at numerous fair events and festivals where her products regularly win awards.

The farm business model is presented by indicating specific findings for the nine building blocks of Business Model Canvas, defined by Osterwalder and Pigneur (2010) (Table 1).

DISCUSSION

Customer Segments

Stressful way of life implies a higher need for recreation and contact with nature for growing number of Serbian city dwellers, particularly of the capital, which is increasingly faced with air pollution in recent years. The Covid-19 crisis only intensified their interest in fleeing the city over the weekend in search of open space and healthy food and wellness items, usually at farmer sale boots near the Krupaja river spring. Locals working abroad order these products from their neighbors and take them on farm, on their return from vacation. Health-conscious people can also find "Natural & Healthy" farm products at the ethno food fairs where the farm is regularly present. Existing and planned tourist capacities in the area could reach significant market share for local traditional foods. Milosava is also planning to enter the European market, but that will require new investments (Vinkić, 2019; RDA-BP, 2019).

Value Propositions

Grozdić farm offers close to forty traditional food products and homemade health remedies – syrups, jams, compotes, sweets, fermented vegetable salads, teas, tinctures and liqueurs of wild herbs, fruits and berries, vegetables and old plum variety. The main success factor of this business strategy is location (as a source of wild plants of organic quality[1] and tourist destination), followed by product innovation. "I start from old recipes and then I experiment to adapt them to the customer demands and I succeed thanks to the love I have for this business" says Milosava (Vinkić, 2019).

This is in line with Galanakis (2019) guidelines for traditional food producers to find innovative ways to promote the nutrition and health advantages of their products by introducing minor modifications to their traditional recipes or innovations that maintain /expand their markets.

The Channels

The main channel to reach customers is on-farm sale. The farm also uses other forms of direct sale such as direct mail order selling and sale boots in tourist resorts, ethno festivals and fairs. Rulebook on the production and trade of small quantities of food of plant origin (2020), has encouraged farmers to develop short food supply chains for traditional food of plant origin. Regarding advertisement, the farm uses Facebook page, regional e-market platform, local TV, newspapers and news portals, food fairs, tasting events and WOM marketing.

The Customer Relationships

Personal and transparent producer-consumer relationships based on trust are the best guarantee of food quality. Direct sale arrangements with personal producer-consumer relations get consumer the opportunity to be informed about the farmer's production practices and to obtain valuable product benefit tips while the farm provides necessary feedback from further product development and innovation.

The Revenue Streams

The farm has diverse product assortment (traditional local food products and homemade health remedies) and customer segments, so the revenue streams are various. Vertical integration enables value addition and premium prices, but there is a lot of untapped potential related to regional branding and organic certification. As registered agricultural holding, the farm is eligible for a range of government subsidies to agriculture and rural development (Directorate for Agrarian Payments, 2022).

The Key Resources

The farm includes orchard with over 100 "čitlovka" variety plum seedlings and vegetable garden. The reintroduction of old crop varieties has helped to revive traditional agro-ecological knowledge and practices (Swiderska et al., 2011), but as Milosava says: "this is an area rich in wild fruits and herbs. Wherever you go - in the field or in the wood, each holding has at least a few trees and hedges, wild and planted, it is accessible to everyone... with no hybrids and pesticides and no additives but prepared in the way our ancestors did, I relied on old recipes" (Ist Media, 2018). She has traditionally equipped on-farm processing and storage capacities. During the season, she hires young people to gather forest fruits, while her colleagues from the women association occasionally help her with processing.

The Key Activities

Wild plant gathering is a vital part of the Grozdić farm business model, but it is also an expression of local identity, social coherence and cultural heritage. Grasser et al. (2012), pointed out that this activity becomes increasingly popular among young and middle-aged people in Europe. Therefore, tourists could be expected in guided mountain hiking tours to make acquaintance with wild plants as well as in food experience workshops and handicraft courses. High-quality niche products foster short supply chains. Participation in food fairs and ethno events and obtained awards improves product promotion and strengthens consumer confidence.

The Key Partnerships

More important cooperation in agricultural entrepreneurship takes place between farmers and other stakeholders within the business networks, small societal groups and platforms on continuing business innovation. Cooperation between women farmers is important for representing common interests in relationships with customers, administration, protected area management and other stakeholders. For Grozdić farm, women association "Homoljke" is of particularly importance as well as cooperation with business society, regional development agencies and local administration (Vinkić, 2019).

The Cost Structure

Cost of fruit and vegetable production and processing, buying ingredients and equipment, salary for seasonal workers for collection of wild herbs and forest fruits, and other running costs are among key farm operating costs. Cost advantages of the value driven Grozdić farm's business model are based on the economy of scope.

SOLUTIONS AND RECOMMENDATIONS

Analysing innovative short food supply chains, participants of the European Innovation Partnership for Agricultural Productivity and Sustainability focus group, relevant to that topic (2015), pointed out that their scaling up is not only achieved through individual business growth, but also through the proliferation, coordination and connection of many small-scale initiatives that take a wide variety of organisational forms, including community-led initiatives and cooperatives. Manikas et al., (2019) elaborate a concept of community-based agro-food hub, which act as knowledge broker and may involve agro-food supply chain partners, tourism sector and research institutions. Schermer (2018) focus attention on cooperative structures and their role in producer network growth and power balancing and therefore, in preserving of small-scale farming and processing structures that are particularly important for traditional food production in tourist regions. Women farmers expressed their positive view about cooperatives, which contribute to upgrading their social status, giving them independence and self-esteem (Koutsou, et al., 2003; Zaridis et al., 2015).

Cooperatives are also crucial for the economic empowerment of Serbian women farmers, helping them reach the market and ensure consistent product quality (Bradaš et al, 2018). In the past few years several women farmers' cooperatives have been formed in Serbia, primarily in the sector of fruit and vegetable processing. Today, these cooperatives successfully produce high quality organic, traditional and innovative food products, increase the number of subcontractors and plan to expand production and processing capacities (Jovičić, 2019; Gavrilović, 2020). The Ministry of Village Care (2021a) supports business and technological development of agricultural cooperatives, including those with diversified activities and particularly federated cooperatives that can provide their members with advanced services such as those related to product marketing, export and research and development. The Ministry plan to offer some extra benefits to women cooperatives in the form of tax exemptions and promotional labelling. Various other national and EU IPARD agriculture and rural development support schemes are also available to cooperatives (Directorate for Agrarian Payments, 2022).

As it is mentioned earlier, Milosava Grozdić is considering new partnerships for the business model optimization, including a supply contract with one of the larger processors /exporters, but she also wants to perceive her farm business as a lifestyle and instrument for active community engagement and not only as a source of profit (Vinkić, 2019; Ist Media, 2018). Having in mind her commitment to the women's association she leads and to which she has already entrusted a part of her business product range, as well as the fact that two other women's associations exist in the area with almost identical program of activities supported by local administration and development agencies, a women cooperative seems to be a good solution for business model optimization. A well-equipped facility for processing fruits, vegetables and medicinal plants, which ensures high quality and safety products, organic certification and branding, collective packaging and labelling and new market niches would reduce costs and competition, enable complementary specialization and increased turnover. Organic certificate and accompanying branding strategy could increase consumer trust in the product quality and provide a higher price premium for farmers (Schunko et al., 2019). Start-up support from the government and the municipality of Žagubica will be necessary and expected, having regard to the possible economic, social and environmental benefits for the local economy and community. With the revenue growth, own investments will be considered, such as those in product innovation, marketing, training, employment of professional management staff and cooperation with research centres and the creative industry. Planned tourist facilities in and around the newly established national park can be a good basis for diversifying cooperative's activities to catering traditional dishes and making handicrafts, including workshops for interested tourists – skills that these women have been preserving / practicing for years. Successful women's cooperative engaged in the production of traditional foods from wild herbs, fruits and vegetables of organic origin in and around the protected area of a tourist region can be a good advocate of a bio-district establishment, as "an innovative approach for a sustainable, integrated and participatory territorial development" (Basile, 2017, p. 1). In the Action plan for organic production development (2021), European Commission encourages member countries to support the development of bio-districts. Scientists consider agroecological peasant territory as a basis of a set of horizontal relations between nature and people, alternative farming and other territorial practices that improve farmers' incomes and foster their emancipation, defending them from destructive political trends (van der Ploeg et al., 2019; van den Berg et al., 2021).

The COVID-19 pandemic, accompanied by the development of on-line services, raises awareness to the benefits of living in sparsely populated areas (Komorowski & Stanny, 2020). With further development of broadband internet, the formation of smart villages should be considered across the rural Serbia (Lukić et al., 2022). The Ministry of Village Care has recently started to buy abandoned houses in rural areas and give them to young married and unmarried couples, single parents and young farmers up to 45 years of age – rural residents and newcomers under the national rural revival program (Mitrović, 2020). The first results are encouraging – 1,631 rural houses with a garden were purchased in 570 villages in 2021-2022, thus providing a home in the countryside for 5,000 people with 2,250 children. The average age of house winners is 29.8 and almost a fifth are newcomers from urban and suburban settlements. In 2023, another 5,000 applications are expected (Ministry of Village Care, 2022). If newcomers have the opportunity to start a successful small farm business, train to produce/prepare or just buy local traditional and/or organic food in the neighbourhood, it can be an additional incentive to relocate. The line minister, Mr. Krkobabić, briefly explained the role of women in rural revival in the following statement: "The fate of Serbian villages depends on women. If young women and girls decide to stay in the villages, to start families there, then we have won the battle, then the village will live. If we want the village to live, then we need to create an environment for young women to engage in entrepreneurship, rural tourism, to establish cooperatives, to have their own sources of income and to be in a position to plan, negotiate and decide" (Ministry of Village Care, 2021b).

FUTURE RESEARCH DIRECTIONS

To create a favourable environment for young women to engage in farm entrepreneurship and to establish cooperatives and other collaborative networks in rural areas, it is necessary to better know the different drivers and motivations faced by different categories of women farmers, especially women newcomers to farm business. The number of newcomers is increasing, as is their role in farm entrepreneurship, innovation and rural renewal (Popović et al., 2022). Their choice of business and entry models depends on resource and market access, investment capacities and skills, but even more on their values and ambitions. Access to land, housing, infrastructure, off-farm employment and rural services and networks is very important for them. To be tailored to different needs of women successors and newcomers, policy must be supported by appropriate monitoring and analysis of different categories of new entrants to farming based on still missing gender-disaggregated statistics.

The post-COVID-19 era gives new business opportunities to young people in rural areas, supported by innovation, smart specialisation and digitalisation of farming and rural services. Numerous studies have confirmed the existence of gender differences in technology adoption, although both women and men farmers are innovators and engaged in farm experiments (Ragasa et al., 2014). More attention to gender-disaggregated analysis is needed to promote the engagement of women farmers in innovation groups and multistakeholder platforms, active in smart local economy and policy dialogues at all levels.

CONCLUSION

The new normal paradigm brings new prospects for an overall rural renewal based on green and digital transition. Women farmers can play crucial role in these dynamics, given their propensity to multifunctional entrepreneurship on family farms and business networking, particularly in cultivation, processing and marketing of local high quality and traditional foods, rural tourism and handicrafts. Innovative business models in these areas provide new opportunities especially for young, skilled and well-educated women farmers and entrepreneurs, but only if they enjoy gender equality and have access to work-life balance services. The case study – female-owned multifunctional farm business in a HNV farmland area of East Serbia, is focused on wild plant gathering and artisanal processing of authentic food and health remedies, prepared with practices that generate added value, respect the environment, preserve local traditions and promote social networking. New market prospects in the area and abroad presuppose business expansion and new investments. The analysis pointed to a women's cooperative as a good solution for business model optimization. Benefits to engaging in collaborative structures include improved product assortment, resource share, easier certification and branding, balanced power relations and facilitated integration of newcomers into agriculture. Women farmers, particularly those engaged in traditional food production, have a positive attitude towards cooperatives that preserve their small-scale farm businesses and improve their social status. Several women's cooperatives are already operating successfully in Serbia, producing high quality organic, traditional and innovative food products and enjoying financial support from the government and development funds and agencies. Investments in women farm businesses, cooperatives and work-life balance services in rural areas should be realized in a way to build synergies with other place-based support schemes, such as those within smart specialization, smart villages and village renewal strategies.

ACKNOWLEDGMENT

Paper is a part of research financed by the MSTDI RS and agreed in decision no. 451-03-47/2023-01/200009 from 03.02.2023. and the project *The Taste of Region – Promoting agri-food products with added value to improve economic capacities of family households* of the Regional Development Agency Braničevo-Podunavlje (Survey data, 2019).

REFERENCES

Action plan for the development of organic production. COM (2021)141 final/2. European Commission.

Addati, L., Cattaneo, U., Esquivel, V., & Valarino, I. (2018). *Care work and care jobs for the future of decent work.* Report. ILO.

Alonso, N., & Trillo, D. (2014). Women, rural environment and entrepreneurship. ICWAR 2014. *Procedia: Social and Behavioral Sciences, 161*, 149–155. doi:10.1016/j.sbspro.2014.12.039

Altieri, M. A., Kat Anderson, M., & Merrick, L. C. (1987). Peasant agriculture and the conservation of crop and wild plant resources. *Conservation Biology*, *1*(1), 49–58. doi:10.1111/j.1523-1739.1987.tb00008.x

Basile, S. (2017). *The experience of bio-districts in Italy*. Case study. I.N.N.E.R Association. FAO. https://www.fao.org/3/bt402e/bt402e.pdf

Baylina, M., Garcia-Ramon, M. D., Porto, A. M., Rodo-de-Zarate, M., Salamana, I., & Villarino, M. (2017). Work-life balance of professional women in rural Spain. *Gender, Place and Culture*, *24*(1), 72–84. doi:10.1080/0966369X.2016.1249345

Beck, A., Haerlin, B., & Richter, L. (Eds.). (2016). *Agriculture at a crossroads – IAASTD findings and recommendations for future farming*. Foundation on Future Farming.

Beker, K. (2017). *Situation of rural women in Serbia*. Shadow Report to the CEDAW Committee regarding the fourth reporting cycle of Serbia. UN Women.

Bock, B. B. (2004). Fitting in and multi-tasking: Dutch farm women's strategies in rural entrepreneurship. *Sociologia Ruralis*, *44*(3), 245–260. doi:10.1111/j.1467-9523.2004.00274.x

Bradaš, S., Petovar, K., & Savić, G. (2018). *Žene na selu – od nevidljivosti do razvojnog potencijala* [Women in the countryside - from invisibility to development potential]. Friedrich-Ebert-Stiftung.

Brandth, B. (2002). Gender identity in European family farming: A literature review. *Sociologia Ruralis*, *42*(3), 181–200. doi:10.1111/1467-9523.00210

Cadiou, F. (2018). *Report on existing business models in EU countries and regions*. Project H2020 LIVERUR Deliverable D2.1. https://liverur.eu/wp-content/uploads/2018/12/D-2.1-Report-of-existing-busi ness-model-in-EU-countries-and-regions.pdf

Carter, S. (1998). Portfolio entrepreneurship in the farm sector: Indigenous growth in rural areas? *Entrepreneurship and Regional Development*, *10*(1), 17–32. doi:10.1080/08985629800000002

De Schutter, O. (2019). *Towards a Common Food Policy for the European Union*. Report. IPES-Food.

Directorate for Agrarian Payments of the Ministry of Agriculture, Forestry and Water Management of the Republic of Serbia. (2022). *Current subsidies*. https://uap.gov.rs/current-subsidies/

European Commission. (2021). *Developing real solutions for smart and resilient rural areas in Europe*. CORDIS Results Pack on rural innovation.

European Innovation Partnership for Agricultural productivity and Sustainability. (2015). *Innovative short food supply chain management*. EIP-AGRI Focus Group. Final report. https://ec.europa.eu/eip/agriculture/ en/publications/eip-agri-focus-group-innovative-short-food-supply

Food and Agriculture Organization of the United Nations. (2011). *Women in agriculture. Closing the gender gap for development*. SOFA 2010-11.

Food and Agriculture Organization of the United Nations & International Fund for Agricultural Development. (2019). *United Nations Decade of Family Farming 2019-2028*. Global Action Plan. Licence: CC BY-NC-SA 3.0 IGO.

Franić, R., & Kovačićek, T. (2019). The professional status of rural women in the EU. Study. European Parliament. Policy Department for Citizens' Rights and Constitutional Affairs.

Galanakis, C. M. (2019). Preface. In C. M. Galanakis (Ed.), *Innovations in traditional foods* (pp. xi–xiii). Elsevier Science. doi:10.1016/B978-0-12-814887-7.00015-0

Gargano, G., Licciardo, F., Verrascina, M., & Zanetti, B. (2021). The agroecological approach as a model for multifunctional agriculture and farming towards the European Green Deal 2030. Some evidence from the Italian experience. *Sustainability (Basel)*, *13*(4), 2215. doi:10.3390u13042215

Gaupp, F., Hall, J., Hochrainer-Stigler, S., & Dadson, S. (2020). Changing risks of simultaneous global breadbasket failure. *Nature Climate Change*, *10*(1), 54–57. doi:10.103841558-019-0600-z

Gavrilović, N. (2020, December 9). *Brašno od dunja, aćeto od maline – pet žena iz Kosjerića osnovalo zadrugu i prave vrhunske proizvode* [Quince flour, raspberry vinegar - five women from Kosjerić founded a cooperative and make top quality products]. RTS. https://www.rts.rs/page/stories/sr/story/125/drustvo/ 4179229/zene-kosjeric-zadruga-brasno-od-dunja-aceto-malina.html

Gomez, M., Mejia, A., Ruddell, B. L., & Rushforth, R. R. (2021). Supply chain diversity buffers cities against food shocks. *Nature*, *595*(7866), 250–254. doi:10.103841586-021-03621-0 PMID:34234337

Grasser, S., Schunko, C., & Vogl, C. R. (2012). Gathering "tea" – from necessity to connectedness with nature. Local knowledge about wild plant gathering in the Biosphere Reserve Grosses Walsertal (Austria). *Journal of Ethnobiology and Ethnomedicine*, *8*(1), 31. doi:10.1186/1746-4269-8-31 PMID:22889066

Howard, P. L. (2003). The major importance of 'minor' resources: women and plant biodiversity. *IIED Gatekeeper Series, 112*, 3-19.

Ist Media. (2018, October 17). *Milosava Grozdić – poslovna žena iz kuhinje* [Milosava Grozdić – business woman from the kitchen]. https://istmedia.rs/milosava-grozdic-poslovna-zena-iz-kuhinje/

Jovičić, B. (2019, August 1). *Ženska zemljoradnička zadruga* [Women's agricultural cooperative]. RTS. https://www.rts.rs/page/stories/sr/story/57/srbija-danas/3609876/zenska-zemljoradnicka-zadruga.html

Khadse, A. (2017). *Women, agroecology & gender equality*. Focus on the Global South.

Komorowski, L., & Stanny, M. (2020). Smart villages: Where can they happen? *Land (Basel)*, *9*(5), 151. doi:10.3390/land9050151

Koutsou, S., Iakovidou, O., & Gotsinas, N. (2003). Women's cooperatives in Greece: An ongoing story of battles, successes and problems. *Journal of Rural Cooperation*, *31*(1), 47–57.

Lans, T., Seuneke, P., & Klerkx, L. (2017). Agricultural entrepreneurship. In E. G. Carayannis (Ed.), *Encyclopedia of Creativity, Invention, Innovation and Entrepreneurship* (pp. 44–49). Springer. doi:10.1007/978-1-4614-6616-1_496-2

Lassithiotaki, A. (2011). Rural women and entrepreneurship: A case study in Heraklion Crete prefecture, Greece. *Journal of Developmental Entrepreneurship*, *16*(02), 269–284. doi:10.1142/S1084946711001835

Lukić, T., Pivac, T., Solarević, M., Blešić, I., Živković, J., Penjišević, I., Golić, R., Kalenjuk Pivarski, B., Bubalo-Živković, M., & Pandžić, A. (2022). Sustainability of Serbian villages in COVID-19 pandemic conditions. *Sustainability (Basel)*, *14*(2), 703. doi:10.3390u14020703

Manikas, I., Malindretos, G., & Moschuris, S. (2019). A community-based agro-food hub model for sustainable farming. *Sustainability (Basel)*, *11*(4), 1017. doi:10.3390u11041017

Mihailović, B., Radić Jean, I., Popović, V., Radosavljević, K., Chroneos Krasavac, B., & Bradić-Martinović, A. (2020). Farm differentiation strategies and sustainable regional development. *Sustainability (Basel)*, *12*(17), 7223. doi:10.3390u12177223

Milone, P., & Ventura, F. (2019). New generation farmers: Rediscovering the peasantry. *Journal of Rural Studies*, *65*, 43–52. doi:10.1016/j.jrurstud.2018.12.009

Ministry of Village Care. (2021a, March 8). *Krkobabić – zajedno do boljeg položaja žena u Srbiji* [Krkobabić–together to a better position of women in Serbia]. https://mbs.gov.rs/aktivnosti-saopstenja.php

Ministry of Village Care. (2021b, October 15). *Garantovana socijalna penzija, naša obaveza* [Guaranteed social pension, our obligation]. https://mbs.gov.rs/aktivnosti-saopstenja.php

Ministry of Village Care. (2022, December, 29). *Za ljude znanja i veština tri puta veće zarade* [For people with knowledge and skills, three times greater earnings]. https://mbs.gov.rs/aktivnosti-saopstenja.php

Mitrović, M. M. (Ed.). (2020). *Nacionalni program za preporod sela Srbije: stanje, problemi i prioriteti održivog razvoja* [National Program for revival of Serbian villages: situation, problems and sustainable development priorities]. IEP.

Montagnoli, L. (2020, October 28). *Italian women are the protagonists of virtuous farming and favor ecological transition.* Gambero Rosso. https://www.gamberorossointernational.com/news/food-news/italian-women-are-the-protagonists-of-virtuous-farming-and-favour-ecological-transition/

Nikolić, M., & Popović, V. (2010). The possibility of safe food production in protected areas. In *Proceedings of the XIV International Eco-Conference Safe Food* (pp. 199-206). Ecological Movement of Novi Sad.

Osterwalder, A., & Pigneur, Y. (2010). *Business model generation. A handbook for visionaries, game changers, and challengers*. John Wiley & Sons, Inc.

Plan razvoja opštine Žagubica 2021-2031 [Development plan of Žagubica municipality 2021-2031]. Official Gazette of the Municipality of Žagubica, 28/2021.

Pölling, B. (2018). *Farm models in region & Food supply chains analysis*. Western Balkans Urban Agriculture Initiative Project. Erasmus Plus Funding Scheme.

Pölling, B., & Mergenthaler, M. (2017). The location matters: Determinants for "deepening" and "broadening" diversification strategies in Ruhr metropolis' urban farming. *Sustainability (Basel)*, *9*(7), 1168. doi:10.3390u9071168

Popović, V., & Mihailović, B. (2020). Business models for urban farming in and around urban protected areas: EkoPark Belgrade case study. In A. Jean Vasile, J. Subić, A. Grubor, & D. Privitera (Eds.), *Handbook of Research on Agricultural Policy, Rural Development, and Entrepreneurship in Contemporary Economies* (pp. 89–107). IGI Global. doi:10.4018/978-1-5225-9837-4.ch005

Popović, V., Mihailović, B., & Radosavljević, K. (2022). Promoting generational renewal in Serbian agriculture. In *Thematic Proceeding of International Scientific Conference Sustainable Agriculture and Rural Development II* (pp. 403-415). IAE, Belgrade.

Popović, V., Milijić, S., & Vuković, P. (2012). Sustainable tourism development in the Carpathian region in Serbia. *Spatium (Belgrade)*, 28(28), 45–52. doi:10.2298/SPAT1228045P

Pravilnik o kontroli i sertifikaciji u organskoj proizvodnji i metodama organske proizvodnje [Rulebook on control and certification in organic production and methods of organic production]. Official Gazette of RS, 95/2020.

Pravilnik o proizvodnji i prometu malih količina hrane biljnog porekla, području za obavljanje tih delatnosti, kao i isključenju, prilagođavanju ili odstupanju od zahteva higijene hrane [Rulebook on the production and trade of small quantities of food of plant origin, on the area for performing these activities, as well as on the exclusion, adjustment or deviation from food hygiene requirements]. Official Gazette of RS, 13/2020.

Ragasa, C., Sengupta, D., Osorio, M., Ourabah Haddad, N., & Mathieson, K. (2014). *Gender-specific approaches, rural institutions and technological innovations*. FAO, IFPRI, & GFAR.

Regional Development Agency Braničevo-Podunavlje. (2019). *The Taste of Region – Promoting agri-food products with added value to improve economic capacities of family households. Project's survey data*. Author.

Romeo, R., Manuelli, S. R., Geringer, M., & Barchiesi, V. (2021). Introduction. In R. Romeo, S. R. Manuelli, M. Geringer, & V. Barchiesi (Eds.), *Mountain farming systems – Seeds for the future. Sustainable agricultural practices for resilient mountain livelihoods* (pp. 11–12). FAO.

Schermer, M. (2018). From 'additive' to 'multiplicative' patterns of growth. *International Journal of Sociology of Agriculture and Food*, 24(1), 57–76.

Schunko, C., Lechthaler, S., & Vogl, C. (2019). Conceptualising the factors that influence the commercialization of non-timber forest products: The case of wild plant gathering by organic herb farmers in South Tyrol (Italy). *Sustainability (Basel)*, *11*(7), 2028. doi:10.3390u11072028

Seuneke, P., & Bock, B. B. (2015). Exploring the roles of women in the development of multifunctional entrepreneurship on family farms: An entrepreneurial learning approach. *NJAS Wageningen Journal of Life Sciences*, *74–75*(1), 41–50. doi:10.1016/j.njas.2015.07.001

Shahraki, H. (2022). Three-dimensional paradigm of rural prosperity: A feast of rural embodiment, post-neoliberalism, and sustainability. *WORLD (Oakland, Calif.)*, *3*(1), 146–161. doi:10.3390/world3010008

Stanković, V. (2014). Srbija u procesu spoljnih migracija [Serbia in the process of external migration]. 2011 Population, Household and Dwelling Census in the Republic of Serbia. Statistical Office of the Republic of Serbia.

Statistical Office of the Republic of Serbia. (2018). *2018 Farm structure survey*. https://www.stat.gov.rs/en-US/oblasti/poljoprivreda-sumarstvo-i-ribarstvo/anketaostrukturipopgazdinstava

Statistical Office of the Republic of Serbia. (2020). *Women and men in the Republic of Serbia*. Author.

Statistical Office of the Republic of Serbia. (2022a). *First results of the 2022 Census of Population, Households and Dwellings*. https://publikacije.stat.gov.rs/G2022/HtmlE/G20221 350.html

Statistical Office of the Republic of Serbia. (2022b). *Opštine i regioni u Republici Srbiji* [Municipalities and regions in the Republic of Serbia]. Author.

Strategija za rodnu ravnopravnost za period 2021-2030 [Gender equality strategy for the period 2021-2030]. Official Gazette of RS, 103/2021.

Sutherland, L.-A., Monllor, N., & Pinto-Correia, T. (2015). *Gender issues among new entrants*. EIP-AGRI Focus Group New entrants into farming: lessons to foster innovation and entrepreneurship. Mini-paper 3. https://ec.europa.eu/eip/agriculture/sites/default/files/fg14_03_minipaper_gender_pdf

Swiderska, K., Song, Y., Li, J., Reid, H., & Mutta, D. (2011). *Adapting agriculture with traditional knowledge*. IIED Briefing Papers.

The U.S. Department of Agriculture. (2022, June 1). *USDA Announces Framework for Shoring Up the Food Supply Chain and Transforming the Food System to Be Fairer, More Competitive, More Resilient.* https://www.usda.gov/media/press-releases/2022/06/01/usda-announces-framework-shoring-food-supply-chain-and-transforming

Tohidyan Far, S., & Rezaei-Moghaddam, K. (2019). Multifunctional agriculture: An approach for entrepreneurship development of agricultural sector. *Journal of Global Entrepreneurship Research*, *9*(1), 23. doi:10.118640497-019-0148-4

Uvarova, I., & Vitola, A. (2019). Innovation challenges and opportunities in European rural SMEs. *Public Policy and Administration*, *18*(1), 152–166. doi:10.5755/j01.ppaa.18.1.23134

van den Berg, L., Goris, M. B., Behagel, J. H., Verschoor, G., Turnhout, E., Botelho, M. I. V., & Silva Lopes, I. (2021). Agroecological peasant territories: Resistance and existence in the struggle for emancipation in Brazil. *The Journal of Peasant Studies*, *48*(3), 658–679. doi:10.1080/03066150.2019.1683001

van der Ploeg, J., Barjolle, D., Bruil, J., Brunori, G., Costa Madureira, L. M., Dessein, J., Drąg, Z., Fink-Kessler, A., Gasselin, P., González de Molina, M., Gorlach, K., Jürgens, K., Kinsella, J., Kirwan, J., Knickel, K., Lucas, V., Marsden, T. K., Maye, D., Migliorini, P., ... Wezel, A. (2019). The economic potential of agroecology: Empirical evidence from Europe. *Journal of Rural Studies*, *71*, 46–61. doi:10.1016/j.jrurstud.2019.09.003

van der Ploeg, J. D. (2010). The peasantries of the twenty-first century: The commoditization debate revisited. *The Journal of Peasant Studies*, *37*(1), 1–30. doi:10.1080/03066150903498721

van der Ploeg, J. D., & Bruil, J. (2020). The economic potential of agroecology in Europe. Opinion. *Farming Matters*, *36*(1), 17.

van der Ploeg, J. D., & Roep, D. (2003). Multifunctionality and rural development: the actual situation in Europe. In G. van Huylenbroeck & G. Durand (Eds.), *Multifunctional Agriculture; A new paradigm for European Agriculture and Rural Development* (pp. 37–53). Ashgate.

van der Schans, J. W., Renting, H., & van Veenhuizen, R. (2014). Innovations in urban agriculture. *Urban Agriculture Magazine*, *28*, 3–12.

Vinkić, V. (2019, November 8). *Žagubičko blago u teglici* [Treasure of the Žagubica in a jar]. Reč naroda. https://recnaroda.co.rs/milosava-grozdic-zagubicko-blago-u-teglici/

Wiesinger, G. (2007). The importance of social capital in rural development, networking and decision-making in rural areas. *Revue de Geographie Alpine*, *95*(4), 43–56. doi:10.4000/rga.354

Wiest, K. (2016). Introduction: Women and migration in rural Europe – explanations and implications. In K. Wiest (Ed.), *Women and migration in rural Europe: labor markets, representations and policies* (pp. 1–22). Palgrave Macmillan. doi:10.1007/978-1-137-48304-1_1

Women and their roles in rural areas. Resolution (2016/2204(INI)), P8_TA (2017) 0099. European Parliament.

Zaremba, H., Elias, M., Rietveld, A., & Bergamini, N. (2021). Toward a feminist agroecology. *Sustainability (Basel)*, *13*(20), 11244. doi:10.3390u132011244

Zaridis, A., Rontogianni, A., & Karamanis, K. (2015). Female entrepreneurship in agricultural sector. The case of municipality of Pogoni in the period of economic crisis. *Journal of Research in Business. Economics and Management*, *4*(4), 486–491.

ADDITIONAL READING

Bock, B. B., & Shortall, S. (Eds.). (2006). *Rural gender relations: issues and case studies*. CABI Publishing. doi:10.1079/9780851990309.0000

Santini, F., & Gomez y Paloma, S. (Eds.). (2013). *Short food supply chains and local food systems in the EU. A State of Play of their Socio-Economic Characteristics*. JRC Scientific and Policy Reports.

Seibert, I. G., Sayeed, A. T., Georgieva, Z., & Guerra, A. (2019). *Without feminism, there is no agroecology*. Civil Society Mechanism for relations to the UN Committee on World Food Security.

Tredinnick-Rowe, J., & Taylor, T. (2015). The use of local culture and sustainability in local food and beverage entrepreneurship: case studies in Cornwall. In P. Sloan, W. Legrand, & C. Hindley (Eds.), The Routledge Handbook of Sustainable Food and Gastronomy (pp. 96-110). Routledge.

Tschirren S. (2021). *Autonomy through agroecology. What women farmers expect from sustainable food systems*. SWISSAID Report to the attention of H.E. António Guterres, UN Secretary-General.

KEY TERMS AND DEFINITIONS

Agricultural Holding: A technically and economically independent production unit with a single management on which an enterprise, cooperative, institution or another legal entity, entrepreneur or family household undertakes agricultural production, either as primary or secondary activity.

Agroecology: A science, set of practices and a social movement aim to build resilient and sustainable local food systems, strongly linked, and adapted to their territories and ecosystems.

Bio-District: Area where farmers, tourist operators, citizens and public authorities work together towards the sustainable management of local resources, based on organic principles and practices and agroecology, with the aim to fulfill the economic and socio-cultural potentials of the territory.

Business Model: A system used to explain how an organization creates, delivers, and captures value.

Entrepreneurship: The creation and development of an economic activity by blending risk-taking, creativity and/or innovation with sound management, within a new or an existing organization.

Multifunctional Agriculture: Umbrella term for farm business models that combine agricultural production with environmental and socio-cultural services for society.

Protected Area: Area recognized, dedicated, and managed to achieve the long-term conservation of nature with associated ecosystem services and cultural values.

Short Food Supply Chain: A food supply chain based on a strong organizational and / or geographical proximity of producers and consumers and on the absence or very few intermediaries.

Traditional Product: Historically recognized food product or produced according to technical specifications in a traditional way or according to traditional methods of production or protected as traditional food by a national or other regulation.

ENDNOTE

[1] According to the Rulebook on control and certification in organic production and methods of organic production (2020), collection of wild plants growing in natural habitats, forests and agricultural areas is considered a method of organic plant production, if those areas have not been treated with agents that are not allowed for use in organic production, for a period of at least three years before collection. Additionally, the collection must not affect the stability of the natural habitat or the maintenance of the species in the collection zone.

Chapter 13

The Influence of Financial Incentives and Other Socio-Economic Factors on Two-Wheeler EV Adoption in the NCR Region

Farah Siraj
Amity University, India

Pooja Mehra
https://orcid.org/0000-0002-5051-5497
Amity School of Economics, Amity University, India

ABSTRACT

Electric vehicles are a technological advancement that has the potential to reduce greenhouse gas emissions and lessen the effects of climate change. However, externalities like knowledge appropriability and pollution reduction produce societal and economic benefits that are not reflected in the cost of electric vehicles. Governments have implemented a few strategies to solve the ensuing market failures. The authors identified a few additional socio-economic parameters based on the research that are anticipated to have an impact on the adoption rates of electric vehicles. They investigated the link between those variables and the effect of socio-economic factors on these variables using structural equation modelling. The model discovered that there is no correlation between financial incentives awareness and two-wheeler EV uptake. The findings indicate that among these socioeconomic characteristics, adoption of two-wheeled electric vehicles was most strongly correlated with age, gender, education, married status, and yearly family income.

DOI: 10.4018/978-1-6684-8810-2.ch013

INTRODUCTION

Background

India is the world's third-largest emitter of greenhouse gases (GHG) after China and the United States, accounting for about 7% of global emissions. The country's emissions have been steadily increasing over the past few decades, largely due to its rapidly growing economy and population. UN-SDG 13 (considering this scenario) urges for prompt action in lowering greenhouse gas emissions and mitigating climate change (Montiel, Cuervo-Cazurra, Park, Antoln-López, & Husted, 2021; Porter, Tuertscher, & Huysman, 2020).

According to the International Energy Agency's (IEA) Global CO2 emissions from fuel combustion report for 2020, the transportation sector accounted for about 24% of global energy-related CO2 emissions.

According to Wang et al (2018), electric vehicles two-wheeler (EVs) is one of the most promising environmentally beneficial technologies against pollution and energy demand from the transportation industry. Two programmes have been started by the Indian government to encourage the use of electric vehicles (EVs) there. By 2030, the National Electric Mobility Mission Plan's (NEMMP) goal is for all vehicles to be electric. Through the Faster acceptance and Manufacturing of Hybrid and Electric Vehicles (FAME) India strategy, EV consumer acceptance is encouraged, and India becomes a hub for EV production.

The market share of electric vehicles (EVs) in India is still relatively low, but it is growing rapidly. According to a report by the Society of Manufacturers of Electric Vehicles (SMEV), EV sales in India increased by 20% in the fiscal year 2020-21, with a total of 2,36,802 units sold (SMEV, 2021).

Practically speaking, as illustrated in Figure 1 (Society of Manufacturers of Electric Vehicles, 2021), sales of electric four-wheelers (E4W) have remained mostly flat while the rise of the EV industry in India is being driven by electric two-wheelers (E2W). In 2022–2023, electric two-wheeler sales accounted for roughly 62% of all EV sales up from 55 percent in 2021–2022 period. This rise has been influenced by elements such as rising gasoline prices, environmental consciousness, and government subsidies.

Despite their significant presence in the transportation industry, research on the deployment of two-wheeler electric vehicles (EVs) in developing nations like India is lacking. While some studies discuss EV adoption difficulties in India, additional research is required to fully understand the opportunities and problems unique to two-wheeler EVs. The goal of this study is to investigate how socioeconomic characteristics and government incentives affect the uptake of electric two-wheelers among Indian customers.

Figure 1. Automobile domestic sales trend
Source: SIAM (Society of Manufacturers of Electric Vehicles)

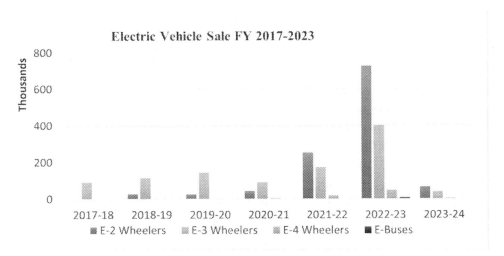

Research Problem Statement

In recent years, several international automobile manufacturers have entered the Indian market, bringing with them new technologies and innovative products. This has led to increased competition in the market, resulting in improved product quality and features, as well as more affordable prices.

India has the world's fastest-growing automobile industry. By 2020, it is anticipated that there would be a demand for 2.7 million commercial vehicles, 34 million two-wheelers, and 10 million passenger vehicles. India will be under further pressure to buy more crude oil, which is already up from 57% in 1997 to 80% in 2014. According to estimates from 2020, oil imports will account for 92% of all imports (Dutta, 2014).

Manufacturers are now focused on alternative energy transportation because of growing environmental pollution and intense pressure on oil imports. For the National Electric Mobility Mission Plan 2020, the government has committed a corpus of INR 14000 crore ($2.25 billion) for incentives for electric vehicles. The electric vehicle business is moving very slowly since end users aren't participating very much.

Scope of the Study

The study's aim was on determining how financial incentives and socioeconomic factors, specifically in India's National Capital Region (NCR), affected the uptake of two-wheeler electric vehicles (EVs). The goal of the study was to examine how financial incentives, such as tax breaks and subsidies, affect the uptake of EVs. The study also looked at how socioeconomic characteristics like income, education, and age influenced how two-wheeler EVs were adopted in the NCR region. The study aims to provide light on the critical elements influencing EV adoption in this region and advance knowledge of tactics for promoting sustainable transportation options in urban environments.

Significance of the Study

For several reasons, the study on the effects of financial incentives and socioeconomic factors on the uptake of electric two-wheelers in the NCR region is important. It supports India's efforts to encourage green mobility and lessen its dependency on fossil fuels. To enable the creation of tailored treatments, the study studies socioeconomic aspects and assesses the effectiveness of financial incentives. Additionally, it closes a study gap and advances knowledge of India's adoption of electric vehicles. In general, the study contributes to the development of efficient policies and interventions to promote the use of electric two-wheelers.

Research Gap

There is a research void regarding the impact of financial incentives and socio-economic factors on the adoption of electric two-wheelers in the National Capital Region (NCR), despite studies already being done on EV adoption in India. Prior studies have mostly concentrated on EVs in general, ignoring the specific factors influencing the adoption of electric two-wheelers in the NCR. Additionally, nothing is known about how financial incentives affect the uptake of electric two-wheelers in the NCR. This study gap is significant given the importance of two-wheelers in India's transportation system and the government's EV adoption goals. Additionally, there are no detailed analyses of electric two-wheelers in the NCR in the literature on socio-economic aspects impacting EV adoption. Additionally, there is a dearth of study on the influence of charging infrastructure, which is crucial in the congested and densely populated NCR region, on the uptake of electric two-wheelers. For successful policies and strategies to promote electric two-wheelers and meet the government's EV adoption targets, it is imperative to close this research gap.

Objectives of the Study

This study investigates how psychological, environmental, and demographic factors affect Indian consumers and buyers of two-wheelers' propensity to buy electric two-wheeler (EVs). It assesses how well-informed they are about EVs and the national electric mobility mission plan with the goal of revealing insights into consumer behaviour and choice-making. To remove the obstacles and hasten the general adoption of EVs in India, more research must be conducted, and cooperative efforts are essential.

1. To assess awareness of government incentives of actual and potential buyers of two-wheeler EV in Delhi NCR.
2. To determine how awareness of government incentives impacts the adoption of two-wheeler electric vehicles in Delhi NCR.
3. To examines the impact of socio-economic factors on the adoption of two-wheeler EV's in Delhi NCR region.

LITERATURE REVIEW

This chapter reviews previous research on the factors that influence consumer purchasing intention (PI) for electric two-wheelers (EVs). The literature review includes studies that have analyzed PI as a dependent variable, as well as related studies with similar dependent variables and similar influencing variables.

Wang N et al. (2018) also divided influencing factors into four broad categories: technical performance (EVs), external environmental factors, consumers' demographics and personalities, and consumer perceived values to EVs.

A study by Sushma and Vijay (2020) aimed to investigate the level of awareness of electric vehicles among consumers in India. The study found that only 25% of the respondents were aware of electric vehicles, and among them, only 15% were aware of electric two-wheelers. Similarly, a study by Teli and Mallick (2019) found that only 22% of the respondents were aware of electric two-wheelers in the city of Pune, India.

However, a study by Ghorbani et al. (2017) in Iran found that while awareness of financial incentives had a positive impact on the intention to purchase electric vehicles, the effect was weaker compared to other factors, such as environmental concerns and performance.

Financial incentives and additional elements involved in the marketing of electric vehicles were examined by Sierzchula et al. (2014). However, they neglected traffic regulatory policies in favour of financial incentives. According to Zhang et al. (2018), prioritising urban public transport development can effectively encourage urban29 sustainable development.

Consumer Characteristics

According to Potoglou and Kanaroglou's 2007 research, different demographic groups have varying preferences when it comes to purchasing electric vehicles (EVs). Age and education were found to significantly correlate with EV adoption by Afroz, Rahman, and Afroz (2013). This finding suggests that younger generations and people with higher education levels are more likely to adopt EVs because they are environmentally conscious and aware of the negative effects of conventional vehicles. Hackbarth and Madlener (2013) asserted that highly educated consumers could be reluctant to buy EVs in developing markets because they are aware of the accompanying disadvantages. In contrast, neither Hidrue et al. (2011) nor Sierzchula et al. (2014) discovered a connection between education, income, or EV adoption. (2011) (Zhang et al.)

Barriers

The relative benefit of new technology, such as electric vehicles (EVs), influences market penetration, according to Potoglou and Kanaroglou (2007b) and Bick (1963). The perceived advantages of conventional two-wheeler (CVs) over battery-powered vehicles (BDVs) may, however, make it more difficult for people to embrace EVs (Bockarjova and Steg, 2014). Despite their lower operating costs and environmental advantages, EVs are hindered by factors such high initial cost, a lack of adequate charging infrastructure, and battery range (Bockarjova and Steg, 2014; Carley et al., 2013; Lebeau et al., 2013). In comparison to CVs, the initial cost of EV purchases is important (Hagman et al., 2016b; Turrentine and Kurani, 2007; Peters and Dütschke, 2014)

Incentives

According to Sierzchula et al. (2014c) and Mersky et al. (2016b), financial incentives, such as tax advantages, are successful ways for increasing the use of electric vehicles (EVs). According to Zhang et al. (2011) b, incentives including tax rebates and access to bus lanes have greatly aided the market penetration of EVs in Norway. Free parking and access to transit lanes, according to Potoglou and Kanaroglou (2007c) and Mersky et al. (2016c), have little effect on consumer behaviour, which could have unfavourable effects like reduced toll revenue and congestion (Langbroek et al., 2016; Ozaki and Sevastyanova, 2011).

Consumer Awareness

According to Ozaki and Sevastyanova (2011b), Potoglou and Kanaroglou (2007d), Steinhilber et al. (2013b), and Steinhilber et al. (2013b), consumer acceptance and comprehension are crucial for the market introduction of electric two-wheeler (EVs). To increase their market share, EVs must address both sociological and technological issues (Egbue and Long, 2012b; Edison WS and Geissler, 2003). customer acceptance of EVs and future purchase intents may be favourably impacted by raising customer awareness and encouraging pleasant EV experiences (Carley et al., 2013; Bunce et al., 2014; Nykvist and Nilsson, 2015b; Larson et al., 2014). Other crucial elements include acknowledging consumer perceptions and reducing perceived risks (Oliver and Rosen, 2010)

RESEARCH METHODOLOGY

The methodology chapter of this research study focuses on the systematic approach adopted to ensure simplicity, accuracy, and validity of the results. It includes the following sections:

3.1 Sampling design
3.2 Collection of data
3.3 Concepts & Variables used
3.4 Analytical tools

Sampling Design

Target Population

This study focuses on persons with driving licences who currently own or have the potential to own a two-wheeler electric vehicle (EV) in the NCR region of India. By analysing the factors impacting the adoption of two-wheeler electric vehicles in the NCR region, the research intends to address air pollution and promote environmentally friendly transportation options. It considers the area's diverse socioeconomic landscape, recognising problems and possibilities across income levels, educational attainment, occupations, and social classes. The study's findings will be helpful to policymakers, industry stakeholders, and researchers who are interested in environmentally friendly transportation and environmental challenges in the NCR region.

Sampling Technique

For obtaining a representative and diverse sample, a combination of probability and non-probability sampling techniques is used. The NCR region is divided using probability sampling approaches including stratified sampling and cluster sampling, considering aspects like topography, income, and education. Additionally, non-probability sampling methods like convenience sampling and snowball sampling are used. The research attempts to increase the validity and generalizability of the results while assuring inclusion and diversity within the sample by integrating multiple sampling procedures.

Sample Size

Using the Krejcie and Morgan formula, the sample size for two-wheeler EV users in Uttar Pradesh is calculated to be 384. There are 1,598,50,002 licenced drivers in India overall, with 19,98,12,341 of those residents living in Uttar Pradesh. The formula is as follows:

$s = X^2.NP (1 - P) \div d^2 (N - 1) + X^2.P (1 - P)$

Where,

s = required sample size
$X^2 = 3.841$
N = population size
$P = 0.5$
$d = 0.05$

By applying the Krejcie and Morgan formula, the appropriate sample size calculated is 365.

Collection of Data

The data collection for the study on the influence of financial incentives and socio-economic factors on two-wheeler EV adoption in the NCR region will involve both primary and secondary data sources.

Primary data was collected through surveys and interviews. Surveys will be conducted to gather quantitative information on variables such as socio-economic status, awareness of incentives, opinions of EVs, and adoption factors. These surveys will be administered to individuals residing in the NCR region who own or have

Figure 2. Proposed model for two-wheeler electric vehicle adoption

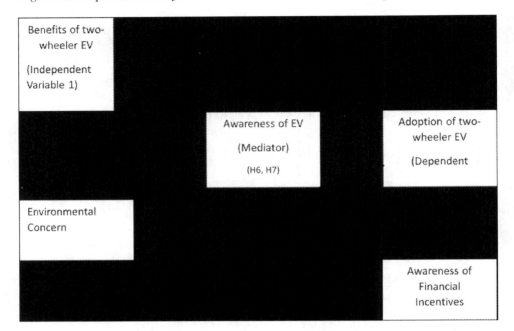

the potential to own a two-wheeler EV. In-depth interviews will be conducted to obtain qualitative insights into the socio-economic determinants and perceptions of incentives among the target population.

Secondary data will be collected from various sources such as academic studies, industry publications, and government papers. Academic research will provide theoretical frameworks and prior findings related to EV adoption and its influencing factors. Industry reporting will offer insights into market trends and consumer behavior in the context of EV adoption. Government papers will provide details on the application of financial incentives and trends in EV uptake in the NCR region.

To obtaining theoretical frameworks, prior findings, market trends, consumer behaviour, and information on financial incentives and EV uptake in the NCR region, secondary data will be gathered from academic research, industry publications, and government papers.

We can see proposed model of the study in Figure 2 and the variables used in the study for analysis in Table 1.

Concepts and Variables Used

1. Financial Incentives: Financial incentives for two-wheeler EV adoption include grants, tax breaks, subsidies, and cost-reduction measures.

Table 1. Variables used in the study for analysis

S. No	Variables		Type of Variable	Expected Impact on Adoption of Two-Wheeler EV
1	Awareness of Financial Incentive (AWF)	Moderator & Independent Variable The adoption of two-wheeler EVs is influenced by knowledge of financial incentives.	Continuous	+
2	Adoption of two-wheeler electric vehicles	Dependent Variable It reflects people's genuine choice to adopt and make use of electric vehicles as their main form of transportation.	Continuous	

Source: Author's own; result of data collection tabulation

2. Socio-economic factors: Two-wheeler EV adoption is influenced by socioeconomic factors such access to charging infrastructure, income, education, occupation, and social position.
3. EV Adoption: When deciding the form of transportation to use, two-wheeler EV adoption entails considering factors including financial incentives, environmental concerns, usability, and accessibility to charging infrastructure.

Analytical Tools

Statistical Package for Social Sciences (SPSS) version 23.0 and Analysis of Moments Structure (AMOS) version 23.0 were used to analyse the data that had been gathered. Descriptive statistics, correlation analysis, Cronbach's alpha computation, and Goodness-of-Fit indices from AMOS 23.0 were all used in the analysis. Targeting "green consumers" interested in two-wheeler EVs, 365 respondents in Delhi NCR were surveyed to gather data. Instead of consumers who expressed a broad interest in sustainability, the study concentrated on those who intended to make a green purchase.

DATA ANALYSIS AND INTERPRETATION

The analysis chapter presents the interpretation of findings, including sample profile, exploratory factor analysis, reliability, convergent validity, discriminant validity, correlation analysis, and the use of statistical tools such as SPSS, AMOS, and descriptive statistics. SEM in AMOS is employed to examine the interaction between independent, mediating, and dependent variables.

Classification of Respondents

As noted from the Table 2, respondents are categorised according to specific demographic characteristics: gender, age, occupation, education, marital status, monthly family income, number of EV's in family, type of EV, and EV use.

Table 2. Classification of respondents based on the demographic profile

Demography	Frequency	Percent
Gender		
Male	242	66.3
Female	123	33.7
Total	365	100
	Frequency	Percent
Age (in years)		
18-30	236	64.7
31-40	54	14.8
41-50	44	12.1
50 and above	31	8.5
Total	365	100
	Frequency	Percent
Occupation		
Home Maker	59	16.16
Employed	87	23.8
Self-employed/ Businessperson	125	34.25
Retired/ Pensioner	26	7.12
Unemployed/Dependent/ unemployed	68	18.63
Total	365	100
	Frequency	Percent
Education		
No formal qualifications	33	9
Up to 10th	30	8.2

The Influence of Financial Incentives

Demography	Frequency	Percent
Above 10th to Graduation	246	67.4
Post-Graduate and above	56	15.3
Total	365	100
	Frequency	Percent
Marital_Status		
Married	242	66.3
Single	123	33.7
Total	365	100
	Frequency	Percent
Annual_Family_Income (in ₹)		
Up to 5 lakhs	105	28.8
Above 5 lakhs to 15 lakhs	191	52.3
Above 15 lakhs to 30 lakhs	4	1.1
Above 30 lakhs	65	17.8
Total	365	100
	Frequency	Percent
Number_of_EV in family		
One or two	242	66.3
More than two	123	33.7
Total	365	100
	Frequency	Percent
Type_Of_EV		
Scooters	242	66.3
Bikes	123	33.7
Total	365	100
	Frequency	Percent
EV_Use		
Commercial Use	242	66.3
Private Use	123	33.7
Total	365	100
Source: Author's own; result of data collection tabulation		

It can be inferred from Table 2 that the total sample size of 365 respondents comprises 242, representing 66.3% of male and 123 representing 33.7% of female users of 2-wheeler Electric Vehicle. The sample respondents are chosen using the multi-stage sampling method, showing a higher percentage of male user of 2-wheeler

Table 3. List of abbreviations for the constructs used in the study

Constructs	Abbreviations
Electric Vehicle	EV
Awareness Of Financial Incentives	AWF
Adoption of 2-wheeler EV	AD
Potential Consumer of two-wheeler EV	PC
Actual Consumer of two-wheeler EV	AC

Source: Author's own; result of data collection tabulation

Electric Vehicle than female users. On classifying the respondents based on age of 2-wheeler Electric Vehicle users, more representation is found to be from the respondents whose age lies among the age group 18-30 implying usage of 2-wheeler Electric Vehicle by adults of the society.

Moreover, half of the respondents (246, or 67.4%) had educations ranging from the tenth to the undergraduate level. Regarding the respondents' occupations, or those who own two-wheel electric vehicles, it was found that roughly 125 (34.25%) came from a business background, and 87 (23.8%) were employed.

On classifying the respondents based on Marital Status of 2-wheeler Electric Vehicle users, more representation is found to be from the respondents who are married i.e., 242 (66.3%) respondents.

Two-wheeler Electric Vehicle users were belonging to the annual income group of above 5 lakhs to 15 lakhs i.e., 191 (52.3%) & up-to 5 lakhs annually i.e., 105 (28.8%) respondents.

Most of the 2-wheeler Electric Vehicle users have one or two electric vehicles in their family 242(66.3%) respondents. Most of the 2-wheeler Electric Vehicle users were using two-wheeler electric scooter 242(66.3%) respondents.

Most of the 2-wheeler Electric Vehicle users were using their two-wheeler electric vehicle for commercial use 242(66.3%) respondents.

To feasible annotation during analysis and interpretation, the constructs are noted in their abbreviations. The expansion of the abbreviation is given below in Table 3.

Table 4. Variance inflation factor values of the variables employed in the study

Variables	Variance Inflation Factor
Awareness Of Financial Incentives	1.41

Source: Author's own; result of data collection tabulation

Table 5. Results of internal consistency reliability and composite reliability

Variables	No of Items	Cronbach Alpha	Composite Reliability
Awareness Of Financial Incentives	5	0.937	0.917
Adoption Of 2-wheeler Electric Vehicles	7	0.915	0.917

Source: Author's own; result of data collection tabulation

Multicollinearity

The assumption of multicollinearity is tested using the Variance Inflation Factor (VIF) (Hair et al., 2019).

It is inferred from table Table 4 that the VIF values obtained for the variables tested in this research study is well below the permissible values, i.e., the VIF values must be ideally less than 3 (Hair et al, 2019). Hence there is found to be no multicollinearity problem among the variables employed in the study.

Reliability

Composite reliability may be thought of as a reliability indicator derived from exploratory factor analysis (Hair et al., 2006). Cronbach's alpha is a reliability coefficient that evaluates the consistency of the scale. The values must fall between 0 and 1. The optimal value to prove the reliability is one that is more than 0.7 (Hair et al, 2006).

Construct Reliability uses the factor loadings of the hypothesised model and is unaffected favourably by the growing number of variables, Fornell & Larcker's (1981) internal consistency measurement is regarded as preferable (Schaffer & Heinemann, 2008).

Table 6. Average Variance Extracted (AVE) values

Variables	AVE
Awareness Of Financial Incentives	0.689
Adoption of 2-wheeler Electric Vehicles	0.615

Source: Author's own; result of data collection tabulation

Table 7. KMO & Bartlett's Test) for the Factor influencing adoption of two-wheeler EV in Delhi NCR region

KMO and Bartlett's Test		
Kaiser-Meyer-Olkin Measure of Sampling Adequacy.		.898
Bartlett's Test of Sphericity	Approx. Chi-Square	3039.902
	df	66
	Sig.	.000

Source: Author's own; result of data collection tabulation

Results of Reliability Analysis

Using validated and tried-and-true questions can increase the reliability of constructs and outcomes, according to Straub (1989) and Boudreau and Gefen (2001). Cronbach's alpha coefficient was used to evaluate the internal consistency (Cronbach, 1951).

From Table 5, the reliability measures, i.e., composite reliability and Cronbach's alpha, are both higher than the necessary value of 0.7 (Nunnally, 1978). The composite reliability scores vary between 0.92 and 0.92, and the Cronbach alpha reliabilities range between 0.0.94 and 0.91, which are found to be over the acceptable threshold.

Validity Analysis

The criteria proposed by Hair et al. (2006) that can be used to determine whether a study has convergent validity: AVE should be greater than 0.5; As a result, the AVE values for the variables examined in this research study ranged between 0.689 and 0.615, yielding results that were satisfactory. The estimations of factor loadings in Table 6 showed that the discovered values to be greater than the desired cut-off value of 0.5 (given regression weights), which is statistically significant to support the convergent validity.

Factor Analysis

After factor extraction, rotation approaches like Promax for correlated factors and varimax and Equimax for uncorrelated factors can be used (Hair et al., 2019).

According to Churchill (1979), variables should be retained if they meet two criteria: they must have a factor loading of at least 0.5 and a difference of at least 0.10 between the highest and second-highest factor loadings.

Table 8. Results of communalities for the factors affecting adoption of two-wheeler EV

	Communalities	
	Initial	Extraction
AD1	1.000	.565
AD2	1.000	.731
AD3	1.000	.796
AD4	1.000	.670
AD5	1.000	.734
AD6	1.000	.538
AD7	1.000	.648
AWF1	1.000	.662
AWF2	1.000	.811
AWF3	1.000	.776
AWF4	1.000	.805
AWF5	1.000	.699

Source: Author's own; result of data collection tabulation

Confirmatory factor analysis (CFA) evaluates how well the measured variables represent an unobservable construct, whereas exploratory factor analysis (EFA) helps find the ideal number of factors and the relationships between measured variables.

Exploratory Factor Analysis (EFA) for the Factor Influencing Adoption of Two-Wheeler EV in Delhi NCR Region

Table 7 holds the results of the tests, which are prerequisites for conducting an exploratory factor analysis. The Kaiser-Meyer-Olkin measure of sampling adequacy value generally varies between 0 and 1, and the values closer to 1 are always considered to be better (Kaiser, 1975). Exploratory factor analysis can be conducted for those datasets whose Kaiser-Meyer-Olkin measure of sampling adequacy value is 0.6 or above. Thus, the value obtained for this study is found to be 0.898, which is very close to 1 and can be interpreted that the sample is adequate for performing exploratory factor analysis.

COMMUNALITIES

Table 8 provides information about the communalities. The percentage of each variable's variance that can be accounted for by the factors (such as the underlying

Table 9. Factor loadings matrix of the factors affecting adoption of 2-wheeler EV in Delhi NCR region

	Rotated Component Matrix	
	Component	
	1	2
AD3	.890	.070
AD2	.848	.108
AD5	.842	.158
AD4	.808	.131
AD7	.795	.123
AD1	.735	.156
AD6	.721	.135
AWF2	.105	.895
AWF4	.132	.888
AWF3	.189	.860
AWF5	.069	.833
AWF1	.183	.793

Source: Author's own; result of data collection tabulation

latent continuum) is shown in this table. The communalities table's extraction values are nothing more than estimates of the variance in each variable that the components are expected to account for. According to Osborne et al. (2008), communalities above 0.4 are acceptable. The communalities in table 4.8 are all high, demonstrating that the variables are accurately reflected by the extracted components.

The items incorporated in this study have been grouped into two factors based on eigenvalues. The overall cumulative percentage is found to be 70.29% which means that the first two factors together account for 71.08% of the total variance.

Rotated Component Matrix

Table 9 contains the rotated factor loadings, which represent how the variables are weighted for each factor. The factor loadings below 0.4 are eliminated. The factor loadings of the awareness of financial incentives affecting adoption of 2-wheeler EV in Delhi NCR region can be noted from table 4.9. The factor, "Awareness of Financial Incentive", holds five items with the following factor loadings 0.793, 0.89, 0.86, 0.88, & 0.83, The second factor, "Adoption of 2-wheeler EV", holds seven

Table 10. Standardised regression weights

			Estimate
AD6	<---	AD	.670
AD5	<---	AD	.827
AD4	<---	AD	.781
AD3	<---	AD	.888
AD2	<---	AD	.844
AD1	<---	AD	.712
AD7	<---	AD	.745
AWF5	<---	AWF	.777
AWF4	<---	AWF	.881
AWF3	<---	AWF	.850
AWF2	<---	AWF	.879
AWF1	<---	AWF	.755

Source: Author's own; result of data collection tabulation

items, and their respective factor loadings are 0.73, 0.85, 0.89, 0.81, 0.84, 0.72 and 0.72. All the factor loadings are above the threshold value, i.e., 0.5 (Hair et al, 2016).

Confirmatory Factor Analysis: Elements of Two-Wheeler EV Adoption in Delhi NCR

The aggregated items of the final structures are subjected to confirmatory factor analysis (CFA) (Marsh et al., 1988). Chi-square (CMIN), RMSEA and baseline fit measures (NFI, CFI), good model comparison; Parsimony measure (PNFI, PCFI), were the minimum number of fit tests that Jaccard and Wan (1996) advised using. In addition, Kline (1998) recommended using the GFI, NFI or CFI, NNFI, and SRMR tests.

Confirmatory Factor Analysis: Elements of two-wheeler EV Adoption in Delhi NCR

According to Hair et al (2010), standardised factor loadings or regression weights should be 0.50 or higher.

From Figure 3, it can be inferred that adoption of two-wheeler EV comprises of seven items viz., AD1, AD2, AD3, AD4, AD5, AD6 and AD7. On looking at the path diagram for adoption of 2-wheeler EV using standardised co-efficient, AD3

Figure 3. Diagrammatic exposition of CFA for the elements of two-wheeler EV adoption in Delhi NCR

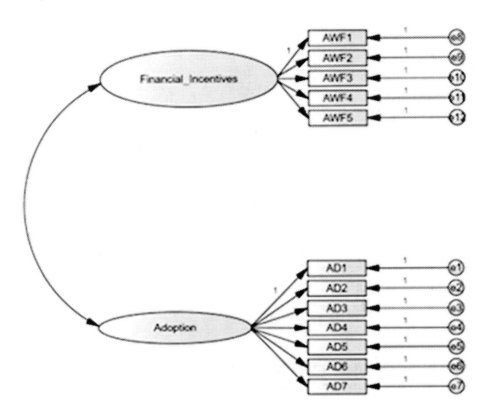

plays a predominant role (0.88) in determining major factor impacting adoption of two-wheeler EV followed by AD1, AD2, AD4, AD5, AD6, AD7.

Awareness of Financial Incentives comprises of five items namely AWF1, AWF2, AWF3, AWF4, AWF5 and AWF6 On looking at the path diagram for adoption of 2-wheeler EV using standardised co-efficient, AWF4 plays a

predominant role (0.88) in determining the impact of financial incentives on two-wheeler EV adoption followed by AWF1, AWF2, AWF4.

Table 11. Summary of model fit – Elements of two-wheeler EV adoption in Delhi NCR

CMIN	DF	CMIN/DF	GFI	AGFI	CFI	RMR	RMSEA	NFI
205.403	53	3.876	0.91	0.87	0.95	0.31	0.71	0.93

Source: Author's own; result of data collection tabulation

Table 12. Correlation

			AD	AWF
Spearman's rho	AD	Correlation Coefficient	1.000	.333**
		Sig. (2-tailed)	.	.000
		N	365	365
	AWF	Correlation Coefficient	.333**	1.000
		Sig. (2-tailed)	.000	.
		N	365	365
**. Correlation is significant at the 0.01 level (2-tailed).				

Source: Author's own; result of data collection tabulation

Table 13. Summary of model fit: Structural equation modeling

CMIN	DF	CMIN/DF	GFI	AGFI	CFI	RMR	RMSEA	NFI
205.403	53	3.876	0.91	0.87	0.95	0.31	0.71	0.93

Source: Author's own; result of data collection tabulation

Model fit summary for the study is presented in Table 11.

Correlation

Spearman bivariate correlation analysis was performed to study the level of association among the independent/predictor variables like "Awareness of financial incentives" and dependent variable namely "Adoption of two-wheeler EV". The results of the correlation analysis are presented in Table 12.

If the value of one variable is greater than the value of the other, there is a negative relationship, which is shown by a value smaller than 0 (Hair et al., 2019).

Table 14. Hypothesis

H.No.	Statement
H1	Adoption of two-wheeler EV have positive and significant effects on awareness of Financial Incentives
H2	Awareness of Financial Incentives have positive and significant effects on adoption of two-wheeler EV

Source: Author's own; result of data collection tabulation

Table 15. Results of structural equation modeling

			Estimate	S.E.	C.R.	P	Hypothesis
Adoption	<---	Awareness_of_ financial_incentives	.248	.047	5.332	***	
AD1	<---	Adoption	1.000				
AD2	<---	Adoption	1.165	.075	15.618	***	
AD3	<---	Adoption	1.249	.076	16.387	***	Hypothesis 1 supported
AD4	<---	Adoption	1.114	.077	14.429	***	
AD5	<---	Adoption	1.105	.073	15.157	***	
AD6	<---	Adoption	.986	.081	12.129	***	
AD7	<---	Adoption	1.029	.076	13.625	***	
AWF1	<---	Awareness_of_ financial_incentives	1.000				
AWF2	<---	Awareness_of_ financial_incentives	1.182	.068	17.461	***	
AWF3	<---	Awareness_of_ financial_incentives	1.113	.066	16.816	***	Hypothesis 2 supported
AWF4	<---	Awareness_of_ financial_incentives	1.046	.060	17.466	***	
AWF5	<---	Awareness_of_ financial_incentives	1.059	.070	15.134	***	

Source: Author's own; result of data collection tabulation

From Table 12, it can be inferred that there is a significant level of correlation among all "Awareness of financial incentives and "Adoption of two-wheeler EV". The level of significance was 0.01 level. The correlation was positively significant among all the variables. The correlation values were also not so close to 0.9 which reveals that there are no multicollinearity issues among the variables tested.

Structural Equation Modeling (SEM)

The measurement model and the structural model are the two basic steps in structural equation modelling (SEM) (Anderson and Gerbing, 1988). The structural model tests the links between constructs, whereas the measurement model looks at how observable variables relate to underlying constructs. The structural model evaluates the importance of path estimations and overall model fit. A sufficient sample size and the assumption of multivariate normality are two requirements for using Maximum Likelihood Estimation (MLE) to evaluate the structural model (Hair et al., 2006; Byrne, 2010).

The Influence of Financial Incentives

Figure 4. The diagrammatic representation of the structural equation model

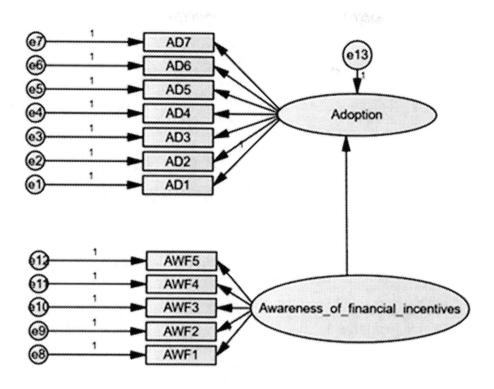

The Structural Equation Model (SEM) is conducted using AMOS 24, and the following results of model fit, and estimates are obtained as shown in Table 13.

Results indicated a good fit for the model presented including RMR of 0.031, GFI of 0.91, and CFI of .95 and RMSEA of 0.71.

From Table 15, it can be observed that Adoption of EV is having a significant impact on Awareness of Financial Incentives with p<0.05. Awareness of Financial Incentives is found to have significant impact on Adoption of two-wheeler EV as the p-value is below 0.05.

Structure equation modelling is shown by the Figure 4.

Figure 5. Awareness of NEMMP (national electricity mobility mission plan)

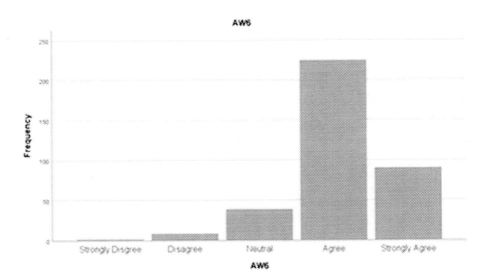

Frequency Analysis

Frequency Analysis: Awareness of NEMMP
(National Electricity Mobility Mission Plan)

In the following Table 16 and Figure 5, it is comprehensible that 86.3% of the respondents are aware of NEMMP and 3% of the respondents are not aware.

Table 16. Awareness of NEMMP (national electricity mobility mission plan

I Am Aware of Indian Govt.'s "National Electric Mobility Mission Plan" (NEMMP)", Made to Protect the Environment by Promoting EVs				
	Frequency	Percent	Valid Percent	Cumulative Percent
2		0.5	0.5	0.5
Disagree	9	2.5	2.5	3
Neutral	39	10.7	10.7	13.7
Agree	225	61.6	61.6	75.3
Strongly Agree	90	24.7	24.7	100
Total	365	100	100	

Source: Author's own; result of data collection tabulation

Figure 6. Type of two-wheeler EV

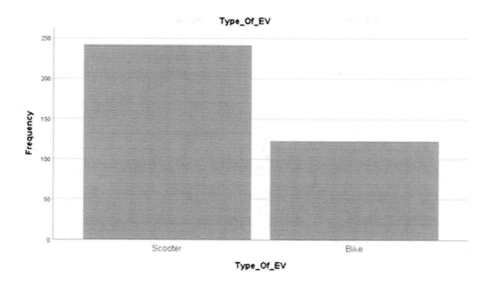

Frequency Analysis: Type of electric two-wheeler vehicle owned by the users.

In Table 17 and Figure 6, it is comprehensible that 66.3% of the respondents own electric two-wheeler scooter and 33.7% of the respondents own electric two-wheeler bike.

Frequency Analysis: Usage Type for Various Electric Two-Wheeler Vehicle User

In Table 18 and Figure 7, it is comprehensible that 66.3% of the use electric two-wheeler for commercial purpose and 33.7% of the respondents use electric two-wheeler for private use.

Table 17. Type of two-wheeler EV

	Frequency	Percent	Valid Percent	Cumulative Percent
Scooter	242	66.3	66.3	66.3
Bike	123	33.7	33.7	100
Total	365	100	100	

Source: Author's own; result of data collection tabulation

Figure 7. Use of two-wheeler EV

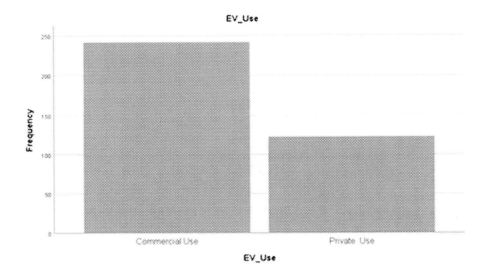

Impact of Socio-Economic Factors on Two-Wheeler EV Adoption

The demographic profile of the 465 respondents is shown in this part through the finalised Table 19 for the final analysis. Gender, age, education, occupation, annual household income, and the respondent's use of an electric two-wheeler were among the demographic factors from the current study that were reviewed.

Table 19 demonstrate the following information on various socio-economic variable:

- Of the total sample size, males made up 242 (or 66.3%) and females 123 (or 33.7%). Given that fewer women than males drive two-wheeler, gender prejudice is unavoidable not only in developing nations like India but also in most industrialised nations. However, this study has made a significant effort

Table 18. Use of two-wheeler EV

	Frequency	Percent	Valid Percent	Cumulative Percent
Commercial Use	242	66.3	66.3	66.3
Private Use	123	33.7	33.7	100
Total	365	100	100	

Source: Author's own; result of data collection tabulation

The Influence of Financial Incentives

Table 19.

	N	Min	Max	Mean	Std	Frequency	Percentage
Gender	365	2	1	1.34	0.47		
Male						242	66.3
Female						123	33.7
Age	365	4	1	2.33	0.83		
18-30						236	64.7
31-40						54	14.8
41-50						44	12.1
50 and above						31	8.5
Occupation	365	4	3	3.10	0.89		
Home Maker						59	16.16
Employed						87	23.8
Self-employed/						125	34.25
Businessperson						26	7.12
Retired/ Pensioner						68	18.63
Education	365	2	3	2.89	0.77		
No formal qualifications						33	9
Up to 10th						30	8.2
Above 10th to Graduation						246	67.4
Post-Graduate and above						56	15.3
Marital Status	365	1	2	1.34	0.47		
Single						242	66.3
Married						123	33.7
Monthly_Family_Income	365	4	2	4.32	0.80		
Up to 5 lakhs						105	28.8
Above 5 lakhs to 15 lakhs						191	52.3
Above 15 lakhs to 30 lakhs						65	17.8
Above 30 lakhs						4	1.1
EV_Use	365	2	1	1.34	0.47		
Commercial Use						242	66.3
Private Use						123	33.7

Source: Author's own; result of data collection tabulation

to reduce it. Therefore, we may draw the conclusion that two-wheeler EV adoption is male dominant by looking at the percentage difference in gender across the industry. The socioeconomic element of gender affects the uptake of electric two-wheelers.

- Most respondents (64.7%) and (14.8%) are between the ages of 18-30 and 31-40. A little over 20.8% of respondents to the entire study's samples—those who agreed to hold a valid driver's license—are slightly older than 50. As a result, by comparing the percentage of respondents between the ages of 18-30 and 31-40 who have adopted two-wheeled electric vehicles, we can draw the conclusion that this age group dominates two-wheeled EV adoption. Age as a socioeconomic determinant affects the uptake of electric two-wheelers.
- Moreover, half of the respondents (246, or 67.4%) had educations ranging from the tenth to the undergraduate level. We can therefore conclude that two-wheeler EV adoption is dominated by respondents who were educated 246 (representing 67%) by looking at the percentage difference in education level of respondents across the adoption of two-wheeler EV.
- Regarding the respondents' occupations, or those who own two-wheel electric vehicles, it was found that roughly 125 (34.25%) came from a business background, and 87 (23.8%) were employed. We can therefore conclude that two-wheeler EV adoption is dominated by respondents who own business and are employed.
- In terms of annual household income, 191 respondents (or 52.3%) fall into the "above 5 lakhs to 15 lakhs" category, followed by 105 respondents (or 28.8%) in the "up to 5 lakhs" category, and 17.8% in the "above 15 lakhs to 30 lakhs" category. The adoption of two-wheeled electric vehicles is therefore dominated by respondents with annual household incomes between up to 5 lakhs and more than 5 lakhs and between 15 lakhs, as shown by the percentage difference in annual household income across the adoption of two-wheeled EVs. The adoption of two-wheeler EVs is influenced by several socioeconomic factors, including household monthly income.
- Nearly half of the respondents—242—were single (representing 66.3%), while 123 (representing 33.7%) of the respondents were married. We can therefore draw the conclusion that respondents who are single are more likely to adopt two-wheeler EVs by looking at the percentage difference in marital status throughout the adoption of two-wheeler EVs. The socioeconomic aspect of marital status affects the uptake of electric two-wheelers.
- After examining the respondents' reasons for purchasing their two-wheeled electric vehicles, we can say that many of them—242 or 66.3 percent—bought their vehicles for business purposes, while 123 or 33. 7 percent bought them for personal usage. We can therefore draw the conclusion that those

respondents who use their two-wheeler EV for commercial purposes, such as for delivering goods, for offering their two-wheeler EV on a rental basis, such as Ola and Uber rides, and for providing fruits and vegetables to customers, dominate the adoption of two-wheeler EV. The adoption of two-wheeler EVs is influenced by the socioeconomic use of these vehicles.

The importance of including respondents with all personal qualities has been highlighted in this study. We can assert the highest level of population representation based on the process and results of data collecting.

CONCLUSION AND RECOMMENDATIONS

Findings and Summary

1. The purpose of the study was to gauge public awareness about electric two-wheelers (EVs). Findings showed that a sizeable percentage of Delhi NCR's actual and potential customers were either fully or somewhat aware of electric vehicles. Increased public awareness is necessary for widespread EV adoption because it relates to a higher possibility of EV adoption.
2. The National Electric Mobility Mission Plan (NEMMP) and electric vehicles (EVs) in general were the subjects of the study. Consumers who are existing or potential consumers in Delhi NCR showed awareness of NEMMP at a rate of above 86.3%. The adoption of two-wheeled electric vehicles and NEMMP were found to be positively correlated, underscoring the importance of vigorously promoting NEMMP incentives.
3. The National Electric Mobility Mission Plan (NEMMP) of India provides several incentives for the use of electric vehicles. Although many people are aware of these incentives, there is no direct correlation between awareness and the adoption of two-wheeler EVs. To hasten EV adoption under NEMMP, active promotion of both financial and non-financial incentives is required.
4. Adoption of two-wheeler electric vehicles (EVs) is significantly influenced by psychosocial factors. Environmental concerns have a detrimental impact on EV adoption, however the benefits of two-wheeler EVs have a positive impact. In Delhi NCR, factors like perceived behaviour control, charging infrastructure, pricing affordability, and driving range also have an impact on customers' intentions to embrace EVs.
5. The study revealed that there is no significant relationship between awareness of EV and environmental consciousness. The study showed positive and significant relationship between the awareness of EV and Environmental consciousness.

6. The factors determining the intention to adopt, and the actual adoption of two-wheeler electric cars are highly influenced by gender, marital status, age, occupation, and education and purpose of two-wheeler EV use.

Strategic Implications

- The study shows that India is encouraging the use of electric vehicles (EVs) without taking the general public's knowledge of technology, attitudes, and interests into account. A thorough awareness campaign is advised to increase the effectiveness of the National Electric Mobility Mission Plan (NEMMP) and promote wide-scale two-wheeler EV adoption. To ensure the campaign's broad reach and impact, the Indian government should work with automakers, marketers, and charity organisations.
- Psychological factors greatly influence the decision to buy electric two-wheeler vehicles (EVs) in India. Individual characteristics play a larger role than social norms, suggesting a need for customer-centric approaches by auto companies and personalized marketing strategies by marketers.
- Addressing environmental issues is essential if electric vehicles (EVs) are to overcome consumer adoption barriers. Targeted tactics, incentives, charging infrastructure, public awareness campaigns, stakeholder collaboration, R&D funding, electrification of public transportation, and battery recycling infrastructure can accomplish this.
- The study's findings give policymakers and automakers useful information about the intentions of current and potential two-wheeler consumers in India about electric vehicles. This knowledge can direct the creation of future models and policy incentives to meet their expectations.
- As perceived behavioural control and perceived usability have such a large impact, marketers should place more emphasis during promotions on the specific and distinctive qualities of electric vehicles, such as their straightforward mechanisms, smooth and easy rides, lack of noise, ability to charge in one's own space, etc.
- It would be very effective if marketers promoted two-wheeler electric vehicles through emotional marketing, citing people antienvironmental activities pertaining to daily mobility or/and transport. This is because past sustainable behaviour and personal norms have a strong influence on the purchase intention for electric vehicles.
- The main barrier to the adoption of two-wheeler electric vehicles is thought to be their high purchase price. To address this problem and lower the cost of electric vehicles, the government, tax authorities, and marketers must

- act. Until electric vehicles are economically competitive with conventional automobiles, corrective actions should be taken at all levels.
- According to the survey, India's plans to acquire two-wheeler electric vehicles are severely impacted by the availability of charging stations. Although consumers feel that the current infrastructure is insufficient, they do think that speedy charging and battery swapping technologies will have a beneficial impact on their decision to purchase electric vehicles.
- The fact that driving range has a favourable effect on two-wheeler electric vehicle purchaser intentions suggests that Indian consumers are OK with the existing range of available options. Misconceptions about EV performance, however, need to be improved.

Contribution of Study Towards Knowledge and Impact on Future Studies

Regarding the significance of financial incentives and infrastructure development in increasing the adoption of two-wheeler electric two-wheeler in the NCR region, the study offers insightful information for businesses and governments. The importance of socioeconomic considerations is also emphasised, and the advantages of EV adoption for sustainability and urban well-being are emphasised. The study offers insightful information on how financial incentives affect the uptake of two-wheeler EVs in India. It emphasises the necessity of comprehensive incentive plans and creates new research opportunities in this area.

The study highlights the requirement for a significant awareness-raising effort to encourage the use of two-wheeled electric vehicles in Delhi NCR, India. It advises including a range of interested parties and incorporating campaign marketing of the National Electric Mobility Mission Plan (NEMMP). These suggestions are intended to address consumer awareness, attitudes, and adoption intentions for EVs.

The study emphasises that people's inclinations to purchase electric two-wheelers in Delhi and the National Capital Region are more influenced by their personal characteristics than by social norms. It recommends using a customer-centric strategy in the auto sector and emphasising the unique benefits of EVs through tailored marketing to boost acceptance.

The study cites the high cost of ownership as a major obstacle to the adoption of electric two-wheelers. To remedy this issue, corrective action is required from all parties, including citizens, governments, taxing agencies, and advertisers. Quick-charging and battery switching are viewed as promising options to improve purchasing intentions, but the current charging infrastructure also raises problems.

Limitation of the Study

Although the study on the impact of financial incentives and other socio-economic factors on the adoption of two-wheeler electric vehicles in the NCR region greatly advances our understanding of EV adoption in India, it also has several limitations that must be recognised. Below are some suggestions for further research as well as a discussion of these limitations and their ramifications.

- The study, which only concentrates on the NCR region, may not be entirely representative of the entire nation. As a result, it may not be possible to generalise the study's results to other parts of India, and more research is required to determine the factors affecting EV adoption there.
- Second, the report excludes other types of EVs and exclusively analyses the adoption of two-wheeler EVs. The results might not be applicable to other EV kinds, such automobiles, and buses. Future studies should look at the variables that affect the uptake of various EV models in India.
- Third, the study relies on survey respondents' self-reported data, which could be biased. Future studies should consider using more impartial indicators of EV uptake, like information on vehicle registration.
- Fourthly, the study does not consider how social and cultural issues may affect the adoption of EVs in India. Therefore, future studies should look at how social and cultural aspects affect EV adoption in India.

REFERENCES

Graham-Rowe, E., Gardner, B., Abraham, C., Skippon, S., Dittmar, H., Hutchins, R. L., & Stannard, J. (2012). Mainstream consumers driving plug-in battery-electric and plug-in hybrid electric cars: A qualitative analysis of responses and evaluations. *Transportation Research Part A, Policy and Practice*, *46*(1), 140–153. doi:10.1016/j.tra.2011.09.008

Hackbarth, A., & Madlener, R. (2013). Consumer preferences for alternative fuel vehicles: A discrete choice analysis. *Consumer Preferences for Alter- Native Fuel Vehicles: A Discrete Choice Analysis.*, *25*, 5–17. doi:10.1016/j.trd.2013.07.002

Hidrue, M. K., Parsons, G. R., Kempton, W., & Gardner, M. P. (2011). Willingness to pay for electric vehicles and their attributes. *Resource and Energy Economics*, *33*(3), 686–705. doi:10.1016/j.reseneeco.2011.02.002

Lai, I. K. W., Liu, Y., Sun, X., Zhang, H., & Xu, W. (2015). Factors Influencing the Behavioural Intention towards Full Electric Vehicles: An Empirical Study in Macau. *Sustainability (Basel)*, *7*(9), 12564–12585. doi:10.3390u70912564

Laroche, M., Bergeron, J., & Barbaro-Forleo, G. (2001). Targeting consumers who are willing to pay more for environmentally friendly products. *Journal of Consumer Marketing*, *18*(6), 503–520. doi:10.1108/EUM0000000006155

Potoglou, D., & Kanaroglou, P. S. (2007). Household demand and willingness to pay for clean vehicles. *Transportation Research Part D, Transport and Environment*, *12*(4), 264–274. doi:10.1016/j.trd.2007.03.001

Rahman, A., & Afroz, R. (2013). *Malaysian perception and attitude towards electric vehicle*. https://www.researchgate.net/publication/280934834_Malaysian_perception_and_attitude_towards_electric_vehicle

Schuitema, G., Anable, J., Skippon, S., & Kinnear, N. (2013). The role of instrumental, hedonic and symbolic attributes in the intention to adopt electric vehicles. *Transportation Research Part A, Policy and Practice*, *48*, 39–49. doi:10.1016/j.tra.2012.10.004

Zhang, Y., Yu, Y., & Zou, B. (2011). Analysing public awareness and acceptance of alternative fuel vehicles in China: The case of EV. *Energy Policy*, *39*(11), 7015–7024. doi:10.1016/j.enpol.2011.07.055

Compilation of References

Abdi, H., & Williams, J. L. (2010). Computational statistics: Principal component analysis. *Wiley Interdisciplinary Reviews: Computational Statistics*, *2*(4), 433–459. doi:10.1002/wics.101

Action plan for the development of organic production. COM (2021)141 final/2. European Commission.

Adamov, T., Ciolac, R., Iancu, T., Brad, I., Pet, E., Popescu, G., & Smuleac, L. (2020). Sustainability of agritourism activity. Initiatives and challenges in Romanian mountain rural regions. *Sustainability (Basel)*, *12*(6), 1–23. doi:10.3390u12062502

Addati, L., Cattaneo, U., Esquivel, V., & Valarino, I. (2018). *Care work and care jobs for the future of decent work.* Report. ILO.

Adekoya, O., Olabode, J., & Rafi, S. (2021). Renewable energy consumption, carbon emissions and human development: Empirical comparison of the trajectories of world regions. *Renewable Energy*, *179*, 1836–1848. doi:10.1016/j.renene.2021.08.019

Aizaz, K., Khan, S. U. R., Khan, J. A., Inayat-Ur-Rehman, & Akhunzada, A. (2021). An Empirical Investigation of Factors Causing Scope Creep in Agile Global Software Development Context: A Conceptual Model for Project Managers. *IEEE Access : Practical Innovations, Open Solutions*, *9*, 109166–109195. doi:10.1109/ACCESS.2021.3100779

Ajmal, K., Khan, M., & Al-Yafei, H. (2020). Exploring factors behind project scope creep – stakeholders' perspective. *International Journal of Managing Projects in Business*, *13*(3), 483–504. doi:10.1108/IJMPB-10-2018-0228

Ajmal, M. M., Khan, M., Gunasekaran, A., & Helo, P. T. (2021). Managing project scope creep in construction industry. *Engineering, Construction, and Architectural Management*.

Akdemir, B. (2013). Agricultural mechanization in Turkey. *IERI Procedia*, *5*, 41–44. doi:10.1016/j.ieri.2013.11.067

Akkaya, B., Guah, M. W., Jermsittiparsert, K., Bulinska-Stangrecka, H., & Koçyiğit, Y. K. (2022). *Agile Management and VUCA-RR.* Emerald Group Publishing. doi:10.1108/9781802623253

Compilation of References

Akman, G., & Yilmaz, C. (2008). Innovative capability, innovation strategy and market orientation: An empirical analysis in Turkish software industry. *International Journal of Innovation Management*, *12*(1), 69–111. doi:10.1142/S1363919608001923

Akshita, A. (2016). *Assessment of Financial literacy among working Indian Women*. https://www.researchgate.net/pubilcation/298790053

Al-Amin, A. Q., & Saidy, C. (2020). Data Analysis Tools in Economics Education: Evidence, Promises, and Challenges. *Journal of Economic Surveys*, *34*(5), 1018–1046.

Albuquerque, R. (2003). The composition of international capital flows: Risk sharing through foreign direct investment. *Journal of International Economics*, *61*(2), 353–383. doi:10.1016/S0022-1996(03)00013-8

Alegre, J., & Chiva, R. (2013). Linking entrepreneurial orientation and firm performance: The role of organizational learning capability and innovation performance. *Journal of Small Business Management*, *51*(4), 491–507. doi:10.1111/jsbm.12005

Alexandros, P. N., & Metaxas, T. (2016). "Porter vs. Krugman": History, analysis and critique of regional competitiveness. *Journal of Economics & Political Economy*, *3*(1), 65–80. doi:10.1453/jepe.v3i1.657

Allianz. (2017). *When will the penny drop? Money, financial literacy and risk in the digital age*. Retrieved from https://gflec.org/initiatives/money-finlit-risk/

Alonso, N., & Trillo, D. (2014). Women, rural environment and entrepreneurship. ICWAR 2014. *Procedia: Social and Behavioral Sciences*, *161*, 149–155. doi:10.1016/j.sbspro.2014.12.039

Altieri, M. A., Kat Anderson, M., & Merrick, L. C. (1987). Peasant agriculture and the conservation of crop and wild plant resources. *Conservation Biology*, *1*(1), 49–58. doi:10.1111/j.1523-1739.1987.tb00008.x

Altinay, L., Madanoglu, M., De Vita, G., Arasli, H., & Ekinci, Y. (2016). The interface between organizational learning capability, entrepreneurial orientation, and SME growth. *Journal of Small Business Management*, *54*(3), 871–891. doi:10.1111/jsbm.12219

Amaranggana, A. (2019). Smart tourism destinations enhancing tourism experience through personalisation of services. In *Information and communication technologies in tourism 2019* (pp. 377–389). Springer.

Amoatey, C. T., & Anson, B. A. (2017). Investigating the major causes of scope creep in real estate construction projects in Ghana. *Journal of Facilities Management*, *15*(4), 393–408. doi:10.1108/JFM-11-2016-0052

Analysis of budget support for the development of rural tourism in Serbia and diversification of economic activities in the countryside. (2009). Ministry of Agriculture, Forestry and Water Management of the Republic of Serbia.

Anderson, J. C., & Gerbing, D. W. (1988). Structural equation modeling in practice: A review and recommended two-step approach. *Psychological Bulletin, 103*(3), 411–423. https://doi.org/.3.411 doi:10.1037/0033-2909.103

Andrei, J., & Drăgoi, M. (2020). A brief analysis of tourism economics in the EU – is there a massive economic potential change? *Tourism International Scientific Conference Vrnjačka Banja - TISC, 5*(1), 59-76. Retrieved February 3, 2023 from http://www.tisc.rs/proceedings/index.php/hitmc/article/view/329

Andrei, J. V., Constantin, M., & de los Ríos Carmenado, I. (2021). Assessing EU's Progress and Performance with Regard to SDG-12 Targets and Indicators. In C. J. Chiappetta Jabbour & S. A. R. Khan (Eds.), *Sustainable Production and Consumption Systems. Industrial Ecology*. Springer. doi:10.1007/978-981-16-4760-4_1

Andrlić, B., Ariwa, E., & Gonçalves Rodrigo Franco. (2022a) Corporate Promotion in the Digital Era: A Conceptual Framework of Tourism Sector. In *Proceedings of IX International Scientific Conference of students and young scholars "Actual problems of Management in Marketing- Current Challenges"*. Lutsk National Technical University. https://doi.org/658.8:338(066)

Andrlić, B., Pandas, A., & Hak, M. (2022b). Market Valuation Models in the Function of Sustainable Rural Tourism. *5th International Rural Tourism Congress*, 772-782.

Andrlić, B., Priyashantha, K., & De Alwis Adambarage, C. (2023). Employee Engagement Management in the COVID-19 Pandemic: A Systematic Literature Review. *Sustainability (Basel), 15*(2), 1–22. doi:10.3390u15020987

Anning-Dorson, T. (2018). Customer involvement capability and service firm performance: The mediating role of innovation. *Journal of Business Research, 86*, 269–280. doi:10.1016/j.jbusres.2017.07.015

Antonetti, P., & Anesa, M. (2017). Consumer reactions to corporate tax strategies: The role of political ideology. *Journal of Business Research, 74*, 1–10. doi:10.1016/j.jbusres.2016.12.011

Arend, R. J. (2014). Entrepreneurship and dynamic capabilities: How firm age and size affect the 'capability enhancement–SME performance' relationship. *Small Business Economics, 42*(1), 33–57. doi:10.100711187-012-9461-9

Ar, I. M., & Baki, B. (2011). Antecedents and performance impacts of product versus process innovation: Empirical evidence from SMEs located in Turkish science and technology parks. *European Journal of Innovation Management, 14*(2), 172–206. doi:10.1108/14601061111124885

Arisman, A. (2018). Determinant of human development index in ASEAN countries. *Jurnal Ilmu Ekonomi, 7*, 113–122.

Atkinson, A., & Messy, F. (2012). *Measuring financial literacy: results of the OECD/international network on financial education (INFE) pilot study*. OECD Working Papers on Finance, Insurance and Private Pensions, No. 15. OECD Publishing. doi:10.1787/20797117

Compilation of References

Atkinson, A., & Messy, F. A. (2011). Assessing financial literacy in 12 countries: An OECD/INFE international pilot exercise. *Journal of Pension Economics and Finance*, *10*(4), 657–665. doi:10.1017/S1474747211000539

Augère-Granier, M.-L. (2016). *Short food supply chains and local food systems in the EU*. Briefing – September 2016, European Parliamentary Research Service. Retrieved from https://www.europarl.europa.eu/RegData/etudes/BRIE/2016/586650/EPRS_BRI(2016)586650_EN.pdf

Augier, M., & Teece, D. J. (2009). Dynamic capabilities and the role of managers in business strategy and economic performance. *Organization Science*, *20*(2), 410–421. doi:10.1287/orsc.1090.0424

Bagozzi, R. P., & Yi, Y. (1988). On the evaluation of structural equation models. *Journal of the Academy of Marketing Science*, *16*(1), 74–94. doi:10.1007/BF02723327

Baker, W. E., Mukherjee, D., & Perin, M. G. (2022). Learning orientation and competitive advantage: A critical synthesis and future directions. *Journal of Business Research*, *144*, 863–873. doi:10.1016/j.jbusres.2022.02.003

Baker, W. E., & Sinkula, J. M. (1999). The synergistic effect of market orientation and learning orientation on organizational performance. *Journal of the Academy of Marketing Science*, *27*(4), 411–427. doi:10.1177/0092070399274002

Balogh, P., Békési, D., Gorton, M., Popp, J., & Lengyel, P. (2016). Consumer willingness to pay for traditional food products. *Food Policy*, *61*, 176–184. doi:10.1016/j.foodpol.2016.03.005

Barczentewicz, M. & Mueller, B. (2021). *More Than Meets The AI: The Hidden Costs of a European Software Law*. Center for Data Innovation. Information Technology and Innovation Foundation (ITIF).

Bardhan, A., & Kroll, C. A. (2007). *Globalization and the real estate industry: Issues, implications, opportunities*. http://web.mit.edu/sis07/www/kroll.pdf

Barjolle, D., Brecic, R., Cerjak, M., & Giraud, G. (2015). Traditional Food in Western Balkan Countries Consumers' Perceptions and Habits. *Intellectual Property Rights for Geographical Indications: What is at Stake in the TTIP?*, 3-15.

Barney, J. B. (1991). Firm resources and sustained competitive advantage. *Journal of Management*, *17*(1), 99–120. doi:10.1177/014920639101700108

Barreto, I. (2010). Dynamic capabilities: A review of past research and an agenda for the future. *Journal of Management*, *36*(1), 256–280. doi:10.1177/0149206309350776

Basile, S. (2017). *The experience of bio-districts in Italy*. Case study. I.N.N.E.R Association. FAO. https://www.fao.org/3/bt402e/bt402e.pdf

Baskentli, S., Sen, S., Du, S., & Bhattacharya, C. (2019). Consumer reactions to corporate social responsibility: The role of CSR domains. *Journal of Business Research*, *95*, 502–513. doi:10.1016/j.jbusres.2018.07.046

Basole, R. C., & Patel, S. S. (2018). Transformation through unbundling: Visualizing the global FinTech ecosystem. *Service Science*, *10*(4), 379–396. doi:10.1287erv.2018.0210

Bayir, B., Charles, A., Sekhari, A., & Ouzrout, Y. (2022). Issues and Challenges in Short Food Supply Chains: A Systematic Literature Review. *Sustainability (Basel)*, *14*(5), 3029. doi:10.3390u14053029

Baylina, M., Garcia-Ramon, M. D., Porto, A. M., Rodo-de-Zarate, M., Salamana, I., & Villarino, M. (2017). Work-life balance of professional women in rural Spain. *Gender, Place and Culture*, *24*(1), 72–84. doi:10.1080/0966369X.2016.1249345

Beck, A., Haerlin, B., & Richter, L. (Eds.). (2016). *Agriculture at a crossroads – IAASTD findings and recommendations for future farming*. Foundation on Future Farming.

Bednarova, M., & Serpeninova, Y. (2023). Corporate digital responsibility: Bibliometric landscape – chronological literature review. *The International Journal of Digital Accounting Research*, Michaela, Bednarova. Advance online publication. doi:10.4192/1577-8517-v23_1

BegoodToday. (n.d.). https://www.begood.today/cvete-s-kauza/?fbclid=IwAR0U_jCxAqtctK3lNYGGad6y6IoUymyV_K011YjISkTkMcLlaYi-TDY-M0g

Beker, K. (2017). *Situation of rural women in Serbia*. Shadow Report to the CEDAW Committee regarding the fourth reporting cycle of Serbia. UN Women.

Bello, M. (2015). Renewable energy for sustainable socio-economic development in developing countries: A case study of Sub-saharan Africa. *Advanced Materials Research*, *1116*, 33–44. doi:10.4028/www.scientific.net/AMR.1116.33

Benigno, G., Fornaro, L., & Wolf, M. (2020). *The global financial resource curse*. FRB of New York Staff Report No. 915.

Benigno, G., Converse, N., & Fornaro, L. (2015). Large capital inflows, sectoral allocation, and economic performance. *Journal of International Money and Finance*, *55*, 60–87. doi:10.1016/j.jimonfin.2015.02.015

BetelBulgaria. (n.d.). https://betelbulgaria.org/bg/

BFBL. (2022). *Bulgarian Business Leader Forum*. Retrieved March 21, 2023 from https://bblf.bg/bg/sabitiya/1637/obyavihme-kso-shampionite-za-2021-a

Bhaskar, A., Saurabh, S., & Manvinder, P. S. (2018). Empowering women through financial literacy in Rajasthan. *International Journal on Computer Science and Engineering*, *6*(9), 20–22. Advance online publication. doi:10.26438/ijcse/v6si9.2022

Bhattacharya, A., Reeves, M., Lang, N., & Augustinraj, R. (2017). *New Business Models for a New Global Landscape*. Boston Consulting Group.

Compilation of References

BIS (2021). *Progress report on adoption of the Basel regulatory framework.* Basel Committee on Banking Supervision.

BIS. (2020). *Implementation of Basel standards A report to G20 Leaders on implementation of the Basel III regulatory reforms.* Basel Committee on Banking Supervision.

Bishop, M., & Green, M. (2010). *Philanthrocapitalism: How giving can save the world.* Bloomsbury Publishing USA.

Bloom, P. N., Hoeffler, S., Keller, K. L., & Meza, C. E. B. (2006). How social-cause marketing affects consumer perceptions. *MIT Sloan Management Review*, *47*(2), 49. Retrieved February 2, 2023, from https://sloanreview.mit.edu/article/how-socialcause-marketing-affects-consumer-perceptions

Blustein, D. L., Kozan, S., & Connors-Kellgren, A. (2013). Unemployment and underemployment: A narrative analysis about loss. *Journal of Vocational Behavior*, *82*(3), 256-265. doi:10.1016/j.jvb.2013.02.005

Blustein, D. L., & Guarino, P. A. (2020). Work and Unemployment in the Time of COVID-19: The Existential Experience of Loss and Fear. *Journal of Humanistic Psychology*, *60*(5), 702–709. doi:10.1177/0022167820934229

BMVJ. (2018). Corporate Digital Responsibility Initiative. *Federal Ministry of Justice and Consumer Protection.* Retrieved February 2, 2023 from https://cdr-initiative.de/en/initiative

Bock, B. B. (2004). Fitting in and multi-tasking: Dutch farm women's strategies in rural entrepreneurship. *Sociologia Ruralis*, *44*(3), 245–260. doi:10.1111/j.1467-9523.2004.00274.x

Bogacz-Wojtanowska, E., Przybysz, I., & Lendzion, M. (2014). Sukces i trwałość ekonomii społecznej w warunkach polskich [Success and sustainability of the social economy in Polish conditions]. Fundacja Instytut Spraw Publicznych.

Bohdanowicz, P., & Zientara, P. (2020). Virtual Reality Applications in Tourism—A Review. *Sustainability*, *12*(7), 2936.

Borowska, A. (2016). The role of outdoor markets in the food supply chain of regional food in Poland. *Handel Wewnętrzny, 362*(3), 50-62. https://www.ceeol.com/search/journal-detail?id=1801

Borychowski, M., Stępień, S., Polcyn, J., Tošović-Stevanović, A., Ćalović, D., Lalić, G., & Žuža, M. (2020). Socio-economic determinants of small family farms' resilience in selected Central and Eastern European countries. *Sustainability (Basel)*, *12*(24), 10362. doi:10.3390u122410362

Bouguerra, A., Mellahi, K., Glaister, K., Sadeghi, A., Temouri, Y., & Tatoglu, E. (2022). Absorptive capacity and organizational performance in an emerging market context: Evidence from the banking industry in Turkey. *Journal of Business Research*, *139*, 1575–1587. doi:10.1016/j.jbusres.2021.10.077

Bradaš, S., Petovar, K., & Savić, G. (2018). *Žene na selu – od nevidljivosti do razvojnog potencijala* [Women in the countryside - from invisibility to development potential]. Friedrich-Ebert-Stiftung.

Brandth, B. (2002). Gender identity in European family farming: A literature review. *Sociologia Ruralis*, *42*(3), 181–200. doi:10.1111/1467-9523.00210

Breslau, J., Finucane, M. L., Locker, A. R., Baird, M. D., Roth, E. A., & Collins, R. L. (2021). A longitudinal study of psychological distress in the United States before and during the COVID-19 pandemic. *Preventive Medicine*, *143*. doi:10.1016/j.ypmed.2020.106362

Brislin, R. W. (1970). Back-translation for cross-cultural research. *Journal of Cross-Cultural Psychology*, *1*(3), 185–216. doi:10.1177/135910457000100301

Broner, F., Didier, T., Erce, A., & Schmukler, S. L. (2013). Gross capital flows: Dynamics and crises. *Journal of Monetary Economics*, *60*(1), 113–133. doi:10.1016/j.jmoneco.2012.12.004

Brunori, G., Galli, F., Barjolle, D., Van Broekhuizen, R., Colombo, L., Giampietro, M., Kirwan, J., Lang, T., Mathijs, E., Maye, D., de Roest, K., Rougoor, C., Schwarz, J., Schmitt, E., Smith, J., Stojanovic, Z., Tisenkopfs, T., & Touzard, J. M. (2016). Are local food chains more sustainable than global food chains? Considerations for assessment. *Sustainability (Basel)*, *8*(5), 449. doi:10.3390u8050449

Bucciol, A., & Zarri, L. (2015). The shadow of the past: Financial risk taking and negative life events. *Journal of Economic Psychology*, *48*, 1–16. doi:10.1016/j.joep.2015.02.006

Buendía-Martínez, I., & Carrasco Monteagudo, I. (2020). The Role of CSR on Social Entrepreneurship: An International Analysis. *Sustainability (Basel)*, *12*(17), 6976. doi:10.3390u12176976

Buhalis, D. (2000). Marketing the competitive destination of the future. *Tourism Management*, *21*(1), 97–116. doi:10.1016/S0261-5177(99)00095-3

Buhalis, D., & Neuhofer, B. (2018). Augmented reality and virtual reality: Redefining tourism experiences. *Journal of Destination Marketing & Management*, *8*, 1–3.

Bui, T. N., Nguyen, A. H., Le, T. T. H., Nguyen, V. P., Le, T. T. H., Tran, T. T. H., Nguyen, N. M., Le, T. K. O., Nguyen, T. K. O., Nguyen, T. T. T., Dao, H. V., Doan, T. N. T., Vu, T. H. N., Bui, V. H., Hoa, H. C., & Lebailly, P. (2021). Can a Short Food Supply Chain Create Sustainable Benefits for Small Farmers in Developing Countries? An Exploratory Study of Vietnam. *Sustainability (Basel)*, *13*(5), 2443. doi:10.3390u13052443

Bulgarian Institute of Social Entrepreneurship. (n.d.). https://sites.google.com/a/piamater.org/theinstistute/exampl es

Business Roundtable. (2019). *Business roundtable redefines the purpose of a corporation to promote 'an economy that serves all Americans'*. Retrieved February 3, 2023 from https://www.businessroundtable.org/business-roundtable-redef ines-the-purpose-of-a-corporation-to-promote-an-economy-that -serves-all-americans

Compilation of References

Cadiou, F. (2018). *Report on existing business models in EU countries and regions.* Project H2020 LIVERUR Deliverable D2.1. https://liverur.eu/wp-content/uploads/2018/12/D-2.1-Report-of-existing-busi ness-model-in-EU-countries-and-regions.pdf

Cakar, N. D., & Erturk, A. (2010). Comparing innovation capability of small and medium-sized enterprises: Examining the effects of organizational culture and empowerment. *Journal of Small Business Management*, *48*(3), 325–359. doi:10.1111/j.1540-627X.2010.00297.x

Calantone, R. J., Cavusgil, S. T., & Zhao, Y. (2002). Learning orientation, firm innovation capability, and firm performance. *Industrial Marketing Management*, *31*(6), 515–524. doi:10.1016/S0019-8501(01)00203-6

Calderwood, L. U., & Soshkin, M. (2019). *The travel & tourism competitiveness report 2019.* The World Economic Forum. https://www3.weforum.org/docs/WEF_TTCR_2019.pdf

Caloghirou, Y., Kastelli, I., & Tsakanikas, A. (2004). Internal capabilities and external knowledge sources: Complements or substitutes for innovative performance? *Technovation*, *24*(1), 29–39. doi:10.1016/S0166-4972(02)00051-2

Camisón, C., & Villar López, A. (2010). An examination of the relationship between manufacturing flexibility and firm performance: The mediating role of innovation. *International Journal of Operations & Production Management*, *30*(8), 853–878. doi:10.1108/01443571011068199

Camisón, C., & Villar-López, A. (2014). Organizational innovation as an enabler of technological innovation capabilities and firm performance. *Journal of Business Research*, *67*(1), 2891–2902. doi:10.1016/j.jbusres.2012.06.004

Caraballo, M., & Garcia, S. (2017). Renewable energy and economic development: An analysis for Spain and the biggest European economies. *El Trimestre Economico*, *84*, 571–609.

Cardinali, P. G., & De Giovanni, P. (2022). Responsible digitalization through digital technologies and green practices. *Corporate Social Responsibility and Environmental Management*, *29*(4), 984–995. doi:10.1002/csr.2249

Carroll, A. B. (1991). The pyramid of corporate social responsibility: Toward the moral management of organizational stakeholders. *Business Horizons*, *34*(4), 39–48. doi:10.1016/0007-6813(91)90005-G

Carter, S. (1998). Portfolio entrepreneurship in the farm sector: Indigenous growth in rural areas? *Entrepreneurship and Regional Development*, *10*(1), 17–32. doi:10.1080/08985629800000002

Cavallo, E., Eichengreen, B., & Panizza, U. (2018). Can countries rely on foreign saving for investment and economic development? *Review of World Economics*, *154*(2), 277–306. doi:10.100710290-017-0301-5

Čechura, L., Kroupová, Z. Ž., & Lekešová, M. (2022). Productivity and efficiency in Czech agriculture: Does farm size matter? *Zemedelská Ekonomika*, *68*(1), 1–10. doi:10.17221/384/2021-AGRICECON

Cenamor, J., Parida, V., & Wincent, J. (2019). How entrepreneurial SMEs compete through digital platforms: The roles of digital platform capability, network capability and ambidexterity. *Journal of Business Research*, *100*, 196–206. doi:10.1016/j.jbusres.2019.03.035

Census of India. (2011). *2011 Census Data*. Office of the Registrar General and Census Commissioner, India. Available at: https://censusindia.gov.in/2011-prov-results/data_files/mp/07Literacy.pdf

Census. (2022). *Republic of Serbia*. https://popis2022.stat.gov.rs/sr-Latn/

Cerqueira, P., Soukiazis, S., & Proença, S. (2021). Assessing the linkages between recycling, renewable energy and sustainable development: Evidence from the OECD countries. *Environment, Development and Sustainability*, *23*(7), 9766–9791. doi:10.100710668-020-00780-4

Chankova, D., & Vasilev, V. (2020). Leadership and deliberative democracy in the changing world: compatible or reconcilable paradigms. *Perspectives of Law and Public Administration*, *9*(2), 209-218. Retrieved March 20, 2023 from http://www.adjuris.ro/revista/an9nr2.html

Chee Hua Chin (2022). Empirical research on the competitiveness of rural tourism destinations: a practical plan for rural tourism industry post–COVID-19. *Consumer Behaviour in Tourism and Hospitality*, *17*(2), 211-231.

Chen, Y. K., Coviello, N., & Ranaweera, C. (2021). How does dynamic network capability operate? A moderated mediation analysis with NPD speed and firm age. *Journal of Business and Industrial Marketing*, *36*(2), 292–306. doi:10.1108/JBIM-01-2020-0050

Chetna, S., & Raj, K. (2017). Study of Women's Financial Literacy- A case of BHU. *Pacific Business Review International*, *10*(4), 128–136.

Chien, S., & Tsai, C. (2012). Dynamic capability, knowledge, learning, and firm performance. *Journal of Organizational Change Management*, *25*(3), 434–444. doi:10.1108/09534811211228148

Chiffoleau, Y., & Dourian, T. (2020). Sustainable food supply chains: Is shortening the answer? A literature review for a research and innovation agenda. *Sustainability (Basel)*, *12*(23), 9831. doi:10.3390u12239831

Chinn, M. D., & Ito, H. (2008). A new measure of financial openness. *Journal of Comparative Policy Analysis*, *10*(3), 309–322. doi:10.1080/13876980802231123

Ciaian, P., Guri, F., Rajcaniova, M., Drabik, D., & Paloma, S. G. (2018). Land fragmentation and production diversification: A case study from rural Albania. *Land Use Policy*, *76*, 589–599. doi:10.1016/j.landusepol.2018.02.039

Ciepielewska-Kowalik, A., Pieliński, B., Starnawska, M., & Szymańska, A. (2015). *Social Enterprise in Poland: Institutional and Historical Context*. ICSEM Working Papers, No. 11, Liege: The International Comparative Social Enterprise Models (ICSEM) Project.

Clarke, L. J. (2000). *Strategies for Agricultural Mechanization Development: The roles of the private sector and the Government*. https://hdl.handle.net/1813/10216

Compilation of References

Coeckelbergh, M. (2021). AI for climate: Freedom, justice, and other ethical and political challenges. *AI and Ethics*, *1*(1), 67–72. doi:10.100743681-020-00007-2

Coile, C. C., Levine, P. B., & McKnight, R. (2014). Recessions, Older Workers, and Longevity: How Long Are Recessions Good for Your Health? *American Economic Journal. Economic Policy*, *6*(3), 92–119. doi:10.1257/pol.6.3.92

Coşkun, H. E., Popescu, C., Şahin Samaraz, D., Tabak, A., & Akkaya, B. (2022). Entrepreneurial University Concept Review from the Perspective of Academicians: A Mixed Method Research Analysis. *Sustainability (Basel)*, *14*(16), 10110. doi:10.3390u141610110

Cristea, M.-A. (2021). Operational Risk Management in Banking Activity. *Journal of Eastern Europe Research in Business and Economics*, 1–16. Advance online publication. doi:10.5171/2021.969612

Cronje, F. D., & du Plessis, E. (2020). A review on tourism destination competitiveness. *Journal of Hospitality and Tourism Management*, *45*, 256–265. doi:10.1016/j.jhtm.2020.06.012

D'Angelo, A., & Presutti, M. (2019). SMEs international growth: The moderating role of experience on entrepreneurial and learning orientations. *International Business Review*, *28*(3), 613–624. doi:10.1016/j.ibusrev.2018.12.006

Damanpour, F. (2010). An integration of research findings of effects of firm size and market competition on product and process innovations. *British Journal of Management*, *21*(4), 996–1010. doi:10.1111/j.1467-8551.2009.00628.x

Dangi, T. B., & Jamal, T. (2016). An Integrated approach to Sustainable community based tourism, journal. *Sustainability (Basel)*, *2016*(8), 2–32. doi:10.3390u8050475

Daum, T. (2023). Mechanization and sustainable agri-food system transformation in the Global South. A review. *Agronomy for Sustainable Development*, *43*(1), 16. doi:10.100713593-023-00868-x

Davis, A. M., Nurmuliani, N., Park, S., & Zowghi, D. (2008, July). Requirements change: What's the alternative? In *2008 32nd Annual IEEE International Computer Software and Applications Conference* (pp. 635-638). IEEE.

Davis, J. S., & Van Wincoop, E. (2018). Globalization and the increasing correlation between capital inflows and outflows. *Journal of Monetary Economics*, *100*, 83–100. doi:10.1016/j.jmoneco.2018.07.009

de Almeida, F. A., Gomes, G. F., & Gaudêncio, J. H. D. (2019). A new multivariate approach based on weighted factor scores and confidence ellipses to precision evaluation of textured fiber bobbins measurement system. *Precision Engineering*, *60*, 520–534. doi:10.1016/j.precisioneng.2019.09.010

de Almeida, F. A., Santos, A. C. O., de Paiva, A. P., Gomes, G. F., & Gomes, J. H. D. F. (2022). Multivariate Taguchi loss function optimization based on principal components analysis and normal boundary intersection. *Engineering with Computers*, *38*(2), 1–17. doi:10.100700366-020-01122-8

De Schutter, O. (2019). *Towards a Common Food Policy for the European Union*. Report. IPES-Food.

de Vries, G., Arfelt, L., Drees, D., Godemann, M., Hamilton, C., Jessen-Thiesen, B., Ihsan Kaya, A., Kruse, H., Mensah, E., & Woltjer, P. (2021). The economic transformation database (ETD): Content, sources, and methods. *WIDER Technical Note 2021/2*. UNU-WIDER. doi:10.35188/UNU-WIDER/WTN/2021-2

Di Pietro, L., Di Virgilio, F., & Pantano, E. (2020). Augmented reality for enhancing customer experiences: Advances and future challenges. *Journal of Business Research*, *109*, 267–276.

Di Stefano, G., Peteraf, M., & Verona, G. (2010). Dynamic capabilities deconstructed: A bibliographic investigation into the origins, development, and future directions of the research domain. *Industrial and Corporate Change*, *19*(4), 1187–1204. doi:10.1093/icc/dtq027

Directorate for Agrarian Payments of the Ministry of Agriculture, Forestry and Water Management of the Republic of Serbia. (2022). *Current subsidies*. https://uap.gov.rs/current-subsidies/

Djordjević Milošević, S., Möllers, J., Marcantonio, F., & Di., & Ciaian, P. (2021). *The best practices and potential of smallholders' participation in short value chains in the Western Balkans and Turkey* (No. JRC125555). JRC Technical Report. Luxembourg. *Publications Office of the European Union*. Advance online publication. doi:10.2760/921512

Doherty, R., Haugh, H., Sahan, E., Wills, T., & Croft, S. (2020). *Creating the new economy: business models that put people and planet first*. WFTO and Traidcraft.

Đoković, A. (2013). *Strukturna korelaciona analiza u interpretaciji vektorskih koeficijenata korelacije* [Structural correlation analysis in the interpretation of vector correlation coefficients] [Doctoral dissertation]. University of Belgrade. https://nardus.mpn.gov.rs/handle/123456789/3059

Double the Donation. (n.d.). *Corporate Philanthropy examples: 15 companies doing it right*. https://doublethedonation.com/corporate-philanthropy-examples/

Dragomir, V. D., Bătae, O. M., Ionescu, B. S., & Ionescu-Feleagă, L. (2022). The Influence of ESG Factors on Financial Performance in the Banking Sector during the Covid-19 Pandemic. *Economic Computation and Economic Cybernetics Studies and Research*, *56*(4), 71–88. doi:10.24818/18423264/56.4.22.05

Drever, A. I., Odders-White, E., Kalish, C. W., Else-Quest, N. M., Hoagland, E. M., & Nelms, E. N. (2015). Foundations of financial well-being: Insights into the role of executive function, financial socialization, and experience-based learning in childhood and youth. *The Journal of Consumer Affairs*, *49*(1), 13–38. doi:10.1111/joca.12068

Du Plessis, E., Saayman, M., & van der Merwe, A. (2015). What makes South African tourism competitive? *African Journal of Hospitality, Tourism and Leisure*, *4*(2), 1–14. https://doaj.org/article/f47353129d7046d3bb772d0535eada2e

Dumitrescu, E., & Hurlin, C. (2012). Testing for Granger non-causality in heterogeneous panels. *Economic Modelling*, *29*(4), 1450–1460. doi:10.1016/j.econmod.2012.02.014

Dunning, J. H. (1980). Toward an eclectic theory of international production: Some empirical tests. *Journal of International Business Studies*, *11*(1), 9–31. doi:10.1057/palgrave.jibs.8490593

Du, S., Yu, K., Bhattacharya, C. B., & Sen, S. (2017). The business case for sustainability reporting: Evidence from stock market reactions. *Journal of Public Policy & Marketing*, *36*(2), 313–330. doi:10.1509/jppm.16.112

Dwyer, L., & Kim, C. (2003). Destination competitiveness: Determinants and indicators. *Current Issues in Tourism*, *6*(5), 369–414. doi:10.1080/13683500308667962

EARS. (2021). *2021 Energy Agency Annual Report*. Energy Agency of the Republic of Serbia.

EC. (2014). Commission delegated regulation (EU) No 807/2014 of 11 March 2014 supplementing Regulation (EU) No 1305/2013 of the European Parliament and of the Council on support for rural development by the European Agricultural Fund for Rural Development (EAFRD) and introducing transitional provisions. *Official Journal of the European Union, L, 227*. https://eur-lex.europa.eu/legal-content/en/ALL/?uri=CELEX:32014R0807

EC. (2020). *A Farm to Fork Strategy for a fair, healthy and environmentally-friendly food system*. Brussels, 20.05.2020. COM(2020) 381 final. Retrieved from https://food.ec.europa.eu/system/files/2020-05/f2f_action-plan_2020_strategy-info_en.pdf

EC. (2021). *A long-term Vision for the EU's Rural Areas – Towards stronger, connected, resilient and prosperous rural areas by 2040*. Brussels, 30.6.2021. COM(2021) 345 final. Retrieved from https://eur-lex.europa.eu/legal-content/EN/TXT/DOC/?uri=CELEX:52021DC0345

Edison, H. J., Levine, R., Ricci, L., & Sløk, T. (2002). International financial integration and economic growth. *Journal of International Money and Finance*, *21*(6), 749–776. doi:10.1016/S0261-5606(02)00021-9

Eichengreen, B., Gupta, P., & Masetti, O. (2018). Are capital flows fickle? Increasingly? And does the answer still depend on type? *Asian Economic Papers*, *17*(1), 22–41. doi:10.1162/asep_a_00583

Elkington, J. (1994). Towards the sustainable corporation: Win-win-win business strategies for sustainable development. *California Management Review*, *36*(2), 90–100. doi:10.2307/41165746

Elkington, J. (2018). 25 years ago I coined the phrase "triple bottom line." Here's why it's time to rethink it. *Harvard Business Review*, *25*, 2–5. Retrieved February 3, 2023, from https://hbr.org/2018/06/25-years-ago-i-coined-the-phrase-triple-bottom-line-heres-why-im-giving-up-on-it

Elkington, J. (2020). *Green Swans: The coming boom in regenerative capitalism*. Fast Company Press.

Elliott, K., Price, R., Shaw, P., Spiliotopoulos, T., Ng, M., Coopamootoo, K., & Van Moorsel, A. (2021). Towards an Equitable Digital Society: Artificial Intelligence (AI) and Corporate Digital Responsibility (CDR). *Society*, *58*(3), 179–188. doi:10.100712115-021-00594-8 PMID:34149122

Enright, M. J., & Newton, J. (2004). Tourism destination competitiveness: A quantitative approach. *Tourism Management*, *25*(6), 777–788. doi:10.1016/j.tourman.2004.06.008

Eom, T., & Han, H. (2019). Community-based tourism (TourDure) experience program: A theoretical approach, pp. 956-968. *Journal of Travel & Tourism Marketing*, *36*(8), 956–968. doi:10.1080/10548408.2019.1665611

Esposito, P., & Ricci, P. (2020). Cultural organizations, digital Corporate Social Responsibility and stakeholder engagement in virtual museums: A multiple case study. How digitization is influencing the attitude toward CSR. *Corporate Social Responsibility and Environmental Management*, *28*(2), 953–964. doi:10.1002/csr.2074

EU. (2012). *Local Food and Short Supply Chains*. EU Rural Review. No 12, Summer 2012. Retrieved from https://enrd.ec.europa.eu/sites/default/files/E8F24E08-0A45-F272-33FB-A6309E3AD601.pdf

EU. (2013). Regulation (EU) No 1305/2013 of the European Parliament and of the Council of 17 December 2013 on support for rural development by the European Agricultural Fund for Rural Development (EAFRD) and repealing Council Regulation (EC) No 1698/2005. *Official Journal of the European Union, L*, *347*. https://eur-lex.europa.eu/legal-content/EN/TXT/PDF/?uri=CELEX:32013R1305

EU. (2021, December). Regulation (EU) 2021/2115 of the European Parliament and of the Council of 2 December 2021establishing rules on support for strategic plans to be drawn up by Member States under the common agricultural policy (CAP Strategic Plans) and financed by the European Agricultural Guarantee Fund (EAGF) and by the European Agricultural Fund for Rural Development (EAFRD) and repealing Regulations (EU) No 1305/2013 and (EU) No 1307/2013. *Official Journal of the European Union, L*, *435*, 6. https://eur-lex.europa.eu/legal-content/EN/TXT/?uri=CELEX%3A32021R2115

European Commission. (2021). *Developing real solutions for smart and resilient rural areas in Europe*. CORDIS Results Pack on rural innovation.

European Innovation Partnership for Agricultural productivity and Sustainability. (2015). *Innovative short food supply chain management*. EIP-AGRI Focus Group. Final report. https://ec.europa.eu/eip/agriculture/ en/publications/eip-agri-focus-group-innovative-short-food-supply

FAO. (2020). *Empowering Smallholders and Family Farms in Europe and Central Asia. Regional Synthesis Report 2019 based on country studies in eight countries in Europe and Central and Asia*. Food and Agriculture Organization of the United Nations., doi:10.4060/ca9586en

Fashina, A. A., Abdilahi, S. M., & Fakunle, F. F. (2020). Examining the challenges associated with the implementation of project scope management in telecommunication projects in Somaliland. *PM World Journal*, *9*(3), 1–16.

Fatima, S. U., Khan, M. A., Siddiqui, F., Mahmood, N., Salman, N., Alamgir, A., & Shaukat, S. S. (2022). Geospatial assessment of water quality using principal components analysis (PCA) and water quality index (WQI) in Basho Valley, Gilgit Baltistan (Northern Areas of Pakistan). *Environmental Monitoring and Assessment*, *194*(3), 151. doi:10.100710661-022-09845-5 PMID:35129685

Feldmann, C., & Hamm, U. (2015). Consumers' perceptions and preferences for local food: A review. *Food Quality and Preference*, *40*, 152–164. doi:10.1016/j.foodqual.2014.09.014

Feng, P., & Ngai, C. (2020). Doing more on the corporate sustainability front: A longitudinal analysis of CSR reporting of global fashion companies. *Sustainability (Basel)*, *12*(6), 2477. doi:10.3390u12062477

Ferreira, Jenkinson, & Wilson. (2019). *From Basel I to Basel III: Sequencing Implementation in Developing Economies*. IMF WP/19/127

Ferreira, J., Coelho, A., & Moutinho, L. (2020). Dynamic capabilities, creativity and innovation capability and their impact on competitive advantage and firm performance: The moderating role of entrepreneurial orientation. *Technovation*, *92*, 102061. doi:10.1016/j.technovation.2018.11.004

Field, A. (2009). *Discovering statistics using SPSS*. Sage Publications.

Fisher, P. J., & Yao, R. (2017). Gender differences in financial risk tolerance. *Journal of Economic Psychology*, *61*, 191–202. doi:10.1016/j.joep.2017.03.006

Fitjar, R. D., Gjelsvik, M., & Rodríguez-Pose, A. (2013). The combined impact of managerial and relational capabilities on innovation in firms. *Entrepreneurship and Regional Development*, *25*(5-6), 500–520. doi:10.1080/08985626.2013.798353

Food and Agriculture Organization of the United Nations & International Fund for Agricultural Development. (2019). *United Nations Decade of Family Farming 2019-2028*. Global Action Plan. Licence: CC BY-NC-SA 3.0 IGO.

Food and Agriculture Organization of the United Nations. (2011). *Women in agriculture. Closing the gender gap for development*. SOFA 2010-11.

Fornell, C., & Larcker, D. (1981). Evaluating structural equation models with unobservable variables and measurement error. *JMR, Journal of Marketing Research*, *18*(1), 39–50. doi:10.1177/002224378101800104

Forstner, K. (2004). Community Ventures and Access to Markets: The Role of Intermediaries in Marketing Rural Tourism Products. *Development Policy Review*, *22*(5), 497–514. doi:10.1111/j.1467-7679.2004.00262.x

Franić, R., & Kovačićek, T. (2019). The professional status of rural women in the EU. Study. European Parliament. Policy Department for Citizens' Rights and Constitutional Affairs.

Frankel, J. A., & Romer, D. (1999). Does Trade Cause Growth? *The American Economic Review*, *89*(3), 379–399. doi:10.1257/aer.89.3.379

Future of Life Institute. (2023). Pause Giant AI Experiments: An Open Letter, ECB. (2016). Understanding the weakness in global trade. What is the new normal? *Occasional Paper Series*, 178. European Central Bank.

Galanakis, C. M. (2019). Preface. In C. M. Galanakis (Ed.), *Innovations in traditional foods* (pp. xi–xiii). Elsevier Science. doi:10.1016/B978-0-12-814887-7.00015-0

Galli, F., & Brunori, G. (Eds.). (2013). *Short Food Supply Chains as drivers of sustainable development.* Document developed in the framework of the FP7 project FOODLINKS (GA No. 265287). Laboratorio di studi rurali Sismondi. Retrieved from https://www.foodlinkscommunity.net/fileadmin/documents_organicresearch/foodlinks/CoPs/evidence-document-sfsc-cop.pdf

Gargano, G., Licciardo, F., Verrascina, M., & Zanetti, B. (2021). The agroecological approach as a model for multifunctional agriculture and farming towards the European Green Deal 2030. Some evidence from the Italian experience. *Sustainability (Basel)*, *13*(4), 2215. doi:10.3390u13042215

Gaupp, F., Hall, J., Hochrainer-Stigler, S., & Dadson, S. (2020). Changing risks of simultaneous global breadbasket failure. *Nature Climate Change*, *10*(1), 54–57. doi:10.103841558-019-0600-z

Gavrilović, N. (2020, December 9). *Brašno od dunja, aćeto od maline – pet žena iz Kosjerića osnovalo zadrugu i prave vrhunske proizvode* [Quince flour, raspberry vinegar - five women from Kosjerić founded a cooperative and make top quality products]. RTS. https://www.rts.rs/page/stories/sr/story/125/drustvo/ 4179229/zene-kosjeric-zadruga-brasno-od-dunja-aceto-malina.html

Gengenbach, C., Urbain, J., & Westerlund, J. (2016). Error correction testing in panels with common sthocastic trends. *Journal of Applied Econometrics*, *31*(6), 982–1004. doi:10.1002/jae.2475

Ghosh, S., & Vinod, D. (2017). What constrains financial inclusion for women? Evidence from Indian micro data. *World Development*, *92*, 60–81. doi:10.1016/j.worlddev.2016.11.011

Gigauri, I., Panait, M., & Palazzo, M. (2021). Teaching Corporate Social Responsibility and Business Ethics at Economic Programs. *LUMEN Proceedings, 15*, 24-37. 10.18662/lumproc/gekos2021/3

Gigauri, I. (2021). Corporate Social Responsibility and COVID-19 Pandemic Crisis: Evidence from Georgia. *International Journal of Sustainable Entrepreneurship and Corporate Social Responsibility*, *6*(1), 30–47. doi:10.4018/IJSECSR.2021010103

Gigauri, I., & Bogacz-Wojtanowska, E. (2022). Effects of the Pandemic Crisis on Social Enterprise: A Case Study from Georgia. *Economics & Sociology (Ternopil)*, *15*(2), 312–334. doi:10.14254/2071-789X.2022/15-2/19

Compilation of References

Gigauri, I., Popescu, C., Panait, M., & Apostu, S. A. (2022). Integrating Sustainability Development Issues into University Curriculum. In E. Hysa & R. Foote (Eds.), *New Perspectives on Using Accreditation to Improve Higher Education* (pp. 69–95). IGI Global. doi:10.4018/978-1-6684-5195-3.ch004

Gneiting, U., & Sonenshine, J. (2018). A living income for small-scale farmers: tackling unequal risks and market power. *Oxfam Discussion Papers*, 1–24. Retrieved from https://oxfamilibrary.openrepository.com/bitstream/handle/10546/620596/dp-living-income-smallscale-farmers-151118-en.pdf

Gomez, M., Mejia, A., Ruddell, B. L., & Rushforth, R. R. (2021). Supply chain diversity buffers cities against food shocks. *Nature*, 595(7866), 250–254. doi:10.103841586-021-03621-0 PMID:34234337

Gorton, M., Salvioni, C., & Hubbard, C. (2014). Semi-subsistence farms and alternative food supply chains. *EuroChoices (Uckfield)*, 13(1), 15–19. doi:10.1111/1746-692X.12045

Gössling, S., Scott, D., & Hall, C. M. (2013). *Tourism and water: Interactions, impacts, and challenges*. Channel View Publications.

Goszczyński, W., & Knieć, W. (2011). Strengthening alternative agro-food networks in the Eastern European Countryside. *Eastern European Countryside*, 17(2011), 5–20. doi:10.2478/v10130-011-0001-4

Grable, J. E. (2000). Financial Risk Tolerance and Additional Factors That Affect Risk Taking in Everyday Money Matters. *Journal of Business and Psychology*, 14(4), 625–630. doi:10.1023/A:1022994314982

Graffelman, J., & Tuft, R. (2004). Site scores and conditional biplots in canonical correspondence analysis. *Environmetrics: The Official Journal of the International Environmetrics Society*, 15(1), 67-80. doi:10.1002/env.629

Graffelman, J., & Aluja-Banet, T. (2003). Optimal representation of supplementary variables in biplots from principal component analysis and correspondence analysis. *Biometrical Journal. Biometrische Zeitschrift*, 45(4), 491–509. doi:10.1002/bimj.200390027

Graham-Rowe, E., Gardner, B., Abraham, C., Skippon, S., Dittmar, H., Hutchins, R. L., & Stannard, J. (2012). Mainstream consumers driving plug-in battery-electric and plug-in hybrid electric cars: A qualitative analysis of responses and evaluations. *Transportation Research Part A, Policy and Practice*, 46(1), 140–153. doi:10.1016/j.tra.2011.09.008

Grasser, S., Schunko, C., & Vogl, C. R. (2012). Gathering "tea" – from necessity to connectedness with nature. Local knowledge about wild plant gathering in the Biosphere Reserve Grosses Walsertal (Austria). *Journal of Ethnobiology and Ethnomedicine*, 8(1), 31. doi:10.1186/1746-4269-8-31 PMID:22889066

Grigore, G., Molesworth, M., & Watkins, R. (2017). New Corporate Responsibilities in the Digital Economy. In A. Theofilou, G. Grigore, & A. Stancu (Eds.), *Corporate Social Responsibility in the Post-Financial Crisis Era*. Palgrave Studies in Governance, Leadership and Responsibility. Palgrave Macmillan. doi:10.1007/978-3-319-40096-9_3

Gronum, S., Verreynne, M. L., & Kastelle, T. (2012). The role of networks in small and medium-sized enterprise innovation and firm performance. *Journal of Small Business Management*, *50*(2), 257–282. doi:10.1111/j.1540-627X.2012.00353.x

Grossman, G. M., & Helpman, D. (1991). *Innovation and Growth in the Global Economy*. MIT Press.

Grujić Vučkovski, B. (2022): *Analiza oblika finansiranja poljoprivrede Republike Srbije, Monografija* [Analysis of forms of financing agriculture in the Republic of Serbia, Monograph]. Institut za ekonomiku poljoprivrede, Beograd. https://www.iep.bg.ac.rs/images/2022/Analiza%20oblika%20finansiranja%20FIN.pdf

Grujić Vučkovski, B., Simonović, Z., Ćurčić, N., & Miletić, V. (2022). The role of agriculture in the economic structure of Serbia and budget support for rural development of Kladovo municipality. *Ekonomika Poljoprivrede*, *69*(3), 863–876. doi:10.5937/ekoPolj2203863G

Guiomar, N., Godinho, S., Pinto-Correia, T., Almeida, M., Bartolini, F., Bezák, P., Biró, M., Bjørkhaug, H., Bojnec, Š., Brunori, G., Corazzin, M., Czekaj, M., Davidova, S., Kania, J., Kristensen, S., Marraccini, E., Molnár, Z., Niedermayr, J., O'Rourke, E., ... Wästfelt, A. (2018). Typology and distribution of small farms in Europe: Towards a better picture. *Land Use Policy*, *75*, 784–798. doi:10.1016/j.landusepol.2018.04.012

Gullo, L. J. (2018). Developing System Safety Requirements. *Design for Safety*, 87-114.

Gunawan, S., Shieh, C., & Pei, Y. (2015). Effects of Crisis Communication Strategies and Media Report on Corporate Image in Catering Industry. *Acta Oeconomica*, *65*(s2), 399–411. doi:10.1556/032.65.2015.s2.29

Gupta, S. D., & Choudhry, N. K. (1997). Globalization, growth and sustainability: An introduction. *Globalization, Growth and Sustainability*, 1-13.

Gupta, A. K., & Gupta, N. (2019). Innovation and culture as a dynamic capability for firm performance: A study from emerging markets. *Global Journal of Flexible Systems Managment*, *20*(4), 323–336. doi:10.100740171-019-00218-5

Haas, R., Imami, D., Miftari, I., Ymeri, P., Grunert, K., & Meixner, O. (2021). Consumer perception of food quality and safety in Western Balkan Countries: Evidence from Albania and Kosovo. *Foods*, *10*(1), 160. doi:10.3390/foods10010160 PMID:33466641

Hackbarth, A., & Madlener, R. (2013). Consumer preferences for alternative fuel vehicles: A discrete choice analysis. *Consumer Preferences for Alter-Native Fuel Vehicles: A Discrete Choice Analysis.*, *25*, 5–17. doi:10.1016/j.trd.2013.07.002

Compilation of References

Hair, J. F. Jr, Black, W. C., Babin, B. J., & Anderson, R. E. (2014). *Multivariate data analysis* (7th ed.). Pearson Education Limited.

Hall, C. M., & Gössling, S. (2016). Tourism and water: Interactions, impacts and challenges: An introduction. In *Tourism and Water* (pp. 1–12). Channel View Publications.

Hanf, J. H., & Gagalyuk, T. (2018). Integration of Small Farmers into Value Chains: Evidence from Eastern Europe and Central Asia. In G. Egilmez (Ed.), *Agricultural Value Chain* (pp. 181–197). IntechOpen. doi:10.5772/intechopen.73191

Hanus, G. (2020). Ethnocentrism in polish consumer food behaviour as a determinant of short supply chain development. *European Journal of Sustainable Development*, 9(4), 169–169. doi:10.14207/ejsd.2020.v9n4p169

Hassan, S. S. (2000). Determinants of market competitiveness in an environmentally sustainable tourism industry. *Journal of Travel Research*, 38(3), 239–245. doi:10.1177/004728750003800305

Hassoun, S., & Ayad, H. (2020). Renewable energy and sustainable development: Evidence from 17 OECD countries. *International Journal of Economics, Business and Politics*, 4, 41–60.

Hayes, A. F. (2018). *Introduction to mediation, moderation, and conditional process analysis: A regression-based approach* (2nd ed.). The Guilford Press.

Heimberger, P. (2022). Does economic globalisation promote economic growth? A meta-analysis. *World Economy*, 45(6), 1690–1712. doi:10.1111/twec.13235

Helfat, C. E., & Peteraf, M. A. (2003). The dynamic resource-based view: Capability lifecycles. *Strategic Management Journal*, (24), 997–1010. doi:10.1002/smj.332

Helms, B. (2006). *Access for all consultative group to assist the poor*. doi:10.1596/978-0-8213-6360-7

Herden, C. J., Alliu, E., Cakici, A., Cormier, T., Deguelle, C., Gambhir, S., Griffiths, C., Gupta, S., Kamani, S. R., Kiratli, Y.-S., Kispataki, M., Lange, G., Moles de Matos, L., Tripero Moreno, L., Betancourt Nunez, H. A., Pilla, V., Raj, B., Roe, J., Skoda, M., ... Edinger-Schons, L. M. (2021). "Corporate Digital Responsibility": New corporate responsibilities in the digital age. *NachhaltigkeitsManagementForum*, 29(1), 13–29. doi:10.100700550-020-00509-x

Hidrue, M. K., Parsons, G. R., Kempton, W., & Gardner, M. P. (2011). Willingness to pay for electric vehicles and their attributes. *Resource and Energy Economics*, 33(3), 686–705. doi:10.1016/j.reseneeco.2011.02.002

Hill, J., & Hill, J. (2018). *Fintech and Government Regulation*. FinTech and the Remaking of Financial Institutions. doi:10.1016/B978-0-12-813497-9.00015-9

Hlioui, Z., & Yousfi, O. (2022). CSR and Innovation: Two Sides of the Same Coin. In B. Orlando (Ed.), *Corporate Social Responsibility*. doi:10.5772/intechopen.94344

Horvat, A. M., Matkovski, B., Zekić, S., & Radovanov, B. (2020). Technical efficiency of agriculture in Western Balkan countries undergoing the process of EU integration. *Agricultural Economics – Czech, 66*(2), 65-73. . doi:10.17221/224/2019-AGRICECON

Howard, P. L. (2003). The major importance of 'minor' resources: women and plant biodiversity. *IIED Gatekeeper Series, 112*, 3-19.

Hult, G. T. M., Hurley, R. F., & Knight, G. A. (2004). Innovativeness: Its antecedents and impact on business performance. *Industrial Marketing Management, 33*(5), 429–438. doi:10.1016/j.indmarman.2003.08.015

Hung, A., Parker, A. M., & Yoong, J. (2009). *Defining and measuring financial literacy*. Working Paper No. WR-708, Rand Corporation. doi:10.2139/ssrn.1498674

Icheva, M., & Vasilev, V. (2021). The time for the next steps is here – from classic to modern paradigms in motivation. *International Journal of Social Science & Economic Research, 6*(3), 913–922. doi:10.46609/IJSSER.2021.v06i03.012

Iddris, F. (2016). Innovation capability: A systematic review and research agenda. *Interdisciplinary Journal of Information, Knowledge, and Management, 11*, 235–260. doi:10.28945/3571

Ilbery, B., & Maye, D. (2005). Alternative (shorter) food supply chains and specialist livestock products in the Scottish–English borders. *Environment & Planning A, 37*(5), 823–844. doi:10.1068/a3717

ILO. (2019). *Rules of the game: An introduction to the standards-related work of the International Labour Organization*. International Labour Office.

Institute of Public Administration. (2021). https://www.ipa.government.bg/bg/publications#cbp=/bg/sbornik-s-dobri-praktiki-2021

Ist Media. (2018, October 17). *Milosava Grozdić – poslovna žena iz kuhinje* [Milosava Grozdić – business woman from the kitchen]. https://istmedia.rs/milosava-grozdic-poslovna-zena-iz-kuhinje/

Jandrić, M., Hadrović, S., Rakonjac, L., & Ćosić, M. Posedovna struktura zemljišta Jugozapadnog dela Srbije [Land ownership structure of the Southwestern part of Serbia]. *Akademski pregled*, 59-65. doi:10.7251/AP2102059J

Jarzębowski, S., Bourlakis, M., & Bezat-Jarzębowska, A. (2020). Short food supply chains (SFSC) as local and sustainable systems. *Sustainability (Basel), 12*(11), 4715. doi:10.3390u12114715

Jaworski, B. J., & Kohli, A. K. (1993). Market orientation: Antecedents and consequences. *Journal of Marketing, 57*(3), 53–70. doi:10.1177/002224299305700304

Jiménez-Jiménez, D., & Sanz-Valle, R. (2011). Innovation, organizational learning, and performance. *Journal of Business Research, 64*(4), 408–417. doi:10.1016/j.jbusres.2010.09.010

Compilation of References

Johnston, J. D. (2005). *Importance of financial literacy in the global economy*. The Financial Education Summit, Kuala Lumpur. https://www.oecd.org/general/35883324.pdf

Joksimović, M., Grujić, B., & Joksimović, D. (2018). Correlation and regression analysis of the impact of leasing on agricultural production in Republic of Serbia. *Ekonomika Poljoprivrede*, *65*(2), 583–600. doi:10.5937/ekoPolj1802583J

Jolly, D., & Grabowski, M. (2018). Virtual and augmented reality in education. *Education and Information Technologies*, *23*(4), 1515–1520.

Jovičić, B. (2019, August 1). *Ženska zemljoradnička zadruga* [Women's agricultural cooperative]. RTS. https://www.rts.rs/page/stories/sr/story/57/srbija-danas/3609876/zenska-zemljoradnicka-zadruga.html

Jung, T. H., & tom Dieck, M. C. (2018). The potential of virtual reality for tourism. In *Information and communication technologies in tourism 2018* (pp. 737–749). Springer.

Kadoya, Y., Khan, M. S. R., Hamada, T., & Dominguez, A. (2018). Financial literacy and anxiety about life in old age: Evidence from the USA. *Review of Economics of the Household*, *16*(3), 859–878. doi:10.100711150-017-9401-1

Kafetzopoulos, D., & Psomas, E. (2015). The impact of innovation capability on the performance of manufacturing companies: The Greek case. *Journal of Manufacturing Technology Management*, *26*(1), 104–130. doi:10.1108/JMTM-12-2012-0117

Kahlor, L. A. (2007). An augmented risk information seeking model: The case of global warming. *Media Psychology*, *10*(3), 414–435. doi:10.1080/15213260701532971

Kaldor, N. (1966). *Causes of the Slow Rate of Growth of the United Kingdom. An Inaugural Lecture*. Cambridge University Press.

Karwowski, M., & Raulinajtys-Grzybek, M. (2021). The application of corporate social responsibility (CSR) actions for mitigation of environmental, social, corporate governance (ESG) and reputational risk in integrated reports. *Corporate Social Responsibility and Environmental Management*, *28*(4), 1270–1284. doi:10.1002/csr.2137

Kazar, G., & Kazar, A. (2014). The renewable energy production-economic development nexus. *International Journal of Energy Economics and Policy*, *4*, 312–319.

Key, N. (2019). Farm size and productivity growth in the United States Corn Belt. *Food Policy*, *84*, 186–195. doi:10.1016/j.foodpol.2018.03.017

Kezar, A., & Yang, H. (2010). The importance of financial literacy. *About Campus*, *14*(6), 15–21. https://doi.org/.20004 doi:10.1002/abc

Khadse, A. (2017). *Women, agroecology & gender equality*. Focus on the Global South.

Kiliyanni, A. L., & Sivaraman, S. (2018). A predictive model for financial literacy among the educated youth in Kerala, India. *Journal of Social Service Research*, *44*(4), 537–547. doi:10.1 080/01488376.2018.1477699

Kindylidi, I., & Cabral, T. S. (2021). Sustainability of AI: The Case of Provision of Information to Consumers. *Sustainability (Basel)*, *13*(21), 12064. doi:10.3390u132112064

Kiss, K., Ruszkai, C., & Takács-György, K. (2019). Examination of Short Supply Chains Based on Circular Economy and Sustainability Aspects. *Resources*, *8*(4), 161. doi:10.3390/resources8040161

Kittilaksanawong, W., & Ren, Z. (2013). Innovation capability building through intermediary organizations: Cases of manufacturing small-and medium-sized enterprises from China's Zhejiang province. *Asian Journal of Technology Innovation*, *21*(2), 62–79. doi:10.1080/19761597.2013.819247

Kneafsey M., Venn, L., Schmutz, U., Balázs, B., Trenchard, L., Eyden-Wood, T., ...Blackett, M. (2013). Short Food Supply Chains and Local Food Systems in the EU. A State of Play of their Socio-Economic Characteristics. In *JRC Scientific and policy reports*. Luxembourg: Publications Office of the European Union. doi:10.2791/88784

Komal, B., Janjua, U. I., Anwar, F., Madni, T. M., Cheema, M. F., Malik, M. N., & Shahid, A. R. (2020). The impact of scope creep on project success: An empirical investigation. *IEEE Access : Practical Innovations, Open Solutions*, *8*, 125755–125775. doi:10.1109/ACCESS.2020.3007098

Komal, B., Janjua, U. I., & Madni, T. M. (2019, April). Identification of scope creep factors and their impact on software project success. In *2019 International Conference on Computer and Information Sciences (ICCIS)* (pp. 1-5). IEEE. 10.1109/ICCISci.2019.8716390

Komorowski, L., & Stanny, M. (2020). Smart villages: Where can they happen? *Land (Basel)*, *9*(5), 151. doi:10.3390/land9050151

Koprivica, R., Veljković, B., Stanimirović, N., & Topisirović, G. Eksplatacione karakteristike kombajna john deere 5820 u pripremi kukuruzne silaže za muzne krave na porodičnim farmama [Silage harvester zmaj 350 productivity in harvesting and chopping of maize silage for dairy cows on a commercial farm]. *Poljoprivredna tehnika*, *34*(3), 23-30. https://scindeks.ceon.rs/article.aspx?artid=0554-55870903023 K

Kose, M. A., Prasad, E., Rogoff, K., & Wei, S. J. (2010). Financial globalization and economic policies. In D. Rodrik, & M. Rosenzweig (Eds.), Handbook of development economics (vol. 5, pp. 4283–4359). Elsevier. doi:10.1016/B978-0-444-52944-2.00003-3

Kose, M. A., Prasad, E., Rogoff, K., & Wei, S. J. (2009). Financial globalization: A reappraisal. *IMF Staff Papers*, *56*(1), 8–62. doi:10.1057/imfsp.2008.36

Kotevska, A., Bogdanov, N., Nikolić, A., Dimitrievski, D., Gjoshevski, D., Georgiev, N., & Martinovska Stojcheska, A. (2015). Consulisons and recommendations. In A. Kotevska & A. Martinovska Stojcheska (Eds.), *The Impact of Socio-Economic Structure of Rural Population on Success of Rural Development Policy* (pp. 117–124). Association of Agricultural Economists of Republic of Macedonia. Retrieved from https://publicpolicy.rs/publikacije/d16435796b8009eb918aa100 c03cfbba0d5423f3.pdf

Kotler, P., Bowen, J. T., Makens, J. T., & Baloglu, S. (2017). Marketing for Hospitality and Tourism (7th ed.). Pearson Education Limited.

Kotschwar, B. R. (2012). *Transportation and communication infrastructure in Latin America: lessons from Asia*. Peterson Institute for International Economics Working Paper No. 12-6.

Koutsou, S., Iakovidou, O., & Gotsinas, N. (2003). Women's cooperatives in Greece: An ongoing story of battles, successes and problems. *Journal of Rural Cooperation*, *31*(1), 47–57.

Kovačević, V., & Jeločnik, M. (2022). *Tržište i trgovanje poljoprivrednim proizvodima/ Market and trading of agricultural products*. Beograd: Institut za ekonomiku poljoprivrede, Begrad, 2022. Retrieved from https://www.iep.bg.ac.rs/images/stories/izdanja/Monografije/ Trziste%20i%20trgovanje%20PP%20LQ.pdf

Kovačević, V., Brenjo, D., Cvetković, S., & Rainović, L. (2022). Comparative analyse of foodstuff geographical indications in the Western Balkans. *Ekonomika Poljoprivrede*, *69*(1), 163–178. doi:10.5937/ekoPolj2201163K

Kuznets, S. (1971). *Economic growth of nations: Total output and production structure*. Harvard University Press. doi:10.4159/harvard.9780674493490

Laforet, S., & Tann, J. (2006). Innovative characteristics of small manufacturing firms. *Journal of Small Business and Enterprise Development*, *13*(3), 363–380. doi:10.1108/14626000610680253

Lai, C. H., Yang, J. C., Chen, F. C., Ho, C. W., & Chan, T. W. (2007). Affordances of mobile technologies for experiential learning: The interplay of technology and pedagogical practices. *Journal of Computer Assisted Learning*, *23*(4), 326–337. doi:10.1111/j.1365-2729.2007.00237.x

Lai, I. K. W., Liu, Y., Sun, X., Zhang, H., & Xu, W. (2015). Factors Influencing the Behavioural Intention towards Full Electric Vehicles: An Empirical Study in Macau. *Sustainability (Basel)*, *7*(9), 12564–12585. doi:10.3390u70912564

Lane, P. R., & Milesi-Ferretti, G. M. (2018). The external wealth of nations revisited: International financial integration in the aftermath of the global financial crisis. *IMF Economic Review*, *66*(1), 189–222. doi:10.105741308-017-0048-y

Lans, T., Seuneke, P., & Klerkx, L. (2017). Agricultural entrepreneurship. In E. G. Carayannis (Ed.), *Encyclopedia of Creativity, Invention, Innovation and Entrepreneurship* (pp. 44–49). Springer. doi:10.1007/978-1-4614-6616-1_496-2

Laroche, M., Bergeron, J., & Barbaro-Forleo, G. (2001). Targeting consumers who are willing to pay more for environmentally friendly products. *Journal of Consumer Marketing*, *18*(6), 503–520. doi:10.1108/EUM0000000006155

Larson, R., & Larson, E. (2009). *Top five causes of scope creep ... and what to do about them.* Paper presented at PMI® Global Congress 2009—North America, Orlando, FL.

Lassithiotaki, A. (2011). Rural women and entrepreneurship: A case study in Heraklion Crete prefecture, Greece. *Journal of Developmental Entrepreneurship*, *16*(02), 269–284. doi:10.1142/S1084946711001835

Lawson, B., & Samson, D. (2001). Developing innovation capability in organisations: A dynamic capabilities approach. *International Journal of Innovation Management*, *5*(3), 377–400. doi:10.1142/S1363919601000427

Lee, M. J., & Xiang, Z. (2019). An empirical investigation of augmented reality and destination marketing. *Journal of Travel Research*, *58*(8), 1289–1307.

Leong, C., Tan, B., Xiao, X., Ter Chian Tan, F., & Sun, Y. (2017). Nurturing a FinTech ecosystem: The case of a youth microloan startup in China. *International Journal of Information Management*, *37*(2), 92–97. doi:10.1016/j.ijinfomgt.2016.11.006

Liao, S. H., Fei, W. C., & Chen, C. C. (2007). Knowledge sharing, absorptive capacity, and innovation capability: An empirical study of Taiwan's knowledge-intensive industries. *Journal of Information Science*, *33*(3), 340–359. doi:10.1177/0165551506070739

Libby, A. M., Ghushchyan, V., McQueen, R. B., & Campbell, J. D. (2010). Economic grand rounds: Psychological distress and depression associated with job loss and gain: The social costs of job instability. *Psychiatric Services (Washington, D.C.)*, *61*(12), 1178–1180. doi:10.1176/ps.2010.61.12.1178 PMID:21123399

Lin, R. J., Chen, R. H., & Chiu, K. K. S. (2010). Customer relationship management and innovation capability: An empirical study. *Industrial Management & Data Systems*, *110*(1), 111–133. doi:10.1108/02635571011008434

Liu, X., & Li, X. (2023). The Influence of Agricultural Production Mechanization on Grain Production Capacity and Efficiency. *Processes (Basel, Switzerland)*, *11*(2), 487. doi:10.3390/pr11020487

Lukić, T., Pivac, T., Solarević, M., Blešić, I., Živković, J., Penjišević, I., Golić, R., Kalenjuk Pivarski, B., Bubalo-Živković, M., & Pandžić, A. (2022). Sustainability of Serbian villages in COVID-19 pandemic conditions. *Sustainability (Basel)*, *14*(2), 703. doi:10.3390u14020703

Lusardi A. And Mitchell, O. (2008). Planning and Financial Literacy: How do Women Fare. *The American Economic Review*, *98*(2), 413–417. doi:10.1257/aer.98.2.413

Machi, L., & McEvoy, B. (2016). *The literature review: Six steps to success* (3rd ed.). Corwin. doi:10.1093/obo/9780199756810-0169

Compilation of References

Madhuri, K. L., Rao, J. J., & Suma, V. (2014). Effect of Scope Creep in Software Projects a [euro]" Its Bearing on Critical Success Factors. *International Journal of Computer Applications*, *106*(2).

Madhuri, K. L., & Suma, V. (2014, October). Influence of domain and technology upon scope creep in software projects. In *International Conference on Advances in Electronics Computers and Communications* (pp. 1-6). IEEE. 10.1109/ICAECC.2014.7002443

Madhuri, K. L., Suma, V., & Mokashi, U. M. (2018). A triangular perception of scope creep influencing the project success. *International Journal of Business Information Systems*, *27*(1), 69–85. doi:10.1504/IJBIS.2018.088571

Majewski, E., Komerska, A., Kwiatkowski, J., Malak-Rawlikowska, A., Wąs, A., Sulewski, P., Gołaś, M., Pogodzińska, K., Lecoeur, J.-L., Tocco, B., Török, Á., Donati, M., & Vittersø, G. (2020). Are short food supply chains more environmentally sustainable than long chains? A life cycle assessment (LCA) of the eco-efficiency of food chains in selected EU countries. *Energies*, *13*(18), 4853. doi:10.3390/en13184853

Malak-Rawlikowska, A., Majewski, E., Wąs, A., Borgen, S. O., Csillag, P., Donati, M., Freeman, R., Hoàng, V., Lecoeur, J.-L., Mancini, M. C., Nguyen, A., Saïdi, M., Tocco, B., Török, Á., Veneziani, M., Vittersø, G., & Wavresky, P. (2019). Measuring the economic, environmental, and social sustainability of short food supply chains. *Sustainability (Basel)*, *11*(15), 4004. doi:10.3390u11154004

Malhotra, N. K. (2010). *Marketing research- An applied orientation* (6th ed.). Pearson Education, Inc.

Manikas, I., Malindretos, G., & Moschuris, S. (2019). A community-based agro-food hub model for sustainable farming. *Sustainability (Basel)*, *11*(4), 1017. doi:10.3390u11041017

Marsden, T., Banks, J., & Bristow, G. (2000). Food supply chain approaches: Exploring their role in rural development. *Sociologia Ruralis*, *40*(4), 424–438. doi:10.1111/1467-9523.00158

Master plan for sustainable development rural tourism in Serbia. (2011). UNWTO, Tourism & Leisure Advisory Services.

Mathias, P. (1969). *The First Industrial Nation: The Economic History of Britain 1700–1914*. Methuen & Co. Ltd.

McKinsey. (2017). *Introducing the next-generation operating model*. McKinsey & Company. www.mckinsey.com

Menicucci, E., & Paolucci, G. (2023). ESG dimensions and bank performance: An empirical investigation in Italy. *Corporate Governance (Bradford)*, *23*(3), 563–586. doi:10.1108/CG-03-2022-0094

Mentzer, J. T., DeWitt, W., Keebler, J. S., Min, S., Nix, N. W., Smith, C. D., & Zacharia, Z. G. (2001). Defining supply chain management. *Journal of Business Logistics*, *22*(2), 1–25. doi:10.1002/j.2158-1592.2001.tb00001.x

Mihailović, B., Radić Jean, I., Popović, V., Radosavljević, K., Chroneos Krasavac, B., & Bradić-Martinović, A. (2020). Farm differentiation strategies and sustainable regional development. *Sustainability (Basel), 12*(17), 7223. doi:10.3390u12177223

Milesi-Ferretti, G. M., & Tille, C. (2011). The great retrenchment: International capital flows during the global financial crisis. *Economic Policy, 26*(66), 289–346. doi:10.1111/j.1468-0327.2011.00263.x

Mileusnic, Z., Djevic, M., Miodragovic, R., & Petrovic, D. (2005). On the Applicabillity of the Single-Shaft Tractors Motocultivators in Serbia. *Poljoprivredna tehnika, 30*(1), 17-25. http://arhiva.nara.ac.rs/handle/123456789/140

Milone, P., & Ventura, F. (2019). New generation farmers: Rediscovering the peasantry. *Journal of Rural Studies, 65*, 43–52. doi:10.1016/j.jrurstud.2018.12.009

Milovanović, Ž. (2017). Primena ELECTRA metode u nabavci poljoprivredne mehanizacij. [Aplication of the ELECTRA method in the purchase of agricultural mechanization]. *Ekonomski signali, 12*(2), 11-21. doi:10.5937/ekonsig1702011M

Ministry of Labor and Social Policy of Bulgaria. (2019). *Strategy for Corporate Social Responsibility 2019-2023*. Retrieved March 21, 2023 from https://www.mlsp.government.bg/uploads/15/spitao/dokumenti/strategii/za-korporativna-sotsialna-otgovornost-2019-2023-g.pdf

Ministry of Village Care. (2021a, March 8). *Krkobabić – zajedno do boljeg položaja žena u Srbiji* [Krkobabić–together to a better position of women in Serbia]. https://mbs.gov.rs/aktivnosti-saopstenja.php

Ministry of Village Care. (2021b, October 15). *Garantovana socijalna penzija, naša obaveza* [Guaranteed social pension, our obligation]. https://mbs.gov.rs/aktivnosti-saopstenja.php

Ministry of Village Care. (2022, December, 29). *Za ljude znanja i veština tri puta veće zarade* [For people with knowledge and skills, three times greater earnings]. https://mbs.gov.rs/aktivnosti-saopstenja.php

Mishkin, F. S. (2006). *The Next Great Globalization: How Disadvantaged Nations Can Harness Their Financial Systems to Get Rich*. Princeton University Press. doi:10.1515/9781400829446

Mitrega, M., Forkmann, S., Zaefarian, G., & Henneberg, S. C. (2017). Networking capability in supplier relationships and its impact on product innovation and firm performance. *International Journal of Operations & Production Management, 37*(5), 577–606. doi:10.1108/IJOPM-11-2014-0517

Mitrović, M. M. (Ed.). (2020). *Nacionalni program za preporod sela Srbije: stanje, problemi i prioriteti održivog razvoja* [National Program for revival of Serbian villages: situation, problems and sustainable development priorities]. IEP.

Compilation of References

Mochales, G., & Blanch, J. (2022). Unlocking the potential of CSR: An explanatory model to determine the strategic character of CSR activities. *Journal of Business Research*, *140*, 310–323. doi:10.1016/j.jbusres.2021.11.002

Montagnoli, L. (2020, October 28). *Italian women are the protagonists of virtuous farming and favor ecological transition*. Gambero Rosso. https://www.gamberorossointernational.com/news/food-news/italian-women-are-the-protagonists-of-virtuous-farming-and-favour-ecological-transition/

Morgan, P., & Trinh, L. (2019). Determinants and impacts of financial literacy in Cambodia and VietNam. *J Risk Financ Manag*, *12*(1), 19. doi:10.3390/jrfm12010019

Morton, A. L., & Tate, G. (1956). *The British Labour Movement 1770–1920*. Lawrence and Wishart.

Mottaleb, K. A., Raheem, R. A., & Ayeh, J. K. (2020). Virtual Reality Tourism: An Effective Way to Promote Tourist Destinations. *Journal of Destination Marketing & Management*, *16*, 100409.

Mottola, G. R. (2013). In our best interest: Women, financial literacy, and credit card behavior. *Numeracy*, *6*(2), 1–15. doi:10.5038/1936-4660.6.2.4

MSCI. (n.d.). *MSCI KLD 400 Social Index*. https://www.msci.com/our-solutions/indexes/kld-400-social-index

Mu, J., & Di Benedetto, A. (2012). Networking capability and new product development. *IEEE Transactions on Engineering Management*, *59*(1), 4–19. doi:10.1109/TEM.2011.2146256

Nabet, A. A., El-Dash, K. M., ElMohr, M. K., & Mohamed, M. A. (2017). Managing scope creep in construction projects in Egypt. *ERJ Faculty Eng Shoubra*, *33*(1), 1–16.

Najafi-Tavani, S., Najafi-Tavani, Z., Naudé, P., Oghazi, P., & Zeynaloo, E. (2018). How collaborative innovation networks affect new product performance: Product innovation capability, process innovation capability, and absorptive capacity. *Industrial Marketing Management*, *73*, 193–205. doi:10.1016/j.indmarman.2018.02.009

National program for renewal villages of Serbia – State, problems and priorities. (2020). Academia Board for Villages, SANU (Serbian Academy of Science and Arts), Ministry for Regional Development. Institute of Agricultural Economics.

NCFE-FLIS. (2013). *Financial Literacy and Inclusion in India*. Final Report, National Institute of Securities Market (NISM), Mumbai. Available https://www.ncfe.org.in/images/pdfs/nasionalsurveyy/NISM_Final%20Report%20%20All%20India.pdf

Neto, D. G., & Veiga, F. J. (2013). Financial globalization, convergence and growth: The role of foreign direct investment. *Journal of International Money and Finance*, *37*, 161–186. doi:10.1016/j.jimonfin.2013.04.005

Neuhofer, B., Buhalis, D., & Ladkin, A. (2015). Technology as a catalyst of change: Enablers and barriers of the tourist experience and their consequences. *The Routledge Handbook of Transport Economics*, 45-58.

Nicolaides, A. (2020). Sustainable ethical tourism (SET) and rural community involvement. *African Journal of Hospitality, Tourism and Leisure*, 9(1), 1–16.

Nikolić, M., & Popović, V. (2010). The possibility of safe food production in protected areas. In *Proceedings of the XIV International Eco-Conference Safe Food* (pp. 199-206). Ecological Movement of Novi Sad.

Nikolic, R., Savin, L., Furman, T., Tomic, M., & Gligoric Radojka, S. M. (2006). Istraživanje podloga i razvoj traktora za poljoprivredu [The advancement of production and development of tractors]. *Letopis naučnih radova strana*, 28-37. https://scindeks.ceon.rs/article.aspx?artid=0350-29530304137 N

Nikolić, R., Savin, L., Furman, T., Tomić, M., Simikić, M., & Gligorić, R. (2005). Pogonske mašine i traktori u poljoprivredi [Power machines and tractors in agriculture]. *Savremena poljoprivredna tehnika*, 31(1-2), 15-23. https://scindeks.ceon.rs/article.aspx?artid=0350-29530502015 N

Nordgren, A. (2023). Artificial intelligence and climate change: Ethical issues. *Journal of Information. Communication and Ethics in Society*, 21(1), 1–15. doi:10.1108/JICES-11-2021-0106

Nunnally, J. C., & Bernstein, I. H. (1994). *Psychometric theory* (3rd ed.). McGraw Hill.

O'Cass, A., & Sok, P. (2014). The role of intellectual resources, product innovation capability, reputational resources and marketing capability combinations in firm growth. *International Small Business Journal*, 32(8), 996–1018. doi:10.1177/0266242613480225

Obstfeld, M. (1998). The global capital market: Benefactor or menace? *The Journal of Economic Perspectives*, 12(4), 9–30. doi:10.1257/jep.12.4.9

Obstfeld, M. (2009). International finance and growth in developing countries: What have we learned? *IMF Staff Papers*, 56(1), 63–111. doi:10.1057/imfsp.2008.32

Osterwalder, A., & Pigneur, Y. (2010). *Business model generation. A handbook for visionaries, game changers, and challengers*. John Wiley & Sons, Inc.

Ouedraogo, N. (2013). Energy consumption and human development: Evidence from a panel cointegration and error correction model. *Energy*, 63, 28–41. doi:10.1016/j.energy.2013.09.067

Pal, S. (2020). Does an Application of Data Analysis Tool Enhance Students' Performance in Macroeconomics? *The Journal of Economic Education*, 51(2), 163–176.

Panait, M. C., Voica, M. C., Hysa, E., Siano, A., & Palazzo, M. (2022). The Bucharest Stock Exchange: A Starting Point in Structuring a Valuable CSR Index. *Journal of Risk and Financial Management*, 15(2), 94. doi:10.3390/jrfm15020094

Compilation of References

Paraušić, V., & Domazet, I. (2018). Cluster development and innovative potential in Serbian agriculture. *Ekonomika Poljoprivrede*, *65*(3), 1159–1170. doi:10.5937/ekoPolj1803159P

Paraušić, V., Domazet, I., & Simeunović, I. (2017). Analysis of the Relationship Between the Stage of Economic Development and the State of Cluster Development. *Argumenta Oeconomica*, *39*(2), 279–305. doi:10.15611/aoe.2017.2.12

Paraušić, V., Kostić, Z., & Subić, J. (2023). Local development initiatives in Serbia's rural communities as rerequisite for the Leader implementation: Agricultural advisors'perceptions. *Ekonomika Poljoprivrede*, *70*(1), 117–130. doi:10.59267/ekoPolj2301117P

Parida, V., & Örtqvist, D. (2015). Interactive effects of network capability, ICT capability, and financial slack on technology-based small firm innovation performance. *Journal of Small Business Management*, *53*(S1), 278–298. doi:10.1111/jsbm.12191

Parida, V., Pesämaa, O., Wincent, J., & Westerberg, M. (2017). Network capability, innovativeness, and performance: A multidimensional extension for entrepreneurship. *Entrepreneurship and Regional Development*, *29*(1-2), 94–115. doi:10.1080/08985626.2016.1255434

Pasricha, G. K., & Nier, E. (2022). *Review of The Institutional View on The Liberalization and Management of Capital Flows—Background Note on Capital Flows and Capital Flow Management Measures—Benefits and Costs (Policy Papers No. 2022/009)*. International Monetary Fund.

Pedroni, P. (2001). Purchasing power parity tests in cointegrated panels. *The Review of Economics and Statistics*, *83*(4), 727–731. doi:10.1162/003465301753237803

Pelević, B. & Ristanović, V. (2011). (Neo)protekcionizam i svetska ekonomska kriza, *Srpska politička misao*, *4*, 237-255. doi:10.22182/spm.3442011.12

Pesaran, H. (2004). *General diagnostic tests for cross-section dependence in panels*. Cambridge University Press. doi:10.2139srn.572504

Pesaran, H. (2007). A simple panel unit root test in the presence of cross-section dependence. *Journal of Applied Econometrics*, *22*(2), 265–312. doi:10.1002/jae.951

Pesaran, H., & Smith, P. (1995). Estimating long-run relationships from dynamic heterogeneous panels. *Journal of Econometrics*, *68*(1), 79–113. doi:10.1016/0304-4076(94)01644-F

Peterson, M., Minton, E. A., Liu, R. L., & Bartholomew, D. E. (2021). Sustainable Marketing and Consumer Support for Sustainable Businesses. *Sustainable Production and Consumption*, *27*, 157–168. doi:10.1016/j.spc.2020.10.018

Pilař, L., Stanislavská, L. K., Moulis, P., Kvasnička, R., Rojík, S., & Tichá, I. (2019). Who spends the most money at farmers' markets? *Zemedelská Ekonomika*, *65*(11), 491–498. doi:10.17221/69/2019-AGRICECON

Pimentel, D., Fauville, G., Frazier, K., McGivney, E., Rosas, S., & Woolsey, E. (2022). *An Introduction to Learning in the Metaverse*. Meridian Treehouse.

Pirlogea, C.Panel Data Evidence. (2012). The human development relies on energy: Panel data evidence. *Procedia Economics and Finance*, *3*, 496–501. doi:10.1016/S2212-5671(12)00186-4

Plan razvoja opštine Žagubica 2021-2031 [Development plan of Žagubica municipality 2021-2031]. Official Gazette of the Municipality of Žagubica, 28/2021.

Podsakoff, P. M., & Organ, D. W. (1986). Self-reports in organizational research: Problems and prospects. *Journal of Management*, *12*(4), 531–544. doi:10.1177/014920638601200408

Pölling, B. (2018). *Farm models in region & Food supply chains analysis*. Western Balkans Urban Agriculture Initiative Project. Erasmus Plus Funding Scheme.

Pölling, B., & Mergenthaler, M. (2017). The location matters: Determinants for "deepening" and "broadening" diversification strategies in Ruhr metropolis' urban farming. *Sustainability (Basel)*, *9*(7), 1168. doi:10.3390u9071168

Popović, V., Mihailović, B., & Radosavljević, K. (2022). Promoting generational renewal in Serbian agriculture. In *Thematic Proceeding of International Scientific Conference Sustainable Agriculture and Rural Development II* (pp. 403-415). IAE, Belgrade.

Popović, V., Sarić, R., & Jovanović, M. (2012). Sustainability of agriculture in Danube basin area. *Economics of Agriculture*, *59*(1), 73-87. https://scindeks.ceon.rs/article.aspx?artid=0352-34621201073P

Popović, V., & Mihailović, B. (2020). Business models for urban farming in and around urban protected areas: EkoPark Belgrade case study. In A. Jean Vasile, J. Subić, A. Grubor, & D. Privitera (Eds.), *Handbook of Research on Agricultural Policy, Rural Development, and Entrepreneurship in Contemporary Economies* (pp. 89–107). IGI Global. doi:10.4018/978-1-5225-9837-4.ch005

Popović, V., Milijić, S., & Vuković, P. (2012). Sustainable tourism development in the Carpathian region in Serbia. *Spatium (Belgrade)*, *28*(28), 45–52. doi:10.2298/SPAT1228045P

Porter, M. E., & Kramer, M. R. (2006). Strategy and Society: The link between competitive advantage and corporate social responsibility. *Harvard Business Review*, *84*(12), 78–92. Retrieved February 2, 2023, from https://hbr.org/2006/12/strategy-and-society-the-link-between-competitive-advantage-and-corporate-social-responsibility PMID:17183795

Porter, M. E., & Van der Linde, C. (1995). Toward a new conception of the environmentcompetitiveness relationship. *The Journal of Economic Perspectives*, *9*(4), 97–118. doi:10.1257/jep.9.4.97

Potoglou, D., & Kanaroglou, P. S. (2007). Household demand and willingness to pay for clean vehicles. *Transportation Research Part D, Transport and Environment*, *12*(4), 264–274. doi:10.1016/j.trd.2007.03.001

Prasad, E. S., Rajan, R. G., & Subramanian, A. (2007). Foreign capital and economic growth. *Brookings Papers on Economic Activity*, *2007*(1), 153–230. doi:10.1353/eca.2007.0016

Compilation of References

Pravilnik o kontroli i sertifikaciji u organskoj proizvodnji i metodama organske proizvodnje [Rulebook on control and certification in organic production and methods of organic production]. Official Gazette of RS, 95/2020.

Pravilnik o proizvodnji i prometu malih količina hrane biljnog porekla, području za obavljanje tih delatnosti, kao i isključenju, prilagođavanju ili odstupanju od zahteva higijene hrane [Rulebook on the production and trade of small quantities of food of plant origin, on the area for performing these activities, as well as on the exclusion, adjustment or deviation from food hygiene requirements]. Official Gazette of RS, 13/2020.

Psichogios, P. (n.d.). If you're not changing you're not growing. *Global Engagement Solutions*. https://www.globalengagementsolutions.com/blog/if-youre-not-changing-youre-not-growing/

Radukić, S., Petrović-Ranđelović, M., & Kostić, Z. (2019). Sustainability-based goals and and achieved results in Western Balkan countries. *Economics of Sustainable Development*, 3(1), 9–18. doi:10.5937/ESD1901009R

Ragasa, C., Sengupta, D., Osorio, M., Ourabah Haddad, N., & Mathieson, K. (2014). *Gender-specific approaches, rural institutions and technological innovations*. FAO, IFPRI, & GFAR.

Rahman, A., & Afroz, R. (2013). *Malaysian perception and attitude towards electric vehicle*. https://www.researchgate.net/publication/280934834_Malaysian_perception_and_attitude_towards_electric_vehicle

Ramos-González, M. D. M., Rubio-Andrés, M., & Sastre-Castillo, M. Á. (2017). Building Corporate Reputation through Sustainable Entrepreneurship: The Mediating Effect of Ethical Behavior. *Sustainability (Basel)*, 9(9), 1663. doi:10.3390u9091663

Regional Development Agency Braničevo-Podunavlje. (2019). *The Taste of Region – Promoting agri-food products with added value to improve economic capacities of family households. Project's survey data*. Author.

REN21. (2007). *Renewables, global status report*. Available at: https://www.ren21.net/wp-content/uploads/2019/05/GSR2007_Full-Report_English.pdf

REN21. (2017). *Renewables, global status report*. Available at: https://www.ren21.net/wp-content/uploads/2019/05/GSR2017_Full-Report_English.pdf

Renting, H., Marsden, T. K., & Banks, J. (2003). Understanding alternative food networks: Exploring the role of short food supply chains in rural development. *Environment & Planning A*, 35(3), 393–411. doi:10.1068/a3510

Republički zavod za statistiku [Statistical Office of the Republic of Serbia]. (2013). *Popis poljoprivrede 2012 Knjiga 1*. Republički zavod za statistiku (RZS).

Republički zavod za statistiku [Statistical Office of the Republic of Serbia]. (2019). *Anketa o stukturi poljoprivrednih gazdinstava 2018*. Author.

Republički zavod za statstiku [Statistical Office of the Republic of Serbia]. (2023). *Metodološko uputstvo: Popis poljoprivrede Republički zavod za statistiku (RZS)*. Academic Press.

Ricart, J.E. (2015). *Business Models for the Companies of the Future, Reinventing the Company in the Digital Age*. Academic Press.

Ricci, A. (2016). *Unequal Exchange in International Trade: A General Model*. WP-EMS no 2016/05, University of Urbino.

Rijk, A. G. (2005). *Agricultural mechanization strategy*. https://www.un-csam.org/sites/default/files/2020-10/CIGR_APC AEM_Website_0.pdf

Ristanović, V., & Knežević, G. (2023). Multi-criteria Decision-Making on Operational Risk in Banks. *Proceedings of the 1st International Conference on Innovation in Information Technology and Business (ICIITB 2022)*, 5–21. doi:10.2991/978-94-6463-110-4_2

Ristanović, V. (2022a, January–April). International Trade Flows of the Balkan States. *The Review of International Affairs*, *73*(1184), 1184. doi:10.18485/iipe_ria.2022.73.1184.1

Ristanović, V. (2022b). Sustainable Development – Where is Serbia in Fulfilling Agenda 2030 Goals? *Serbian Review of European Studies*, *I*(1), 119–152.

Ristanović, V. (2023). Sustainable development in the new methodology of Serbia's accession to the EU. *International Problems*, *75*(1), 7–37. doi:10.2298/MEDJP2301007R

Ritchie, J. R. B., & Crouch, G. I. (2003). *The competitive destination: A sustainable tourism perspective*. CABI Publishing. doi:10.1079/9780851996646.0000

Ritter, T., & Gemünden, H. G. (2003). Network competence: Its impact on innovation success and its antecedents. *Journal of Business Research*, *56*(9), 745–755. doi:10.1016/S0148-2963(01)00259-4

Roberts, L., & Hall, D. (2003). Rural Tourism and Recreation: principles to practice. In Leisure and Tourism Management Department. CABI Publishing.

Rodriguez-Gomez, S., Arco-Castro, M. L., Lopez-Perez, M. V., & Rodríguez-Ariza, L. (2020). Where Does CSR Come from and Where Does It Go? A Review of the State of the Art. *Administrative Sciences*, *10*(3), 60. doi:10.3390/admsci10030060

Rodrik, D. (2016). Premature deindustrialization. *Journal of Economic Growth*, *21*(1), 1–33. doi:10.100710887-015-9122-3

Rodrik, D., & Subramanian, A. (2009). Why did financial globalization disappoint? *IMF Staff Papers*, *56*(1), 112–138. doi:10.1057/imfsp.2008.29

Romeo, R., Manuelli, S. R., Geringer, M., & Barchiesi, V. (2021). Introduction. In R. Romeo, S. R. Manuelli, M. Geringer, & V. Barchiesi (Eds.), *Mountain farming systems – Seeds for the future. Sustainable agricultural practices for resilient mountain livelihoods* (pp. 11–12). FAO.

Romer, P. M. (1990). Endogenous technological change. *Journal of Political Economy*, *98*(5, Part 2), 71–102. doi:10.1086/261725

Romijn, H., & Albaladejo, M. (2002). Determinants of innovation capability in small electronics and software firms in southeast England. *Research Policy*, *21*(7), 1053–1067. doi:10.1016/S0048-7333(01)00176-7

Roy, & Searle, M. (2020). Scope Creep and Purposeful Pivots in Developmental Evaluation. *Canadian Journal of Program Evaluation*, *35*(1), 92–103. . doi:10.3138/cjpe.56898

Rucabado-Palomar, T., & Cuéllar-Padilla, M. (2020). Short food supply chains for local food: A difficult path. *Renewable Agriculture and Food Systems*, *35*(2), 182–191. doi:10.1017/S174217051800039X

Ryan, C., & Page, S. J. (Eds.). (2016). *The Routledge handbook of transport economics*. Routledge.

Sachs, G. (2023). *Generative AI could raise global GDP by 7%*. Author.

Sadorsky, P. (2009). Renewable energy consumption and income in emerging economies. *Energy Policy*, *37*(10), 4021–2028. doi:10.1016/j.enpol.2009.05.003

Safapour, E., & Kermanshachi, S. (2019, June). Identifying manageable scope creep indicators and selecting best practice strategies for construction projects. In *Proceedings of the 7th CSCE International Construction Specialty Conference* (pp. 12-15). Academic Press.

Salavou, H., Baltas, G., & Lioukas, S. (2004). Organisational innovation in SMEs: The importance of strategic orientation and competitive structure. *European Journal of Marketing*, *38*(9/10), 1091–1112. doi:10.1108/03090560410548889

Sari Hassoun, S., & Mekidiche, M. (2018). Does renewable energy affect the economic growth in Algeria. *Journal of Applied Quantitative Methods*, *13*.

Sasmaz, M., Sakar, E., Yayla, E., & Akkucuk, U. (2020). The relationship between renewable energy and human development in OECD countries: A panel data analysis. *Sustainability (Basel)*, *12*(18), 1–16. doi:10.3390u12187450

Satrovic, E. (2018). The human development relies on renewable energy: evidence from Turkey. *Proceedings of the 3rd International Energy & Engineering*, 19-27.

Schermer, M. (2018). From 'additive' to 'multiplicative' patterns of growth. *International Journal of Sociology of Agriculture and Food*, *24*(1), 57–76.

Schmukler, S. L. (2004). Financial globalization: Gain and pain for developing countries. *Federal Reserve Bank of Atlanta Economic Review*, *89*(2), 39–66.

Schuitema, G., Anable, J., Skippon, S., & Kinnear, N. (2013). The role of instrumental, hedonic and symbolic attributes in the intention to adopt electric vehicles. *Transportation Research Part A, Policy and Practice*, *48*, 39–49. doi:10.1016/j.tra.2012.10.004

Schunko, C., Lechthaler, S., & Vogl, C. (2019). Conceptualising the factors that influence the commercialization of non-timber forest products: The case of wild plant gathering by organic herb farmers in South Tyrol (Italy). *Sustainability (Basel)*, *11*(7), 2028. doi:10.3390u11072028

Schwab, K., & Malleret, T. (2020). *COVID-19: The Great Reset*. World Economic Forum.

Sen, S., & Bhattacharya, C. B. (2001). Does doing good always lead to doing better? Consumer reactions to corporate social responsibility. *JMR, Journal of Marketing Research*, *38*(2), 225–243. doi:10.1509/jmkr.38.2.225.18838

Seuneke, P., & Bock, B. B. (2015). Exploring the roles of women in the development of multifunctional entrepreneurship on family farms: An entrepreneurial learning approach. *NJAS Wageningen Journal of Life Sciences*, *74–75*(1), 41–50. doi:10.1016/j.njas.2015.07.001

Shahraki, H. (2022). Three-dimensional paradigm of rural prosperity: A feast of rural embodiment, post-neoliberalism, and sustainability. *WORLD (Oakland, Calif.)*, *3*(1), 146–161. doi:10.3390/world3010008

Sima, E. (2019). Economic, social and environmental impact of Romanian rural tourism. *Agricultural Economics and Rural Development*, *16*(1), 137–146.

Simonović, Z., Mihailović, B., & Ćurčić, N. (2017). Struktura poljoprivrednih gazdinstava u Republici Srbiji prema površini poljoprivrednog zemljišta [Structure of agricultural distributions in the Republic of Serbia, by the surface of agricultural land]. *Poslovna ekonomija: časopis za poslovnu ekonomiju, preduzetništvo i finansije*, *11*(2), 247-259. doi:10.5937/poseko12-15416

Sindi, M. (2018). Scope creep in construction industry of Saudi Arabia. *Int. Res. J. Adv. Eng. Sci.*, *3*(2), 277–281.

Sinha, S., Pandey, K. R., & Madan, N. (2018). Fintech and the demand side challenge in financial inclusion. *Enterprise Development & Microfinance*, *29*(1), 94–98. doi:10.3362/1755-1986.17-00016

Sinkula, J. M., Baker, W. E., & Noordewier, T. (1997). A framework for market-based organizational learning: Linking values, knowledge and behavior. *Journal of the Academy of Marketing Science*, *25*(4), 305–318. doi:10.1177/0092070397254003

Smith, N. C. (2003). Corporate social responsibility: Whether or how? *California Management Review*, *45*(4), 52–76. doi:10.2307/41166188

Soukiazis, E., Proença, S., & Cerqueira, P. (2017). The interconnections between renewable energy, *Economic development and environmental pollution: A simultaneous equation system approach. Centre for Business and Economics Research*, *10*, 1–26.

Compilation of References

Sousa, R. D., Karimova, B. & Gorlov, S. (2020). Digitalization as a New Direction in Education Sphere. *E3S Web of Conferences, 159*. doi:10.1051/e3sconf/202015909014

Stanković, V. (2014). Srbija u procesu spoljnih migracija [Serbia in the process of external migration]. 2011 Population, Household and Dwelling Census in the Republic of Serbia. Statistical Office of the Republic of Serbia.

Statistical Office of the Republic of Serbia. (2018). *2018 Farm structure survey*. https://www.stat.gov.rs/en-US/oblasti/poljoprivreda-sumarstvo-i-ribarstvo/anketaostrukturipopgazdinstava

Statistical Office of the Republic of Serbia. (2020). *Women and men in the Republic of Serbia*. Author.

Statistical Office of the Republic of Serbia. (2022a). *First results of the 2022 Census of Population, Households and Dwellings*. https://publikacije.stat.gov.rs/G2022/HtmlE/G20221 350.html

Statistical Office of the Republic of Serbia. (2022b). *Opštine i regioni u Republici Srbiji* [Municipalities and regions in the Republic of Serbia]. Author.

Stein, P. (2010). Towards universal access: financial inclusion: addressing the global challenge of financial inclusion. Korea-World Bank high level conference on post-crisis growth and development, 1–35.

Stein, A. J., & Santini, F. (2021). The sustainability of "local" food: A review for policy-makers. *Review of Agricultural, Food and Environmental Studies*, 1–13. doi:10.100741130-021-00148-w

Storm, S. (2017). *The political economy of industrialization: Introduction to Development and Change*. Academic Press.

Stoykov, S., & Vasilev, V. (2021). Prerequisites for efficiency of human resources management in crisis situations (from classic theories to a new vision). *Politics & Security, 5*(3), 15–21. doi:10.5281/zenodo.6402953

Strategija za rodnu ravnopravnost za period 2021-2030 [Gender equality strategy for the period 2021-2030]. Official Gazette of RS, 103/2021.

Strategy for development tourism in the Republic of Serbia for the period 2016 – 2025 (Official Gazete, RS, No. 98, 08th December 2016).

Šūmane, S., Miranda, D. O., Pinto-Correia, T., Czekaj, M., Duckett, D., Galli, F., ... Tsiligiridis, T. (2021). Supporting the role of small farms in the European regional food systems: What role for the science-policy interface? *Global Food Security, 28*, 100433. doi:10.1016/j.gfs.2020.100433

Sung, B., & Park, D. (2018). Who drives the transition to a renewable-energy economy? multi-actor perspective on social innovation. *Sustainability (Basel), 10*(2), 1–32. doi:10.3390u10020448

SungJ.HannaS. D. (1996). *Factors Related to Risk Tolerance. Financial Counseling and Planning*. https://ssrn.com/abstract=8284

Sun, H., Yuen, D. C. Y., Zhang, J., & Zhang, X. (2020). Is knowledge powerful? Evidence from financial education and earnings quality. *Research in International Business and Finance*, *52*, 101179. doi:10.1016/j.ribaf.2019.101179

Sun, T. (2017). Balancing innovation and risks in digital financial inclusion-experiences of ant financial services group. In *Handbook of blockchain, digital finance, and inclusion* (1st ed., Vol. 2). Elsevier Inc. doi:10.1016/B978-0-12-812282-2.00002-4

Suresh Babu, C. V. (2023). *Introduction to Data Science*. Anniyappa Publications.

Sutherland, L.-A., Monllor, N., & Pinto-Correia, T. (2015). *Gender issues among new entrants*. EIP-AGRI Focus Group New entrants into farming: lessons to foster innovation and entrepreneurship. Mini-paper 3. https://ec.europa.eu/eip/agriculture/sites/default/files/fg1 4_03_minipaper_gender_pdf

Swamy, P. (1971). *Statistical inference in random coefficient regression models*. Springer. Available at: https://www.tr.undp.org/content/turkey/tr/home/sustainable-d evelopment-goals.html

Swiderska, K., Song, Y., Li, J., Reid, H., & Mutta, D. (2011). *Adapting agriculture with traditional knowledge*. IIED Briefing Papers.

Sylla, M., Olszewska, J., & Świąder, M. (2017). Status and possibilities of the development of community supported agriculture in Poland as an example of short food supply chain. *Journal of Agribusiness and Rural Development*, *43*(1), 201–207. doi:10.17306/J.JARD.2017.00266

Szegedi, K., Fülöp, G., & Bereczk, Á. (2016). Relationships between social entrepreneurship, CSR and social innovation: In theory and practice. *International Journal of Social, Behavioral, Educational, Economic, Business and Industrial Engineering*, *10*(5), 1402–1407.

Taşdemir, F. (2023). International financial integration: Too much? *Borsa Istanbul Review*, *23*(2), 402–411. doi:10.1016/j.bir.2022.11.005

Teece, D. J. (2007). Explicating dynamic capabilities: The nature and microfoundations of (sustainable) enterprise performance. *Strategic Management Journal*, *28*(13), 1319–1350. doi:10.1002mj.640

Teece, D. J. (2014). The foundations of enterprise performance: Dynamic and ordinary capabilities in an (economic) theory of firms. *The Academy of Management Perspectives*, *28*(4), 328–352. doi:10.5465/amp.2013.0116

Teece, D. J., Pisano, G., & Shuen, A. (1997). Dynamic capabilities and strategic management. *Strategic Management Journal*, *18*(7), 509–533. doi:10.1002/(SICI)1097-0266(199708)18:7<509::AID-SMJ882>3.0.CO;2-Z

Tepavac, R., & Brzaković, T. (2013). Suffering of wild animals in hunting-grounds from application of agricultural mechanization and pesticides. *Sustainable agriculture and rural development in terms of the republic of Serbia strategic goals realization within the Danube region. Achieving regional competitiveness*, 539-556. https://mpra.ub.uni-muenchen.de/52472/1/MPRA_paper_52472.pdf

Thakurta, R. (2013). Impact of Scope Creep on Software Project Quality. Vilakshan: The XIMB. *Journal of Management*, *10*(1).

Thanvi & Appalla. (2016). A study on the financial literacy of Professional Women in the district of Ernakulum, Kerala. *International Journal of Technology Enhancements and Emerging Engineering Research*, *4*(7), 4-8. https://www.coursehero.com/file/63540321/A-Study-On-The-Financial-Literacy-Of-Professional-Women-In-The-District-Of-Ernakulum-Keralapdf/

The U.S. Department of Agriculture. (2022, June 1). *USDA Announces Framework for Shoring Up the Food Supply Chain and Transforming the Food System to Be Fairer, More Competitive, More Resilient*. https://www.usda.gov/media/press-releases/2022/06/01/usda-announces-framework-shoring-food-supply-chain-and-transforming

Thung. (2012). *Determinants of saving behavior among university students in Malaysia*. Final Year Project. UTAR. http://eprints.utar.edu.my/607/1/AC-2011-0907445.pdf

Tohidyan Far, S., & Rezaei-Moghaddam, K. (2019). Multifunctional agriculture: An approach for entrepreneurship development of agricultural sector. *Journal of Global Entrepreneurship Research*, *9*(1), 23. doi:10.118640497-019-0148-4

Tregenna, F. (2015). *Deindustrialization, structural change and sustainable economic growth*. Inclusive and Sustainable Industrial Development Working Paper Series, Working Paper 02–2015.

Trygg, J., Holmes, E., & Lundstedt, T. (2007). Chemometrics in metabonomics. *Journal of Proteome Research*, *6*(2), 469–479. doi:10.1021/pr060594q PMID:17269704

Turk, W. (2010). Scope creep horror. *Defense AT&L*, *39*(2), 53-55.

Umuhoza, B. F., & An, S.-H. (2021). Causes and preventive strategies of scope creep for building construction projects in democratic republic of Congo and Rwanda. *International Journal of Construction Management*, 1–12. . doi:10.1080/15623599.2021.1967576

UN WTO. (2017). *Report of Secretary-General*. A/22/10(I) rev.1, Madrid, 01st September 2017, General Assembly, Twenty-Second Sessions, Chengdu, China.

UN. (2020). *United Nations Sustainable Development Goals*. United Nations. Retrieved February 3, 2023 from https://www.undp.org/content/undp/en/home/sustainable- development-goals.html

UNCTAD. (2021). Handbook of Statistics 2021. doi:10.18356/9789210010610

UNIDO. (2020). *Short food supply chains for promoting local food on local markets*. UNIDO. Retrieved from https://suster.org/wp-content/uploads/2020/06/SHORT-FOOD-SUPPLY-CHAINS.pdf

United Nations. (2015). *Transforming our world: the 2030 Agenda for Sustainable Development*. General Assembly. United Nations, 21 October 2015, A/RES/70/1. Retrieved from https://www.un.org/ga/search/view_doc.asp?symbol=A/RES/70/1&Lang=E

Urban, C., Schmeiser, M., Collins, J. M., & Brown, A. (2018). The effects of high school personal financial education policies on financial behavior. *Economics of Education Review*. https://www.sciencedirect.com/science/article/abs/pii/

Uvarova, I., & Vitola, A. (2019). Innovation challenges and opportunities in European rural SMEs. *Public Policy and Administration*, *18*(1), 152–166. doi:10.5755/j01.ppaa.18.1.23134

Valls Martínez, M., Martín-Cervantes, P. A., & Miralles-Quirós, M. M. (2022). Sustainable development and the limits of gender policies on corporate boards in Europe. A comparative analysis between developed and emerging markets. *European Research on Management and Business Economics*, *28*(1), 100168. doi:10.1016/j.iedeen.2021.100168

van den Berg, L., Goris, M. B., Behagel, J. H., Verschoor, G., Turnhout, E., Botelho, M. I. V., & Silva Lopes, I. (2021). Agroecological peasant territories: Resistance and existence in the struggle for emancipation in Brazil. *The Journal of Peasant Studies*, *48*(3), 658–679. doi:10.1080/03066150.2019.1683001

van der Ploeg, J. D., & Bruil, J. (2020). The economic potential of agroecology in Europe. Opinion. *Farming Matters*, *36*(1), 17.

van der Ploeg, J. D. (2010). The peasantries of the twenty-first century: The commoditization debate revisited. *The Journal of Peasant Studies*, *37*(1), 1–30. doi:10.1080/03066150903498721

Van der Ploeg, J. D., Renting, H., Brunori, G., Knickel, K., Mannion, J., Marsden, T., de Roest, K., Sevilla-Guzman, E., & Ventura, F. (2000). Rural development: From practices and policies towards theory. *Sociologia Ruralis*, *40*(4), 391–408. doi:10.1111/1467-9523.00156

van der Ploeg, J. D., & Roep, D. (2003). Multifunctionality and rural development: the actual situation in Europe. In G. van Huylenbroeck & G. Durand (Eds.), *Multifunctional Agriculture; A new paradigm for European Agriculture and Rural Development* (pp. 37–53). Ashgate.

van der Ploeg, J., Barjolle, D., Bruil, J., Brunori, G., Costa Madureira, L. M., Dessein, J., Drąg, Z., Fink-Kessler, A., Gasselin, P., González de Molina, M., Gorlach, K., Jürgens, K., Kinsella, J., Kirwan, J., Knickel, K., Lucas, V., Marsden, T. K., Maye, D., Migliorini, P., ... Wezel, A. (2019). The economic potential of agroecology: Empirical evidence from Europe. *Journal of Rural Studies*, *71*, 46–61. doi:10.1016/j.jrurstud.2019.09.003

van der Schans, J. W., Renting, H., & van Veenhuizen, R. (2014). Innovations in urban agriculture. *Urban Agriculture Magazine*, *28*, 3–12.

van Wynsberghe, A., Vandemeulebroucke, T., Bolte, L., & Nachid, J. (2022). Towards the Sustainability of AI; Multi-Disciplinary Approaches to Investigate the Hidden Costs of AI. *Sustainability (Basel)*, *14*(24), 16352. doi:10.3390u142416352

Vanhove, N. (2022). *The Economics of Tourism Destinations – Theory and Practice* (4th ed.). Routledge.

VarnaUtre. (2013). https://varna.utre.bg/2013/09/02/184053-otvoriha_purvia_sotsialen_magazin

Compilation of References

Vasilev, V., & Stefanova, D. (2021). Complex communication barriers in the organisation in a crisis context. *KNOWLEDGE - International Journal (Toronto, Ont.), 49*(1), 29–33. Retrieved March 20, 2023, from https://ikm.mk/ojs/index.php/kij/article/view/4617

Vasiliev, I. I., Smelov, P. A., Klimovskih, N. V., Shevashkevich, M. G., & Donskaya, E. N. (2018). Operational Risk Management in A Commercial Bank. *International Journal of Engineering and Technology (UAE), 7*, 524–529. doi:10.14419/ijet.v7i4.36.24130

Vasiljević, Z., Todorović, S., & Popović, N. (2008). Uticaj promene cene goriva na optimizaciju ukupnih troškova upotrebe poljoprivredne mehanizacije za obradu zemljišta [An influence of the fuel price change on optimization of total operating costs of the tillage agricultural machinery]. *Poljoprivredna tehnika, 33*(4), 69-77. https://scindeks.ceon.rs/article.aspx?artid=0554-55870804069V

Venkatraman, N., & Ramanujan, V. (1987). Planning system success: A conceptualization and an operational model. *Management Science, 33*(6), 687–705. doi:10.1287/mnsc.33.6.687

Vial, G. (2019). Understanding digital transformation: A review and a research agenda. *The Journal of Strategic Information Systems, 28*(2), 118–144. doi:10.1016/j.jsis.2019.01.003

Vinkić, V. (2019, November 8). *Žagubičko blago u teglici* [Treasure of the Žagubica in a jar]. Reč naroda. https://recnaroda.co.rs/milosava-grozdic-zagubicko-blago-u-teglici/

Vittersø, G., Torjusen, H., Laitala, K., Tocco, B., Biasini, B., Csillag, P., de Labarre, M. D., Lecoeur, J.-L., Maj, A., Majewski, E., Malak-Rawlikowska, A., Menozzi, D., Török, Á., & Wavresky, P. (2019). Short food supply chains and their contributions to sustainability: Participants' views and perceptions from 12 European cases. *Sustainability (Basel), 11*(17), 4800. doi:10.3390u11174800

Vuković, P, (2017). Character and dynamics of development rural tourism in the Republic of Serbia. *Ekonomika/Economics, 63*(4), 53 – 60.

Vuković, P., Kljajić, N., & Sredojević, Z. (2022). The future of development rural tourism in the Republic of Serbia. Agro*ekonomika/Agroeconomic, 63*(4).

Vuković, P. (2019). *Competitiveness of rural tourist destinations in area of the Lower Danube region in the Republic of Serbia. Institute of Agricultural Economics*. Serbia.

Vuković, P., & Kljajić, N. (2013). Education and training employees and local residents as presumption to develop rural tourism. In *International Scientific Conference Sustainable Agriculture and Rural Development in Terms of the Republic of Serbia Strategic Goals Realization within the Danube Region: Achieving Regional Competitiveness.* Institute of Agricultural Economics.

Vuković, P., Kljajić, N., & Roljević, S. (2009). Strategic determinations of tourism development in the process of transition in the Republic of Serbia. *Ekonomika/Economic, 3-4*, 168–177.

Wade, M. (2020). Corporate Responsibility in the Digital Era. *MIT Sloan Management Review*. Retrieved February 3, 2023 from https://sloanreview.mit.edu/article/corporate-responsibility-in-the-digital-era/

Walter, A., Auer, M., & Ritter, T. (2006). The impact of network capabilities and entrepreneurial orientation on university spin-off performance. *Journal of Business Venturing*, *21*(4), 541–567. doi:10.1016/j.jbusvent.2005.02.005

Wang, C. L., & Ahmed, P. K. (2007). Dynamic capabilities: A review and research agenda. *International Journal of Management Reviews*, *9*(1), 31–51. doi:10.1111/j.1468-2370.2007.00201.x

Wang, Z., Bui, Q., Zhang, C., Nawarathna, C., & Mombeuil, C. (2021). The nexus between renewable energy consumption and human development in BRICS countries: The moderating role of public debt. *Renewable Energy*, *165*, 381–390. doi:10.1016/j.renene.2020.10.144

Wang, Z., Danish, B., Zhang, B., & Wang, B. (2018). Renewable energy consumption, economic growth and human development index in Pakistan: Evidence form simultaneous equation model. *Journal of Cleaner Production*, *184*, 1081–1090. doi:10.1016/j.jclepro.2018.02.260

WB. (2016). *Development Goals in an Era of Demographic Change*. Global Monitoring Report 2015/2016, The World Bank. doi:10.1596/978-1-4648-0669-8

WCED. (1987). *Our Common Future: The World Commission on Environment and Development*. Oxford University Press.

Weatherell, C., Tregear, A., & Allinson, J. (2003). In search of the concerned consumer: UK public perceptions of food, farming and buying local. *Journal of Rural Studies*, *19*(2), 233–244. doi:10.1016/S0743-0167(02)00083-9

Weber, M. (2008). The business case for corporate social responsibility: A company-level measurement approach for CSR. *European Management Journal*, *26*(4), 247–261. doi:10.1016/j.emj.2008.01.006

Wei, A.-P., Peng, C.-L., Huang, H.-C., & Yeh, S.-P. (2020). Effects of Corporate Social Responsibility on Firm Performance: Does Customer Satisfaction Matter? *Sustainability (Basel)*, *12*(18), 7545. doi:10.3390u12187545

Wiesinger, G. (2007). The importance of social capital in rural development, networking and decision-making in rural areas. *Revue de Geographie Alpine*, *95*(4), 43–56. doi:10.4000/rga.354

Wiest, K. (2016). Introduction: Women and migration in rural Europe – explanations and implications. In K. Wiest (Ed.), *Women and migration in rural Europe: labor markets, representations and policies* (pp. 1–22). Palgrave Macmillan. doi:10.1007/978-1-137-48304-1_1

Wiklund, J., & Shepherd, D. (2005). Entrepreneurial orientation and small business performance: A configurational approach. *Journal of Business Venturing*, *20*(1), 71–91. doi:10.1016/j.jbusvent.2004.01.001

Wilden, R., Devinney, T. M., & Dowling, G. R. (2016). The architecture of dynamic capability research identifying the building blocks of a configurational approach. *The Academy of Management Annals*, *10*(1), 997–1076. doi:10.5465/19416520.2016.1161966

Compilation of References

Williams, O. J., & Satchell, S. E. (2011). Social welfare issues of financial literacy and their implications for regulation. *Journal of Regulatory Economics*, *40*(1), 1–40. doi:10.100711149-011-9151-6

Wnuk, K., & Kollu, R. K. (2016, June). A systematic mapping study on requirements scoping. In *Proceedings of the 20th International Conference on Evaluation and Assessment in Software Engineering* (pp. 1-11). 10.1145/2915970.2915985

Women and their roles in rural areas. Resolution (2016/2204(INI)), P8_TA (2017) 0099. European Parliament.

Wood, D. J. (1991). Corporate social performance revisited. *Academy of Management Review*, *16*(4), 691–718. doi:10.2307/258977

Worthington, A. C. (2016). Financial literacy and financial literacy programmes in Australia. *Finance Lit Limits Finance DecisMak*, *18*, 281–301. doi:10.1007/978-3-319-30886-9_14

WTO. (2020). World Trade Report 2020. World Trade Organisation.

Wu, Q., Masyluk, S., & Clulow, V. (2010). *Energy consumption transition and human development*. Monash University Press.

Xie, Y., & Zheng, X. (2020). How does corporate learning orientation enhance industrial brand equity? The roles of firm capabilities and size. *Journal of Business and Industrial Marketing*, *35*(2), 231–243. doi:10.1108/JBIM-10-2018-0320

Yang, J. (2012). Innovation capability and corporate growth: An empirical investigation in China. *Journal of Engineering and Technology Management*, *29*(1), 34–46. doi:10.1016/j.jengtecman.2011.09.004

Zacca, R., Dayan, M., & Ahrens, T. (2015). Impact of network capability on small business performance. *Management Decision*, *53*(1), 2–23. doi:10.1108/MD-11-2013-0587

Zahoor, N., & Lew, Y. K. (2022). Sustaining superior international performance: Strategic orientations and dynamic capability of environmentally concerned small-and medium-sized enterprises. *Business Strategy and the Environment*, *31*(3), 1002–1017. doi:10.1002/bse.2931

Zahra, S. A., Sapienza, H. J., & Davidsson, P. (2006). Entrepreneurship and dynamic capabilities: A review, model and research agenda. *Journal of Management Studies*, *43*(4), 917–955. doi:10.1111/j.1467-6486.2006.00616.x

Zakić, V., Nikolić, M., & Kovačević, V. (2018). International experiences in cooperative audit and lessons for Serbia. *Ekonomika Poljoprivrede*, *65*(3), 1111–1122. doi:10.5937/ekoPolj1803111Z

Zaremba, H., Elias, M., Rietveld, A., & Bergamini, N. (2021). Toward a feminist agroecology. *Sustainability (Basel)*, *13*(20), 11244. doi:10.3390u132011244

Zaridis, A., Rontogianni, A., & Karamanis, K. (2015). Female entrepreneurship in agricultural sector. The case of municipality of Pogoni in the period of economic crisis. *Journal of Research in Business. Economics and Management*, *4*(4), 486–491.

Zavolokina, L., Dolata, M., & Schwabe, G. (2016). The FinTech phenomenon: Antecedents of financial innovation perceived by the popular press. *Financial Innovation*, *2*(1), 16. doi:10.118640854-016-0036-7

Zdorov, A. B. (2009). Comprehensive Development of Tourism in the Countryside. Studies on Russian Economic Development, 20(4), 453–455.

Zengeni, T. (2015). *The Competitiveness and performance of the Zimbabwe poultry industry* [MA dissertation]. University of the Witwatersrand.

Zhang, X., Qing, P., & Yu, X. (2019). Short supply chain participation and market performance for vegetable farmers in China. *The Australian Journal of Agricultural and Resource Economics*, *63*(2), 282–306. doi:10.1111/1467-8489.12299

Zhang, Y., Yu, Y., & Zou, B. (2011). Analysing public awareness and acceptance of alternative fuel vehicles in China: The case of EV. *Energy Policy*, *39*(11), 7015–7024. doi:10.1016/j.enpol.2011.07.055

Zhao, H., Guo, S., & Zhao, H. (2018). Impacts of gdp, fossil fuel energy consumption, energy consumption intensity, and economic structure on SO2 emissions: A multi-variate panel data model analysis on selected Chinese provinces. *Sustainability (Basel)*, *10*(3), 1–20. doi:10.3390u10030657

Zhou, S. S., Zhou, A. J., Feng, J., & Jiang, S. (2019). Dynamic capabilities and organizational performance: The mediating role of innovation. *Journal of Management & Organization*, *25*(5), 731–747. doi:10.1017/jmo.2017.20

Zivkov, G. (2013). *Association of farmers in the Western Balkan countries*. Policy Studies on Rural Transition (No 2013-1). FAO Regional Office for Europe and Central Asia. Retrieved from https://www.fao.org/3/ar592e/ar592e.pdf

Zollo, M., & Winter, S. G. (2002). Deliberate learning and the evolution of dynamic capabilities. *Organization Science*, *13*(3), 339–351. doi:10.1287/orsc.13.3.339.2780

Compilation of References

About the Contributors

Andrei Jean Vasile is full professor at Petroleum-Gas University of Ploiesti, Department of Business Administration and Ph.D mentor in economics at Bucharest University of Economic Studies, Romania. He is co-founder and scientific coordinator of the Research Network on Resources Economics and Bioeconomy. Andrei Jean-Vasile holds a Ph.D. in Economics from the National Institute of Economics Research – Romanian Academy of Sciences. He has earned a BA degree in Administrative Sciences (2005) and in Banks and Finances (2007) from the Petroleum-Gas University of Ploiesti. He has an MA degree in Economics, Administrative and Business Management (2007) earned at the same university. Jean Andrei is also Associate Editor of Economics of Agriculture (Serbia), scientific reviewer and committee member for numerous international conferences. He is member of scientific organizations: The Balkan Scientific Association of Agrarian Economists, Serbia (2008), DAAAM Vienna and Information Resources Management Association (2011). Issues like: agricultural economics and rural development, energy and resource economics and business economics are among his research and scientific interests.

Mile Vasic obtained his MA and PhD in the field of Human Resources Management. He has acted as a Dean of Faculty of Technical Sciences, Dean of Faculty of Economics and Management, Vice-Rector of PIM University and Vice-Rector and Rector of Slobomir P University. He was a guest lecture in Greece, Romania, Slovenia, Serbia, and the United Kingdom. Besides academic work, his passion is the implementation of scientific knowledge and skills in practice. He has been consulting and providing in-company training worldwide and most important clients were Coca-Cola, Renault, BH Mont Trade Srl., Johnson & Johnson, McDonald's, OMV. Between 2015 and 2018 professor Vasic served as an Ambassador Extraordinary and Plenipotentiary of Bosnia and Herzegovina to Romania. Dr. Mile Vasic is currently President of European Marketing and Management Association (EUMMAS).

Predrag Vuković is senior research associate. Graduated 2003 on the Faculty of Economics, University of Belgrade. Postgraduate specialist studies finished

About the Contributors

2006 and Master's thesis degree 2008. Doctoral thesis 2016 degreed at the Faculty of Economics, University of Kragujevac. He has been working in the Institute of Agricultural Economics, Belgrade since 2004. He has been actively engaging as a member of the research team on projects of the Ministry of Education, Science and Technological Development of the Republic of Serbia. He has also been engaged in numerous projects of the Institute of Agricultural Economics, as well as the development of a numerous of development strategies of cities, municipalities and local communities as a member of research teams and manager of project teams. In doctoral thesis, master thesis, specialist thesis and numerous scientific articles published in national and international professional journals, presented at scientific conferences of national and international importance, he dealing with the issues of tourism marketing, management of tourist destinations, rural tourism, rural development and agriculture issues of economics. He is member of scientific organizations: Balkan Scientific Association of Agricultural Economists (B.S.A.A.E); Serbian Association of Agricultural Economist (S.A.A.E.); European Rural Development Network (ERDN); Research Network on Resources Economics and Bio-economy Association (RebResNet).

* * *

Nilay Aluftekin Sakarya is a retired professor from Ankara Yıldırım Beyazit University, Department of Business Administration. She received her PhD from Ankara University in Agricultural Economics field. She has worked as an academic at Ankara Yıldırım Beyazit University and Çankaya University. During her time at Ankara Yıldırım Beyazit University, she worked as department head, vice dean and head of Cluster Academy and Competition Research Centre. Her research areas include entrepreneurship, innovation, and cluster development.

Berislav Andrlic has been in higher education for over 18 years, involved in the teaching of marketing, promotion, project management, and branding. From 2007 to 2012 he served as Head of the Social Department. In 2012, and from 2014 he is Vice Dean for Development of the Faculty of Tourism and Rural Development in Pozega. His research interests include marketing management, EU project management, internet marketing, and tourism. He is a member of the CROMAR (The Croatian Marketing Association) and DAAAM Vienna.

Dr. C.V. Suresh Babu is a pioneer in content development. A true entrepreneur, he founded Anniyappa Publications, a company that is highly active in publishing books related to Computer Science and Management. Dr. C.V. Suresh Babu has also ventured into SB Institute, a center for knowledge transfer. He holds a Ph.D. in

Engineering Education from the National Institute of Technical Teachers Training & Research in Chennai, along with seven master's degrees in various disciplines such as Engineering, Computer Applications, Management, Commerce, Economics, Psychology, Law, and Education. Additionally, he has UGC-NET/SET qualifications in the fields of Computer Science, Management, Commerce, and Education. Currently, Dr. C.V. Suresh Babu is a Professor in the Department of Information Technology at the School of Computing Science, Hindustan Institute of Technology and Science (Hindustan University) in Padur, Chennai, Tamil Nadu, India. For more information, you can visit his personal blog at .

Marisa Cleveland, with more than two decades in the education and publishing industries, is adamant about supporting efforts toward the betterment of the human condition. Cleveland is the executive director for The Seymour Agency, a trustee for Hodges University Board of Trustees, and co-author of the leadership book, There Is No Box. Cleveland holds an Ed.D. in Organizational Leadership from Northeastern University, and an M.A. in Educational Administration and a B.A. in Speech Communication from George Mason University.

Simon Cleveland is a professor of project management Purdue University Global. Dr. Cleveland is a graduate of George Mason University with Bachelor of Science degree in Business, of the George Washington University with a Master of Science degree in Project Management, of the City University of Seattle with a Master of Arts degree in Leadership, with a Ph.D. in Information Systems from Nova Southeastern University, and with a Ed.D. in Organizational Leadership from Northeastern University. He is also certified as a project management professional (PMP), Six Sigma Black Belt (SSBB) expert, and Information Technology Infrastructure Library (ITIL) foundations expert. Dr. Cleveland is the author of over 50 peer-reviewed publications in journals and conferences, and is a three-time recipient of the prestigious Dr. Harold Kerzner Scholarship which is awarded by the Project Management Institute Educational Foundation. Professionally, Dr. Cleveland has worked as both technology manager, program manager and PMO Director for organizations such as MD Anderson Cancer Center, Department of Homeland Security, NASA, Accenture, and AOL.

Iza Gigauri is based at St. Andrew the First-Called Georgian University in Tbilisi, Georgia. She has a Ph.D. in Business Administration from Ivane Javakhishvili Tbilisi State University, Georgia. She holds an MBA from Business School Netherlands and an MBA from American University for Humanities Tbilisi Campus. She graduated from Ilia State University (Georgia) and Ruhr-University Bochum (Germany). She delivers lectures and teaches seminars at all three levels of higher education. She has more than 70 scientific publications in international journals and books, participated in more than 30 international scientific conferences. She is a member of the editorial and reviewer boards of more than 35 international journals within Emerald Publishing, IGI Global, Inderscience, Frontiers, Taylor & Francis, and Springer. Her research interests include marketing, corporate responsibility and business ethics, sustainable development, organizational behavior, leadership, human resource management, entrepreneurship and social entrepreneurship.

Biljana Grujic Vuckovski graduated 2010 on the Faculty of Agriculture, University of Belgrade. Doctoral thesis degree 2017 at the Faculty of Business Studies, Megatrend University (John Naisbitt University), and gained title a Ph.D. of Economic Sciences. She is employed in the Insitute of Agricultural Economics in Belgrade from 2011. She was also involved in numerous projects of Institute and strategies of local community development as a member of the research team.

Marijana Jovanović Todorović, PhD in Biotechnology, currently working in Institute of Agricultural Economics Belgrade on possition of Research Assistant in scientific sector. The main area of research is plant production, organic production and sustainable agriculture.

Pelin Karaca Kalkan works as an Assistant Professor in the department of Business Administration in Ankara Science University. She completed her Bachelor's degree in Business Administration at Hacettepe University. After that, she obtained her Master's degree in the field of Management and Organization from Gazi University in 2016. At the end of the 2022, she earned her PhD in Management and Organization from Ankara Yıldırım Beyazıt University. Her research areas encompass Strategic Management, Organizational Behavior, Innovation Management, and Small Business Management.

Vlado Kovačević completed his basic studies in 1997 at the Faculty of Agriculture - University of Belgrade. At the Faculty of Economics -University of Belgrade, he completed his master degree. At the Faculty of Agriculture - University of Belgrade, completed PhD. Professional experience Fellow of the Ministry of Science and Technology of the Republic of Serbia, worked within the Ministry of Agriculture, Forestry and Water Management - advisor in the sector for international cooperation. In TD Waterhouse Edmonton. Canada – worked as Financial Market Analyst. Worked in the Ministry of Agriculture, Trade, Forestry and Water Management as an advisor to the Minister. Since 2016 he has been working as a Senior research associate at the Institute for Agricultural Economics Belgrade.

Irina Marina, graduated 2020 on the Faculty of Agriculture, University of Belgrade, Department of Agricultural machinery. She completed her master studies in 2021 at the Faculty of Agricultural, University of Belgrade, Department of Biotechnical and information engineering. After that, in the year 2021, PhD studies are enrolled at the Agricultural faculty in Belgrade, University of Belgrade, Department of Biotehnology. She is employed in the Institute of Agricultural Economics in Belgrade from 2022, on possition Research Trainee. The main area of research is agricultural mechanization, biotechnology sustainable agriculture and precision agriculture.

Branko Mihailović is Ph.D. in Economics and works as principal research fellow at the Institute of Agricultural Economics in Belgrade, Serbia. He deals with issues related to consulting, enterprise restructuring and agricultural economics.

Vesna Popović is PhD in Economics and works as principal research fellow at the Institute of Agricultural Economics (IAE), Belgrade, Serbia. She deals with issues related to agricultural trade and trade policy, sustainable agriculture and rural development, and land use policy and planning.

Vladimir Ristanović is a research associate at the Institute for European Studies and an associate professor. He graduated from the Faculty of Economics of the University of Belgrade in 2000. He obtained his master's degree at the same faculty in 2004. He defended his doctorate in International Economy and Finance in 2010 at the Faculty of International Economics of Megatrend University. Part of his research and analytical experience comes from the strategic and analytical affairs of the Government of the Republic of Serbia. As a civil servant, through the technical rounds of the accession agreement, he acquired numerous certified knowledge of the EU legal acquis (Acquis communautaire). He built his teaching career at the Faculty of International Economics of Megatrend University, first as an assistant professor in 2010, then as an associate professor in 2015 in the narrow scientific field of International Economics and Finance. During his teaching career, he was a visiting professor at Erasmus+ programs (University West Timisoara, Romania, 2018, and Universitatea "Lucian Blaga" din Sibiu, Romania, 2019) and a visiting lecturer at the University Technique de Monterey Mexico in 2018. He participated in numerous international conferences in Romania, Bulgaria, Ukraine, and Mexico.

Fatma Taşdemir is a faculty member at Sinop University, Department of International Trade and Business since 2021. She completed her MSc in 2014 and received her PhD in 2019 from the Department of Economics at the Middle East

About the Contributors

Technical University. She is an applied economist and her main research areas include growth, international finance and macroeconomics.

Mustafa Batuhan Tufaner is an Assoc. Prof. Dr. at Beykent University. Batuhan's research focuses on the economic development and central bank independence in developing and developed countries. Batuhan is the author of various international articles. Batuhan received his PhD from the Marmara University, Istanbul.

Index

3D Modelling 8-9

A

Adoption 1-2, 4-10, 13, 15-21, 23, 27-31
African Economies 5, 7, 12, 17, 19, 21, 28
Agricultural Holding 9-10, 23
Agricultural Mechanization 1-2, 4, 6-7, 10, 14, 17, 19-22, 24-25
Agriculture 1-7, 9, 11-25
Agroecology 2, 4, 17, 21-23
Areas of Serbia 1, 7, 17-18
Asian Economies 1, 5-6, 10-11, 15-19, 22, 24, 28
Augmented Reality 1-2, 8-12, 17-18

B

Bio-District 12, 23
Biplot 1, 8, 13-14, 16-18, 21
Business Model Canvas 1, 3, 8
Business Models 1-2, 4-6, 8, 12-13, 15-20, 23

C

Caution in Glorifying SFSCs 9, 22
Characteristics of SFSCs 22
Competitiveness 1-4, 6-7, 15-21, 23, 25
Construction Project 4
Consumer Behaviour 1, 5-6, 9, 19
Consumers 1-17, 19, 22-23, 28-30
CSR 1-2, 4-9, 13-20

D

Development 1-30, 32
Digital Transformation 1-6, 14, 20
Digitalization 1-6, 9, 16, 20
Direct Sales 1, 6-7, 10, 12-13
Dynamic Capabilities Theory 1-3, 12, 23

E

Emergent Economy 31
Emerging Market and Developing Economies 1, 3-11, 13-19, 21-23, 28
Entrepreneurship 1-3, 5-6, 9-17, 19-23, 25, 27, 29, 31
Environment 1-8, 10-18, 20-21, 31
ESG 1-4, 6-7, 14, 18-19
EV 1-2, 4-11, 15-16, 18-21, 23-25, 27-31

F

Females 2-3, 5-6, 8, 27
Financial Globalization 1-10, 14-27
Financial Incentives 1, 3-6, 8-10, 17, 20-21, 23, 30-31
Financial Literacy 1-8, 11-14
Financial Markets 1-2, 11
Food Safety 7, 14, 23
Food Systems 1-3, 5, 7, 9, 13, 15, 19-20, 22-23
Friend-Shoring Business Model 21

G

Gender Inequalities 1

Index

Growth 1-19, 22-29, 31

H

High-Technology Sector 8, 23, 31
Human Development 1-2, 7, 11-13

I

Immersive Experience 10
Immersive Learning 21
Importance of SFSCs for Sustainable Rural Development in Central and Eastern European Countries 23
Industrialization 7, 27
Information 1-11, 13, 15-23, 27-31
Investment 1-5, 8, 10-11, 13-16, 21-25, 27, 31

L

Latin American Economies 5-7, 10-11, 14, 16-19, 21-24, 28
Learning Orientation 1-2, 4, 11, 15, 25-26, 31-32
Loading Plot 1, 8, 12-15, 17, 21
Long-Tail Economy 6, 21

M

Management Model 1
Marketing Channels 1, 4-5, 9, 12, 14, 22
Megaplatforms 21
Metaverse 1, 5, 10, 20-21
Multifunctional Agriculture 1-4, 16, 21, 23
Multifunctional Entrepreneurship 1, 5, 13, 20

N

NCR 3-5, 7-10, 15-16, 18-19, 28-31
Nearshoring Business Model 21
Nemmp 1-2, 23-24, 28-29, 31
Neo-Traditional Type of SFSCs 23
Network Capability 1-2, 4, 11, 14, 26-27, 29, 31-32
New Normal 1-3, 5, 7-9, 13-15, 17, 19, 21

New Normal Paradigm 1-3, 7, 13, 17, 21

O

OECD Countries 1, 3-5, 7-8, 10-12
Off-Farm Sales 5, 23
Operating System 3, 5
Operational Risks 21

P

Panel Data Analysis 3-4, 12
Principal Components Analysis (PCA) 7, 23
Process Innovation Capability 1, 5-7, 11, 13, 18-23, 29, 32
Product Innovation Capability 1, 5-7, 11, 18-19, 21-23, 29, 32
Protected Area 10, 12, 23

R

Regions of Serbia 1, 17
Renewable Energy 1-4, 10-13, 16
Risk Tolerance 1-8, 11-14
Rural Area 1, 4
Rural Renewal 13

S

Scope Creep Causes 1
SDGs 1-3, 6-7, 9, 11
Serbia 1-25
SFSCs as a Part of Value-Added Agriculture 23
Short Food Supply Chain 16, 21, 23
Short Supply Circuits 1-2
Short vs. Global Food Supply Chains 23
Small and Medium Enterprises 32
Small-Scale Farmers 2, 7, 12-14, 17
Social and Cultural Distance 2, 22
Social Entrepreneurship 1-3, 6, 8-9, 11-14, 16, 20
Society 1-3, 5-11, 13, 15, 17, 19-20, 22-23
Socio-Economic 1, 4-5, 8-11, 15, 19, 22, 27, 31
Sustainability 1-26, 30
Sustainable Production Process 1, 14

Sustainable Tourism 1-5, 11, 19-20
System Changes 4

T

Technology Projects 1-2, 4-5
Tourism 1-21
Tourist Destination 1-4, 8
Traditional Foods 5, 8, 12-13, 16
Traditional Product 23
Traditional Type of SFSCs 23
Trust 2-3, 7, 9-10, 12-13, 22

U

User Interface 6-7, 13

V

Virtual Reality 1-5, 8, 10, 12, 17-18

W

Wild Plant Gathering 10, 14, 17, 20
Women Cooperatives 11
Women Farmers 1-3, 5, 10-11, 13-14, 22

Index

Recommended Reference Books

IGI Global's reference books are available in three unique pricing formats:
Print Only, E-Book Only, or Print + E-Book.
Order direct through IGI Global's Online Bookstore at **www.igi-global.com** or through your preferred provider.

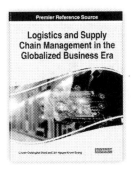

Logistics and Supply Chain Management in the Globalized Business Era

ISBN: 9781799887096
EISBN: 9781799887119
© 2022; 413 pp.
List Price: US$ **250**

Food Safety Practices in the Restaurant Industry

ISBN: 9781799874157
EISBN: 9781799874164
© 2022; 334 pp.
List Price: US$ **240**

Implementing Diversity, Equity, Inclusion, and Belonging Management in Organizational Change Initiatives

ISBN: 9781668440230
EISBN: 9781668440254
© 2022; 320 pp.
List Price: US$ **215**

Analyzing Telework, Trustworthiness, and Performance Using Leader-Member Exchange: COVID-19 Perspective

ISBN: 9781799889502
EISBN: 9781799889526
© 2022; 263 pp.
List Price: US$ **240**

Digital Communications, Internet of Things, and the Future of Cultural Tourism

ISBN: 9781799885283
EISBN: 9781799885306
© 2022; 587 pp.
List Price: US$ **360**

Research Anthology on Developing Socially Responsible Businesses

ISBN: 9781668455906
EISBN: 9781668455913
© 2022; 2,235 pp.
List Price: US$ **1,865**

Do you want to stay current on the latest research trends, product announcements, news, and special offers?
Join IGI Global's mailing list to receive customized recommendations, exclusive discounts, and more.
Sign up at: **www.igi-global.com/newsletters**.

Publisher of Timely, Peer-Reviewed Inclusive Research Since 1988

www.igi-global.com | Sign up at www.igi-global.com/newsletters | facebook.com/igiglobal | twitter.com/igiglobal

Ensure Quality Research is Introduced to the Academic Community

Become an Evaluator for IGI Global Authored Book Projects

   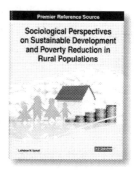

The overall success of an authored book project is dependent on quality and timely manuscript evaluations.

Applications and Inquiries may be sent to:
development@igi-global.com

Applicants must have a doctorate (or equivalent degree) as well as publishing, research, and reviewing experience. Authored Book Evaluators are appointed for one-year terms and are expected to complete at least three evaluations per term. Upon successful completion of this term, evaluators can be considered for an additional term.

If you have a colleague that may be interested in this opportunity, we encourage you to share this information with them.

Easily Identify, Acquire, and Utilize Published Peer-Reviewed Findings in Support of Your Current Research

IGI Global OnDemand

Purchase Individual IGI Global OnDemand Book Chapters and Journal Articles

For More Information:
www.igi-global.com/e-resources/ondemand/

Browse through 150,000+ Articles and Chapters!

Find specific research related to your current studies and projects that have been contributed by international researchers from prestigious institutions, including:

- Accurate and Advanced Search
- Affordably Acquire Research
- Instantly Access Your Content
- Benefit from the InfoSci Platform Features

« *It really provides* an excellent entry into the research literature of the field. *It presents a manageable number of* highly relevant sources *on topics of interest to a wide range of researchers. The sources are* scholarly, but also accessible *to 'practitioners'.* »

- Ms. Lisa Stimatz, MLS, University of North Carolina at Chapel Hill, USA

Interested in Additional Savings?

Subscribe to
IGI Global OnDemand *Plus*

Learn More

Acquire content from over 128,000+ research-focused book chapters and 33,000+ scholarly journal articles for as low as US$ 5 per article/chapter (original retail price for an article/chapter: US$ 37.50).

7,300+ E-BOOKS.
ADVANCED RESEARCH.
INCLUSIVE & AFFORDABLE.

IGI Global e-Book Collection

- Flexible Purchasing Options (Perpetual, Subscription, EBA, etc.)
- Multi-Year Agreements with No Price Increases Guaranteed
- No Additional Charge for Multi-User Licensing
- No Maintenance, Hosting, or Archiving Fees
- Continually Enhanced & Innovated Accessibility Compliance Features (WCAG)

Handbook of Research on Digital Transformation, Industry Use Cases, and the Impact of Disruptive Technologies
ISBN: 9781799877127
EISBN: 9781799877141

Handbook of Research on New Investigations in Artificial Life, AI, and Machine Learning
ISBN: 9781799886860
EISBN: 9781799886877

Handbook of Research on Future of Work and Education
ISBN: 9781799882756
EISBN: 9781799882770

Research Anthology on Physical and Intellectual Disabilities in an Inclusive Society (4 Vols.)
ISBN: 9781668435427
EISBN: 9781668435434

Innovative Economic, Social, and Environmental Practices for Progressing Future Sustainability
ISBN: 9781799895909
EISBN: 9781799895923

Applied Guide for Event Study Research in Supply Chain Management
ISBN: 9781799889694
EISBN: 9781799889717

Mental Health and Wellness in Healthcare Workers
ISBN: 9781799888130
EISBN: 9781799888147

Clean Technologies and Sustainable Development in Civil Engineering
ISBN: 9781799898108
EISBN: 9781799898122

Request More Information, or Recommend the IGI Global e-Book Collection to Your Institution's Librarian

For More Information or to Request a Free Trial, Contact IGI Global's e-Collections Team: eresources@igi-global.com | 1-866-342-6657 ext. 100 | 717-533-8845 ext. 100